Pocket Guide to the
Birds of
Britain and North-West Europe

Chris Kightley and Steve Madge

Illustrated by
Dave Nurney

Pica
PRESS

PICA PRESS
SUSSEX

In association with the British Trust for Ornithology

© 1998 Chris Kightley, Steve Madge and Dave Nurney

Pica Press
(an imprint of Helm Information Ltd.)
The Banks, Mountfield
Nr. Robertsbridge
East Sussex TN32 5JY

ISBN 1-873403-49-6

A CIP catalogue record for this book is available from the British Library.

For our children

Sophie, James, Bryony, Elysia and Chris

Computer graphics and typesetting by Fluke Art, Great Britain
Printed by Midas Printing, Hong Kong

Osprey p.76
Pandionidae

Swifts pp.174-175
Apodidae

Falcons pp.70-75
Falconidae

Owls pp.165-173
Tytonidae & Strigidae

Vultures, Eagles,
Buzzards and Hawks
pp.56-69
Accipitridae

Woodpeckers &
Wryneck
pp.180-186
Picidae

Parakeet p.179
Psittacidae

Roller p.178
Coraciidae

Bee-eater p.178
Meropidae

Hoopoe p.179
Upupidae

Nightjar p.176
Caprimulgidae

Storks p.22
Ciconiidae

Spoonbill p.21
Threskiornithidae

Cuckoos pp.163-164
Cuculidae

Pigeons & Doves pp.158-162
Columbidae

Bustards p.92 Otididae

Sandgrouse p.163
Pteroclidae

Grouse pp.77, 80-83
Tetraonidae

Partridges, Pheasants &
Quail pp.77-79, 84-86
Phasianidae

CONTENTS

ACKNOWLEDGEMENTS   vi

INTRODUCTION   vii
   Area of coverage; How to use this book; What's in a name; Races or
   subspecies; Size; Layout of the book; Status and population

TOPOGRAPHY AND GLOSSARY   xi

IMPROVING YOUR FIELDCRAFT   xvii

EXPANDING YOUR INTEREST   xix

SPECIES ACCOUNTS (arranged by family)

Divers	1	Owls	166
Grebes	4	Swifts	174
Petrels and Shearwaters	9	Nightjars	176
Storm Petrels	12	Kingfishers	177
Gannets	13	Bee-eaters	178
Cormorants	14	Rollers	178
Herons, Bitterns and Egrets	16	Hoopoe	179
Spoonbills	21	Parrots	179
Storks	22	Woodpeckers and Wrynecks	180
Flamingos	23	Larks	187
Cranes	23	Swallows and Martins	192
Swans, Geese and Ducks	24	Pipits and Wagtails	196
Kites, Eagles, Vultures, Harriers,		Waxwings	204
Buzzards and Hawks	56	Dippers	205
Falcons	70	Accentors	206
Osprey	76	Wrens	207
Grouse	77	Chats and Thrushes	207
Partridges, Pheasants and Quail	77	Warblers	223
Rails and Crakes	87	Flycatchers	245
Bustards	92	Babblers	248
Stone-curlews	93	Long-tailed Tits	249
Oystercatchers	94	Tits	250
Pratincoles	94	Nuthatches	256
Stilts and Avocets	95	Treecreepers	257
Plovers	96	Wallcreeper	258
Sandpipers, Snipes, Godwits,		Penduline Tits	258
Curlews and Phalaropes	103	Orioles	259
Skuas	128	Shrikes	260
Gulls	132	Starlings	263
Terns	145	Crows and Jays	264
Auks	154	Sparrows	272
Pigeons and Doves	158	Finches	275
Sandgrouse	163	Buntings	289
Cuckoos	163		
Barn Owls	165	INDEX	297

ACKNOWLEDGEMENTS

Throughout the life of this project publisher Christopher Helm and editor Nigel Redman have been patient, constructive and encouraging in their belief and support for this book (even though there have been many occasions when they must have all but despaired that the project would ever reach a conclusion). We also would like to thank Marc Dando and Julie Reynolds of Fluke Art who have so capably handled the graphic design and typesetting.

Special thanks also go to our families and to the many other people with whom we have watched birds and travelled over the years, especially those friends who inspired us with ideas, discussion and enthusiasm: David Christie, Darrell Clegg, David Cottridge, Dennis Cox, Steve Dudley, Dick Forsman, Roy Hargreaves, Sara McMahon and Arnoud van den Berg.

Finally, to everyone who has contributed, either directly or indirectly, to the content of this book, but whose names we may have overlooked (or might simply never have known), we offer our very sincere thanks.

INTRODUCTION

Area of coverage

This book deals fully with the 385 species that occur regularly in Britain and North-West Europe, a region that includes Norway, Sweden, Denmark, Germany, the Czech Republic, Austria, Switzerland, France, Luxembourg, Belgium, the Netherlands, and Britain and Ireland. This effectively covers all of Western Europe other than Iceland, Spain, Portugal and Italy, although the great majority of species to be found there are, in fact, included within this book, as are the bulk of those occurring in neighbouring eastern European countries such as Poland, Hungary, Slovakia, Croatia and Slovenia.

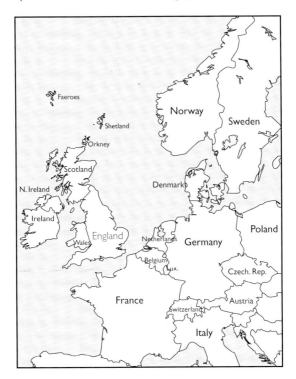

How to use this book

The birds are arranged in systematic order – a recognised, scientifically accepted sequence based on evolution – rather than being grouped alphabetically, or by size, colour or habitat. It is good practice to become familiar with this sequence of bird families (i.e. starting with divers, and ending with buntings), as it groups like with like and will be similar to the systematic sequence adopted by most works of reference, be it a comprehensive handbook or simply a county bird report. Where we have departed slightly from the strict order of things, we have only done so when we have felt it advantageous to compare two similar looking but unrelated birds together, placing such species on the same page or on facing pages for ease of comparison.

Use the differently coloured highlights behind the bird's name at the top of each page to help locate the different groups as you thumb through the pages of this book (see inside front cover).

What's in a name?

A bird's name is important. It does more than merely enable us to label a particular species, it is also a reflection of their relationships to one another. All birds have both an English name and a scientific name. In recent years, there have been several attempts to standardise the English names of birds mainly in order to achieve a common nomenclature between North America and Britain. With a few exceptions, however, we have used the traditional English names.

A bird's scientific name, which is in Latin or latinised Greek, is unique to a particular species and is the same in every language. *Phylloscopus collybita*, for example, will always be recognised as the same species, regardless of whether you would normally call it by its English name (Chiffchaff), French name (Pouillot véloce) or Swedish name (Gransångare), and so on. Each scientific name comprises two parts – a generic name and a specific name. The generic name always comes first and begins with a capital letter. Chiffchaffs, for example, belong to the genus *Phylloscopus* (Greek, leaf-searcher). The second name is the specific name; it begins with a small letter – in the case of Chiffchaff, its specific name is *collybita* (Greek, money-changer – from its chinking song!).

The scientific name also clearly indicates the relationships between species. This is not always clear from the English name alone: for example, the Stone-curlew *Burhinus oedicnemus* is quite unrelated to the Curlew *Numenius arquata*, a fact that is immediately apparent when reading the scientific generic name. The fact that the Chiffchaff is a member of the genus *Phylloscopus*, however, immediately suggests its relationship to the closely-related Willow Warbler, *Phylloscopus trochilus*.

Races or subspecies

Many species can be split into recognisable races or subspecies. To enable birdwatchers to distinguish between them, a third name is added – the subspecific name. In the case of the Chiffchaff, three different races can occur in Britain: those that breed here belong to a different race from those breeding in North-East Europe, which are different again from those found east of the Ural mountains in Russia. Though the differences between the various races may not always be apparent in the field, each will have its own subspecific name – *Phylloscopus collybita collybita* in the case of West European Chiffchaffs, while those from North-East Europe belong to the race *Phylloscopus collybita abietinus*; those from eastern Russia are noticeably paler and belong to the race *Phylloscopus collybita tristis*.

Evolution is by definition a continuing gradual process. In many cases the dividing line between what constitutes a separate species rather than a well-marked subspecies is a fine one. Some subspecies differ markedly from each other and could indeed be considered as different species (and have been so treated at times); Carrion and Hooded Crows and Red and Willow Grouse are good examples. Scientific studies on speciation follow several diverging definitions, with the current trend being to split more named forms (or taxa) as species. Examples include the subspecies of both Bean and Brent Geese, which are considered to be good species by some recent authors, whilst Yellow-legged Gull, Rock Pipit, Mediterranean Shearwater and Scottish Crossbill are now universally accepted as full species.

Size

Both metric and imperial measurements are shown. In most cases, an average length is given. This is a useful way to compare similar species. A range of measurements is generally only given where there is a marked size difference between individuals or sexes. It is important to realise that although birds may seem to us to be very close in terms of actual measurements, these small differences in size are often quite marked in the field, particularly with small birds.

For species which are typically seen on the wing, such as birds of prey and seabirds, the total wingspan (i.e. wing-tip to wing-tip) is also indicated.

| Tufted Duck | Ferruginous Duck | Scaup |

Sleeping female diving ducks, illustrating subtle differences in size and crown shape.

Layout of the Book

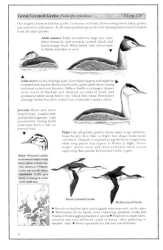

The text We want this book to be easy to use and understand. Hence, we have broken the text up into separate sections. Each account typically opens with a short scene setting paragraph, often focussing attention on the most important fieldmarks to look for. This is followed by descriptions of the salient plumage characteristics placed alongside the appropriate colour picture. Each account concludes with a bulleted list of key pointers, including hints on when and where to look, voice and behaviour.

Successful identification involves a process of elimination; knowing what to find and when helps narrow down the field of possible contenders. To help you in this, we have opted for a concise approach aimed at picking up on the most important characters, or key differences where similar species are involved.

If you are unfamiliar with any of the terms used, you should refer to the topographical diagrams on page xv and/or the glossary of terms on page xi.

The illustrations Although the number of illustrations used varies from plate to plate, we have tried to cover as many different plumage stages as space allows. Where there are significant differences, illustrations are clearly labelled to show at a glance whether the bird depicted is in breeding or non-breeding plumage, male, female or juvenile.

The maps The maps aim to give a broad indication of the likelihood of seeing a particular bird within a particular area at a particular time of year.

The maps are colour-coded as follows (see also inside back cover):

Green = resident: present all year throughout the area.
Yellow = summer visitor: birds which occur chiefly during the months April-September.
Blue = winter visitor: birds which occur chiefly during the months October-March.

Unfortunately, maps do have limitations. An accurate assessment of distribution is, of course, impossible to achieve on such small scale maps, which can give no indication of relative abundance. For instance, a species may be locally common in one area but scarce somewhere else, and yet still be shown to be present by the map. The Crossbill is a good example, being shown as present throughout the British Isles; in practice its numbers are low and thinly spread. Conversely, the map for Sedge Warbler appears to indicate that this species never occurs over much of southern Europe; the map here is simply blank. Despite this, however, the Sedge Warbler occurs widely throughout this blank zone on migration. Since none of this information is evident from the maps, they should be treated only as an indication of breeding and winter ranges.

Status A brief written statement summarising and complementing the information portrayed by the maps.

Population The figures quoted are in most cases estimates. Their aim is to give a broad indication of the relative abundance and hence likelihood of seeing a particular bird. **Note that the figures given refer only to Britain and Ireland**. Population figures for North-West Europe as a whole are not given. Most figures refer to an estimate of the number of pairs of birds, but in some cases the term 'territories' or 'singing males' is considered more appropriate for breeding birds. For others (e.g. winter visitors), the population may be expressed in terms of the actual number of individual birds. Do bear in mind that birds may be locally common in one area, but scarce or absent elsewhere. For some species where there is no reliable estimate of numbers a '?' is used.

For those wishing to know more about the population and number of birds within Britain and Ireland, we refer readers to the following key references: *The New Atlas of Breeding Birds in Britain and Ireland: 1988-1991* (Gibbons 1993); and *The Atlas of Wintering Birds in Britain and Ireland* (Lack 1986). In addition, a recent paper in *British Birds* (Stone *et al.* 1997) summarises population estimates for the United Kingdom. For a wider picture of distribution, we recommend *The EBCC Atlas of European Breeding Birds: Their Distribution and Abundance* (Hagemeijer and Blair 1997).

TOPOGRAPHY

Feathers are, of course, unique to birds, setting them apart from all other creatures in the animal kingdom. Feathers are not just evenly scattered over the body surface of a bird, they grow in defined lines or tracts. Though differing widely in size, shape, colour, function and form, a basic knowledge of the main feather tracts (which fortunately are similar in most birds) will not only enhance your understanding and enjoyment of birds in general, but considerably sharpen your field skills. Close attention to such features as pale-tipped greater coverts or a white trailing edge to the wings may be essential to identify a new or unfamiliar bird. Other aspects, such as wing shape, length of tail and primary projection, can provide the key to separating some of the trickier look-alike species. Use the topographical diagrams below as a reference point when making a description of an unfamiliar bird's appearance.

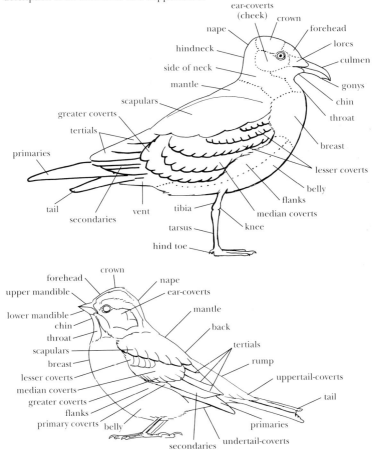

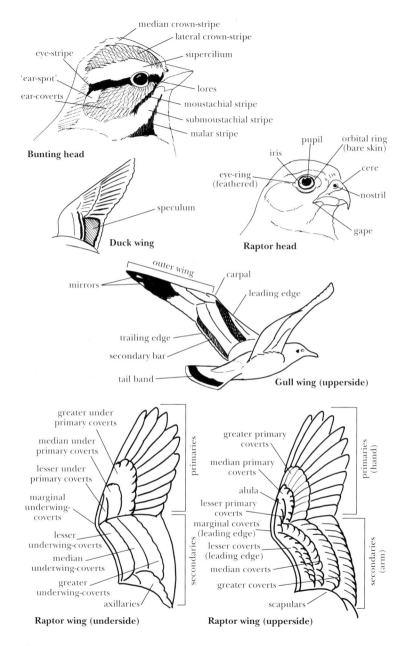

median crown-stripe
lateral crown-stripe
eye-stripe
supercilium
'ear-spot'
lores
ear-coverts
moustachial stripe
submoustachial stripe
malar stripe

Bunting head

speculum

Duck wing

pupil
iris
orbital ring (bare skin)
eye-ring (feathered)
cere
nostril
gape

Raptor head

outer wing
mirrors
carpal
leading edge
trailing edge
secondary bar
tail band

Gull wing (upperside)

greater under primary coverts
median under primary coverts
lesser under primary coverts
marginal underwing-coverts
lesser underwing-coverts
median underwing-coverts
greater underwing-coverts
axillaries
primaries
secondaries

Raptor wing (underside)

greater primary coverts
median primary coverts
alula
lesser primary coverts
marginal coverts (leading edge)
lesser coverts (leading edge)
median coverts
greater coverts
scapulars
primaries (hand)
secondaries (arm)

Raptor wing (upperside)

GLOSSARY

Refer also to the topograpical diagrams on pages xi-xii.

Accidental A species that has occurred only a handful of times within a particular geographical area (see also Vagrant).

Adult A bird that has passed through the various plumages of immaturity and is capable of breeding. The length of time this takes varies widely according to species: in many passerines, for example, this may be only 12 months; in gulls, the process may take 2, 3 or 4 years depending on size, and in White-tailed Eagle 5 or more years.

Arm Inner section of wing, between the body and carpal joint (wrist); often used in describing seabirds and birds of prey.

Axillaries Group of feathers on the underwing between wing and body that form the 'armpit'. Differences in colour of axillaries between certain species (e.g. Grey and Golden Plovers) provide a key fieldmark.

Breeding plumage Also called adult summer plumage. This is the plumage in which a bird breeds. It may be acquired through processes of moult or abrasion – the latter is the gradual wearing away of pale feather fringes during the autumn and winter to reveal the bright colours of summer (breeding) plumage.

Carpal joint The wrist or bend of the wing.

Carpal patch Dark patch on the wrist of the underwing. Often a prominent fieldmark on certain species in flight (e.g. Osprey, buzzards)

Cere Area of bare skin at the base of the upper mandible clearly visible on certain species (e.g. raptors, pigeons). Colour of skin may change as bird matures.

Colour phase Colour variants, not subspecies, which freely occur within the same population, such as light and dark phase skuas and Fulmar, and hepatic female Cuckoos.

Conspecific Belonging to the same species.

Cryptic Markings and colours that render perfect camouflage, allowing a bird to blend with its surroundings, such as Bittern, the snipes, Woodcock and Nightjar.

Culmen The ridge along the top of the upper mandible, from forehead to bill tip.

Eclipse Drab, female-type plumage stage acquired by male ducks during the summer months; provides good camouflage during period in which simultaneous shedding of flight feathers for renewal renders them flightless.

Eye-stripe Line (typically dark in colour) running from the bill *through* the eye, along the upper border of the ear-coverts. Not to be confused with supercilium or eyebrow.

Eyebrow See supercilium.

Feral Populations originating in captivity but now established in a wild state.

First-winter Transitional plumage stage acquired by many birds when juvenile plumage is shed (typically August-October), and recognised by presence of retained juvenile feathers in wing and tail (e.g. gulls; first-winter male Blackbird shows dark head and body but retains brown wings and tail of juvenile plumage).

Gonys Point along the ridge of the lower mandible of some birds at which a visible bulge or change of angle occurs; it is seen most clearly in the larger gulls.

Gorget A distinct band of colour or streaks across the throat or upper breast.

Hand Outer section of wing, between the carpal joint (wrist) and wing tip; often used in describing seabirds and birds of prey. The tendency for some species, particularly raptors, to 'drop their hand' in flight can provide a useful clue to identity.

Hirundine A member of the swallow family.

Immature A bird that is not yet adult; may be in juvenile or any one of its various subadult plumages. A rather vague term often used by birdwatchers when the age of a bird has not or cannot be precisely determined.

Introduced species Species that have been released by man into an area where they were not previously found.

Irruption Term to describe the periodic but generally irregular mass movements of certain species (e.g. Nutcracker, Waxwing) *into* an area outside the normal range; typically in late summer or autumn, in response to food shortages.

Juvenile A bird's first plumage of feathers, in which it fledges from the nest.

Lek Communal display ground at which males congregate to attract, woo and mate with females. Derives from Swedish 'leka', to play. Birds that lek include Black Grouse, Capercaillie, Great Snipe and Ruff.

Mirrors White ovals near tips of longest primaries of larger gulls; chiefly on inner webs and generally concealed when wing closed (but may often be seen by carefully looking at the folded underside of the tip of the far wing). Do not confuse with white spots at tips of fresh primaries (these are not the mirrors).

Morph Colour phase.

Moult Regular process of renewal of a bird's feathers to replace those lost or damaged through wear. Moult may be complete (head, body, wing and tail feathers replaced at same time) or partial (moult of most feathers, excepting wings and tail). The timing, duration and sequence of moult varies between species.

Nominate The first-named form of a species which has been divided into subspecies; the nominate subspecies carries the same subspecific name as the species name e.g. *Phylloscopus collybita collybita* .

Non-breeding plumage This is the plumage in which a bird spends the winter. Typically acquired through complete moult at the end of the breeding season. (Though it generally refers to an adult bird in winter plumage, the term is rather loose and is often used to embrace any bird, young or old, that is not in breeding plumage.)

Passage migrant A bird which regularly passes through an area in which it neither normally breeds nor winters.

Pelagic A boat trip out to sea specifically to look for seabirds.

Pelagic species Bird that spends the bulk of its life at sea, normally well away from land.

Pishing Onomatopoeic word to describe the gentle '*psshh-ing*' noises made by bird-watchers to coax warblers and other small birds into view. See page xviii.

Primaries The large flight feathers that form the outer half of the wing (typically 10 in number).

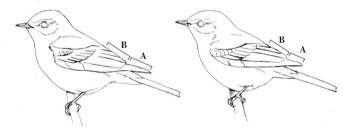

Primary Projection This is the distance that the primaries project beyond the tip of the longest tertial (labelled 'A'), compared to the visible length of the tertials (labelled 'B'). In the example above, Willow Warbler (left) has a relatively long primary projection (A & B are about equal) but Chiffchaff's relatively short (A is only about half the length of B). Though not always easy to see, primary projection is an especially useful aid to identification in several tricky groups or species 'pairs' – notably Little and Baillon's Crakes, Great Grey and Lesser Grey Shrikes, and various waders, larks, pipits and warblers.

Race See Subspecies.

Raptor Another word for bird of prey; generally refers to diurnal hawks, etc. rather than owls.

Rectrices The main tail feathers (singular Rectrix).

Redhead Word used for the similar female, juvenile and immature plumages of Goosander, Red-breasted Merganser and Smew, which all show brownish-red heads (not to be confused with the vagrant North American diving duck of the same name).

Remiges The main flight feathers (i.e. primaries and secondaries)

Sawbill Goosander, Red-breasted Merganser and Smew are all sawbills, a term derived from the serrated edges along both mandibles.

Secondaries The large flight feathers forming the inner half (or arm) of the wing.

Spatulate Refers mainly to the bill being shaped like a spoon (as in Spoonbill).

Speculum A patch of distinctive colour on the wing (secondaries), referring particularly to the bright metallic patches shown by dabbling (surface-feeding) ducks.

Subadult A general term for a bird in the later stages of immaturity, which has acquired some or most, but not all, features of adulthood.

Subspecies A population or group of birds which can be distinguished from other members of the same species, such as Pied and White Wagtails or Carrion and Hooded Crows. In many cases the distinctions are slight and may not be readily apparent in the field. See also page viii.

Supercilium Sometimes referred to as the eyebrow. A line of variable length and width (often pale in colour) running from the bill *above* the eye and upper border of the ear-coverts. Do not confuse with eye-stripe (see above).

Tail shapes Tails come in all shapes and sizes, and often provide useful clues to a bird's identity. When faced with something unusual, make a note of the length and shape of its tail. Use the diagrams below to help you describe what you see.

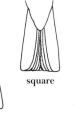

rounded square notched forked graduated (wedge-shaped) pointed

Tail patterns The presence (or absence) of a distinctive colour or pattern on the rump and/or tail can be important in establishing the identity of a bird. Use the diagrams below to help you describe what you see.

white wedges at base · white outer tail feathers · white corners · inverted 'T' · banded/barred · subterminal band · terminal band (black tip)

Tertials The elongated innermost secondaries. On the closed wing, the tertials cloak the remainder of the secondaries and may conceal or partially conceal the primaries too. Their colour, size, pattern and form can provide important clues to age and identity in certain birds, e.g. as when used to evaluate primary projection (see above).

Trailing edge (see below) Many species of birds show distinctive markings along the trailing or rear edge of the wing in flight. The presence or absence of such a feature can be useful in distinguishing between certain species (e.g. Redshank and Spotted Redshank, Skylark and Woodlark), and in ageing others (e.g. buzzards, which show a solid dark trailing edge to the underwing in adults, but a diffuse band in juveniles).

Vagrant A species that has occurred only rarely within a particular geographical area.

Wing-bar Sometimes called a wing-stripe. May be visible at rest and/or in flight, as either a light or dark band that is generally formed by pale tips to the greater coverts and/or base of the primaries. On species that also show pale tips to the median coverts, a double wing-bar is created.

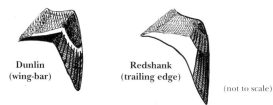

**Dunlin
(wing-bar)**

**Redshank
(trailing edge)**

(not to scale)

Wing panel Can be interpreted in several ways, e.g.: (i) a bold area of colour (often pale) within the wing that would not more accurately be described as a wing-bar or trailing edge (examples include drake Wigeon, Black Guillemot, Pied Flycatcher, Snow Bunting); (ii) a distinctive pale band or panel visible across the upperwing in flight (as in various raptors, such as Booted Eagle, Black Kite); (iii) pale margins to the tertials/secondaries forming a more or less discrete panel on the closed wing, notably of some passerines (such as Icterine Warbler, Willow Tit).

**Booted Eagle
(wing panel)**

**Willow Tit
(wing panel)**

**Black Guillemot
(wing panel)**

(not to scale)

Wing shape Wings come in all shapes and sizes, and can provide useful clues to a bird's identity. When faced with something unusual, make a note of the length and shape of its wings. Use the diagrams below to help you describe what you see.

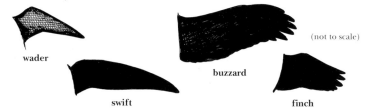

(not to scale)

wader

buzzard

swift

finch

Wreck Term used to describe the occurrence of pelagic birds (often in large numbers) blown ashore or deposited inland by severe storms.

IMPROVING YOUR FIELDCRAFT

Experience will teach you a number of techniques to improve your bird-watching skills. Below are some tips which have helped us when in the field.

Size illusion It is easy to be fooled by size. When watching birds through a powerful telescope be aware that, with two same-sized birds, the eye can deceive you into believing the one farther away is bigger than the one in front.

Finding birds in woodland When searching for woodland birds, first use your naked eye to locate the movement of birds in the trees, then raise your binoculars. This is generally a more successful technique than optimistically scanning with binoculars in the hope of finding a bird, as even low power binoculars will narrow your field of view.

Seawatching Unless they are close inshore, birds are invariably hard to spot with the naked eye against an expanse of sea. Instead, try using your binoculars or telescope to scan for movement, or to watch a fixed point, then follow any birds that move across your field of view. Select a sheltered position that is not too high above sea-level. The higher you are, the narrower your field of view over the sea will be and the greater the chance of birds slipping past. A plastic bag is useful to pop over your telescope during showers, but good birds often seem to fly ahead of incoming squalls, so be extra vigilant just before popping your bag over your telescope.

Pointing birds out Different habitats call for different techniques. When sea-watching or in other open terrain use the 'clock system' to give directions to other birdwatchers or refer to obvious prearranged landmarks. If you plan to sit and watch from one spot for a while, it's a good idea to establish your 12 o'clock position at the outset, so everyone knows precisely where to look when that special bird comes by. This is far better than pointing in a frantic and rather aimless fashion with one hand whilst still trying to look through your binoculars held in the other.

Back this up with easily understood descriptions. In woodland, for example, it is no use exclaiming to a friend who is valiantly struggling to find 'your' bird that 'it's in that tree over there!' or to 'look where I'm looking!' Advising your companion that the bird is 'in the third elder to the left of the cherry' isn't going to help much either if he or she can't tell an oak from a birch. Instead, go for a quick thinking and more imaginative approach – 'it's in the tree shaped like a giraffe' or 'it's just passing above the cloud shaped like Africa' often works well. Of course, there will always be someone who can't find the bird no matter how hard you try. Though some may scoff at your efforts, such ploys can significantly improve your chances of getting onto a bird quickly enough to enjoy it.

Never be afraid to get it wrong Making mistakes is a vital part of the learning process. If you commit an absolute howler (everybody does, though few have the courage or honesty to own up), don't crawl sheepishly into the corner and hide; ask yourself why you got it wrong and you may be wiser next time.

Be positive Whilst you can't simply conjure a bird out of thin air, a positive mental attitude very often pays off. Don't be downhearted that the Bittern or Golden Eagle fails to show the moment you arrive – more often than not you will need to apply yourself a little to the task. Be watchful, attentive and patient, look in the most likely places and success will often follow. Don't be put of by those who say 'we've been here hours and haven't seen a thing' – you may be more lucky, and perhaps they haven't really tried.

Learn the common birds first Familiarity with the common birds is the key to furthering both your enjoyment and your skill as a birdwatcher. Only by building and drawing upon a sound basic knowledge will you start to acquire the essential skills needed when confronted by some of birdwatching's knottier and more intriguing identification problems.

Check flocks carefully Get into the habit of looking through all those flocks of Lapwings and thrushes out in the fields, gulls on the beach, tit flocks in woodland and waders on the mud. There is no better way to acquaint yourself with the more common species, their field marks, actions and different plumages. As a bonus, every once in a while you may be rewarded with something rare or unexpected; flocks of Long-tailed Tits, for instance, often carry other species with them, which occasionally includes gems such as Pallas's and Yellow-browed Warblers.

Don't despair If you miss a bird first time round, be patient; birds are very much creatures of habit. Flocks of tits, for example, typically rove on a circuit around a wood. Though they can be frustrating to observe, moving quickly on before you've had a chance to watch them all or to check for that elusive Lesser Spotted Woodpecker within, don't despair; it may not be long before the flock returns, giving you another chance.

Keep a notebook Field sketches with notes (no matter how bad an artist you think you may be) are by far the best way to learn. By forcing accurate observation they help to commit detail to memory.

Use your ears Experienced birdwatchers pick up a great many of their birds by sound. First learn to tune in to bird calls. There is no real short cut to learning bird song, but you don't need to have a good ear or be musical to succeed. Practice and familiarity are the cornerstones on which to build. That doesn't mean having to listen to hour after hour of bird song tapes, which is rather like trying to become an expert by simply reading all the right books. Some things will stick of course, but the only real way to master the art is to get out into the field and practice.

At first, the task seems daunting – almost everything you hear will be unfamiliar. But persevere, following up any interesting sounds (even if 9 out 10 woodland birds do prove to be Great Tits!). As a rule, the longer it takes to track a bird down and identify it, the more likely you are to remember it next time. As an aid, try and associate a song or call with something quite unrelated – e.g. a coin spinning to rest on a saucer (Wood Warbler). And whilst 'a little bit of bread and no cheese' may not be the most accurate rendition of a Yellowhammer's song, it does at least stick in the memory.

One of the best ways to get to grips with bird song is to undertake a common bird census (CBC) or breeding birds survey (BBS) of the birds on your local patch. Run by the BTO (the British Trust for Ornithology – see below), your contribution to this scheme will be welcomed. You will not only be making a valuable contribution to our knowledge of breeding birds in the UK, it's also fun.

'Pishing' The art of 'pishing' originated in North America and involves making gentle '*pshh*-ing' sounds in an attempt to coax a small warbler or hitherto unseen skulker from the depths of thick cover. Once you overcome the initial embarrassment of pishing in public, the rest comes easy. The traditional method is to repeat the word *pish* or *pshh* thus: *pshh-pshh-pshh-pshh*.... But you can make almost any squeaking or loud kissing sound. The key is not to make too much noise or you will risk scaring away the very bird you are hoping to see. Instead, stand quietly and make soft, gentle sounds (though these obviously have to be loud enough for the bird to hear), which can increase a little in intensity if you like. What attracts the birds we do not know, but pishing often works. Tits, Nuthatches, Chaffinches, Bearded Tits and many warblers will respond (pishing is just about your only chance of seeing those skulking reedbed warblers in autumn). Used in moderation, it's a useful tool; but the effect soon wears off and most birds will only respond once or twice before retiring back into cover.

EXPANDING YOUR INTEREST

To get an insight into what species are likely in your home area it is well worth joining a local birdwatching club. Most cities and counties have their own clubs, the majority of which produce annual publications on the status of local birds and have regular outdoor and indoor meetings. A list of these clubs, together with other vital information about birds, can be found in *The Birdwatcher's Yearbook and Diary* published annually by Buckingham Press.

British Trust for Ornithology
The Nunnery, Thetford, Norfolk IP24 2PU Tel: 01842 750050

The British Trust for Ornithology studies Britain's birds and their habitats. Since 1933, tens of thousands of BTO members have monitored bird populations in the UK. This remarkable network of volunteers produces the raw data which is then rendered statistically valid by the BTO's scientists in Thetford. Their impartial research has an important role, as it often shapes subsequent conservation measures.

The BTO conducts many surveys including Garden BirdWatch – an ongoing nationwide survey of garden birds; Breeding Bird Survey (jointly funded by the Joint Nature Conservation Committee and the RSPB) – annual nationwide survey of breeding birds; Nest Records Scheme – a survey of the breeding success of Britain's birds.

The BTO also administers the national Bird Ringing Scheme. Bird ringing (or banding as it is known in North America) can become a major interest. Ringers set mist nets or other traps in order to catch birds, often at first light. After weighing and measuring the trapped birds, they are ringed (or banded) and then released. Each country has its own ringing scheme and birds that are ringed in Europe may (for instance) turn up in southern Africa, thus giving valuable information about the movement of bird populations.

Any birdwatcher can join the BTO and the keen beginner is as welcome as the seasoned expert. To find out how easy it is to get involved contact the Membership Secretary for further details.

Royal Society for the Protection of Birds
The Lodge, Sandy, Bedfordshire SG19 2DL Tel: 01767 680551

All birdwatchers should belong to the RSPB or its junior wing, the YOC (Young Ornithologists Club). It is Europe's largest voluntary conservation body, and membership brings free entry to the huge numbers of RSPB reserves throughout the UK, the option of joining a local members' group and the magazines *Birds* (RSPB) and *Bird Life* (YOC).

Scottish Ornithologists' Club
21 Regent Terrace, Edinburgh EH7 5BT Tel: 0131 556 6042
Welsh Ornithological Society
Crud yr Awel, Bowls Road, Blaenporth, Cardigan SA43 2AR Tel: 01239 811561
Irish Wildbird Conservancy
Ruttledge House, 8 Longford Place, Monkstown, Co Dublin Tel: (01) 280 4322

Scotland, Wales and Ireland each has its own ornithological society which promotes the study of birds and their conservation within its territory.
Wildfowl and Wetlands Trust
Slimbridge, Gloucestershire GL2 7BT Tel: 01453 890333

Founded by the late Sir Peter Scott half a century ago, the WWT carries out research on wildfowl and maintains a network of eight reserves and collections. Membership brings free entry to their wildfowl refuges.

Bird journals and magazines

British Birds
Published monthly and available only on subscription, *British Birds* includes identification articles, bird reports, recent news, book and equipment reviews, short notes, letters and detailed scientific papers. A free sample copy is available from British Birds, Fountains, Park Lane, Blunham, Bedford MK44 3NJ.

Birding World
Published monthly and available only on subscription, *Birding World* provides identification arctiles and hot news about rarities throughout Britain and Europe. It is closely associated with *Birdline*, a telephone service giving daily reports of sightings in the British Isles. Available from Bird Information Service, Stonerunner, Coast Road, Cley next the Sea, Norfolk NR25 7RZ.

BirdWatching and Birdwatch
These two large format monthly magazines aim for a more popular market. Both contain a heady mix of topical news, regional reports and feature articles, in full colour throughout. *BirdWatching* is available on subscription from EMAP, Tower House, Sovereign Park, Market Harborough, Leics LE16 9EF, and *Birdwatch* from Fulham House, Goldsworth Road, Woking, Surrey GU21 1LY; both are also available from newsagents.

The smallest and most numerous diver. At sea distant birds can be confused with winter Guillemot, though latter is considerably smaller. Habitually inclines head and bill in decidedly snooty manner (Black-throated sometimes carries head slightly up). Sexes alike, although males often noticeably larger.

Adult summer Combination of grey head, 'pyjama-striped' hindcrown and plain, dark brown upperparts unique among divers. Rust-red throat appears dark at distance. ▶

Adult winter White on face and neck more extensive than other divers, extending above eye, with grey more or less confined to dark stripe over crown and hindneck. Appears elegant and thin-necked. Dark grey upperparts distinctively peppered with white speckles at close quarters. ◀

First-winter Variable moult. Some become like adult, others show ashy face and foreneck. Upperparts show weaker spotting than adult; flanks browner and bill paler. Indistinct rusty patch on throat of juvenile. ◀

Characteristic 'nose up' attitude enhanced by gently sloping forehead and slender, chisel-tipped bill.

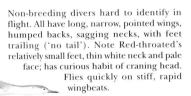

Non-breeding divers hard to identify in flight. All have long, narrow, pointed wings, humped backs, sagging necks, with feet trailing ('no tail'). Note Red-throated's relatively small feet, thin white neck and pale face; has curious habit of craning head. Flies quickly on stiff, rapid wingbeats.

Status Widespread but thinly distributed breeder in north. Scarce breeder in NW Scotland and Donegal; in winter, most numerous along eastern coasts. **Population** c1500 pairs; 15,000-20,000 birds in winter.

◆ Nests inland on smaller lochans in moorland and 'flow country', but fishes mainly at sea, attracting attention with cackling *kak-kak-kak* on flights to and fro ◆ Song a mournful, gull-like wailing and goose-like clamour ◆ In winter, favours shallower inshore waters. Often seen in small, loose flocks ◆ Like all divers, submerges frequently, for up to 60 seconds ◆ Watch for glint of white belly as birds 'roll-preen' their underside.

1

Black-throated Diver *Gavia arctica* 58-73cm (23-31")

Unmistakable in summer plumage. Between Red-throated and Great Northern in size but marked individual size variation so careful separation needed from both in non-breeding plumage. Clean white 'rising-sun' patch on rear flank – usually visible above waterline when swimming low – is a useful pointer, especially at long range (less sharply defined on other divers). Sexes alike.

Adult summer Combination of silken grey hood, 'zebra-striped' neck-sides, and white slatted back unique. Black throat patch diagnostic (but beware Red-throated also looks dark at distance). Characteristic is the way face can appear one moment grey, then black – changing like the sheen on velvet.

Adult winter Note sharp split between white foreneck and dark hindneck (cf. other divers). Check for flank patch. Slaty nape contrasts slightly with otherwise plain blackish back and forehead.

First-winter When close, upper-parts show weak grey 'scales', lacking in winter adult.

Dark crown extends below eye (cf. Great Northern). Pale grey bill with dark culmen and tip, heavier, straighter and more evenly tapering than Red-throated.

Neck fuller, more elegantly curving than other divers. Curiously, head shape often seems more angular in winter plumage.

Status Breeds in N Europe and NW Scotland (rare). Winters off coasts, but very local (chiefly W Scotland & Cornwall); occasionally strays inland. **Population** c150 pairs; 2,000 birds in winter.

Flight Identification difficult in winter; note Black-throated's neck pattern, centrally-placed wings, less drooped neck, and contrasting appearance. Larger feet than Red-throat but toes less 'bundled' than in Great Northern.

◆ Nests on larger freshwater lochs, often with wooded islands ◆ Scarcest and most localised of the three divers in Britain in winter, preferring larger deep-water bays and inlets ◆ Behaviour much as Red-throated, often swimming with bill held up ◆ Call is even more desolate and echoing, with mournful, dog-like howls.

Great Northern Diver *Gavia immer* 69-91cm (27-36")

Largest and bulkiest diver found regularly in our region. Size of goose but swims low in water. Notice heavy head and dagger-like bill pointing straight ahead. Might be confused with Cormorant, but latter has long tail and uptilted head and bill. Sexes alike. Compare rare White-billed Diver.

Adult summer The only diver with black bill, head and neck, and boldly chequered back. Notice narrow broken collar of white stripes.

Adult winter Uniformly sooty crown and nape generally darker than back (*contra* Black-throated). Diffuse eye-ring. Steel-grey bill can look pale at times (cf. White-billed). White notch above broad dark half-collar creates irregular divide between light and dark ('ghost of breeding pattern'). Differs further from Black-throat in its bigger, more angular head (often with 'bump' on forecrown), thicker neck and heavier bill.

First-winter From winter adult by paler, more rounded margins to back feathers.

Status Winter visitor (Oct-May) chiefly to W coast. Most breed N America (a few nest Iceland). Handful summer in Scotland (has bred). **Population** 4,000 birds in winter.

Flight Heavier, more goose-like than the smaller divers. Trailing feet noticeable, with fat toes.

◆ Occurs alone or in loose aggregations, principally over coastal reefs and inter-island waters in north and west of region. Occasional inland on larger reservoirs ◆ Slides beneath surface with powerful rolling lunge. Surfaces again up to 60 seconds later, some considerable distance away ◆ Usually silent away from breeding grounds.

White-billed Diver *Gavia adamsii* 75-100cm (30-39")

Scarce in winter along coast of Norway, rarer south Baltic. Vagrant elsewhere; in Britain most likely Scotland and north-east England, February-May. Averages larger than Great Northern and similar in all plumages but for striking ivory upturned bill (even pale-billed Great Northerns always show a dark culmen and dark cutting edges). First-winter birds (shown) are much paler than Great Northern, with wider pale scaling above and paler clouding on sides of head and neck.

3

Great Crested Grebe *Podiceps cristatus*   51cm (20")

Our largest and most familiar grebe. Common on broad, slow-moving rivers, lakes, gravel pits and other still waters. At all times pinkish spear-like bill distinguishes Great Crested from all other grebes.

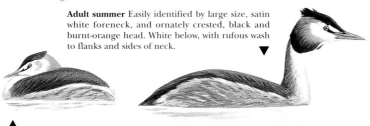

Adult summer Easily identified by large size, satin white foreneck, and ornately crested, black and burnt-orange head. White below, with rufous wash to flanks and sides of neck.

Adult winter Looks strikingly pale. Loses fancy tippets and might be confused with stockier Red-necked Grebe, particularly when resting with head tucked into shoulder. Differs chiefly in its longer, cleaner neck, traces of blackish and chestnut on sides of head, and prominent white streak before eye. Check bill colour. First-winter plumage similar but often retains hint of juvenile's stripey cheek.

Juvenile Black and white striped head, coupled with pinkish bill diagnostic. Calls persistently. Young birds sometimes hitch a ride on parent's back.

Status Widespread resident, found mainly in lowlands. Avoids barren uplands. In British Isles, most numerous in Midlands, London area and NE Ireland. **Population** >6,000 pairs (slowly increasing). In winter 10,000-20,000 birds.

Flight Like all grebes, patters across water to get airborne. Superficially diver-like in flight but shape looks more 'stretched'. Instantly recognised as a grebe by its conspicuous white wing panels that appear to flicker in flight. Notice longer, whiter neck and more extensive white across upperwing than similar Red-necked Grebe (right).

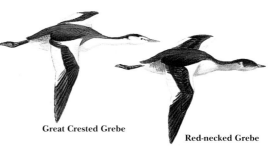

Great Crested Grebe

Red-necked Grebe

◆ Breeds on shallow lakes and sluggish waterways with reedy edges
◆ Well-known for its harsh, noisy chattering, guttural croaks and ritualised head-waggling displays in spring ◆ Disperses to larger lakes, estuaries and even sheltered coasts in winter, often gathering in sizeable 'rafts' ◆ Dives repeatedly for fish and invertebrates.

Scarce. Stockier and darker in all plumages than Great Crested. Black bill with yellow base diagnostic but pattern less clear in first-winter birds. Distant birds appear front-heavy, with relatively large wedge-shaped head and dagger-like bill providing easy distinctions from similarly dull Black-necked.

Adult summer Highly distinctive (but rarely seen in Britain), with black cap and chestnut-red neck. Contrastingly pale grey cheeks are edged white, like cloud with silver lining. ▶

◀ **Adult winter** Always more dingy than Great Crested, with proportionately shorter, thicker neck and overall 'smoky' appearance. If in doubt, scrutinise head:

Winter Red-necked Lacks white supercilium but has more extensive dark cap, which embraces the eye. Notice dirty white cheeks and 'unwashed' smoky foreneck. In good light, adult's dark eyes and yellow base to bill confirm identification. ▶

Winter Great Crested By comparison, is invariably paler, with longer, more slender, 'well-scrubbed' white foreneck. Notice reduced black crown and clean white cheeks, with prominent white streak before eye. Pink bill and crimson eyes unique amongst grebes. ▶

◀ **Juvenile** Rufous wash over foreneck recalls summer adult, but notice smudgy dark stripes across cheek. First-winter birds may be distinguished from adults by yellowish eyes and less strongly patterned bill.

Status Breeds sparsely in N & E of region. Winter visitor elsewhere. In Britain, best looked for along E coast of Scotland and E & S England (peak numbers Oct-Mar). **Population** Yet to nest successfully in Britain (1-3 pairs present most years since 1985). Winter: c100-500 birds.

◆ Nests on shallow marshy lakes and reedy backwaters ◆ Mainly coastal in winter, favouring estuaries and sheltered bays. Occasionally on inland waters in Britain, especially early in New Year following onset of hard weather on Continent ◆ Usually solitary or in company with divers or other grebes, but seldom more than two or three Red-necks together ◆ Usually silent in winter; on breeding grounds wailing cries recall screaming of Water Rail.

Marginally the largest and most robust of the smaller grebes. Unmistakable in summer. Looks most like Black-necked in winter, but rides lower in water and has flatter forehead, sleeker crown and stronger, evenly tapering bill.

Adult summer Only grebe with dark cheeks and chestnut-red foreneck, breast and flanks. Neck appears black at distance. Dense golden tufts behind eye (aptly likened to 'shaving brushes') much more conspicuous than Black-necked's wispy fans. Head larger, more bulbous than in winter plumage; lacks steep crown-peak of Black-necked.

Adult winter Looks strikingly black and white – not unlike a small Great Crested. Overall impression typically cleaner and more contrasting than Black-necked, with important differences in head shape and markings. At closest ranges, pale greyish loral spot, strip of bare red skin running from gape to eye, and clear white tip to bill diagnostic.

Juvenile/First-winter Like winter adult, but head pattern more diffuse and sides of neck more dingy (cf. Black-necked).

Flight Slavonian (left) skims over waves, with bulky feet trailing (like all grebes). Combines white panel along rear of wing with white 'landing lights' at shoulder. Similar Black-necked (right) shows a touch more white along trailing edge but forewing is plain.

Status Rare breeder northern Scotland, more numerous in Scandinavia. Winter visitor to coasts elsewhere. In Britain, chiefly a local winter visitor (October-April). Small numbers regular in Ireland. **Population** c80 pairs. Winter c500-1,000 birds.

Slavonian Grebe

Black-necked Grebe

◆ Nests on freshwater lochs fringed with sedges, reed and willow ◆ 'Song' includes a loud accelerating trill and nasal, rattling *ij-aarrr* ◆ Essentially maritime in winter, occurring singly or in small groups in estuaries, inlets and bays (in Britain, favours 'traditional' sites off Scotland and southern England). Most likely inland during hard weather ◆ Silent in winter.

Distinctive in summer plumage. In winter, very like Slavonian but has different head shape, more slender 'waisted' neck, and slimmer bill with chiselled tip that gives characteristic uptilted look. Often sits high on water with tail puffed-up like Little Grebe.

Adult summer All black neck and rather sparse, fanning spray of golden plumes behind eye (like combed wet hair) diagnostic. Has chestnut flanks and white stern, but seems all dark at distance.

Adult winter Glistening red eyes and distinctly monochrome appearance preclude confusion with Little Grebe. Trickier to separate from Slavonian but seems 'scruffier'. Head provides the key.

Black-necked Note steep forehead and peaked 'riding hat' crown; has extensively dark ear-coverts smudging onto white cheek, sullied grey foreneck and thin, uptilted bill.

Slavonian Compare sleeker 'flat-capped' appearance; has sharper contrast between clean-cut black crown and gleaming white cheeks, (usually) much whiter foreneck, and straighter bill with clear white tip. Pale loral spot is lacking in Black-necked.

Juvenile/first-winter From winter adult by brownish tone to grey sides of face and neck.

Status Breeding distribution decidedly patchy in NW Europe. In Britain, occurs principally Aug-Apr, in mainly southern counties. Handful nest N England/Scotland. Now also rare in Ireland (formerly bred). **Population** c30-60 pairs. Winter 120+ birds.

◆ Breeds on well-vegetated freshwater lakes, preferably amongst nesting Black-headed Gulls ◆ In winter on reservoirs, gravel pits and sheltered estuaries and bays ◆ Often occurs singly or in company with other grebes. Gathers in small flocks at favoured sites (e.g. some London reservoirs) ◆ Swims quickly away or submerges when danger threatens ◆ More likely on freshwater in winter than Slavonian ◆ Pattern of white in wing separates flying birds on seawatches ◆ Breeding birds have whinnying trill like Little Grebe.

Little Grebe *Tachybaptus ruficollis*   25cm (10")

Smallest of Europe's grebes. Pint-sized, 'powder-puff' form, short neck and stubby bill diagnostic at all seasons. Loud, tittering trill (like whinny of a tiny horse) emanating from some secluded backwater is one of the most distinctive of all waterbird calls. Sexes alike.

Adult summer Brilliant yellow gape spot (visible at surprisingly long range), chestnut face panels and 'fluffy cottontail' prevent confusion with slightly larger Black-necked and Slavonian Grebes. Bill black, tipped white.

Winter plumage is more subdued. Combination of dull brown cap and upperparts with mainly buffy underparts unique among European grebes. Juvenile is similar, but has dark and light striped face, and rufescent neck.

Winter Dark eyes and buffy face separates from other small grebes in winter (cf. 'bloodshot' eyes of winter Black-necked and Slavonian.).

Status Resident. Our most numerous and widely distributed grebe. Shuns barren upland lakes and largely replaced by Slavonian in N of range.
Population c8,000-16,000 pairs.

Flight Timid and easily disturbed. Dives to escape danger (often skulking beneath bank until coast is clear) or skitters across water, half-running, half-flying, to safety of reedy cover. Note upperwing usually lacks white panels shown by all four larger grebes, but secondaries are whitish in some individuals.

◆ Breeds on slow-moving rivers and inland waters with well-vegetated margins. Watch for bird swimming close to swampy margins ◆ Buoyant. Rides high on water, with characteristic rounded back and 'sawn-off' tail ◆ Dives frequently (sometimes with a jump), but soon bobs to the surface again, like a cork ◆ Disperses in winter to form small flocks on larger, more open waters, in harbours and on sheltered estuaries ◆ Flocks keep in contact with sharp 'asdic' bleeping.

Thickset seabird with a stout, hooked bill. In flight the narrow, stiffly-straight wings and bursts of rapid flapping, or bounding, between long glides gives action quite unlike the flexed, slower wing beats of gulls. Wingspan 105cm (41").

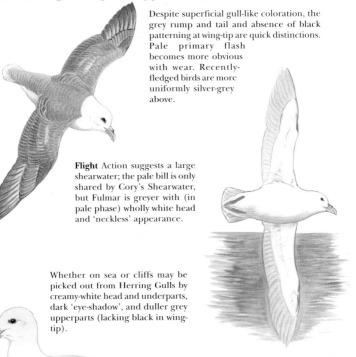

Despite superficial gull-like coloration, the grey rump and tail and absence of black patterning at wing-tip are quick distinctions. Pale primary flash becomes more obvious with wear. Recently-fledged birds are more uniformly silver-grey above.

Flight Action suggests a large shearwater; the pale bill is only shared by Cory's Shearwater, but Fulmar is greyer with (in pale phase) wholly white head and 'neckless' appearance.

Whether on sea or cliffs may be picked out from Herring Gulls by creamy-white head and underparts, dark 'eye-shadow', and duller grey upperparts (lacking black in wing-tip).

Status Present throughout year. Visits breeding cliffs from mid-winter to late summer; pelagic after breeding. Exceptional inland. Rare south of mapped range. **Population** 570,000 pairs (increasing).

◆ Spends long periods gliding effortlessly along cliff-tops, with wings slightly depressed (end-on, distant birds can suggest Peregrine) ◆ Pairs squat close together on sea-cliff ledges, billing and cackling. Occasionally nests some distance inland ◆ Young Fulmars deserted after being fattened-up by their parents in late summer, are forced to 'fast' until the down is lost, and hunger drives them away to sea ◆ Small parties gather on sea off breeding cliffs; also forms larger congregations to scavenge around fishing-boats at sea ◆ Patters across water's surface to take to the air (unlike gulls) ◆ Most birds in our region are pale phase, but wholly grey individuals (blue phase) become increasingly frequent in the far north.

9

Cory's Shearwater *Calonectris diomedea*   48cm (19")

Bulkiest shearwater. Heavy head and uniformly brown upperparts, some with narrow pale crescent on rump (cf. Great). Thick yellow bill diagnostic.

Head and neck duller and more diffuse than Great. Broad wings characteristically bowed, wingspan 100-125cm; in calm weather hugs water with flap-flap-glide action.

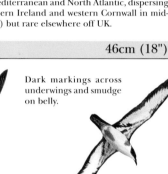

In rough weather, soars high, then sweeps down into wave-troughs much like an immature Gannet.

♦ Breeds on islands in Mediterranean and North Atlantic, dispersing north to waters off southern Ireland and western Cornwall in mid-summer (July-September) but rare elsewhere off UK.

Great Shearwater *Puffinus gravis*   46cm (18")

Large shearwater, wingspan 100-118cm. Distinguished from Cory's by clean-cut dark cap, white collar, and distinct white horseshoe at base of tail. Black bill.

Dark markings across underwings and smudge on belly.

Flight action tends to be rather stiffer than Cory's.

♦ Breeds in South Atlantic. Found off Ireland and Western Isles in mid-summer (July-September) but rare elsewhere off UK ♦ Highly pelagic.

Sooty Shearwater *Puffinus griseus*   43cm (17")

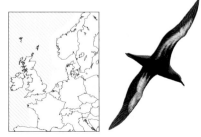

Larger and longer-winged than Manx and Mediterranean, wingspan 94-109cm. Sooty all over with silvery wing-linings. Absence of white in upperwing distinguishes Sooty from distant dark phase skua. In calm weather flies fast and low, making short glides between rapid beats of narrow, swept back wings; bounds high over rough seas. Breeds in southern hemisphere. Most often seen off western seaboard and northern North Sea, July-October. Highly pelagic.

Manx Shearwater *Puffinus puffinus* 34cm (13")

Clean appearance obvious in good light; note white vent.

Slender bill, 'low shoulder' and long wings make it look rather odd on water (cf. auks), wingspan 76-82cm (30-32").

Distant birds flash black and white as they swing from side to side.

Status Common summer visitor (late Mar-Sep), wintering S Atlantic. Most abundant off western seaboard, but parties of non-breeders likely off all coasts. **Population** 250,000 pairs (95% of world population).

◆ Slender-winged, black and white seabird with little variation in size or plumage ◆ Only auks are similarly patterned but are smaller-winged and have direct whirring flight ◆ Pelagic but comes to land under cover of darkness to nest in burrows on grassy islands off north and west coasts ◆ Sociable; flocks travel in lines or small groups ◆ In strong winds progresses with bounding, swinging glides and short bursts of rapid flapping. In calm weather flaps for longer periods, with short swinging glides, hugging the surface.

Mediterranean Shearwater *Puffinus yelkouan* 36cm (14")

Slightly larger and shorter-tailed than Manx. Palest birds similar to Manx but have browner upperparts and duskier foreneck and vent; often also with duller underwing. Wingspan 78-89cm (31-35").

Status Nests colonially on Mediterraean islands. Regular visitor off British Isles, May-Oct (rarely even in winter). Numbers vary, but often quite common in SW waters (rare elsewhere).

The darkest birds are easily confused with Sooty Shearwater, but latter is larger, with longer, more angled wings and has a more bulging forehead. Mediterranean also always has a pale centre to the belly centre.

◆ Formerly treated as a race of Manx, when termed 'Balearic Shearwater' ◆ Plumage variable but always browner than Manx ◆ Breeds in Mediterranean but visits Britain each autumn.

11

Storm Petrel *Hydrobates pelagicus* 15cm (6")

Tiny size renders it almost invisible on water, like tiny piece of flotsam.

Flight Rapid, low over water like a small dark wader ▼ or bat (looks blacker overall and square white rump more obvious than that of Leach's). Wings lack tern-like impression and show only trace of pale line on upperside, wingspan 37cm (15"). Tail is square.

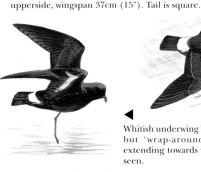

Status Summer visitor (May-Sept), wintering S Atlantic. Most abundant off western seaboard, but possible off all coasts. **Population** 70,000-250,000 pairs.

Whitish underwing bar is diagnostic, but 'wrap-around' white rump extending towards vent more easily seen.

◆ Tiny dark seabird, typically seen from boats at sea as rarely near land in daytime ◆ Breeds in large numbers on rocky islets, but only visits under cover of darkness. Proclaims presence at night by guttural purring from beneath boulders or within stone walls ◆ Feeds on surface plankton in fluttering and dancing motion, picking at surface. Attends fishing boats.

Leach's Petrel *Oceanodroma leucorhoa* 22cm (9")

In good light, underwing brown (lacks whitish band of Storm); often shows contrast with darker flight feathers, wingspan 48cm (19"). Rump patch does not extend round body as in Storm.

Status Very local summer visitor (May-Nov). Winters in tropical Atlantic. **Population** 10,000-100,000 pairs (8 known colonies).

In good light, browner than Storm; pale panel across upperwing often conspicuous (lightens with wear). Rump patch less obvious, often broken in centre. Forked tail not apparent unless bird close.

◆ Larger than Storm Petrel, with longer, angled wings (has wing-shape and buoyant action reminiscent of Black Tern) ◆ When feeding, swoops and wheels to patter on surface with wings held flat, or dips with briefly-raised wings like Black Tern. Seldom attends fishing boats ◆ Nesting habits similar to Storm, but confined to more remote islands ◆ Most likely to be seen from Atlantic seawatching points after severe storms, October-December. Weakened birds may be 'wrecked' inland.

Our largest seabird, wingspan 170cm (67"). In flight the dagger-like bill and sharp tail give the cigar-shaped body the appearance of being pointed at both ends. Head and tail ends project equally fore and aft of long, pointed wings – thus overall shape is distinctly 'pointed at all corners' and quite unlike that of gulls, skuas or shearwaters. Sexes similar. Fully adult plumage attained in stages by fourth or fifth year.

Adult Stunning whiteness visible at long ▶ range. Yellow-buff head of breeding plumage becomes whitish in winter.

◀ **Second-year** Unmistakably patchy above. The head is normally whitish until the third year.

Sits buoyantly on sea, with pointed tail cocked. Takes off with short splashing run over surface to get airborne.

Juvenile Blackish-brown, with white belly and tail crescent, and grey-brown breast. Can suggest rare Cory's or Great Shearwater when distant, but shape and darker underwing distinctive. ▶

Status Common at sea, but only locally close inshore. Nonbreeders present off all coasts throughout most of the year. In British Isles, breeds in dense colonies at 22 sites in N and W but only one English colony (Bempton, Yorkshire with 1250 pairs). **Population** 187,700 pairs but 75% of these in 5 huge colonies: St Kilda, Grassholm (Dyfed), Ailsa Craig (Strathcyde), Little Skellig (Co Kerry) and Bass Rock (Lothian).

Third-year 'Piano-keyboard' wing pattern identifies. ▶

Executes spectacular dives from a great height, with neck outstretched like an arrow. The splash is visible over long distances.

◆ Sociable. Nests on small islands in dense, noisy and smelly concentrations ◆ Flight action steady on measured wing-beats. Flocks usually travel in lines or small groups ◆ In strong head-winds, progresses with prolonged banking glides like enormous shearwater. In calm weather readily soars high over sea ◆ Dolphin schools are often found near feeding Gannet flocks.

Large blackish waterbird, equally at home on both fresh and salt water. Long neck and tail, slim bill and bulky body. Both Cormorant and similar Shag stand upright on waterside rocks, buoys and posts, often with outstretched wings. Cormorants also perch on dead trees and power lines.

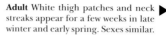

Adult White thigh patches and neck streaks appear for a few weeks in late winter and early spring. Sexes similar. ▶

◀ Tree-nesting Continental race *sinensis* is white-headed in spring. Visits east coast of Britain, but many (possibly older) birds of nominate race *carbo* are very similar.

Swims low in water, with bill carried upwards. Shows glimpse of long tail as it rolls forwards into dive (cf. divers).

◀ **Immature** Most are mottled below, with some whitish on breast; a few are almost entirely white below. Fully adult plumage attained by third winter.

Juvenile Head and bill shape a flattened-wedge in profile. Orange-yellow of throat skin extends over lower cheeks and upper lores (cf. Shag).

Flight Recalls a blackish goose, especially when high, but long tail of Cormorant provides a quick diagnosis. Wings and rear body longer and neck thicker than Shag. Immature (right) lacks pale wing panel of immature Shag.

Status Common resident, partial migrant and winter visitor. Widespread in Britain, but thinly distributed. **Population** 11,700 breeding pairs

◆ Sociable, found on coasts, estuaries and inland lakes and rivers ◆ Nests in small colonies on coastal cliffs and slopes, especially on islets. There are a few inland colonies in waterside trees (e.g. 350 pairs at Abberton Reservoir, Essex) ◆ Flies fast and direct when low over water but generally flies higher than Shag, the quick wing-beats interrupted by short glides ◆ Parties moving overland from roost to feeding waters form lines or chevrons like geese ◆ Feeds on fish, normally diving with forward-roll from surface. (When feeding over deep water sometimes jumps clear in manner of Shag) ◆ Fish are brought to the surface to swallow. ◆ Patters over surface on take-off.

Very similar to Cormorant, but Shag is smaller (not always apparent unless the two are together) with less chunky head and neck, steeper forehead and thinner bill (less of a tapering wedge). Unlike Cormorant, is almost exclusively coastal. Sexes similar.

Adult breeding Curly crest diagnostic, but only worn from January-April; yellow only on gape (Cormorant has orange-yellow face and white cheeks). ▶

Typically (but not always) dives by jumping clear of water. (Cormorant usually sinks forward, but occasionally jumps).

▲ Look for short head with steep forecrown and slim bill.

Immature Usually browner than Cormorant, with distinctive pale scaling on forewing (can bleach very pale when worn). Underparts vary from extensively off-whitish to brown with white only on throat. Legs often fleshy-pink. Fully adult plumage attained by third winter. ◀

▲ **Juvenile** Lacks orange-yellow on face but pale eye-ring often obvious; brown (not whitish) cheeks contrast cleanly (not diffusely) with white throat.

Flight Rear body ends abruptly behind wings (longer rear body of Cormorant tapers into tail). Wings also shorter. In immatures, contrasting light forewing panel aids identification.

Status Fairly common resident, breeding along rocky coasts. Very local in NE England; uncommon visitor rest of E and SE England. **Population** 47,000 breeding pairs.

◆ Sociable seabird of rocky coasts and islands, harbours and lower reaches of estuaries ◆ Nests in small loose colonies, amongst boulders or in caves ◆ Juveniles often very approachable in harbours and will sit on waterside rocks with fishermen ◆ Not normally on freshwater, but occasionally 'wrecks' of birds (usually juveniles) inland after prolonged gales ◆ Flight rapid, typically hugging surface of sea, overtaking Cormorant if flying together. Does not normally fly very high and avoids going overland (cf. Cormorant). Flies round, rather than taking short-cut over, headlands ◆ Gathers into rafts on sea in favoured feeding bays ◆ Freely mixes with Cormorants when standing on rocks.

15

Secretive marsh bird, seldom seen in open. Plumage highly cryptic, blending buffs, browns and intricate blackish markings that perfectly match its reedbed habitat and render the bird all but invisible – even when close. Crown and moustache black. Legs and bill greenish-yellow. Sexes alike; juveniles have indistinct brownish moustache.

Often appears surprisingly small on ground, with crouching walk, head held low (not standing tall like heron). Seen head-on, has laterally-compressed body like Water Rail. Inches slowly and deliberately forward, 'nosing' gently through emergent vegetation and peering intently at water. 'Freezes' with neck and bill pointing skyward, to merge imperceptibly with surroundings.

Looks large in flight, characteristically low over reedtops. Mottled buffy appearance and broad, rounded wings give owl-like impression but legs trail in true heron-fashion and thick neck often hunched. Flight feathers rufous, barred black.

Status Scarce resident, range very fragmented in NW Europe. Rare and extremely localised resident in Britain, nesting at a few sites in E Anglia/Lancs. Vulnerable in severe winters; dwindling British population bolstered by small-scale influxes from continent (Nov-Feb).
Population <20 booming males.

◆ Breeds in large, unpolluted wetlands with extensive reedbeds ◆ Presence is usually only betrayed by deep booming song (February-June) – like sound produced by blowing across top of an empty bottle (no two birds sound quite alike) ◆ Sound carries c5kms but when close is clearly preceded by audible intakes of breath: *uh uh uh-WOOMP, uh-WOOMP* ◆ Most easily seen in June-July, when making regular flights to nest ◆ More widespread in winter, dispersing to smaller marshes, lakes, even gravel pits; sometimes forced into open during cold snaps ◆ Flight call a short *kow* ◆ Similar juvenile Purple Heron has longer bill, snakier neck and unmarked, dark-brown flight feathers.

16

Little Bittern *Ixobrychus minutus* 36cm (14")

◀ **Male** Black upperparts and flight feathers with rich buff underparts and buff-white wing patches. Yellow bill and greenish legs.

Similar female (not shown) has browner back and more striped chest; wing patches duller.

Juvenile Browner, more streaked ▶ and spotted; looks like a miniature Bittern, but has pale wing patches.

Status Summer visitor. Winters in tropial Africa. Rare spring overshoot to S Britain (has bred).

◆ Europe's smallest heron ◆ Locally common in stands of *Typha* and reed fringing freshwater wetlands and sluggish backwaters ◆ Sometimes seen clambering up tall reedy stems at water's edge, freezing to escape notice ◆ Note tiny size and striking pale oval on black wing, conspicuous at rest and in brief flights low over reedtops ◆ Male's spring song is frog-like *wogh*, repeated every few seconds ◆ Hunts fish, frogs, insects.

Night Heron *Nycticorax nycticorax* 60cm (24")

Adult Sexes alike. Black crown and back, grey wings and tail, ▼ and white face and underparts. In breeding season, wears 2-3 white plumes on nape; yellow legs become red for a time.

Immature Brown, with bold white spotting above and untidy streaking below. Bill mainly yellowish. Might be confused with much larger Bittern.

◀

Status Summer visitor (Mar-Nov). Winters in tropical Africa. Annual vagrant to Britain.

Flight Has compact flight silhouette, with bunched neck and rounded wings.

◆ Small squat heron with large red eyes and black bill ◆ Nests colonially in thickets by slow-moving rivers and marshes ◆ Largely nocturnal, but sometimes unwittingly flushed from daytime roost in leafy waterside trees ◆ Flies out to hunt fish and frogs at dusk, just as other herons are returning ◆ Distinctive flight call a gruff croaking, *kwok*.

Squacco Heron *Ardeola ralloides*   46cm (18")

Adult summer Rich buff body with long ▶ drooping mane of black and white feathers hanging from nape, and bluish spear bill with dark tip, unique among European herons.

Flight Transformed into a surprisingly white heron with characteristic brown 'saddle'.

Status Scarce summer visitor (Apr-Sep). Winters in Africa. Vagrant to Britain.

Winter/immature Plumages clearly streaked brownish on head, neck and breast. Legs and dark-tipped bill, greenish-yellow.

◆ Small, white-winged heron, locally common in wetlands in south/east of region ◆ Nests sparingly with other herons, in bushy wetland clumps ◆ At rest, buff (summer) or brownish (winter/juvenile) plumage blends perfectly with swampy vegetation, so often overlooked until it flies ◆ Stalks fish, frogs and insects in shallows ◆ Usually silent; occasionally a harsh, duck-like quack in flight.

Cattle Egret *Bubulcus ibis*   50cm (20")

Adult summer Orange-buff on crown, lower ▶ throat and mantle. Legs, bill and eyes become red when breeding, then 'fade' to yellow.

Flight Looks stubby in flight. Notice dark feet (Little Egret's are yellow).

Status Mainly resident. Has spread from Iberia to S France (range slowly expanding northwards). Vagrant to Britain.

Winter/juvenile White with yellow eyes and bill, and blackish legs. Differs from Little Egret in its stout pale bill (dusky in very young birds), shorter neck and stockier build.

◆ Small, sociable white heron; in our region mainly in the Camargue ◆ Conspicuous and rather tame ◆ Breeds near water but unlike other herons, feeds mainly in pastures, picking off insects disturbed by grazing stock or plough ◆ Jerks head as it walks, jabbing at prey ◆ Mostly silent.

Little Egret *Egretta garzetta*   60cm (24")

A slim heron with slender bill, black legs and diagnostic yellow feet. Breeding adult acquires two long nape plumes, feathery aigrettes on back, and orange lores – all absent in non-breeding/immature plumages, when lores bluish.

Flight Leisurely; neck hunched but legs trail to reveal bright yellow 'socks'. (Juvenile has greyish-green feet).

Status Common in southern wetlands. Most winter in Africa. In Britain formerly a rare visitor but dramatic recent increase following northward range extension in France. Several hundreds now 'resident', forming substantial roosts at favoured coastal sites in S and SW. Has bred.

◆ Frequents estuaries, lakes, marshes ◆ Makes erratic, darting runs through shallows in pursuit of small fry ◆ Dazzling white plumage stands out, but often hides in creeks and is surprisingly easy to dismiss as a gull when hunched or roosting.

Great White Egret *Egretta alba*   85-102cm (33-40")

Breeding adult Yellowish legs, black bill and long feathery plumes (aigrettes) on back. Lacks head plumes shown by Little Egret.

Flight Slow, flapping steadily like Grey Heron. (cf. Spoonbill, which flaps and glides, with long neck extended.)

Status Rare and extremely local breeder. Increasing in winter, notably in Camargue. Vagrant to Britain.

Winter/juvenile Distinguished from Little Egret by its large yellow bill, longer neck and longer legs with dark feet. Unlike other white herons, gape-line finishes well behind eye.

◆ Much the largest white heron. When seen with Little Egret looks almost twice as big, with characteristically long, snaky neck distinctly kinked in middle (like Purple Heron) ◆ Breeds in reedy eastern European wetlands, few elsewhere ◆ Walks tall and sedately, often stealing thigh-deep through water (cf. Little Egret's erratic runs).

19

Grey Heron *Ardea cinerea* 94cm (37")

Tall, familiar and easily recognised bird of rivers, lakes, marshes, estuaries and creeks. Apart from strays, the only heron in Britain. Long neck and predominantly grey and white plumage distinguish it from all other birds except rare Crane, but note Heron's long yellowish legs and dagger-like yellow bill. Elsewhere in Europe, confusion also possible with darker Purple Heron.

Adult Head, neck and underparts mainly white, with black hindcrown and dark streaks on foreneck. Blue-grey upperparts relieved by solid black patch at shoulder on standing bird (lacking on immature). Breeding adult has pale scapular plumes, elongated wispy black plumes on nape and bill and legs become 'blushing' red for a short time. Sexes alike. ▶

Juvenile Differs in dark grey legs and forecrown (latter white in adult), dark upper mandible, and duskier ('unwashed') grey face and underparts. Sub-adult ◀ retains grey crown.

Easily overlooked when hunched motionless in field or stock-still beside water.

Flight Large; long neck drawn into shoulders but legs trailing. Dark grey underwing and white 'landing lights' on leading edge of wing (conspicuous on approaching bird, but buffy on juvenile) are characteristic.

Status Common and widespread resident, frequenting all waters (inc. urban areas and uplands). **Population** c14,000 nests in Britain & Ireland. Some continental birds winter here.

Flies with slow, deep beats of long, broad and strongly arched wings.

◆ Nests colonially (February onwards) in traditional heronries. Bulky stick nest placed high in treetops; sometimes in reedbeds ◆ Mainly solitary outside breeding season, but gathers in loose aggregations at favoured spots ◆ Walks tall in slow, stealthy quest for fish, frogs, even worms and birds ◆ Call distinctive: a loud, harsh *frarnk* given in flight or alarm as bird takes wing.

Purple Heron *Ardea purpurea*

80cm (32")

Adult Purplish-slate above with black crown and nape plumes, maroon 'shoulders' and elongated cinnamon scapulars. Rufous-buff face and neck, striped black. Underparts chestnut, shading to black. Juvenile browner (cf. Bittern).

Status Localised ummer visitor. Nests Netherlands, eastwards. In Britain, rare visitor (April-October), mainly eastern & southern England.

Flight Like Grey Heron, but slighter body often lifts on downstroke. Look for characteristic 'U-bend' bulge in hunched neck, untidy feet trailing like bundle of twigs, and buffy 'landing lights'. Underwing dark – adult with chestnut underwing-coverts. Upperwing of adults more uniformly dark than Grey Heron.

◆ Furtive skulker in dense reedbeds and swamps ◆ Often stands motionless 'like dead branch' until unwittingly flushed ◆ Smaller and darker than Grey Heron, with more spear-like yellow bill and kinked, 'broken' neck giving different jizz – like snake about to strike.

Spoonbill *Platalea leucorodia*

85cm (34")

Adult summer Shaggy crest, yellow tip to bill, bare yellow throat and tawny-yellow band at base of neck – all lacking in non-breeding plumages.

Juvenile Pinkish bill and legs which darken during first year.

Status Uncommon; extremely localised colonial nester. Winters Mediterranean/Africa. Scarce visitor (esp. in spring) to coastal counties in S & E England, where a few also overwinter.

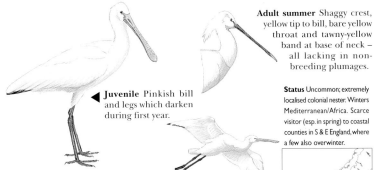

Flight Legs trail, flies with neck extended and stiff, shallow beats followed by glide. Immature (shown) has black primary tips.

◆ Frequents estuaries, marshes ◆ Heron-like, but long dark bill with spatulate tip unique. Appreciably larger than Little Egret and more creamy-white ◆ Feeds by sweeping bill from side-to-side in shallows – an excellent fieldmark, even at great distance ◆ Rests with head and bill tucked into back, when easily overlooked ◆ Silent.

Black Stork *Ciconia nigra* 97cm (38")

Flight Entirely black above. From below, 'white waistcoat' is diagnostic.

Status Summer visitor mainly to E Europe (Apr-Sep). Rare in our region but slowly increasing. Rare vagrant to Britain.

Adult When white chest is hidden, overall dark appearance makes it tricky to spot on ground. Plumage looks glossy at close range, with red eye patch, bill and legs. Similar juvenile is blackish-brown with greenish legs and bill.

◆ Slightly shorter and more sinister looking than White Stork, as though wearing black cloak ◆ Generally shy and wary ◆ Sometimes seen in fields with White Stork, but prefers to forage alone by rivers and in forest clearings ◆ Solitary breeder, concealing bulky stick nest within canopy of leafy forest tree or cliff cave ◆ Migrates to Africa, travelling in family groups or flocks.

White Stork *Ciconia ciconia* 110cm (43")

Flight Broad, fingered wings flapped slowly in flight, with frequent glides. Often soars, like a raptor. White forewing and tail always distinguishes from Black Stork, though both species appear dark at long range. Unlike herons, flies with neck extended.

Status Lost to most of NW Europe this century; more frequent in east. Winters mainly in Africa. Annual vagrant to Britain.

Adult Unmistakable; white with black wings, and long red bill and legs. When close, white looks dirty, as if tobacco stained.

◆ Conspicuous summer visitor (February-August/September), well-known for its habit of constructing huge stick nests on rooftops, old trees and pylons ◆ Not shy ◆ Walks quietly and sedately in open fields, damp meadows and marshy edges, feeding on frogs, fish, reptiles, insects ◆ Noisy bill-clattering from pairs at nest can be heard some distance away, otherwise silent ◆ Migrates in big flocks.

Greater Flamingo *Phoenicopterus ruber*   125-145cm (49-57")

Adult Unmistakable; a familiar zoo bird, distinguished from escapes of other species by bill pattern and all red legs.

Pale pink adult shows rose red forewing in flight.

Juvenile Dirty grey-brown, with dark legs.
▼

Status Breeds in Camargue, mainly a summer visitor but some overwinter.

◆ Restricted to saltpans and coast of southern France, with single colony in Camargue (20,000 birds). Heads south in winter (c5,000 remain) ◆ Goose-like honking characteristic of flocks ◆ Probably a vagrant to Britain, although majority are escapes of pinker American races.

Common Crane *Grus grus*   112cm (44")

Adult Bushy black 'bustle', long black legs and pale bill diagnostic. Striking head pattern, although red crown patch hard to see in field. Juvenile browner with reduced 'bustle' and plain sandy head and neck.

Flight Strong with measured beats and glides on flat, rectangular, fingered wings. Legs trail but unlike Heron, neck is extended. Flocks travel in Vs or lines.

Status Breeds bogs and marshes across N/C Eurasia; winters S Europe/Africa. Vagrant to Britain and very rare resident (Norfolk, 2-12 birds).

◆ Huge bird of marshes, open fields ◆ Substantially larger than Grey Heron, but looks mainly grey at distance ◆ Loud throaty, bugling *krroo* (like an echoing Whooper Swan) carries over 2kms, often first sign that cranes are about ◆ Slow, stately walk, picking at plant and animal matter.

Mute Swan *Cygnus olor*   140-152cm (56-60")

The familiar swan. A majestic inhabitant of ponds and waterways throughout much of region; also estuaries and locally in sheltered coastal bays. Easily distinguished from the two 'wild' swans by bill pattern, pointed tail (useful when bird asleep), and in flight by the throbbing drone of its wings (silent in the other two swans).

Adult Graceful curving 'swan-neck', and orange-red bill with black basal surround and knob, diagnostic of Mute. Sexes similar, but male rather larger and with a more bulbous knob at bill base.

Adult Habit of swimming with arched wings is unique to Mute; this threat posture is exaggerated by territorial males in spring (as shown).

First-year Mute Darker and browner than either Bewick's or Whooper. Blackish face and longer tail can be evident even at long range. Adult plumage attained by second winter in all swans.

◀**First-year Whooper** Paler, cinnamon-toned grey-brown. Has a short, blunt tail and pale-based rose-pink bill (cf. similar Bewick's).

Heads of first-year swans Mute (top) is the only swan with black at base of greyish-pink bill. The other two have rose-pink bills with pale flesh towards the base (shape of pale area a 'ghost' of forthcoming adult yellow pattern). By first spring, the plumage whitens and the rosy area of the bill becomes black, making the precise pattern obvious (basal area remains whitish flesh). Whooper (bottom) has a longer head and bill than Bewick's (centre), with a distinct high peak to rear crown creating a 'Roman-nosed' appearance.

Status Common and wide-spread resident over lowland areas; avoids upland waters.
Population 33,000 individuals (absent Shetland).

◆ More restricted to water than other swans but will graze nearby meadows (Bewick's and Whooper habitually feed in fields, but roost on water) ◆ When swimming, bill typically points at water (other swans look straight ahead) ◆ Nest a large platform of vegetation, close to water ◆ Family groups keep together until following spring, when parents chase them from their territory ◆ Nonbreeders form flocks throughout the year ◆ Only vocalisations are snorts, grunts and hisses. Lacks noisy bugling of other swans in flight, but wing beats produce a throbbing or whistling sound which is audible over a considerable distance.

Bewick's Swan *Cygnus columbianus* 120-135cm (47-53")

Whooper and Bewick's Swans are very similar, and often difficult to separate. Bill pattern is crucial to diagnosis of adults, but relative sizes and head and bill shapes also differ. Lone first-years can be problematic. ▶

Adult Bill pattern varies, but always more black than yellow; black sometimes extends right up culmen to forehead. The yellow patch is quite rounded (does not project as a point like Whooper).

Adult Smaller, shorter-bodied and shorter necked than other swans, with smaller, rounder head and shorter bill than Whooper. Bill appears black with yellow base (cf. Whooper).

Status Winter visitor from Siberian tundra. In British Isles, chiefly to England and S Ireland; few elsewhere. **Population** A significant proportion of the western population increasingly winters – up to 9,000 (1250 in Ireland), with the Ouse Washes holding up to 5000.

Flying adults Separation from Whooper tricky, although blacker bill of Bewick's (top) often evident. Bugling calls, but quiet wings, distinguish both from Mute.

◆ Similar habits to Whooper but more agile, takes-off and lands with greater ease; birds dropping towards ground come in at a steeper angle ◆ Groups joining flock indulge in noisy greeting displays ◆ Voice higher in pitch than Whooper but both have various calls; distant fying flock recalls yelping pack of small dogs.

Whooper Swan *Cygnus cygnus* 140-165cm (55-62")

◀

Adult Bill pattern varies little, with more yellow than black. Yellow extends into the black in an obvious point (cf. Bewick's).

Adult Larger size, longer neck, peaked crown and long 'Roman-nose' bill aid separation from Bewick's. Bill appears yellow with black tip (cf. Bewick's). Head and neck often stained rusty, less frequently so with the other two swans.

Status Winter visitor from Iceland and N Europe. Most of Icelandic population winters in Ireland and Scotland, with significant numbers N & E England; rare S England. **Population** Increasing, up to 15,000 winter (12,000 in Ireland); a few pairs nest Scotland but some are feral.

◆ In winter, frequents open fields, shallow lakes and estuarine flats
◆ Usually in family parties, which gather into herds (locally in hundreds). Small numbers occur with herds of Bewick's in East Anglia
◆ At distance, impression of mainly pale bill can be useful pointer – Bewick's typically seems dark.

Bean Goose *Anser fabalis*   70-90cm (27-35")

Larger and darker relative of the Pinkfoot, and the only dark-billed grey goose with orange legs. Two forms occur which may be specifically distinct. Most seen in Britain are of the nominate race *fabalis*, which is larger with a noticeably longer neck and snout than Pinkfoot, the long upstanding neck being especially striking when alert. Smaller individuals of the rarer race *rossicus* approach Pinkfoot in size and structure, but have darker upper flanks, ashy-brown (not cinnamon-buff) breast and lack silvery tone to upperparts of Pinkfoot. First-winter birds can be aged by flank and wing-feather shapes (see Pinkfoot). Compare also first-winter Whitefront, which can be confusing at times.

Adult *fabalis* Almost as large as Greylag. When alert the neck is long and slim, with the forecrown sloping into a long bill to give a 'Roman-nosed' appearance. The dark head and patterned bill recall Pinkfoot, but in Bean the legs are typically bright orange (duller yellowish-orange in immatures).

Flight Bean has dark forewing and a mostly dark tail (with narrow white border), like Whitefront. Pinkfoot shows pale grey forewing and a much whiter tail, with small dark grey centre.

Adult *fabalis* Bill pattern varies – typically blackish over basal half and tip, with wide orange subterminal area, but some have much less black (suggesting young Whitefront). Both races and Pinkfoot often show a narrow white line at base of bill.

Status Rare and very localised winter visitor (Nov-Feb) from N Europe (declining) and Siberia. **Population** Nominate race *fabalis* (Taiga Bean): 500 birds. Race *rossicus* (Tundra Bean): very sporadic in appearance.

Adult *rossicus* Smaller and shorter-necked than nominate with a shorter bill and steeper forehead, recalling Pinkfoot. Bill often more blackish than in nominate race but pattern equally as variable.

◆ When identifying distant geese, beware of tricks of the light which can make pink legs appear orange (and *vice versa*); this can be particularly problematic under very bright winter light conditions. ◆ Voice lower in pitch than Pinkfoot, the latter's diagnostic *wink-wink* phrase being replaced by a deeper *hank-hank* ◆ Two regular winter concentrations in Britian: Norfolk (Yare Valley) and southern Scotland (Carron Valley); sporadic elsewhere.

Pink-footed Goose *Anser brachyrhynchus* 60-75cm (24-30")

Small grey goose, though size not always easy to gauge in the field. Better to concentrate on structure: note Pinkfoot has a stubby bill and neat, rounded head atop rather short dark neck. Dusky-pink legs and small, mainly black bill with variable pink band near tip diagnostic. First-winter has more yellowish feet.

Adult Marked contrast between uniformly dark head and neck and distinctly paler, grey-buff chest picks out Pinkfoot, even at distance. In good light, blue-grey wash across upperparts gives distinctly frosted look, lacking in other grey geese.

All adult grey geese can be recognised by their prominent 'gill-slits' (distinctly ruffled neck feathers that look as though they've been combed whilst wet), and square-cut back feathers with narrow buff-white tips (dividing upperparts into pattern of regular 'bands').

First-winter Duller, with more 'bland-looking' faces, smoother neck feathers, and more rounded feathers on back and flanks, giving rather mottled or 'scaly' appearance.

Status Locally common winter visitor (breeds Iceland/Greenland). Keeps mainly to established haunts. In Britain, majority occur S/E Scotland (mid Sep-Apr, with stragglers to end May). Smaller concentrations Lancs and NW Norfolk (Oct-Mar); few elsewhere. **Population** c200,000 birds.

Flight Shows conspicuous lavender-grey forewing and dark underwing (darker than Greylag). Small head and short, waisted neck are important pointers, but pale tail and voice offer best clues to identification.

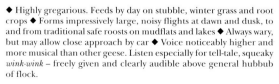

◆ Highly gregarious. Feeds by day on stubble, winter grass and root crops ◆ Forms impressively large, noisy flights at dawn and dusk, to and from traditional safe roosts on mudflats and lakes ◆ Always wary, but may allow close approach by car ◆ Voice noticeably higher and more musical than other geese. Listen especially for tell-tale, squeaky *wink-wink* – freely given and clearly audible above general hubbub of flock.

White-fronted Goose *Anser albifrons*   65-80cm (25-30")

Chunky, medium-sized grey goose with a square head and orange legs. Two distinct races occur. Black belly bands of adults are usually visible long before the white frontal shield behind the bill is apparent. First-winter birds identifed by combination of pinkish or yellow-orange bills (depending on race) and dull orange feet.

Adult *albifrons* (Siberian) White 'front' rather variable in extent (most obvious when bird is head-on) and head darkest immediately behind frontal band. Dark belly bands are variable in size and shape. Bill pinkish becoming yellowish at very base. Only Bean Goose shares orange feet.

First-winter *albifrons* Lacks white 'front' and belly banding of adult. Often shows a dusky nail at tip of bill and greyish shading on the bill suggesting rarer Bean; latter has different head and bill shape and bold blackish bill markings.

Adult *flavirostris* (Greenland) Slightly larger, with a longer 'snout' than Siberian birds and darker head and upperparts. Belly barring typically bolder and broader. Bill orange-yellow, becoming pinkish only towards tip.

Status Localised winter visitor (Oct-Mar/Apr). Siberian race winters mainly at Slimbridge, Norfolk and the Swale; Greenland race winters Ireland, W Scotland, and a few in W Wales (Dyfi estuary). **Population** Siberian race: 5000-7000 birds; Greenland race: 30,000 birds.

Flight Dark forewing and underwing like Bean, but belly barring of adults provides an easy distinction.

◆ Flocks graze fields and estuarine saltings, Greenland race also amidst peat-bogs ◆ Roosts on tidal flats and lakes ◆ Entire world population of Greenland race winters in the British Isles, mainly Wexford Slobs and Islay ◆ Winter numbers of Siberian birds in England fluctuate, may increase dramatically following severe weather on the continent ◆ Noisy; calls include distinctive musical yelping phrase *kow-lyou* or *lyo-lyok* .

Lesser White-fronted Goose *Anser erythropus*   53-66cm (21-26")

Very rare. A few pairs breed in Lapland and migrate with flocks of White-fronted. Note more conspicuous white forehead blaze projecting higher onto crown; yellow eye-ring is diagnostic. Small individuals markedly daintier than White-front, with smaller head and bill, shorter neck and longer primaries. Large individuals are particularly problematic. First-winters lack white forehead but show pale eye-ring. Note quicker feeding action and higher-pitched voice than White-fronted Goose.

Greylag Goose *Anser anser* — 75-90cm (30-35")

Largest grey goose and ancestor of most domestic geese. Apart from introduced Canada Goose, and odd injured birds or escapes of other species, the only goose likely to be seen over most of the region in summer. Majority are of nominate race *anser*, with orange bills. Paler eastern race *rubrirostris* (nests in east of region) has pink bill.

Adult Distinguished from all other grey geese by weightier build and unique combination of outsize 'carrot' bill and pink legs. At a distance, can often be picked out by contrast between grey-brown upperparts and pale and rather uniform head, foreneck and underparts – chest may appear almost white at times. Narrow orange eye-ring at close range. Juvenile similar.

Flight Strikingly pale grey forewing makes this the easiest *Anser* goose to identify in flight. Heavy head and big pale bill conspicuous. Flies strongly, making spectacular whiffling descents to land. Grey rump coupled with dark tail band are reliable fieldmarks.

Viewed overhead (top), Greylag's underwing coverts much paler than other grey geese (e.g. Bean Goose, bottom).

Status Breeds patchily in N & E of region. Winter visitor elsewhere (Sep-Apr). **Population** Entire Icelandic population of >100,000 birds winters in Britain, chiefly on farmland across Scotland. In summer 25,000 birds (mainly feral, but indigenous population of c3000 birds confined to N Scotland/W Isles).

◆ Nests beside lochs, reedy lakes, marshes. Also a common feral introduction on lakes, gravel pits and broads across southern Britain ◆ Gregarious, forming large flocks on farmland in winter ◆ Roosts on water, flighting out noisily at dawn to crop nearby fields ◆ Heavy, rolling gait ◆ Take-off ponderous – broad wings sound stiffly starched ◆ Noisy. Loud calls include distinctive farmyard goose cackling and an angry honking in flight: *aahng-ahng-ung*. Always sounds bad-tempered – an excellent pointer.

29

Canada Goose *Branta canadensis* — 90-100cm (35-40")

The most familiar goose over much of inland England. A large brown goose, with distinctive long black neck, topped by broad white chin strap and contrasting with whitish breast. All plumages similar. Noisy honking voice.

Adult Long black neck contrasts with pale breast. Less white on head than Barnacle (which has black breast), more of a wide white grin.

Flight White 'U' separates black rump and tail, useful on rear views of rising birds (cf. rear-patterns of Greylag and Whitefronts).

Status Well-established introduction from N America, mainly to Sweden (these birds wintering south to Netherlands) and British Isles. Common in England, but local in Wales and Scotland; few in Ireland. **Population** 60,000 birds (increasing rapidly).

Loud, resonant, trumpeting *ah-honk* heralds flying flock. Flocks form lines or chevrons when high. In silhouette long, slender neck evident.

◆ Noisy inhabitant of farmland, parks, gravel pits, lakes and estuaries. ◆ Nonbreeders form large flocks ◆ Many northern birds fly to Beauly Firth (southern Scotland) to moult in mid-summer, returning south in autumn ◆ Flocks attract both escaped and wild geese of various kinds. Such birds also often hybridise with Canada Geese, producing peculiar offspring ◆ Very small, shorter-necked birds rarely occur; these may be of pale-breasted race *hutchinsii* (known as Richardson's Goose) or brown-breasted race *minima* (known as Cackling Goose), but their status here as either true vagrants or escapes is unknown.

Bar-headed Goose *Anser indicus* — 75cm (30")

Native of central Asia, popular in collections. Escaped or feral birds (even family groups) frequently turn up in flocks of Canada Geese.

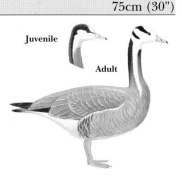

Adult Beautiful silvery-grey goose with unusual transverse black bands on back of white head. Orange bill and legs add to distinctive appearance. In flight, forewing very pale grey, both above and below. Head pattern is lacking in juveniles but yellow-orange bill and legs aid identification.

Barnacle Goose *Branta leucopsis* 64cm (25")

Adult An immaculate, sociable little goose, only slightly larger than a Mallard. Tiny bill and white face peering out of black 'balaclava' diagnostic. Unlike much larger Canada Goose, black extends over breast and body is grey (not brown). All plumages similar, but juvenile duller with plain, unbarred flanks.

Status Increasing. Winter visitor (Oct-Apr), chiefly to coastal Netherlands, W & N Ireland, W Scotland and Solway Firth (Dumfries/Cumbria). Uncommon elsewhere. **Population** 50,000 birds (60% of world population). Irish (8,000) and W Scottish birds (mostly on Islay; 26,000) are from Greenland, whereas entire Svalbard population (12,000) winters on Solway. (Dutch population breeds in Novaya Zemlya.)

Flight Compact shape and white 'U' separating black rump and tail useful when bird flying away. (Similarly small Brent has almost wholly white rear-end.)

Flying flocks tend to form masses or lines, rather than chevrons.

◆ Despite relative abundance is very local. In Scotland grazing flocks carpet fields in dense concentrations, but Irish birds tend to be in smaller scattered flocks ◆ Noisy, even when feeding, their high-pitched, yelping barks reaching a crescendo as the shimmering flock rises – sounds not unlike a pack of chasing hounds ◆ Feral or escaped birds are also frequent at inland sites in England, often with Canadas.

Snow Goose *Anser caerulescens* 65-80cm (26-31")

Escaped or feral birds (even family groups) are widespread, typically mixed with flocks of Canada Geese. Vagrancy from North America possible in some cases, but small feral population on Mull obscures status of birds found in western Scotland. Occurs in two colour phases (but intermediates frequent); all have snarling reddish-pink bill and feet when adult, dusky when juvenile.

Adult white phase Black primaries and thin, pointed tertials rule out occasional white individuals of other geese. Adult blue phase is a dark grey goose with a white head. Some have much white on underparts, others are simply white-headed.

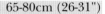

Small, dark, dumpy goose of estuaries and adjacent fields. Conspicuous white rear body contrasts with mud-brown upperparts (and fore flanks in nominate race). Black head, neck and breast (without white on face) an easy distinction from similar-sized Barnacle Goose, but adults show a white mark at sides of neck. Sexes similar. Two distinct races occur.

Adult Dark-bellied race *bernicla* from Siberia ▶
shows variably paler rear flanks which are
otherwise slaty-brown like upperparts.

◀ **Adult** Light-bellied race *hrota* from
Svalbard, Greenland and Canada
has pale (often almost silvery) flanks
giving strong contrast with black
breast. Cleaner and purer brown upperparts help separate duller flanked
individuals from even the palest Dark-
bellied race.

Flight Small, duck-like goose that flies in
ragged flocks not V formation. Black tail
almost hidden by stunning white rear so
that often looks tailless in flight.

Status Locally common winter
visitor (Sept-Apr) to coasts.
Rare inland. **Population** Dark-
bellied 100,000-130,000 (S & SE
England plus Low Countries).
Pale-bellied 17,000-22,000 (NE
England, Ireland and Denmark).

Juvenile Lacks neck patch in autumn but this soon acquired;
by winter many are more safely aged by narrow pale bars
across wings (absent in adults). Flanks are more uniformly
brown than adults, indeed even juvenile Light-bellied has
brownish wash on flanks which can be confusing. Numbers
vary according to breeding success in Arctic.

◆ Rarely mixes with other geese, but groups of either race sometimes
join with each other ◆ Isolated small groups or lone birds are often
remarkably confiding ◆ Dense packs feed over tidal mudflats and
adjacent fields, at high tide often joining roosting waders ◆ Distant
flocks appear as blackish mass in fields ◆ Call is a low, throaty, rolling
kr-runk – the confidential grumblings of birds feeding and in flight
being quite unlike the honking notes of other geese.

Egyptian Goose *Alopochen aegyptiacus* 68cm (27")

Distinctive ornamental 'misfit' from Africa that looks as though it's made of parts left over from other ducks! Popular in captivity and well established in eastern England. Basic plumage tone of upperparts varies between rufous and grey, but not enough to confuse. Sexes similar.

Juvenile Lacks belly patch. ▶ Has brownish crown and nape, and greyish legs.

◀ **Adult** Very pale, with small dark patch on centre of belly. Dark 'blinkers' around eyes, foxy tertials and long pink legs are easy field-marks.

Status Introduced to and resident in E England and the Netherlands. **Population** Around 800 birds.

Flight (grey individual shown) Bold white forewing obvious from above and below.

◆ Low-lying freshwater lakes, grassland and parks ◆ Grazes in pairs or family parties in waterside fields, but nests and perches freely in trees ◆ Territorial males are noisy, uttering loud, donkey-like braying *hah-hah-hah-hah*. Aggressive towards other waterfowl in the breeding season.

Ruddy Shelduck *Tadorna ferruginea* 63cm (25")

Distinctive ginger shelduck, with rusty-orange body and pale head in all plumages. Some wild vagrants from Asia occur, but most are escapes. Popular in captivity and on park lakes, with a small feral population established in the Netherlands. Found on lakes, estuaries and waterside fields.

Breeding male Has narrow black ring around neck (lacking in female).

Flight Shows white forewing contrasting with black flight feathers, rump and tail – much like Egyptian Goose.

Common Shelduck *Tadorna tadorna* 61cm (24")

Large, mostly white duck of estuaries, conspicuous with its glossy green-black head and neck, waxy-red bill and rusty-chestnut breast band. Unlike other ducks, the sexes are similar. Juveniles and eclipse adults lack the rusty breast band and have whitish face and foreneck.

▶

Adult female Although basically similar, females are smaller and drabber than males, with reduced breast and belly patterns, some whitish on the face and duller bills, without basal knob.

Adult male In spring males the basal knob becomes swollen and more vivid in coloration. ◀

Up-ending Patterned bottom and reddish-pink legs are another unique combination but compare drake Shoveler.

◀ **Juvenile** Lacks rusty breast band, has a greyish bill and legs and whitish face and foreneck; adults plumage similar for a few weeks following the post-breeding moult (eclipse). Such birds can appear most peculiar, especially lone partly-grown youngsters (cf. distant birds with Avocets)

Flight White forewing and body distinctive; only drake Goosander and Red-breasted Merganser have similar pattern but both these have much faster, more direct flight and dark rumps and uppertails.

Status Widespread around all coasts. **Population** 50,000 birds present in breeding season (including a good percentage of nonbreeders); with 84,000 in mid-winter (30% of European total).

◆ Muddy and sandy estuaries; not infrequent during passage times on inland waters ◆ Most adults leave most British estuaries in July to migrate to northern Germany (Waddensee) to moult, leaving creche of chicks in charge of one or two adults which stay behind. Smaller moult gatherings also occur on 4 or 5 larger British estuary systems. Vanguard return to UK estuaries October-December ◆ Nests in holes, especially fond of rabbit burrows. Frequently nests far from water, both parents then escort brood of chicks overland for 1km or more to reach water ◆ In courtship male bows to female, or follows her in flight, uttering series of mellow twittering whistles; female has a guttural, almost 'laughing' *ahng-ahng-ahng* ◆ Feeds by skimming bill over mud surface and readily up-ends whilst swimming.

Smaller than Mallard, with dark legs and a highly characteristic outline created by short blue-grey bill, steep forehead and sharply pointed tail. Drake is grey-bodied, with bold black and white rear-end, and often shows white shoulders. Female unmarked rich brown on breast and flanks, with clear white belly and distinctive head shape as give-away features.

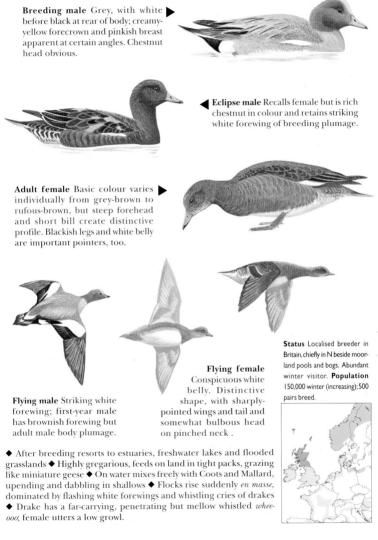

Breeding male Grey, with white before black at rear of body; creamy-yellow forecrown and pinkish breast apparent at certain angles. Chestnut head obvious.

Eclipse male Recalls female but is rich chestnut in colour and retains striking white forewing of breeding plumage.

Adult female Basic colour varies individually from grey-brown to rufous-brown, but steep forehead and short bill create distinctive profile. Blackish legs and white belly are important pointers, too.

Flying male Striking white forewing; first-year male has brownish forewing but adult male body plumage.

Flying female Conspicuous white belly. Distinctive shape, with sharply-pointed wings and tail and somewhat bulbous head on pinched neck .

Status Localised breeder in Britain, chiefly in N beside moorland pools and bogs. Abundant winter visitor. **Population** 150,000 winter (increasing); 500 pairs breed.

◆ After breeding resorts to estuaries, freshwater lakes and flooded grasslands ◆ Highly gregarious, feeds on land in tight packs, grazing like miniature geese ◆ On water mixes freely with Coots and Mallard, upending and dabbling in shallows ◆ Flocks rise suddenly *en masse*, dominated by flashing white forewings and whistling cries of drakes ◆ Drake has a far-carrying, penetrating but mellow whistled *whee-ooo*; female utters a low growl.

Drake an inconspicuous dark grey dabbling duck, rather smaller than a Mallard, with an inky-black stern and diagnostic (but often partially hidden) white speculum. Females have a smaller white speculum and can be difficult to separate from Mallard, but note clean-cut bill pattern and, when ashore, show much whiter belly (cf. Wigeon). Swimming birds often seem to be leaning forward – a useful pointer at a distance.

Breeding male Dark grey, shading blackish at rear of body, contrasting with pale tail; white and chestnut speculum may be partially hidden. In eclipse much as female but retains male wing pattern. ▶

◀ **Adult female** Smaller, with neater head and bill, and whiter belly than Mallard (visible when upending). Juvenile, however, has mottled belly which can be confusing. Well-defined orange bill sides and dark culmen readily distinguishes Gadwall from female Mallard, which has more patchy bill.

Flight Gadwall (below) is rather smaller and sleeker than Mallard (top), with striking white belly in adults (mottled in juveniles). ▶

Mallard

◀ **Flying male** Striking white speculum, underwing and belly contrast well with darkness of rest of plumage.

Gadwall

Status Localised resident and partial migrant in Britain; chiefly England. **Population** 9,000 winter (increasing); 800 pairs breed.

◀ **Flying female** Smaller speculum patch than male (may even be absent in juvenile females).

◆ Shallow freshwater lakes, reservoirs, gravel pits, etc. Small numbers locally on upper reaches of estuaries ◆ Generally singly or in small parties with other ducks, often close to emergent vegetation or in quiet backwaters away from main lakes ◆ Often associates with feeding Coots ◆ Drake utters peculiar nasal *angh* accompanied by a shrill whistle *pyee*. Female has a typical Mallard-like decrescendo of *kwaks* but rather high in pitch.

Mallard *Anas platyrhynchos* 58cm (23")

Our most familiar duck, the archetypal duck of cartoons, park lakes and the dinner plate! Our largest dabbling duck; males (drakes) are distinctive but females can be easily confused with others of the genus, notably Gadwall and Shoveler, both of which share Mallard's orange feet. Juveniles and eclipse males resemble females.

Breeding male Grey-bodied and pale-billed, with ▶ distinctive combination of bottle-green head, purplish-brown breast and narrow white collar. Note short, curly tail centre when close.

Adult female Combination of dark crown and eyestripe, pale tail, and black and orange patches on bill useful. Check for orange legs and mottled belly when out of the water (cf. Gadwall). ▼

Eclipse male In late summer male resembles female but has more rusty breast and plain yellowish bill.

Female Gadwall Slightly smaller, with plainer head than Mallard. Note clean-cut pattern on bill, which shows orange sides and black culmen stripe (rather than patches).

Flight Both sexes show double white wing-bars, one each side of metallic purple-blue speculum; from below white underwing coverts contrast with mottled brown underbody of female.

◆ Freshwater bodies of all kinds favoured, from streams and small ponds to large reservoirs; locally in sheltered coastal bays and on estuaries ◆ Nests both on ground and in holes, including tree holes and disused nests of large birds (e.g. crows) ◆ Ancestor of many forms of domestic ducks, most of which look nothing like the original ◆ Introductions of birds for both shooting and ornamental purposes has given a 'farmyard' influence to many of our wild populations ◆ Female alone tends ducklings (as with most other ducks) ◆ Male utters soft, rasping *kreep*; female has the well-known mocking decrescendo *KWAAK-KWAK-KWAK-kwak-kwak......* ◆ Short legs gives awkward waddling gait on land, prefers feeding in water by dabbling and upending.

Status Common & widespread throughout Britain and Ireland.
Population 120,000 breeding pairs but true wild population becoming increasingly invaded by domestic strains.

37

The smallest dabbling duck. Neatly proportioned, with oval head and slightly upturned, slim dark bill. Short dark legs noticeable when upending or standing. Flight fast, with sharply pointed wings showing white central bar and green speculum in all plumages, but generally looks dark at a distance. Garganey is the most likely confusion species.

Breeding male Grey-bodied and dark-headed, with white stripe along scapulars and triangular yellow-buff patches on vent. Chestnut and green of head often difficult to discern. ▶

Adult female Note small size, dark bill and legs, green speculum and weak head pattern. Creamy stripe at sides of tail (actually along under-tail-coverts), absent on similar Garganey. Eclipse male similar but darker, with eyestripe less distinct. ◀

Green-winged Teal Breeding male of vagrant ▶ American race *carolinensis* has vertical white stripe at breast sides and lacks white scapular stripe. Females indistinguishable from those of resident race.

◀ **Female** Weaker facial pattern than Garganey, with smaller bill; when close note fleshy-orange tones at gape – not shown by Garganey.

Status Fairly common. Small numbers breed throughout Britain and Ireland; abundant after autumn and winter influxes. **Population** 6,000 breeding pairs; 150,000 in winter. Vagrant *carolinensis* possible amongst flocks in winter and spring.

Flight Both sexes show white mid-wing bar, green speculum and narrow white trailing edge. Underwing greyish with white area in centre following dark band along leading edge – a pattern shared only by Garganey.

◆ Breeds by freshwater marshes and moorland bogs. Non-breeders resort to flooded meadows, shallow edges of reservoirs and lakes, upper reaches of estuaries and locally in sheltered coastal bays ◆ Forms enormous flocks in winter at key sites, often with Wigeon and Mallard. Feeds by dabbling over mud surface or in shallows and by upending ◆ Rises suddenly from water, flying swiftly and with great agility, typically in small, twisting groups that can look rather wader-like in the distance ◆ Far-carrying call of male, a mellow *proop-proop*, is a typical sound of winter wildfowl gatherings.

This little duck is a summer visitor to freshwater marshes. Only marginally bulkier than Teal, but with head more angular in outline and the bill distinctly heavier. Male is the only duck (apart from Mandarin) with a conspicuous white supercilium. Forewing of drake appears pale silvery-grey in flight, unlike any other duck. Female easily confused with female Teal but head pattern bolder and belly whiter (see below).

Breeding male Bold white swirl of a supercilium and pale lavender flanks contrast with chestnut-brown of head and breast. ▶

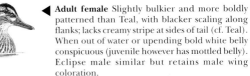

◀ **Adult female** Slightly bulkier and more boldly patterned than Teal, with blacker scaling along flanks; lacks creamy stripe at sides of tail (cf. Teal). When out of water or upending bold white belly conspicuous (juvenile however has mottled belly). Eclipse male similar but retains male wing coloration.

Flying male Pale grey of forewing extends onto primaries (indeed very distant birds may appear strangely white-winged). Speculum narrow and green, with broad white borders. (Shoveler has bluer grey forewing and whiter underwing.)

Female Distinct pale supercilium and dusky lower cheek enhances blackish eyestripe and white 'spot' at base of bill. Bill is wholly grey and larger than that of Common Teal. Note that female Common Teal often shows a palish spot at base of bill.

Female Forewing brownish-grey with white border to often dull (but can be green) speculum obvious only at trailing edge (*vice versa* in Teal, which shows prominent white bar across midwing), as in female Pintail. Underwing similar to that of Teal but leading edge even blacker, giving more pronounced striped effect.

Status Scarce summer visitor, chiefly England, Mar.-Sept. **Population** 40-100 pairs, depending on strength of spring influx. Higher numbers at passage times, but still uncommon.

Juvenile male Forewing paler than female with both speculum borders narrow. ▶

◆ Freshwater marshes and wet meadows; in spring especially favours cover of emergent vegetation ◆ In late summer and autumn may join parties of Common Teal in shallow bays of reservoirs and lakes ◆ Males remain in eclipse plumage until late in autumn or winter, acquiring breeding plumage in Africa prior to spring migration.

Large but slender dabbling duck, with a relatively long neck, pointed tail and rounded crown. Overall shape and slim lead-grey bill useful features at all times. Name refers to male's elongated central tail feathers which may be up to 10cm (4") additional to the body length, although they can be difficult to see unless close. Female recalls outsized, stretched female Common Teal, with which they often associate.

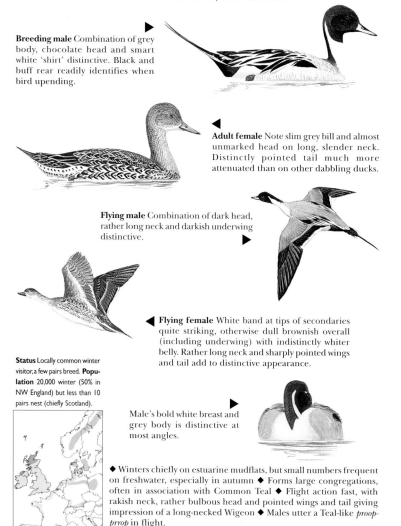

Breeding male Combination of grey body, chocolate head and smart white 'shirt' distinctive. Black and buff rear readily identifies when bird upending.

Adult female Note slim grey bill and almost unmarked head on long, slender neck. Distinctly pointed tail much more attenuated than on other dabbling ducks.

Flying male Combination of dark head, rather long neck and darkish underwing distinctive.

Flying female White band at tips of secondaries quite striking, otherwise dull brownish overall (including underwing) with indistinctly whiter belly. Rather long neck and sharply pointed wings and tail add to distinctive appearance.

Status Locally common winter visitor, a few pairs breed. **Population** 20,000 winter (50% in NW England) but less than 10 pairs nest (chiefly Scotland).

Male's bold white breast and grey body is distinctive at most angles.

◆ Winters chiefly on estuarine mudflats, but small numbers frequent on freshwater, especially in autumn ◆ Forms large congregations, often in association with Common Teal ◆ Flight action fast, with rakish neck, rather bulbous head and pointed wings and tail giving impression of a long-necked Wigeon ◆ Males utter a Teal-like *proop-prrop* in flight.

40

Front-heavy freshwater duck, usually found dabbling in small groups near water's edge. At all times outsized, long broad bill distinctive but strikingly patterned male is quite unmistakable. Sleeping birds on shore show orange legs like Gadwall and Mallard, females of all three being easily confused if bills hidden.

Breeding male White breast contrasts ▶ with chestnut flanks and dark green head.

◀ **Adult female** Like female Mallard but head plainer and bill much larger and longer, often with tip touching water when head relaxed. Eyes dark.

Eclipse male Rustier flanks and bluer ▶ forewing than female, also pale eye. In autumn head darkens but leaves whitish facial crescent; full colour attained in early winter.

Flight Faster than other dabbling ducks, the rather long neck and bill and relatively short tail creating a top-heavy appearance.

◀ **Male** Blue forewing and chestnut belly distinguish from similarly patterned Shelduck.

Status Fairly common. Thinly scattered over Britain and Ireland, but few in west. **Population** 1000-1500 breeding pairs, 8000 in winter (few sites support more than 75 birds even in winter).

Female Large bill gives rather long, ▶ front-heavy appearance in flight when compared to Mallard. Forewing greyer than male, with narrower white bar; young females duller still, with forewing grey-brown.

◆ Shallow freshwater lakes with fringing and emergent vegetation, gravel pits and reservoir margins, more locally by tidal estuaries ◆ Typically found in small parties, feeding closely one behind the other, sifting sediment stirred up by feet of bird ahead ◆ Males utter nasal grunting *g'dunk-g'dunk-g'dunk* during spring courtship, even in flight.

Red-crested Pochard *Netta rufina* 55cm (22")

This large diving duck behaves more like a dabbling duck. Almost unmistakable although female head pattern superficially resembles that of female Common Scoter (unusual on inland waters in south). Favours large, shallow freshwater lakes.

Breeding male Stunning marmalade-orange head, black breast and intense red bill. In eclipse, resembles female but bill remains red. ▶

Status Breeds in small numbers over S and C Europe but uncommon or rare overall. Small numbers breed E England; otherwise scarce visitor elsewhere in UK, most likely on lowland lakes in England (most assumed to be escapes).

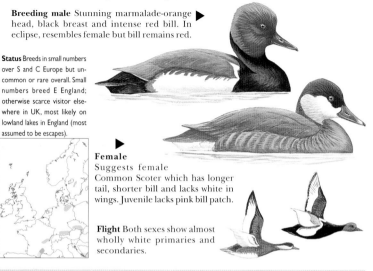

▶ **Female** Suggests female Common Scoter which has longer tail, shorter bill and lacks white in wings. Juvenile lacks pink bill patch.

Flight Both sexes show almost wholly white primaries and secondaries.

Ferruginous Duck *Aythya nyroca* 40cm (16")

Compact rich dark chestnut or brown diving duck with snowy-white undertail. The peaked crown, enhanced by sloping forehead and rather long bill, should be apparent even if the bird is asleep. Some Tufteds are similarly white-vented but the white is rarely so clean; and they also show a lump at the rear of the flatter crown and a wider bill with more black at the tip. Keeps close to cover of aquatic vegetation in breeding season. Non-breeders mix with flocks of Tufted and Pochard.

Status Scarce breeder C Europe. Rare but annual in UK, most likely lowland lakes in SE and N England in autumn and winter (most thought to be escapes).

Breeding male White eyes. In poor light ▶ appears dark with white vent; latter forms square (tail raised) or triangle (tail depressed). Peaked crown important.

◀ **Female** Duller than male, with dark eye and less clean vent, but head and bill shape distinctive.

Flight Both sexes look highly contrasting in flight; shows bolder belly patch and wider and whiter wing-bars than Tufted, although not quite so much as Red-crested Pochard.

Medium-sized freshwater diving duck with smoothly-peaked head shape, enhanced by sloping forehead and longish, slightly retrousse bill. Breeding plumaged drakes distinctive but other plumages most easily diagnosed by 'ski-jump' head shape and lack of white wing-bar.

Breeding male More uniformly pale grey than Scaup and with red head; black breast and lack of white on ventral area prevents confusion with drake Wigeon. Eye red.

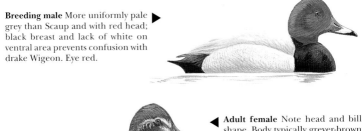

Adult female Note head and bill shape. Body typically greyer-brown than Tufted or Scaup, with variable pale facial shading (sometimes none). Eye brown. First-year birds have all dark bills.

Eclipse male In late summer males resemble females but have reddish eyes, more uniform reddish-brown head and paler bill band.

Male

Female

Flight Both sexes lack white wing-bars shown by others of genus.

Status Widespread breeder and common winter visitor. **Population** 400 pairs (chiefly in lowland England), with numbers building in autumn and winter to c50,000 birds.

◆ Nests close to water's edge on shallow, reedy freshwater lakes ◆ In winter, occurs on gravel pits, reservoirs and locally on wide estuaries ◆ Generally found sleeping in rafts with Tufted Ducks and Coots on open water ◆ In late spring, most flocks will be male-only; these flocks form whilst females incubate ◆ Female utters a harsh *kraah*, but male relatively quiet except for low, wheezy whistle ◆ Patters over water whilst rising, followed by fast direct flight – wholly grey upperwing then an easy feature to see ◆ Short rear-end and legs make walking difficult, but readily 'loafs' on shore with other ducks.

Medium-sized freshwater diving duck. Females in particular are rather variable, with many showing quite extensive white on face (cf. Scaup) and on undertail coverts (cf. rare Ferruginous Duck). Useful clues with difficult birds include Tufted's more extensive black at tip of bill and rather flat-crowned appearance, but with diagnostic ruffled angle or scruffy lump at rear of crown.

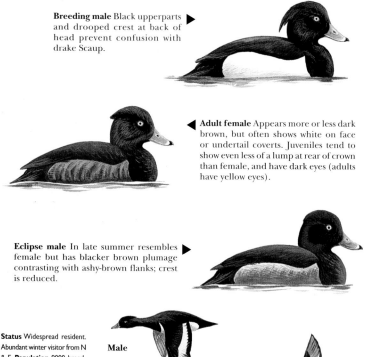

Breeding male Black upperparts and drooped crest at back of head prevent confusion with drake Scaup.

Adult female Appears more or less dark brown, but often shows white on face or undertail coverts. Juveniles tend to show even less of a lump at rear of crown than female, and have dark eyes (adults have yellow eyes).

Eclipse male In late summer resembles female but has blacker brown plumage contrasting with ashy-brown flanks; crest is reduced.

Male

Female

Status Widespread resident. Abundant winter visitor from N & E. **Population** 9000 breeding pairs, with numbers building in autumn and winter to 90,000 birds.

Flight Both sexes show white wing-bars, similar in extent to those of Scaup, but less extensive than in Ferruginous.

◆ Freshwater lakes and gravel pits, park lakes and locally on wide estuaries in winter ◆ Generally found sleeping in rafts with Pochards and Coots ◆ Breeds in scattered groups, often near colonies of Black-headed Gulls (the gulls tend to chase away potential predators) ◆ General behaviour similar to that of Pochard.

Medium-sized diving duck. The saltwater counterpart of Tufted Duck, which it recalls in all plumages but drakes have 'silver' back and females typically more white on face. Both sexes distinctly larger and broader in the beam than Tufted, with longer and larger bill and a gently rounded crown (lacking peak or bump).

Breeding male Note contrast between white ▶ flanks and grey upperparts (cf. Pochard). In eclipse, flanks and scapulars become browner and head and breast duller.

◀ **Adult female** White face also shown by many Tufteds but on Scaup is usually bolder, more extensive. Pale 'ear-muffs' (if present) are diagnostic but are not always obvious. Note head and bill shape. Juveniles lack white on face and are even more similar to Tufted.

First-winter male Blackish-brown head and ▶ breast; grey 'frosting' appears on upperparts and eyes become yellow as winter progresses.

Flight Both sexes show similar wing pattern to Tufted Duck.

Female

Male

Female Scaup (upper) and Tufted (lower) heads: Note longer, larger bill of Scaup, with black restricted to nail, smoothly-rounded crown and larger size. In fresh plumage the 'ear-muffs' are obscured by brown feather tipping.

Status Breeds mainly in N Europe, but widespread off coasts in winter. **Population** 0-5 pairs (chiefly Scotland). Up to 9000 birds in winter, most in Scotland and N Ireland (few in S and SW England or Wales).

◆ Individuals occur on inland lakes with other diving ducks, but the majority winter in sheltered coastal bays and estuaries ◆ At favoured sites forms dense rafts along shallow coasts ◆ On inland waters, odd birds may be picked out from amongst rafts of Tufted (even when asleep) by rather larger, longer body and more sloping rear end ◆ Female shows a little more black at bill tip than does male, but 'inland Scaups' with extensive black are most likely hybrids with Tufted or Pochard.

Common Eider *Somateria mollissima*   61cm (24")

Large, well-built sea-duck, both sexes with triangular head shape created by long sloping forehead and peaked crown. This impression only shared with Velvet Scoter, but approached by rare Surf Scoter and King Eider. Generally seen inshore, flocks typically consisting of piebald drakes of various ages and all-brown females.

Breeding male Not fully adult until third or fourth winter. ▶ Black and white head pattern with pale green nape diagnostic. Breast pale pink.

Adult female Rusty-buff and brown. ▶ Compare wedge of feathering protruding onto sides of bill with blunt lobe of 'happier' female King Eider.

Eclipse male White forewing and blackish breast are chief differences from first-summer birds. ▼

First-winter male Similar to female but darker and ▶ more finely barred. White begins to appear on breast in early winter. By end of first winter, drakes have much white on breast and scapulars but forewing not white until second winter (cf. eclipse male)

Status Resident along coasts in N & W. In Britain, locally abundant resident in north, chiefly offshore N Scotland and islands but likely off all coasts. **Population** 72,000 birds in winter (50% mainland E Scotland), few S and W England but scattered birds and small parties possible all coasts. 30,000 breeding females.

Flight Barrel-bodied duck with rather wide wings and heavy head, often held low. Adult females have dingy underwing, which whitens with wear.

Male

Female

◆ Favours sheltered coastal bays and estuary mouths, where loafs on reefs, islets and sandbars. Rarely inland in UK, but regular on Swiss lakes ◆ Breeds colonially on islets. Females line nest with dense down self-plucked from their breasts (eider-down) ◆ Often dives with a flurried-splash; bringing up crabs which are swallowed on surface ◆ From late winter drakes display in the flocks, throwing head back and uttering endearing, purred *coo-AAOW*.

King Eider *Somateria spectablis* 54cm (21")

Slightly smaller than Common Eider, amongst which it is usually found. Unmistakable adult male plumage. Females identifiable with care.

Breeding male Note lilac head, green cheeks, and ▶ bright red bill 'crowned' by orange sail – latter visible at long range. Black back with twin 'shark fins' diagnostic. Pinkish bill distinguishes immature (not shown) from similar immature Common Eider.

Female From female Common Eider by scaly flank markings, head shape, and happier expression created by unique dolphin-like 'smile'. Notice blunt lobe of feathers at bill base (wedge-shaped in Common Eider), and two-tone head with grain of nape feathers cutting across grain of cheek feathers.

Status Rare winter visitor from Arctic to northern coasts (including Scotland); exceptionally rare further south. Strays often take up residence for long periods.

Flight Black back and isolated white wing ovals readily identify flying male.

Steller's Eider *Polysticta stelleri* 45cm (18")

A small eider (half size of Common Eider), breeding in eastern Siberia. Parties mix loosely with flocks of Common and King Eiders.

Breeding male Distinctive with combination ▶ of pale apricot underparts, black rear body and collar, and white head with 'greengage' on nape.

Status Recently found to winter in large numbers on coast of extreme NE Norway and in smaller numbers in the Baltic Sea. Exceptional vagrant to N Britain.

Female Unlike other eiders, ▼ sooty-brown females have a relatively square head, pale eye-ring and a conventional duck bill.

Blue speculum is bordered fore and aft with white (like Mallard), but is dull and bars narrower in first-year birds.

47

Long-tailed Duck *Clangula hyemalis* 36-46cm (14-19")

Small, squat sea-duck with short bill and pointed tail, extremely long in adult male, up to 13cm (5") additional to body length. In winter overall pale, neckless appearance and habit of opening its wings as it dives suggests an auk, particularly winter Black Guillemot. Plumage stages are complex, and ageing and sexing of birds other than adult males unreliable.

Winter male Chocolate and grey cheek patch on white head identifies. Note bright pink band across stubby grey bill. Long whip tail often trails on water, only flicking into view as bird dives.

Winter female Lacks tail streamers; has brownish back and pale patch around eye. First-winter birds (of both sexes) tend to be paler, with less-defined cheek patch than adult females, but variable.

First-spring male By March young males show pink on bill and dusky breast, but do not get their full male plumage until second winter.

Breeding male (April-August) Very dark with pale 'goggles' and white belly.

Breeding female Shape distinctive even though head pattern often obscured. Compact size, short tail and palest 'teardrop' face can sometimes suggest Puffin.

Female

Male

Status Breeds in N Europe. Winter visitor to coasts, especially Baltic and offshore N Scotland and islands, but small numbers likely all coasts of British Isles. **Population** Up to 20,000 birds in winter (50% in Moray Firth); has very rarely nested in N Isles.

Flight Both sexes have all dark wings, contrasting with white belly. Winter drake shows white sides to back. Flight action rapid and swinging on slightly bowed wings. Splashes down heavily onto water when landing.

◆ Breeds on tundra pools ◆ In winter, occurs mainly on sheltered coastal bays and estuaries. Odd birds not infrequent on inland lakes, but mixes little with other ducks ◆ Typically seen in small scattered flocks of 10-12 birds, even in favoured areas, belying overall abundance ◆ An avid and adept diver, spending more time below than on top of the water when feeding ◆ Often swims very low and difficult to see if water choppy ◆ Small size, rapid, shallow wing-beats and piebald coloration may give auk-like impression ◆ From late winter drakes display, throwing head back, raising tail and uttering far-carrying wailing cries, *ah-OWa-lee* – in chorus.

Chunky, neckless diving duck with small bill and triangular or 'baked potato' head shape. Drakes and females are quite unmistakable, but drab immatures are best identified by head and bill shape. Golden eye can be striking against dark head.

Breeding male Appears very white with bold ▶ black back-stripe and large green-black head. Look for diagnostic white face spot.

Displaying male Pairs form in winter quarters, when drakes avidly display by throwing head back and uttering shrill, speeded-up quack.

Adult female Typically looks dark and squat on water at distance, but block of white along wing is useful pointer. Note pale bill band and contrast between warm brown head and grey body, separated by distinct white collar. First-winter birds (not illustrated) are similar but much drabber-brown overall, lacking both collar and bill band. Head and bill ◀ shape are important features.

Flight A stocky, short-necked duck, both sexes with blackish underwings and white secondary patch. Female (below) has less white on upper-wing (although still very obvious). Rapid wing-beats produce a characteristic whistling noise (loudest in adult male), like sound of pebble skimming across ice.

Male

Status Widespread winter visitor from N Europe. Found in small flocks throughout British Isles in winter, and now breeding in Scotland. **Population** First bred 1970; provision of nest-boxes increased Scottish population to 100+ pairs by 1994. 30,000 birds in winter.

Female

Female upperwing

◆ Summers in northern Europe, nesting in tree-holes and nest-boxes (up to 3km from water) ◆ Females fly with remarkable agility through forest trees ◆ In winter, occurs on freshwater lakes, estuaries and in shallow coastal bays ◆ Usually in very small parties but at some northern coastal sites quite large congregations form. Mixes little with other ducks ◆ An adept diver, spending more time beneath the water than on top when feeding ◆ Often loafs on water with tail cocked, like a scoter.

Common Scoter *Melanitta nigra* — 48cm (19")

Dark, compact sea-duck with a slender neck and rounded head. Often swims with rather long, pointed tail cocked. Flocks frequently observed passing well offshore, either as straggling line of low-flying dark blobs or in more compact bunch with snaking tail. Unlike other scoters, eyes and feet dark. The most numerous of the three scoter species in the region.

Breeding male Entirely black plumage makes this the darkest scoter. Yellow spot-light on bill can be obvious at surprisingly long ranges. Only adult drake has black lump at base of bill.

Adult female Dark brown body and cap with contrasting 'milky coffee' cheeks, obvious even at long range. (Only female Red-crested Pochard similar, but that is a freshwater duck). First-winter like female, but more whitish on belly. By January, immature drake increasingly blackish on sides of head (beware confusion of birds with patchy cheeks with rarer Surf Scoter).

Female Surf Scoter

Flight Contrast between dark wing-coverts and paler flight feathers is a good fieldmark of Common Scoter – primaries of both sexes looking silvery in flight, even at considerable range. Compare uniformly dark wings of Surf Scoter and white wing panel of Velvet Scoter.

Female Common Scoter

Female Velvet Scoter

Status In NW Europe, nests mainly Scandinavia. Rare breeder also on handful of lochs in N Scotland/Ireland. Winter visitor to most coasts, sometimes massing in flocks of thousands (e.g. NE Scotland). **Population** c150 pairs, plus 1000+ summering non-breeders. Winter 25,000-30,000 birds.

◆ Breeds sparsely on freshwater lochs and pools, but spends most of year at sea ◆ Marked midsummer moult migration off English coasts and even overland northern England, when occasional on inland waters ◆ Congregates offshore in large flocks or slick-like rafts which bob into view then vanish again on the swell ◆ Dives to sea-bed for mussels, typically submerging with wings closed (cf. Velvet) ◆ Flocks usually dive in unison, springing back to surface after 20-30 secs ◆ Mainly silent; drake has soft whistled *cu*.

Velvet Scoter *Melanitta fusca* · 56cm (22")

Largest and bulkiest scoter, and the only one with white in wing – obvious in flight, but hidden or reduced to narrow wedge on swimming bird. More akin to Common Eider than Common Scoter in size and shape, with thickish neck, heavy bill and shelving forehead.

Breeding male Check for extensive orange sides to bill, visible at surprisingly long range. White iris 'shedding tear' confirms identity when close.

Status Nests Scandinavia/N Europe. Winter visitor (Sep-May) to most coasts. Erratic inland in south. **Population** 3,000-10,000 birds in winter; <500 summering non-breeders.

Female Sooty-brown, with dark grey bill. Note two whitish cheek patches, variable in extent (occasionally lacking). Lobe of feathering protrudes onto sides of bill unlike other female scoters.

First-winter As female, but belly whiter. By January, young male has blackish head with yellow in bill.

◆ Breeds on taiga pools and tree-lined Baltic coasts ◆ Winters mainly at sea ◆ Unlike Common, typically swims in single file or loose groups of 10-50 birds, although thousands may assemble at favoured spots ◆ Mixes freely with bigger and more tightly-packed flocks of Commons – Velvets often left stranded on surface when Commons dive in unison.

Surf Scoter *Melanitta perspicillata* · 51cm (20")

Rare but regular winter visitor from North America, chiefly to coasts of north and east Scotland. Look for in flocks of other scoters. Slightly larger than Common Scoter, and seems all head, with thicker neck. Male's swollen bill appears luminous orange, even at distance. Female resembles Common but has angular head, with tongue of feathering extending along top of bill. Flicks open wings to dive – watch for red legs. Wings uniformly dark in flight. Occurs singly (occasionally 2-6).

Breeding male Brilliant white nape and fore-head patch conspicuous at extreme range. Uniquely patterned bill red, yellow and white, with characteristic black 'hole'. Iris white.

◀ **Adult female** Typically dark-capped, with whitish patches on face and nape. Heavy grey bill abuts squarely onto face (cf. Velvet). Iris usually pale.

First-winter Like adult female but belly whitish, and eye and nape dark. By New Year, young males blackish with ghost of bill pattern and whitish nape. ▶

Red-breasted Merganser *Mergus serrator* 52-58cm (20-23")

Low, sleek sawbill (the genus *Mergus* has serrated edges to mandibles). Elegance suggests diver or large grebe but slender bill and wispy double crest diagnostic. Eyes red. Commonest of the three sawbills in British Isles, but outnumbered elsewhere in region by Goosander.

Breeeding male Smart appearance somewhat marred by shaggy ▶ crest. Slighter than Goosander with even thinner red bill. Streaked rufous-buff breast, white 'dog-collar' and bottle-green head with unique straggling crest. Black breast-sides enclosing white windows, and broad white wing patch sandwiched between black mantle and vermiculated grey flanks, conspicuous features at rest.

Female From similar female Goosander by scruffier ▶ 'hair-do', lack of sharp contrast between gingery head and pale chest, diffuse white chin patch and grubbier grey-brown body. At close range, look for dusky loral streak and reddish eyes (cf. Goosander). Juvenile duller than female – eyes, bill and legs brownish.

Eclipse male Quite scruffy by early June when head brownish with buffy collar. Increasingly like female as ◀ moult progresses, but has sootier mantle and retains extensive white in wing.

Flying female White on upper-wing crossed by single dark bar (cf. Goosander). ▼

Status Widespread resident in N and W. Winter visitor, principally to coasts elsewhere.
Population c3,000 pairs. Winter c10,000 birds.

▲
Flying male White collar, dark chest and mainly white innerwing crossed by twin black bar always distinguish drake Red-breasted Merganser from paler Goosander. Patters across surface to get airborne. Flight swift with neck held stiffly out.

◆ Nests close to water, in crevice or vegetation on ground ◆ Gathers in numbers on sheltered coasts for summer moult, when often seen loafing on shore ◆ Almost exclusively maritime in winter, occurring mainly in small groups within estuaries and inshore waters ◆ Feeds by diving for fish ◆ Usually silent, except in communal bowing display.

Goosander *Mergus merganser* — 58-66cm (23-26")

Freshwater counterpart of Red-breasted Merganser. However, both sexes are larger and bulkier, with neater head-shape, stouter base to red bill and brown eyes.

Breeding male Looks strikingly black and white at any distance. Quickly separated from drake Merganser by creamy-white underparts with delicate pink flush, and more bulbous, bottle-green head with full, bushy 'mane' hanging down towards back. Eclipse male is like female but mantle blacker, flanks paler, and larger white wing panel embraces forewing. ▶

Female Tricky to distinguish from female Merganser at ▶ longer ranges. Heavier build and neater, more bushy crest are useful pointers but better to look instead for darker chestnut-brown head with sharply defined white chin, clean-cut division between dark head and pale chest, and cleaner blue-grey body. When close, notice brown eyes and absence of dusky loral streak.

◀ **Juvenile** Dingier than female. Distinct loral streak and smudgy white chin provoke confusion with female Merganser, but eyes are yellowish.

◀ **Flying male** Conspicuous pale chest and extensive white 'arm-bands' identify (cf. male Merganser). Flight fast and direct after laboured, pattering take-off run.

Status Breeds across N Europe, shifting south as lakes freeze over in winter. In Britain, increasing resident:, chiefly nests Scotland (but spreading to N and W England and Wales); more widespread in winter. Rare Ireland. **Population** c2,700 pairs. Winter c8,000 birds.

Flying female Difficult to separate from female Merganser – best field-marks are Goosander's lack of obvious dark band across white wing-panel, and sharp divide between brown head and pale neck.

◆ In summer, nests in tree-holes beside forested rivers and lakes ◆ Winters mainly on freshwater, avoiding coasts and estuaries favoured by Merganser ◆ Typically encountered in small groups (upto c50 birds) on lakes and reservoirs ◆ Feeds chiefly on streams and rivers, assembling to roost on lakes ◆ Mostly silent, though wings make an audible hum in flight.

Smallest of the three sawbills, female scarcely bigger than a Common Teal. Compact diving duck recognised by its narrow grey bill, steep forehead, slight crest and striking plumage pattern. Male is unmistakable, but easily overlooked on broken water.

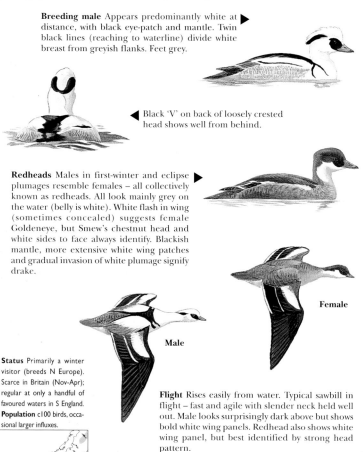

Breeding male Appears predominantly white at distance, with black eye-patch and mantle. Twin black lines (reaching to waterline) divide white breast from greyish flanks. Feet grey.

Black 'V' on back of loosely crested head shows well from behind.

Redheads Males in first-winter and eclipse plumages resemble females – all collectively known as redheads. All look mainly grey on the water (belly is white). White flash in wing (sometimes concealed) suggests female Goldeneye, but Smew's chestnut head and white sides to face always identify. Blackish mantle, more extensive white wing patches and gradual invasion of white plumage signify drake.

Female

Male

Status Primarily a winter visitor (breeds N Europe). Scarce in Britain (Nov-Apr); regular at only a handful of favoured waters in S England.
Population c100 birds, occasional larger influxes.

Flight Rises easily from water. Typical sawbill in flight – fast and agile with slender neck held well out. Male looks surprisingly dark above but shows bold white wing panels. Redhead also shows white wing panel, but best identified by strong head pattern.

◆ Nests in tree-holes beside wooded taiga lakes and rivers ◆ Winters mainly on shallow freshwater lakes, reservoirs; less often on saltwater ◆ Seldom numerous – typically seen singly or in small parties though hard weather in eastern Europe can trigger big influxes (especially to the Netherlands) ◆ At distance, redhead can be confused with winter Ruddy Duck or non-breeding Slavonian Grebe ◆ Male looks a little like winter Black Guillemot, but latter strictly maritime and has red feet ◆ Feeds mostly on fish.

Mandarin Duck *Aix galericulata* — 45cm (18")

Familiar ornamental duck, a native of East Asia. Female basically dark grey but no less distinctive, with its dappled flanks and maned nape.

Breeding male Exotic male unmistakable ▶ with its ginger sails and whiskers. Bill is red.

Female Grey bill, narrow white spectacles, ▼ and white chin and vent. Tail rather square. Male in eclipse plumage looks similar, but retains its red bill.

Status Introduced from East Asia, now well-established resident in southern England. **Population** 7,000 birds in winter.

Flight Both sexes show a similar pattern of clean white belly and contrasting dark upper- and underwings.

◆ Rivers and lakes in parts of Britain, especially wooded country in southern England ◆ Can be surprisingly difficult to see when resting amongst shade of waterside trees or on dappled water ◆ Nests in tree holes ◆ Often in small parties, flushing suddenly in manner of Common Teal and flying rapidly amongst trees.

Ruddy Duck *Oxyura jamaicensis* — 40cm (16")

Plump little freshwater diving duck. Spends much time asleep on open water with long tail partly cocked, in small parties or amongst other diving ducks. Regular now in Europe where sporadic breeding has taken place.

◀ **Breeding male** Shown in partial display, with tail held high. Unmistakable with its chestnut body, black cap and showy white cheeks. Sweeping sky-blue bill.

Status Introduced from North America, now widespread in England. Some local movement in winter. **Population** 600 breeding pairs. Winter 3,500 birds.

Female Duller than male and with dark bar across cheek. At times may recall a small grebe, but tail shows clearly when diving or at rest.

Winter male Resembles female, but retains white cheeks through the year. Bill becomes dark grey.

Flight Flies little, taking off with much pattering; when on the wing, flight is fast, rather jerky and the posture distinctly tail-heavy.

Honey Buzzard *Pernis apivorus*   50-58cm (20-23")

A variable buzzard of lowland and foothill forests. Perches inside canopy (shuns exposed perches), so almost always seen in flight. Easily passed-off as a Common Buzzard, but is distinctively shaped to the practiced eye with a smaller 'cuckoo head' on a more projecting neck, a longer tail and narrower body. Latter emphasises Honey's relatively longer, wider wings, which are rather pinched-in at base. Wingspan 125-145cm (49-57").

Adult Tail pattern is characteristic, showing a bold subterminal band with two narrower bars at the base (partially concealed from below by the undertail-coverts). Male sexed by distinctly grey head, broad dark trailing edge to wing, inky 'fingertips' and wide pale band before the barring of the central and forewing.

Adult female Flight-feather barring duller, more even than on male, with more diffuse trailing edge to wing, more extensively dark 'fingers' and browner head.

Adult Dark bill and cere. Yellow eye. Beware juvenile has yellow cere and dark eye, like Common Buzzard.

Juvenile Less frequent whitish bird depicted, but note dusky secondaries (typical of juveniles), extensive black on fingers and finer tail bars than adults – more akin to that of Common Buzzard. Note tail and head shape.

Status Widespread summer visitor, but rare in Britain (breeds mainly S/E England; rare migrant elsewhere). Winters tropical Africa. **Population** >20 pairs.

Flight Soars on flattish wings, twisting tail in kite-like fashion (tail-twisting less obvious on Common Buzzard, which soars with wings in a 'V').

◆ Purely a summer visitor, rarely arriving before mid May ◆ Rather solitary but during migration crosses land-bridges (e.g. southern Sweden/Denmark) in thousands ◆ In direct flight, action is slower than in Common, with emphasis on the upstroke, breaking into a floppy circling as birds begin to soar on forward-pressed wings. (Wings that suddenly 'go limp' and hang at the wrist can be useful pointer.) ◆ During looping aerial display uniquely lifts and shakes wings almost vertically over back, appearing to wing-clap ◆ Has a passion for wasp and bee grubs, hence name ◆ Can be confused with big female Goshawk.

Red Kite *Milvus milvus*   60-70cm (24-28")

Long broad wings, typically angled forwards and held slightly arched, and rather long tail (frequently twisted like a rudder) are key features of distant Red and Black Kites.

Status Chiefly resident. Very local in Britain, but not uncommon in mid Wales; recently reintroduced central England and northern Scotland. Wandering birds likely elsewhere.
Population 120 pairs .

From below note much bolder wing patch and longer, more deeply forked tail than Black (Red's tail shows a distinct notch even when fanned).

◆ An elegant, yet wide-winged, raptor with buoyant wing action and long trailing rusty tail ◆ Soars effortlessly showing bright white patches on underside of primaries and deeply forked tail ◆ Locally numerous about wooded hillsides and valleys; sociable at roost and favoured feeding locations (feeds chiefly on carrion, its weak feet being hardly adept at killing) ◆ Only likely to be confused with Black Kite (especialy paler juveniles) ◆ Wingspan 140-165cm (55-65").

Black Kite *Milvus migrans*   50-63cm (20-25")

Adult Note when tail is fanned it appears straight-edged and sharp-cornered. ▶

Darker brown (but hardly black) and with a shallower tail fork than Red Kite. Nevertheless, in bright light Black Kites can appear deceptively rufous, and the tail quite well-forked if tightly closed.

Status Locally numerous summer visitor, spreading northwards. Winters in Africa. Increasingly frequent vagrant Britain and Ireland.

◀
Adult The pale midwing band (most striking in juveniles) is also shared by Booted Eagle (check for latter's diagnostic white 'landing lights').

◆ Juveniles are paler, with fine whitish streaking on body and edges of wing-feathers ◆ Soaring birds can be confused with female Marsh Harrier (but latter soars with wings upturned) and particularly dark phase Booted Eagle (latter is stockier with less arched and angled wings) ◆ Prefers lakesides and rivers, in lightly wooded country. Sociable at times, scavenging at rubbish dumps and picnic sites ◆ Wingspan 135-152cm (53-60").

White-tailed Eagle *Haliaeetus albicilla* 77-92cm (30-36")

Adult Large yellow bill and short white tail diagnostic. Fully adult at about five years of age, but older birds have paler buff head. May appear tailless when viewed overhead against a pale sky.

Status Local resident, with young birds dispersing in autumn and winter. In UK and Ireland 2-5 breeding pairs on west Scottish islands (recently re-introduced); vagrant elsewhere.

Juvenile Dark bill and chocolate brown hood, contrasting with mottled breast and wing coverts. Short dark tail concealed by wings when perched, but shows white feather centres ('windows') when spread or low overhead.

◆ Our biggest eagle, with wide rectangular 'barn-door' wings, prominent projecting head and neck and relatively short, wedge-shaped tail ◆ Frequents rugged coastlines, lowland lakes and rivers. In winter, gatherings of 12 or more may form at favoured waters ◆ Soars on flat, or slightly bowed wings ◆ The most vulture-like of the eagles when in the air, but massive head and neck identifies (cf. Griffon Vulture) ◆ Wingspan 200-245cm (78-96").

Golden Eagle *Aquila chrysaetos* 75-86cm (30-34")

The only eagle of the region to soar on upswept 'V' wings. Much longer-winged and much more stable in flight (does not rock and tilt) than buzzards. (cf. Griffon Vulture in southern Europe).

Adult Dark and rather featureless, but relatively long tail and long rectangular wings contribute to a distinctive shape, enhanced by soaring habit.

Status Sparsely distributed resident. In winter young birds may wander to lowlands in east of region. In Britain, local resident Scotland, with odd pairs in NW England. **Population** 420 pairs.

Juvenile Striking whitish wing patches and basal portion of tail render it quite unmistakable. Plumage becomes progressively darker as bird ages. Fully adult plumage acquired at 5-7 years of age.

◆ Large, evenly-proportioned eagle, only likely to be confused with immature White-tailed but relatively long, round-tipped tail and feathered (not bare) legs are important distinctions ◆ Typically found soaring over high ridges in rugged, mountainous country ◆ Wingspan 190-230cm (75-90").

Short-toed Eagle *Circaetus gallicus* 68cm (27")

Adult The only eagle to habitually hover (cf. Rough-legged Buzzard); does so in between bouts of soaring on flat wings with tips of fingers just curling-up.

Greyish upperparts and whitish underside renders Short-toed one of the easiest eagles to identify. Dark hood is typical, but plumage varies considerably. Many are less patterned than shown and have paler head and chest.

Status Localised summer visitor, wintering in Africa. Not in UK or Ireland.

◆ Pale, long-winged eagle of open country and mountain foothills ◆ Has a relatively large, broad head, especially obvious when perched – frequently does so on roadside poles ◆ Tail pattern recalls Honey Buzzard, but Short-toed lacks dark carpal patches and trailing edge to secondaries (shown by even palest Honey) ◆ Nests in canopy of tall tree ◆ Feeds principally on snakes, therefore confined to south of region ◆ Wingspan 170cm (67").

Lammergeier *Gypaetus barbatus* 110cm (43")

Adult Rusty-buff body contrasts with blackish underwing and tail (cf. Bonelli's Eagle). Rustiness due to feather staining; some birds are whitish.

Status Provision of vulture feeding-stations has ensured its tenuous survival in the Pyrenees. Reintroduction in progress in Switzerland. Not in UK or Ireland.

Juvenile Sooty overall, with paler belly contrasting somewhat with balaclava helmet of a black hood (cf. juvenile Egyptian Vulture).

◆ Very rare ◆ Size and shape distinctive. Enormous 'bearded' vulture, with long, wide and strangely pointed wings and long, full, diamond-shaped tail ◆ A magnificent bird, prized among birders and others who share its mountain wilderness ◆ Glides along high ridges on flat wings ◆ Nests in cave on sheer rock face ◆ Specialised feeder on bone marrow, smashing bones by dropping them from great height ◆ Wingspan 254cm (100").

Egyptian Vulture *Neophron percnopterus*   55-65cm (21-25")

Juvenile Dark and blotchy appearance is quite different but tail shape remains most useful feature of flying birds. Compare bigger, longer-winged and longer-tailed juvenile Lammergeier. ▶

Adult Suggests both distant White Stork and pale phase Booted Eagle, but note tail shape and small orange-yellow head. ▶

White of plumage, especially ruff and breast, becomes ginger and grey with 'soiling'. ▶

◆ Relatively stocky raptor, with distinctive wedge-shaped tail and small head in all plumages. Typically soars and glides on flat wings along hill ridges and cliff-faces ◆ Attends feeding stations with Griffons, or rubbish dumps with Black Kites. On ground looks chunky and short-legged, hopping or striding with waddling gait. Then slender bill and naked head framed by scruffy ruff should be apparent ◆ Adult plumage attained by fourth year. Wingspan 155-165cm (61-65").

Griffon Vulture *Gyps fulvus*   95-105cm (37-41")

Adult All plumages rather similar, but juvenile is darker brown above and has more contrasting pale underwing coverts than adult.

◆ Massive, wide-winged raptor with 'flying-door' wings, a relatively short tail and small head (cf. young White-tailed Eagle). Soars and glides on flat or slightly upturned wings along hill ridges and cliff-faces ◆ Sociable; breeding colonies and roosting sites given away by extensive whitewash ◆ On ground appears like a sandy-brown box with pale downy snake of a neck and whitish ruff. Dwarfs Egyptian Vultures at feeding stations ◆ Wingspan 230-265cm (91-104").

Largest and most easily recognised of the harriers. Medium-sized birds of prey characterised by their long tails and 'floating' low-level flight on long wings held in shallow V. Adult male distinctive, but dark female/immatures sometimes mistaken for Black Kite – note latter's different tail, arched wings and pale upperwing panel.

Adult male Note pale ▶ buffish head and grey tail.

▲

Adult male Even at distance, tricoloured upperwing (brown forewing, grey hindwing, black wingtip) is striking. This pattern, acquired after two years, grows successively paler with age; many also develop a whitish rump.

◀ **Male** Variable rufous belly and underwing coverts identify most adult males seen coasting overhead. Old males, however, can appear almost white below with black wingtips and are sometimes difficult to tell from male Hen save for touch of rufous between legs.

Juvenile More blackish than ▶ female, with all-dark forewing and richer, orange-buff head markings (head all dark on some).

Status Mainly summer visitor (April-October). Winters mostly in Mediterranean/Africa but increasing numbers remain in NW Europe at favoured spots.
Population 160 'pairs' (male harriers often polygamous).

▲   ▶

Female Bigger than male; chocolate brown with dark eye stripe and prominent creamy-buff crown, throat and epaulettes. When seen from below, 'palm of hand' often appears silvery.

◆ Locally common in larger reedbeds. Nests increasingly in farmland (especially with reedy dykes) in some regions, including parts of eastern Britain ◆ May turn up almost anywhere on passage ◆ Usually seen patrolling just above reed-tops in easy, buoyant flight, often with long legs dangling; rocks gently on the breeze ◆ Drops with lightning agility onto small animals, birds, frogs ◆ In spring, male performs 'sky-dancing' display at great height, drawing attention with Lapwing-like calls, *vee-it...*

61

Hen Harrier *Circus cyaneus*   43-50cm (17-20")

In size falls between Marsh and Montagu's Harriers; all occur widely on passage and confusion with latter is then a distinct possibility. Females and immatures of both are especially similar – brownish with a white rump and dark bands on the tail; birdwatchers often refer to them collectively as ringtails. Hen is, however, always a bigger, heavier bird with broader, more rounded wings and broader white rump patch. Wingspan 100-120cm (39-47").

Adult male Blue-grey upperparts look cleaner and more ghostly than those of male Montagu's – a useful pointer at long range; differs further in its bold white rump patch, dusky trailing edge to wings and no wing-bars.

Adult male Appears strikingly pale below, the unmarked white body and innerwing contrasting with inky wing-tips (cf. old male Marsh Harrier).

Female Bigger than male, with more owl-like face. Very like female Montagu's, showing similarly banded tail and under-wing, and buffish underparts streaked with brown. Best distinguished by its broader white rump and broader wings without dark bar across upperwing.

Status Patchy resident (sum-mer visitor to Scandinavia) and widespread winter visitor.
Population 630 'pairs' (male harriers often polygamous).

Juvenile Closely resembles female but a touch warmer below (a few distinctly rusty). Sexes alike, though females larger.

◆ Breeds on moors, bogs and extensive young conifer plantations ◆ Adults indulge in noisy and spectacular aerobatics over territory ◆ In winter, deserts higher ground for rough fields, marshes and low-lying coasts; watch for small roost gatherings at dusk over favoured reedbeds and other rough ground ◆ Usually seen sailing just above ground in typical harrier fashion, wings upheld in classic V ◆ Effortless gliding belies swiftness of active flight ◆ Skilled at seizing small birds disturbed from low cover.

Smallest of the three harriers. Always appears very lean and lightweight in flight, especially the smaller male, rocking and tilting as if upset by the merest draught. Both sexes distinguished from similar but noticeably bulkier Hen Harrier by their decidedly thin bodies and distinctly narrower and more pointed wings – apparent even at distance. Wingspan 105-120cm (41-47").

Adult male Lacks uniformly clean grey appearance of male Hen ▶ Harrier. Instead, the upperparts look rather dirty, appearing more as a patchwork of different greys – obvious at surprisingly long range. Diagnostic is the single black bar across upperwing. Rump pale grey (whitish on some, but never so bold as male Hen).

◀ **Adult male** Double black bar across underwing and streaks of marmalade on belly/underwing coverts unique among male harriers.

Female Best separated from female/immature ▶ Hen Harrier by its narrower white rump and markedly more slender wing and body. Dark bar across upperwing characteristic, mirroring that of male.

◀ **Juvenile** Differs from female Montagu's and all ringtail Hen Harriers in its unmarked rusty-orange body and underwing-coverts. Sexes alike (females larger).

Status Summer visitor (April-August/October). Rare in Britain (confined to southern England, arriving in May). Winters in tropical Africa. **Population** <10 'pairs'.

◆ Breeds in extensive croplands, lowland heath and grassland ◆ Quarters low to ground, wavering on V-wings in true harrier fashion, but looks unstable ◆ Preys mainly on smaller birds (up to Cuckoo size), voles, lizards and insects ◆ Year-old males exhibit a perplexing mix of immature and adult plumage features and care is needed to avoid confusing the three species.

Goshawk *Accipiter gentilis* 48-60cm (19-24")

Large, powerfully-built hawk of mature forests, especially coniferous. Many females are almost buzzard-sized, but smaller males are only a little larger than a big Sparrowhawk. Latter frequently misidentified as Goshawks, but genuine Goshawks show relatively longer wings and neck, wider rear-body, and rounder tail tip.

Adult female Underparts whiter and ▶ uppersparts more slate than Sparrowhawk. Note dark hood and bold white supercilium. Wide-bellied look is typical of Goshawk, whether perched or in flight.

◀ **Adult male** Much smaller than female, but similar in pattern. Eye more red.

Juvenile Browner above, buffer below and much more boldly streaked than juvenile Sparrowhawk. Note also tail shape and ◀ longer wing.

Male Wide rear body gives ▶ impression that tail is an extension of body without visible join.

Status Uncommon but widespread on Continent. Rare but increasing in Britain (easily overlooked); also a rare migrant. Vagrant Ireland. **Population** 200+ pairs.

◀ **Male** Dark hood and white vent often surprisingly conspicuous. Latter fluffed out in aerial display in spring (much like Sparrowhawk).

◆ Solitary, shy and elusive ◆ Keeps hidden within forest, venturing more widely away from tree cover in autumn and winter, when migrants also possible on coast ◆ Flies with strong, steady beats and swift glides (cf. Sparrowhawk's rapid pulses and glides) ◆ Never hovers but often soars for short periods. Largest individuals can suggest Honey Buzzard or even Gyrfalcon ◆ Indulges in aerial display on fine days in early spring, swooping and diving at great height over breeding forest or patrols its patch with slow flapping flight – the easiest ways to locate this elusive hawk ◆ Hunts fast and low, sweeping through dense forest trees with remarkable agility ◆ Feeds chiefly on Woodpigeons and rabbits – but also takes Sparrowhawks!

Widespread small hawk, easily distinguished from Common Kestrel and other small falcons by short, blunt wings. The smallest males are half size of biggest females. Cuckoos are often mistaken for Sparrowhawks, but have slim head and bill and pointed wings.

Adult male Barred rufous underparts ▶ and plain bluish upperparts often striking. Can be confused with male Merlin, but latter is streaked below.

▲
Juvenile Slightly browner than female (more rufous when close), with band of streaks across chest breaking into barring over rest of underparts. Scapulars often with prominent white markings.

Adult female Much bigger than male – can easily be confused with much rarer Goshawk. Apart from pale nape patch and supercilium, almost plain grey-brown above, with finely ◀ barred, pale underparts.

Female Uniform grey-brown upperparts lack two-tone effect of similar-sized but more gingery Common Kestrel.

◀

Male Showing characteristic brown barring on underwing.

▶

Flight Hunts fast and low, relying on surprise to catch prey. Skims down woodland rides, hedge-hopping at speed, side-slipping to grab small birds.

Status Widespread resident and passage migrant. **Population** 43,000 pairs.

◆ Common in forests and wooded farmland, especially in valleys ◆ Hunts alone, often along coastal hedges in autumn and winter ◆ In normal 'flap-flap-glide' flight wings seem to be half-closed. Unlike Goshawk, wing-beats come in rapid flurries ◆ Never hovers but often soars for short periods ◆ Frequently mobbed by small birds, such as swallows, whose frantic calls often forewarn of approach ◆ Sharp tail corners and shorter neck useful clues for separating large females from male Goshawk ◆ Usually perches in cover of trees or hedges, rarely in open where very nervous and alert.

Common Buzzard *Buteo buteo*   43-53cm (17-22")

Broad-winged hawk typically noticed as a large, dumpy 'eagle' sitting atop a roadside pole or swirling slowly on broad, upswept wings over a wooded valley or hillside. Buzzards are very variable in plumage (two frequent forms shown here), a feature shared by similar Honey Buzzard (rare in Britain). Wingspan 100-135cm (39-53").

Typical brown individual Usually has whitish ▶ band across lower breast. Note tail is only a little longer than wingtips when perched upright.

◀ **Pale individual** Especially striking. Note bare yellow tarsus visible below baggy trousers (cf. Rough-legged Buzzard).

Brown adult Despite much variation the two-toned underwing, with neat dark border and carpal patch, are features of them all. The prominent dark trailing edge and indication of a wider sub-terminal tail bar on this bird is typical of adults.

Pale juvenile The more diffuse ▶ greyish trailing edge to the wing and fine bars at tail tip suggest juvenile. Shape and V-winged soaring habit an important distinction from other large pale raptors.

Brown adult A rather dark individual. Note that pale birds may show pale upperwing coverts and whitish rump area.

Status Widespread resident, but Scandinavian populations highly migratory, forming large flocks to cross narrowest points of sea (e.g. S Sweden/N Denmark). Common in W Britain; uncommon migrant E England. In Ireland, only in NE. **Population** 12,000-17,000 territories.

Flight Soars on upswept wings (most other raptors soar on flat wings), but glides with wings held flat. Often looks a little unstable, rocking on the breeze.

◆ Favours hilly country with wooded valleys, also sparsely wooded farmland ◆ Nests in trees, rarely on cliffs ◆ Vocal both in spring and especially young birds in late summer/autumn, which call persistently with a plaintive *meeooo* ◆ Often in pairs or family parties. Larger congregations form in autumn ◆ Hangs on updraughts over hills and readily hovers, but is less persistent in doing so than Rough-legged ◆ Indulges in aerial display in spring, swooping and diving over breeding area, but does not wing-clap like Honey Buzzard ◆ Feeds chiefly on rabbits; also takes carrion and spends much time on ground in open fields searching for worms.

Rough-legged Buzzard *Buteo lagopus* 50-60cm (20-24")

A large buzzard of the Arctic tundra, wintering south over eastern Europe in open country. Plumage less variable than the other two buzzards, but both can approach Rough-legged in basic pattern. Whitish tail with broad dark terminal band is most important plumage feature as diagnostic feathered tarsus ('rough legs') very difficult to discern in the field. Wingspan 125-145cm (49-57").

Juvenile Contrast between blackish belly and ▶ whitish head and breast most marked in juveniles. Check for feathered tarsus (often hidden). Common Buzzards with pale head and breast should show pale on wing coverts, too (as do some juvenile Rough-legged Buzzards).

◀ **Adult** Note heavily marked head and breast separated from dark belly by pale 'U'. More important age features are the wider border to secondaries and blacker tail band (with 2-3 narrow subterminal bars) than juvenile. Eyes brown.

◀ The whitish tail base may give the impression of a white rump when seen from above. Note very dark upperparts and whitish patch on upperside of primaries (especially juveniles), latter rarely shown by western Common Buzzards.

Juvenile Aged by paler eyes and blacker belly ▶ patch than adult, diffuse border to secondaries and greyer tail band without subterminal bars.

Status Scarce visitor to North Sea coasts (October-April). Very rarely in W Britain. **Population** 20-200 birds in winter.

Flight Rough-legged habitually hovers like a giant ponderous kestrel. Common Buzzard does so less persistently.

◆ Breeds amongst Scandinavian uplands. Winters on open plains, marshes and heathland ◆ The large size and longer wings can impart the feel of an eagle at long range. Wing action less stiff than Common Buzzard, with deeper, more pliable beats in level flight ◆ Population varies according to abundance of voles and lemmings ◆ Less dependent on thermals than most other big raptors, regularly crossing North Sea ◆ Often in small parties in invasion years.

Lesser Spotted Eagle *Aquila pomarina*   57-64cm (22-25")

Adult From below lighter brown head and body than Spotted, usually with underwing coverts paler than secondaries. Adult has slightly shorter, more wedge-shaped tail than juvenile, without whitish tip.

Status Scarce summer visitor to forests in extreme east of region. Winters in tropical Africa. Not in UK or Ireland.

Juvenile Age differences less marked than in other *Aquilas*. Juvenile has whitish tail tip and one or two lines of spots across lower part of wing. Adults have paler brown upperwing coverts than juveniles. All show whitish rump patch and primary flash.

◆ A relatively chunky, short-winged dark eagle. Bulkier than dark phase Booted, with a shorter, often wedge-shaped, tail ◆ Soars on flat or often slightly drooped wings, like rarer Spotted, which can be very similar ◆ Wingspan 134-160cm (53-63").

Spotted Eagle *Aquila clanga*   62-74cm (24-29")

Adult Very dark head and underwing coverts (latter darker than the flight feathers) gives reverse of normal pattern shown by Lesser Spotted. Adult has shorter tail than juvenile, and lacks whitish tip.

First-year Striking, with rows of white tear-drops across most of wingcoverts (quite unlike all other eagles). Adults are plain brown above, except for whitish 'rump' patch.

◆ Chunky dark eagle, closely associated with wetlands. Typically perches on waterside trees ◆ Adult's dark plumage makes yellow cere, gape and feet conspicuous. Note thicker thighs, heavier head and bill, and shaggier nape than Lesser Spotted ◆ Soaring birds may suggest White-tailed Eagle in shape, but are shorter-winged and have shorter necks. See also Lesser Spotted Eagle ◆ An uncommon variant ('*fulvescens*') has buff body and wing-coverts, and is quite perplexing ◆ Rare winter visitor to southern wetlands from breeding grounds in forests of eastern Europe (has bred Sweden) and Siberia. Almost annual in the Camargue in winter ◆ Accidental UK (no recent records) ◆ Wingspan 158-182cm (62-71").

Booted Eagle *Hieraaetus pennatus* 45cm (18")

Dark morph Suggests both Marsh Harrier and Black Kite, but soars on flat wings and has square-tipped tail. Note translucent inner primaries.

Pale morph Two-tone wing pattern recalls only adult Egyptian Vulture, but latter has wedge-shaped tail and smaller yellow head.

Both morphs have distinctive pale band across upperwing (like Black Kite). When bird head-on look for diagnostic 'landing-lights' where wing joins body.

◆ A dimorphic buzzard-sized eagle ◆ More frequent pale phase can be suggested by palest buzzards or Honey Buzzards, but note Booted's blackish flight feathers ◆ Rarer dark phase less striking but quite distinct ◆ Juveniles are strangely similar to adults ◆ Swoops and dives in spectacular aerial display over wooded valleys in spring, uttering wader-like whistles ◆ Wingspan 122cm (48").

Bonelli's Eagle *Hieraaetus fasciatus* 63cm (25")

Adult Most birds show inconspicuous whitish leading edge. In general underside appears blackish with greyer flights and white body – a diagnostic combination.

Juvenile Not unlike a chunky, large Honey Buzzard, but lacks strong barring or dark carpal patches. Body can look surprisingly rosy.

Adult plumage gradually attained by fourth year through variety of intermediate stages.

◆ Typically seen in pairs, gliding along faces of deep gorges or cruising over wooded mountains and crags; soars little ◆ Notice flat wings with straight trailing edge but carpals pushed well forward giving characteristic bulging look ◆ Adults overhead show unique combination of blackish underwings contrasting with whitish body ◆ Very different juvenile recalls large, unbarred, gingery Common Buzzard ◆ Perches on trees on cliff faces (check dark upperparts for distinctive whitish saddle on adults) ◆ Wingspan 148cm (58").

Common Kestrel *Falco tinnunculus*   33-39cm (13-15")

The commonest falcon. Habit of persistently hovering generally distinctive but shared by rarer Lesser Kestrel and Red-footed Falcon. Easily separated from widespread (but less conspicuous) Sparrowhawk by pointed wings which have distinctive two-tone contrast on upperside. Although females are slightly larger than males, the difference is less marked than in most other falcons. Wingspan 65-80cm (26-31").

Adult male Blue-grey head and tail (with bold black sub-terminal bar) contrasts with rufous upperparts. Note black moustaches, spotted mantle and wingtips that fall well short of tail tip (compare Lesser Kestrel).

Adult female Dark-barring on brown upperparts and tail is distinctive; older birds often become greyish on the head. Juvenile similar.

Flight Two-tone wings are distinctive in all plumages. Kestrels are relatively longer-tailed than most other falcons.

Hangs as if suspended on an invisible wire, hovering with flickering wings and depressed, fanned tail.

Male

Female

Status Widespread resident and passage migrant. **Population** 60,000 pairs.

Soaring Common Kestrel (top) and Sparrow-hawk (bottom) can be confusing but neither soar for very long; note bold subterminal tail band and spotting and streaking on underside of Common Kestrel (rather than barring).

◆ Widespread in open or lightly-wooded country. Favours un-improved grassland, including motorway embankments and city parks ◆ Feeds chiefly on voles, but also takes small birds ◆ Perches in open on posts and crags (contra Sparrowhawk) ◆ Rarely catches and eats flying insects on the wing (unlike Lesser Kestrel) ◆ Nests in disused crow nests, on cliff ledges and even on buildings in city centres ◆ Generally solitary ◆ Call a rising, ringing *kee-kee-kee-kee*.

Lesser Kestrel *Falco naumanni*   29-32cm (11-13")

Male Brighter than Kestrel, unspotted above, lacks moustache and has warmer (less marked) orange-buff breast. Older birds have a diagnostic blue-grey panel across the wing, lacking in first-years which are very like Common Kestrels.

▼

◄ **Female** Almost identical to female Common Kestrel in plumage but note that wing-tips reach black subterminal tail band and head generally paler and more finely streaked.

Status Rare and declining summer visitor to southern France (still relatively common in Iberia). Very rare vagrant to Britain.

Female Central tail feathers often appear to project slightly when tail is spread. Tail appears pencil-thin when closed. The whiter underwing and disjointed tail band offer further clues.

◆ Smaller and daintier, with relatively shorter tail than Common Kestrel ◆ Diagnostic pale (not black) claws but this feature is virtually useless in the field ◆ Sociable behaviour a good clue to identity, as flocks hover scattered over grassland; nests colonially in cliffs and old buildings ◆ Readily 'hawks' and eats flying insects on the wing ◆ Its dry, hoarse calls are distinctive ◆ Wingspan 58-72m (23-28").

Red-footed Falcon *Falco vespertinus*   28-31cm (11-12")

Juvenile Resembles juvenile Hobby, but has much paler and more ► extensive creamy fore-crown, less black at sides of head, prominently barred upper tail and distinct dark trailing edge to underwing in flight.

Adult male Dark grey with silvery flight feathers. Check for rusty vent, red legs and red cere if birds close (orange on female). ►

Status Gregarious summer visitor to eastern Europe, with some overshoots in May-July reaching as far west as Britain (chiefly east England)

◄ **Adult female** Extensive orange-buff on head and underparts (note black mask); the grey upperparts are barred, including the tail but latter lacks a subterminal band.

◆ Feeds over open country, hovering like a kestrel or 'hawking' flying insects like a Hobby ◆ Breeds colonially in old crow or Rook nests, even within active rookery ◆ Wingspan 65-75cm (26-30").

Male is smallest falcon of the region. Both sexes recall Sparrowhawk in colour and hunting technique, but Merlin perches on posts and rocks in open country and has longer wings that extend well down tail at rest. Juvenile very similar to female, both differing from Hobby in diffuse head pattern (not a defined hood) and absence of bright white throat and collar. Wingspan 60-65cm (22-25").

Adult male Rufous underparts and bluish upperparts suggest male Sparrowhawk but Merlin has dark eyes and is streaked (not barred) below. ▶

◀ **Adult female** Larger female is closer to Common Kestrel in size but differs in diffuse head pattern and unmarked dark brownish upperparts.

Adult male Notice black subterminal tail band and sharply pointed wings in flight. ▶

◀ **Female** Compare dark brownish upperparts (showing only weak contrast with wingtip) with more contrasting and gingery tones of Common Kestrel.

Status Scarce breeder in north and west, more widespread, but still uncommon, in winter and on passage. **Population** 1,500 pairs.

Flight Merlin's rapid, dashing flight readily identifies. Hunts fast and low in open country, relying on surprise to catch small birds such as larks and pipits as they rise or 'locking on' to follow every twist and turn in pursuit.

◆ Likely at any season on open moorland, but in winter moves to lowland plains, marshes and coastal fields ◆ Solitary but forms communal roosts on ground in winter ◆ Nests on ground amongst heather or in disused crow nests in low trees ◆ Call a shrill chattering *chik-ik-ik-ik...* only likley to be heard on breeding grounds ◆ A difficult bird to get good views of; typically flashes over a field and lost to sight before you can get your binoculars onto it ◆ Sometimes briefly hovers (like Common Kestrel) and may soar for short periods (when silhouette remarkably close to Peregrine).

Nippy little falcon of forestry clearings, heathland, open woodland and farmland with copses; on passage also along coasts. Recalls a small Peregrine in plumage (especially head pattern) but sharply-tipped wings always a give-away even on poor views. Female larger than male. Wingspan 70-84cm (27-33").

Juvenile Browner than adult, without rusty vent. Pale forehead and scaly back can suggest rarer juvenile Red-footed Falcon but note Hobby's unbarred upperside of tail (except for pale tip) and, in flight, lack of obvious dark trailing edge to underwing. First summer birds similar.

Adult Rufous vent and streaked underparts coupled with black and white hood make it unmistakable.

Flight Relatively short tail and finely-pointed wing-tip are features of Hobby as it dashes overhead. At certain angles, swept back appearance of wings on distant birds may even suggest a large swift.

Note black hood and white collar contrast with streaked underparts. Habit of hawking flying insects and eating them on the wing is typical of Hobby (but also shared by rarer Lesser Kestrel and Red-footed Falcon; Hobby, however rarely hovers and then only very briefly and seemingly uncomfortably).

Status Uncommon summer visitor. In Britain nests locally in England, scarce on passage elsewhere. Winters in tropical Africa. **Population** 500-900 pairs, increasing.

◆ Tremendous agility allows it to catch swallows, swifts and even bats on the wing ◆ Presence often indicated by swallows bunching together in noisy alarm ◆ Often hunts by wetlands in evenings, taking dragonflies and hirundines assembling for roost ◆ Favours perching on prominent branch near top of tree ◆ Nesting pairs usually take-over unoccupied crow nest, typically in top of tall pine ◆ Quite vocal in breeding season, cry a rising, ringing *kee-kee-kee-kee*, higher in pitch than similar call of Common Kestrel – much like song of Wryneck ◆ Solitary or in pairs.

Saker *Falco cherrug* — 45-55cm (18-22")

Adult Brownish, with distinctly ▶ whitish head. Note that the wings fall well short of tail tip at rest (contra Peregrine). Saker has dusky underwing-coverts contrasting with pale primaries (Peregrine has uniform underwing).

▲
Paler brown upperparts than young Peregrine, with distinctly darker wingtip.

◆ Larger and relatively longer tailed than Peregrine, but not quite as massive as Gyrfalcon. Brown coloration, rather than grey, a useful difference between the two but ranges unlikely to overlap ◆ Soaring birds are longer-winged than Peregrine, with primary tips upturned (not flat or drooped) ◆ Darker juveniles easily confused with large young Peregrine; it is important to note position of wing and tail tip at rest, and underwing pattern in such birds. Scarce resident (with some dispersal) in steppe and mountains of south-east Europe (including western Hungary and extreme eastern Austria). Sometimes recorded as a (presumed) escape in north-west Europe, including UK ◆ Wingspan 102-126cm (40-50").

Gyrfalcon *Falco rusticolus* — 53-62cm (21-24")

Adult Not unlike a large drab Peregrine, but Gyr has ▶ broader wings and a longer tail; wing-tips fall far short of tail when perched.

Status A powerful Arctic hunter, small numbers of which breed south into the mountains of Norway. Vagrants to Britain and Ireland occur almost annually in winter; most are of the almost wholly white form which predominates in Greenland and Canada.

▲
Juvenile Dark juveniles have dusky underwing-coverts contrasting with pale undersides to primaries and secondaries.

◆ Biggest and bulkiest falcon (females as big as a Buzzard) ◆ Most likely to be mistaken as a large immature Peregrine, but Gyr has broader wings and a longer tail (shape may even suggest Goshawk when soaring) ◆ Scandinavian birds (depicted) are often almost uniformly mottled drab greyish, others have paler underparts ◆ Wingspan 105-130cm (41-51").

Powerfully-built falcon of wild open country, from rocky coasts and estuaries to mountains and moorland. Stockier and fuller-chested than other falcons (except rarer Gyr and Saker, which see), with tapered wings and medium-length tail. Blackish hood evident in all plumages. When soaring has distinctive anchor shape. Adult plumage attained in second calendar year. Wingspan 95-115cm (37-45").

Adults Barred below and have slate upperparts, rather paler on rump. Blackish hood and white throat only shared by smaller and slimmer Hobby. On size this is a female.

Flight Fast and direct, typically a few quick beats and a long glide, but can swiftly accelerate.

Juvenile Streaked underparts and is dark brown above, with clear pale tip to tail (latter surprisingly obvious even if upperpart colour not discernible). On size this is a male.

Flight Soars on flat or slightly drooped wings (distant birds from behind resemble gliding Fulmar). Magnificent in the air, enjoying swooping and gliding on air currents and often chasing birds for fun and devilment.

Status Increasing, but sparsely-distributed, resident and winter visitor (northern populations migratory). Numbers increasing after sudden decimation through use of powerful pesticides in 1950s. **Population** 1500 pairs.

◆ Perches upright and hunched on favoured rock or ledge (look for whitewash on cliff face) ◆ Pairs often hunt in partnership, the smaller male moving prey towards larger female hanging high; she stoops swiftly from above and makes the kill ◆ Estuaries are favourite hunting areas, panic amongst waders and ducks often betraying the sudden appearance of a Peregrine ◆ Prey carried to favoured ledge or rock to be plucked ◆ Noisy in breeding season, uttering shrill whining *keeah-keeah-keeah*. Otherwise silent ◆ Nests on cliff ledges, even on tall buildings in some city centres (where feral pigeons are easy prey). Rarely in disused tree nest of crow ◆ Solitary away from nesting site.

Osprey *Pandion haliaetus*   55-69cm (22-27")

Large raptor that hunts exclusively for fish in lochs, rivers and bays. Flies on long, relatively narrow and typically bowed wings, angled at the wrist. Easily taken for an immature large gull as it circles high above water, but differs in characteristic dark carpal patch and bouts of clumsy hovering, legs dangling – silvery underside to primaries seem to flash with each wingbeat, making bird conspicuous at great distance. Wingspan 145-160cm (57-63").

Adult Dark brown above, gleaming white below, ▶ with ragged crest, dark band through eye and winkle-picker bill. Sexes similar, but females average broader and more distinct brownish breast-band than males.

◀ **Juvenile** Appears blacker above with prominent white scaling. When cruising overhead, differs from adult in more distinct and even banding on secondaries, buff tint to white wing-linings, and pale tips to flight feathers and tail.

In southern Europe, confusable with larger ▶ Short-toed Eagle (also pale and hovers), but Osprey's mainly white head with white eye-stripe, shining white belly and wing-linings, and dark carpal patches unique among raptors.

Status Summer visitor (April-September). In Britain, rare but increasing Scotland (reintroduction England). Winters mainly in Africa. **Population** 100 pairs.

Hovers to fix prey, often dropping lower then hovering again before executing spectacular splash-dive with outstretched feet. May submerge briefly before rising again, fish slung torpedo-fashion beneath body.

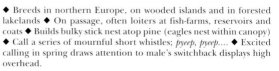

◆ Breeds in northern Europe, on wooded islands and in forested lakelands ◆ On passage, often loiters at fish-farms, reservoirs and coats ◆ Builds bulky stick nest atop pine (eagles nest within canopy) ◆ Call a series of mournful short whistles; *pyeep, pyeep....* ◆ Excited calling in spring draws attention to male's switchback displays high overhead.

Hazel Grouse *Bonasa bonasia* 36cm (14")

Shy forest grouse. Frustrating to observe, invariably seen only as a 'partridge' whirring away between trunks of close-growing forest trees. Sometimes perches in trees after a short flight. A glimpse of the spread tail will reveal the dark subterminal band and whitish rim suggestive of Turtle Dove.

Male Black bib and boldly spotted underparts. Both sexes show the distinctive tail pattern.

Status Resident but sedentary and localised. Absent from Britain and Ireland.

Female Browner. Lacks black throat of male.

◆ Best located by listening for distinctive, very high-pitched, thin whistle *peeeeiiii* (like a dog-whistle) and then patiently tracking down source of call ◆ Favours mixed forest, especially streamside alders and birches, where it feeds in the trees as well as on the ground.

Rock Partridge *Alectoris graeca* 33cm (13")

Overlaps (and even hybridises) with similar Red-legged in the French Alps. Rock, however, typically occurs at higher altitudes, favouring craggy alpine slopes. Closely-related Chukar (*A. chukar*) of Asia has been introduced into UK and France, and hybridises with both species.

Adult Greyer above, and lacks streaking on neck and breast of Red-legged. Flanks are more closely and evenly-barred with longer stripes, lacking obvious rufous and violet-grey bands Red-legged.

Status Scarce alpine partridge. Absent from Britain and Ireland.

Chukar Differs from Rock in having fewer, more spaced, and less continuous flank bars, V shaped (rather than U-shaped) lower border to black gorget, and a more prominent black gape spot (isolated by the white, not black, lores).

Red-legged Partridge *Alectoris rufa* 33cm (13")

Bulkier than Grey Partridge. Striking black-border to white throat, whitish supercilium and very strong flank barring provide easier distinctions from Grey than do the red legs and bill. Old name is French Partridge.

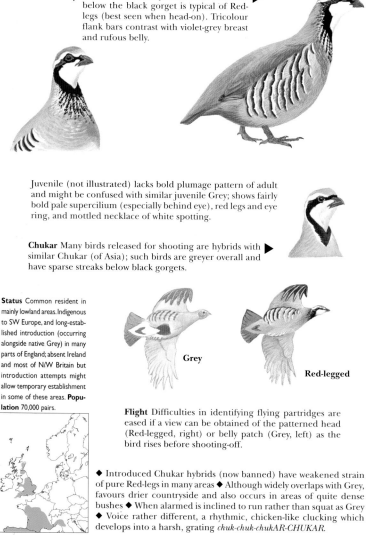

▼ **Adult** A well-developed necklace of streaks below the black gorget is typical of Red-legs (best seen when head-on). Tricolour flank bars contrast with violet-grey breast and rufous belly. ▶

Juvenile (not illustrated) lacks bold plumage pattern of adult and might be confused with similar juvenile Grey; shows fairly bold pale supercilium (especially behind eye), red legs and eye ring, and mottled necklace of white spotting.

Chukar Many birds released for shooting are hybrids with ▶ similar Chukar (of Asia); such birds are greyer overall and have sparse streaks below black gorgets.

Status Common resident in mainly lowland areas. Indigenous to SW Europe, and long-established introduction (occurring alongside native Grey) in many parts of England; absent Ireland and most of N/W Britain but introduction attempts might allow temporary establishment in some of these areas. **Population** 70,000 pairs.

Grey

Red-legged

Flight Difficulties in identifying flying partridges are eased if a view can be obtained of the patterned head (Red-legged, right) or belly patch (Grey, left) as the bird rises before shooting-off.

◆ Introduced Chukar hybrids (now banned) have weakened strain of pure Red-legs in many areas ◆ Although widely overlaps with Grey, favours drier countryside and also occurs in areas of quite dense bushes ◆ When alarmed is inclined to run rather than squat as Grey ◆ Voice rather different, a rhythmic, chicken-like clucking which develops into a harsh, grating *chuk-chuk-chukAR-CHUKAR*.

Partridges are rotund, small-headed birds usually found in small parties (coveys) in open farmland. Grey easily separated from Red-legged by its finely barred and buff-streaked upperparts, orange face, duller flank barring and distinctive dark chestnut belly patch. Legs dull fleshy grey. Juveniles of both species are drab and featureless, but normally accompany parents at least until adult plumage features acquired.

Adult male Large dark belly patch (usually concealed by squat posture) exhibited by territorial male when standing erect. Face has bright ruddy complexion. ▶

Adult female Sexes similar but duller female has paler face and smaller, much less defined, belly patch.

Flight Sudden explosion of rising birds and speed of flight makes assessment of differences in upperside pattern difficult. Both show rufous tails. Grey (upper) has buff streaks on back and barring on flight feathers; plain-backed Red-legged (lower) is bulkier, more earthy-brown above and shows characteristic buff and dark wedges on primaries (see Red-legged for under-sides).

Grey

Red-legged

Juvenile Drab and featureless, lacking orange face.

Adult Well-camouflaged when feeding – resembles clod of earth but head periodically lifted to check for predators.

Status Widespread resident in lowland areas, but massive decrease attributed to agricultural change. Native to British Isles (absent N and W Scotland, inc. islands); very local Ireland (dramatic decrease), Wales, Cornwall. **Population** 150,000 pairs in 1990 (500,000 in 1970).

◆ Inhabits open fields with hedgerows, generally in flat country but also in gentle hills, favouring weedy cultivation and stubbles ◆ When alarmed squats or crouches and walks or runs away from danger. Flushes as a last resort, with explosive whirr of wings, interspersed with glides, dropping just out of view ◆ Coveys of both species often feed in the same field, but keep apart ◆ Presence proclaimed on fine evenings by far-carrying, grating *kerrrr-ik* (like rusty gate being opened) ◆ Chicks explode into the air and fly, even when tiny, suggesting rarer Quail ◆ Half-grown juvenile pheasant suggests partridge but has pointed, wedge-shaped, brown tail and is more spotted overall.

Red Grouse *Lagopus lagopus scoticus*   38cm (15")

A dark, partridge-like bird of open heather moors. Generally distinctive in its specialised habitat but can be confused with both Ptarmigan and female Black Grouse. Young birds resemble females after fledging.

Adult male Chestnut plumage appears very dark at a distance, ▶
the woolly white feet seldom visible. In spring, red eye wattles
become swollen and project above the crown. Face shows
white whisker, like drooping moustache.

Flight Explodes from the heather
with a whirr of wings, uttering a
cackling series of calls. Flight
rapid, interrupted by brief glides
on stiffly bowed wings, banking to
show whitish underwing.

Status Locally common resident
in Scotland, Wales, N England
and Ireland, with isolated introduced populations in Devon
(now scarce). **Population** Has
declined to c250,000 pairs,
chiefly through less widespread
moorland management.

◀
Adult female
Smaller than male,
without moustache.
Wattles vestigial and
often invisible. Paler and
browner than male, with
intense yellowish feather tipping.

◆ Favours extensive tracts of upland heather moors, but found down
to sea-level in some areas and may descend to edges of cultivation in
cold weather ◆ Most likely to be encountered by hillwalkers. Search
for head and neck of birds peering above the heather ◆ In spring
males are noisy, uttering a variety of barked and nasal calls, including
an angry ('grousing') guttural *go-bak, go-bak, go-bak-ak-ak-ak...* ◆ Forms
flocks outside the breeding season, particularly in the winter ◆
Formerly considered as species endemic to the British Isles but now
treated as a race of the circumpolar Willow Grouse.

Willow Grouse *Lagopus lagopus lagopus*   40cm (16")

Replaces Red Grouse in Scandinavia. Unlike Red,
has white wings and belly in summer and is all
white in winter (like Ptarmigan). Rather larger
and bulkier than Ptarmigan, with slightly stouter
bill and is much more chestnut in summer. Winter
male lacks black loral stripe of male Ptarmigan,
but females are very similar. Shuns barren, rocky
ground favoured by Ptarmigan, preferring birch
and willow scrub in boggy areas of open taiga.
Voice as Red Grouse (cf. Ptarmigan).

Superbly camouflaged mountain and tundra counterpart of Willow Grouse, sharing latter's snowy white plumage in winter and white wings at other times. This makes for easy identification of the relict populations of Scotland, the Alps and the Pyrenees, but not so in Scandinavia where it meets similar Willow Grouse – here habitat and voice often the best clues to identity.

Summer male Stone-grey body plumage, intricately barred 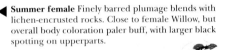 black – indeed almost blackish-grey in spring. Lacks the rich chestnut tones of Willow. Note prominence of red 'comb' in spring.

◄ **Summer female** Finely barred plumage blends with lichen-encrusted rocks. Close to female Willow, but overall body coloration paler buff, with larger black spotting on upperparts.

Winter male Very similar to Willow, but note male Ptarmigan ► has black lores. Black tail virtually hidden when at rest.

Winter female Most lack black lores of ▼ male; only separable from Willow by slighter build, habitat and voice.

Best found by carefully scanning ahead for head and neck of birds peering above rocks and crags.

Status Localised resident. In Britain, only in N & C Scotland. **Population** Up to 10,000 pairs.

◆ Inhabits barren mountain ridges and boulder-strewn slopes, almost down to sea level in northern parts of range ◆ Announces presence with low creaking call, like door slowly opening ◆ Generally exceedingly tame ◆ Squats when alarmed, then walks or scuttles to rock outcrop from which it glides away downhill ◆ In flight utters distinctive dry, rattling belch – quite unlike Willow Grouse ◆ Forms small flocks, especially in winter.

Black Grouse *Tetrao tetrix*   40-55cm (16-22")

Spectacular grouse of forested uplands, most likely to be seen on rough hilly fields near woodland edge. Handsome males ('Blackcock') are larger and longer-tailed than brownish female ('Greyhen'). Compare female with larger female Capercaillie and smaller Hazel Grouse.

Displaying male Stunning blue-black plumage, topped by bright scarlet wattles and dazzling white undertail coverts that billow in 'boiling' display. In normal posture, the tail is long and lyre-shaped. ▶

◀ **Female** A little larger than Red Grouse, with relatively longer, notched tail. Eclipse male (June/July) similar but has black tail and whitish undertail coverts.

Flying female Much whiter underwing than Red Grouse. Note full, notched tail. Eclipse male similar but has black tail and often a whitish bar on the upperwing. ▼

Flying male Brilliant white underwing and upperwing bar, plus lyre-shaped tail render breeding male unmistakable in flight.

Status Declining resident in N/E Europe. In Britain, chiefly Scotland and N Wales. **Population** (1991 census) 25,000 displaying males.

◆ Inhabits open coniferous and birch woods, mixed with rough heathland and boggy moors. Recently-planted hillsides often favoured ◆ Usually in small, often single sex, parties ◆ Chiefly in spring, males gather at dawn and dusk on traditional display grounds or leks. Uttering low but far-carrying bubbling and whooshing cries (like distant babble of brook and hisses of steam), they jump and spar with wings drooped and tail elevated to expose frothing white undertail coverts ◆ Females visit lek to select a mate ◆ Readily perches in trees, feeding on buds – at times almost hanging from branches, like a gigantic finch ◆ Shy and wary; best to observe quietly from a vehicle than on foot ◆ Flushes easily with rather silent wing beats, typically flying higher and further than Red Grouse (usually above tree height) ◆ Wild hybrids have occasionally been recorded with Pheasant, Capercaillie and Willow/Red Grouse.

Huge grouse confined to old, open pine forests with lush ericaceous ground cover. Male an enormous turkey-like bird (a third larger than female), dark in plumage with ivory bill, shaggy throat and long, broad tail. Smaller, mottled brown female recalls outsize female Black Grouse.

Male Unmistakable with rich brown back and wings, velvet-green shield on chest, slaty beard and fearsome hooked bill. In display, struts with tail fanned like a turkey and massive, loosely-feathered head and neck erect, uttering a bizarre sequence of belching sounds which quicken into a loud *plop*, followed by a series of harsh, scraping wheezes. Old males are biggest, with broader tails than younger birds.

◀ **Female** Markedly larger than (and twice weight of) female Black Grouse, with paler, more clearly marked underparts. Cinnamon throat and unmarked rufous chest band diagnostic.

◀ **Flying male** Distinctive, but typical view is frustratingly brief; invariably of huge, dark shape crashing noisily out of nearby treetops (each beat of wings can be heard). Looks very dark, with white underwing and bill, and long thick neck and tail.

Status Resident in N and in mountains of C/E Europe; outposts in Pyrenees and Scottish highlands. **Population** 2200 individuals (autumn); recent rapid decline reported.

Flying female Bigger-winged than Black ▶ Grouse, with longer, blunt-ended tail that shows rusty as bird flies away – a good fieldmark.

◆ Despite their size, Capercaillies are shy forest birds and almost impossible to see well ◆ Best looked for March-May when males are lekking or in early mornings along undisturbed forest trails ◆ Beware: some old cocks can be very aggressive – even attacking birdwatchers! ◆ Except at lek, is remarkably silent, adding to its almost mythical nature. Female calls include one recalling the 'crow' of a Pheasant ◆ Both sexes readily perch in trees (eats pine needles), but freeze as people approach ◆ Flushed birds fly with surprising agility between trees, even in dense forest. Sometimes flies high across valleys and lochs ◆ Occasionally hybridises with Black Grouse and even Pheasant.

Common Pheasant *Phasianus colchicus*   55-85cm (22-33")

Familiar long-tailed gamebird of farmland. Males with their goggles of bare red skin and highly glossed, colourful plumage are unmistakable. Females can only be confused with those of the other pheasants. Note measurement above includes a tail of 25-45cm (10-18").

▶

Adult male Colour varies due to racial mixing; many have white collars, whilst others are extremely dark green and purple-copper overall.

◀

Female Varies in colour saturation – typical bird shown (many are darker, others paler). Juvenile similar but with tail hardly elongated (cf. Grey Partridge).

Flight Flushed birds explode from underfoot with startling clatter of wings, although most prefer to run rather than fly from danger. Most males show pale blue upper forewing in flight. Long pointed tail separates female from flying partridges.

Status Widespread, well-established introduction. A native of Asia, widely reared and released for shooting. **Population** 2 million females.

◆ Favours relatively open country with some form of cover, including lowland farmland with hedges, woodland edge, and coastal and waterside scrub (including reedbeds) ◆ Feeds in open fields, often running for cover with tail cocked and head high ◆ Female explodes from ground nest almost underfoot, or indulges in 'broken-winged' distraction display as chicks fly in all directions ◆ Chicks can fly when quite small (beware confusing them with Quail) ◆ After noisy initial rise into the air, towers to clear hedges and continues with speedy flap-flap-glide action over short distance ◆ Roosts in trees. Rather noisy at roost times ◆ Males give a loud, grating squawk *ku-tok*, accompanied by a noisy wing-flutter in display.

Lady Amherst's Pheasant *Chrysolophus amherstiae* 60-120cm (23-47")

Established introduction (native to China) in a few woodlands in southern Britain (especially Beds, Herts and Bucks). Similar in size to Golden, but with longer tail. Normally skulking, keeping under the cover of dense, half-grown coniferous plantations. Male's distinctive strident, harsh spring call is the best clue to its presence; unlike that of Golden it consists of three notes (not two), with the emphasis on the first note (not the last): *chee ik-ik*. Population c100-200 birds. Note measurement above includes tail of 30-95cm (12-37").

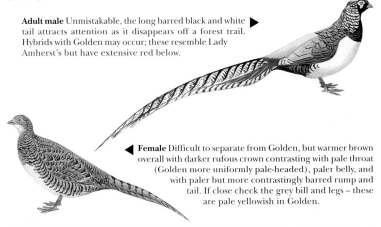

Adult male Unmistakable, the long barred black and white tail attracts attention as it disappears off a forest trail. Hybrids with Golden may occur; these resemble Lady Amherst's but have extensive red below.

Female Difficult to separate from Golden, but warmer brown overall with darker rufous crown contrasting with pale throat (Golden more uniformly pale-headed), paler belly, and with paler but more contrastingly barred rump and tail. If close check the grey bill and legs – these are pale yellowish in Golden.

Golden Pheasant *Chrysolophus pictus* 60-115cm (23-45")

Small ornamental pheasant, native to China. Widely kept in collections and an established introduction in a few forests in Britain (notably East Anglia; also south-west Scotland, South Downs and Gloucester). Inhabits dense, half-grown coniferous plantations, usually with rhododendron thickets. Keeps to cover of dense, dark forest but look out for them on tracks in the early morning. Far more often heard than seen. Male calls February-May, with a loud strident *ka-cheek*, the second note louder and higher in pitch than the first. Population c1,000-2,000 birds. Note measurement above includes tail of 30-75cm (12-29").

Adult male Unmistakable flame-coloured exotic. In display the golden shawl is fanned forwards and upwards to conceal the face. Hybrids with Lady Amherst's may show black chin.

Female Small size, closely-barred (unspotted) body plumage and longer tail are useful distinctions from female Common Pheasant. Very similar to female Lady Amherst's; check for plainer rump and yellowish bill and legs.

Common Quail *Coturnix coturnix*   18cm (7")

A miniature partridge (size of Starling), frustratingly difficult to see unless accidentally flushed. The distinctive call is normally the only clue to its presence. Easily confused with partially-grown young partridges, which can fly even when quite small, but Quail have longer and more pointed wings (an adaptation for long distance migration).

Adult male Pale buff and whitish body streaking and striped crown (pale central stripe divides dark brown sides) may be visible as the bird slips furtively through the grass in crouching ('quailing') posture. Some males have chestnut face and throat, lacking the typical bridled pattern. ▶

◀ **Adult female** Quail sometimes peep above short grasses. Females lack the black throat of males and have less marked facial bridles.

Status Widespread summer visitor (Apr-Sept), wintering in Africa. Numbers fluctuate greatly from year to year depending on size of migratory influx. In Britain, most likely in S England but in 'quail years' calling birds penetrate to the far north (including Shetland). **Population** Varies between some 20 & 2,000 territorial males; good years are an exception, and are usually followed by several poor ones.

Flight The sudden, snipe-like explosion of a rising bird is often accompanied by a low trilled call. Relatively long wings and short pointed tail are useful aids to exclude baby partridges.

Quail scud fast and low for a considerable distance, before dropping back into cover and running. They can rarely be flushed a second time.

◆ The only migratory gamebird ◆ Favours open rolling, and preferably weedy, cornfields and meadows ◆ Listen for persitent and distinctive call, especially at dawn or dusk: a series of rapid staccato, but liquid, notes *qwip-qwip, qw-qwip* ("wet my lips") ◆ Will only be seen with a great deal of luck, possibly dust-bathing on tracks in the early morning.

Slim, skulking marshbird, appreciably smaller and more secretive than Moorhen. Swims well but usually seen picking at muddy margins of reedbeds or wading in swampy fresh-water shallows. The only European rail or crake with a long red bill.

Adult Handsome, with plain slate-grey face and chest (cf. Spotted Crake), and bold black and white barring on flanks. Sexes alike.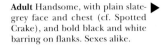

 **Juvenile** Duller than adult, with whitish super-cilium and muddy streak through eye. More brownish-buff and mottled below. Dull bill gradually becomes brighter and reddens with age.

Flight When flushed flies only a short distance before dropping into cover. Flight is low and weak, on fluttering wings. Notice long flesh-brown legs and toes, dangling behind like a Moorhen's. ▶

Status Common resident, though birds breeding in N/E of region migrate S/W in winter. In British Isles, widespread but rather scarce resident. More numerous in winter when native birds augmented by continental immigrants (Sep-Apr). **Population** c1300-2500 pairs.

Looks remarkably slender when viewed from behind – body is laterally compressed to slip easily through dense reeds. Short, cocked tail jerked nervously to reveal conspicuous buff-white undertail.

◆ Inhabits reed swamps, bogs and marshes ◆ In winter, also found locally in brackish creeks and saltmarsh on coasts ◆ Usually seen in ones or twos, seldom far from water ◆ Walks and runs about. Typically freezes or darts head down into cover when approached, but can be amazingly tame at times ◆ Loud calls give unseen birds away – an unmistakable outburst of grunting, agonised groans and pig-like squealing (latter can also suggest sound of a cork being twisted in the neck of a bottle) ◆ Abrupt, repeated *pik, pik, pik...* also frequently given, but often overlooked ◆ Omnivorous – sometimes catching and killing small birds.

Spotted Crake *Porzana porzana* 23cm (9")

Adult Short yellowish bill (variable orange patch at base, brightest in spring males) is distinctive. If views are reasonable, white freckles over the body plumage may be evident (most obvious on breast and upperparts), but can disappear with wear on late summer adults. Sexes similar.

Status Localised summer visitor. Some winter in S/W Europe, most in tropical Africa. In Britain, a scarce migrant, most frequent Aug/Sept in E/S England; very rare breeder (chiefly Scotland). **Population** 10-20 pairs.

Undertail coverts generally buffer than those of Water Rail (but colour varies in both species and identity should not be based on this feature alone). Juveniles, and many females, have an olive-brown bill.

◆ Easily confused with Water Rail on a disappearing rear-view, but smaller, browner below, with greenish legs ◆ Uncommon in sedge bogs and marshes ◆ Calls mostly at night – a far-carrying, 'whiplashed' *whit,* repeated at one second intervals ◆ Not shy, but sighting any crake is a rare event; be aware of the possibility of rarer, even smaller, Little and Baillon's Crakes.

Corncrake *Crex crex* 26cm (11")

Flight Most likely to be seen when inadvertently flushed from underfoot; rarely flushes twice. Flies low, with legs dangling – resembles a buffy Moorhen. Long rufous wings are diagnostic.

Status Diminishing summer visitor (mid Apr-Sep). Now rare and extremely local in Britain and Ireland; rare on passage elsewhere. Winters SE Africa. **Population** 650 pairs.

Adult Often stands on mounds and stones to call – look for greyish head and neck above tops of grasses, especially in spring when vegetation shorter.

◆ Fast-declining inhabitant of hay meadows, rank grass and fringes of marshland ◆ Rarely seen; betrays its presence with distinctive dry, rasping *crake-crake* – like running thumb along teeth of comb (loud rasping voice of Grey Partridge can confuse the unwary).

Little Crake *Porzana parva*   19cm (7.5")

Smaller and plainer than Spotted. Very similar to Baillon's but Little has long wings and light tertial stripe: long primary extension beyond tertials, the latter having a pale buff upper border (shows as stripe either side of rump, even in flight). The tail is also rather longer. Tiny red area at base of slimmer bill a helpful distinction from Baillon's but red difficult to see and absent in juveniles. Sexes differ.

Adult female Sandy-buff body distinctive in spring (both sexes resemble male in Baillon's). ▼

▼ **Adult male** Bluish-grey flanks look unbarred if wings drooped, as barring begins behind legs. Red at bill base, buff tertial stripe, long wing-tips and spiked tail.

Juvenile like female but shows some barring on flanks; best told from young Baillon's by structure.

◆ Reed and *Typha* beds by margins of lakes and pools ◆ Song a series of clucking notes, starting slow but accelerating into a rapid stammer ◆ Often feeds amongst flattened reed platforms over deep water, scampering for cover when alarmed ◆ Swims quite readily for short distances.

Baillon's Crake *Porzana pusilla*   18cm (7")

Like Little but plumper, with redder-brown upperparts, quite profusely marked with white, and strongly barred flanks (Baillon's has barred flanks and blunt wings). Short primary point beyond tertials very important (cf. Little) but beware effects of moult (when tertials might be missing, or primaries of Little incompletely grown). Bill stouter than that of Little, wholly green. Legs (especially of western adults) often distinctively pinkish, but many have greenish legs like Little. Sexes similar.

Juvenile Underparts duller and more spotted and barred than adult. Juvenile Little less barred below. ▼

▼ **Adult** Rear half of bird barred and spotted. Note short primaries and barred flanks; lacks buff tertial stripe. Leg colour varies.

◆ Sedge bogs and swampy meadows ◆ Local summer visitor (scarce but easily overlooked) ◆ Song given mostly at night, a repeated short, dry rasping *trrrr-trrrr-trrr..*; easily confused with some frogs.

89

Moorhen *Gallinula chloropus*   33cm (13")

Familiar tail-jerking waterbird, chicken-like both in shape and actions on land. Often confused with Coot, but never forms flocks on open water. White flank streak and white stern diagnostic in adult and juvenile. On water, back much flatter than Coot. Tail raised and frequently jerked in time with incessantly nodding head.

Adult Combination of bright red frontal shield and yellow-tipped bill is unique. On adult, white flash along flank divides slate-black head and body from dark brown wings. Sexes similar (slightly smaller female more whitish on belly).

Juvenile Much browner than adult, with buff-white lateral line and undertail. Whitish chin persists throughout much of first year. Greenish-brown bill lacks frontal plate.

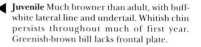

Skitters over water to escape danger. Flights usually brief, with legs dangling or feet trailing noticeably beyond short tail. On land, runs headlong for cover or safety of water, wings flailing.

Constantly cocks and flirts tail, showing white stern with black central divide. Takes elegant steps on long yellow-green legs (duller in juvenile) with outsize toes.

Status Widespread resident, but sparse or absent in north. British birds mainly sedentary, but northern populations migrate in winter – many to British Isles.
Population c315,000 pairs.

◆ Common on ponds, ditches, lakes and other still or slow-moving freshwater ◆ Usually solitary or in pairs. Occasionally gathers in loose groups to feed beside water and in nearby fields ◆ Generally wary, except where used to people (e.g. town parks)◆ Shuns expansive open waters, keeping instead to well-vegetated margins and banks ◆ Rarely dives but climbs well, sometimes to considerable height in trees and bushes ◆ Commonest call an explosive, throaty *kurr-uk!*◆ Alarm an anxious *kit-tik* or stuttering *kik-kik-kik-kik* ◆ When predator such as Stoat or Sparrowhawk nearby utters a peculiar loud, strained alarm, like sound produced by pulling reed leaf firmly between fingers.

A plump and quarrelsome waterbird. Noticeably bigger and more rotund than Moorhen, with entirely black plumage. Swims very buoyantly, with back more arched than Moorhen's. Noisy, belligerent and strongly territorial in summer – but highly gregarious in winter, massing in large compact flocks or rafts on exposed lakes and reservoirs.

Adult Brilliant white bill and frontal ▶ shield distinguishes Coot from all other birds in the region. Dark-slate plumage looks black at any distance.

◀ **Juvenile** Body duller, more brownish than adult. Whitish belly and foreneck (can be confusingly grebe-like) darkens by first autumn. Differs further from adult in dusky pink bill; frontal plate present but smaller and greyish.

Watch for splashing, wing-flailing run across water to escape danger or achieve take-off. Broad, rounded wings show narrow white trailing edge to secondaries (lacking in Moorhen). Outsize grey-green feet trail behind in typical rail fashion.

Walks and runs well on land, despite its clumsy looking feet.

Status Common and widespread resident. Mainly sedentary in Britain, with big influx of birds from continent (Oct-Mar). **Population** c55,000 pairs. Winter >200,000 birds.

◆ Distribution mirrors that of Moorhen, but has preference for larger, more open bodies of water ◆ Nests on slow rivers and still freshwater with reedy fringes ◆ Typically swims with hunched neck and bobbing head ◆ Feeds largely on plant matter, making frequent short dives with forward leap or up-ending like a duck in shallows. Also comes ashore in packs to graze ◆ Distinctive voice includes loud, penetrating *kowk* or *kut* (hence name), and an explosive, jarring *tizz* (so high it sets nerves on edge) ◆ Juvenile utters an incessant, pleading *quee-ip*.

91

Little Bustard *Tetrax tetrax*   40-45cm (16-18")

Flight Quick, fluttery wingbeats like a grouse. Black and white wing markings are striking and distant flocks appear to shimmer (can look oddly wader-like).

Male summer Black and white banded neck unmistakable.

Male has shorter fourth primary, producing characteristic whistling noise.

Status Scarce resident (migratory in N). Accidental Britain.

Female/winter male Mottled upperparts provide excellent camouflage on ground. Distant flock in fields can suggest winter Golden Plovers.

◆ In NW Europe, breeds only in France ◆ Dwarfed by Great Bustard ◆ In spring, males stand out on low mounds in grassy fields, uncultivated land and crops, blowing raspberries: *prrrt!*, with neck inflated (as though swallowing jam jar) and head thrown back. Occasionally 'flutter-jumps' into air ◆ Flocks in winter, but elusive.

Great Bustard *Otis tarda*   75-105cm (30-41")

Male Massive, matures after 5-6 years; has broad fan-tail, long thick neck and obvious chestnut collar. Long, white hussar-like whiskers worn only in summer.

Female Half size of male; lacks whiskers and rusty collar.

Status Rare and local resident in E Europe (formerly more widespread); occasionally strays west in winter. Accidental Britain (extirpated in 1830s).

Flight Powerful beats of extensively white wings. Old males have wingspan of 2.5m, and weigh up to 16kgs.

◆ Huge, gregarious, turkey-like bird of open grassy plains and cultivations ◆ Both sexes have ashen head and neck; cinnamon upperparts, boldly barred black ◆ Extremely wary, moving off with head held high in stately walk (seems almost to glide) ◆ In bizarre display (March-May) male turns 'inside-out'; becomes mass of white feathers, like a foaming bath, visible at great range ◆ Eats plants, insects, voles.

Strange bug-eyed wader of open, dry country. Rarely seen away from traditional haunts. Cryptic plumage and crepuscular activity render it difficult to find, but listen for wild, curlew-like calls at dusk. All plumages similar, juvenile has less-defined wing panel than adults.

Adult Round-shouldered stance but can look suprisingly sleek and upright at times. Rufous-buff vent, long yellow legs and short yellow bill with black tip are characterisitc. Black border highlighting wing panel is strongest in males.

Flight Prefers to crouch or jog away from danger, but if ▶ pressed, flies low with deliberate beats of long, bowed wings. Striking black and white pattern and long tail unlikely to be confused.

During day rests in depression on ground or squats awkwardly on tarsi. Watch then for hawk-like eye and distinctive bill.

Status Thinly distributed summer visitor. Rare and local in S England, late Mar-Oct. Exceptional elsewhere. **Population** 160 pairs (chiefly E Anglia), now stable after long decline.

◆ Bare flinty fields, sandy heaths, rabbit-cropped grassland and downs. On passage also by dry lakesides and stubbles ◆ Actions plover-like, but gives unique downward flick of tail. Trots forward, then pauses motionless to simply 'melt' into surroundings ◆ Loud *kur-LEE* calls suggest those of Curlew; often builds to an eerie, frenetic crescendo before dying away ◆ Gathers in flocks at favoured sites prior to southward migration (September-October).

Oystercatcher *Haematopus ostralegus* 43cm (17")

Large, noisy shorebird. Easily recognised by its boldly pied plumage, sturdy pink legs and long orange bill. Shrill, piping *k-leep!* and excited chorus of *pik, pik...* calls demand attention. Female has longer bill.

Adult summer Upperparts glossier black. ▶
No 'scarf' but legs and bill brighter.

▲
Adult winter Wears white 'scarf' around neck. Iris red with bright orange eye-ring.

◀ **Juvenile/first-winter** Browner than winter adult with greyish legs, duller eyes; more pointed bill has duskier tip. Bare parts gradually brighten with age, but white collar retained until third calendar year.

Status Resident. Many N European birds winter in Britain. **Population** 40,000+ pairs; winter c300,000.

Flight Striking pattern of white wing-stripe, black tail and white V on back unmistakable. Underwing white, with dark trailing edge.

♦ Nests on coasts and locally inland beside stony rivers, loch shores, even roadsides ♦ Essentially coastal in winter, often forming large flocks ♦ Feeds on cockles and mussels, hammered or prised open with its powerful, blade-like bill. Also seeks worms on coastal fields and riverbanks ♦ Watch for curious 'piping ceremony' in which groups trot along, bills pointing at ground, calling furiously.

Collared Pratincole *Glareola pratincola* 25cm (10")

Adult On ground, easily dismissed as 'cowpat' but for occasional short runs and head bobbing. Buff-yellow throat neat bordered black (like Chinese mandarin's moustache) and red base to stubby black bill characteristic. Juvenile scaly, without defined throat patch.

Status Summer visitor to S Europe (Apr-Sep). Winters tropical Africa. Annual vagrant to Britain.

Flight Pale belly, dark underwing (chestnut in good light) and white rump. 'Swallowtail' conspicuous in adults. If close check for diagnostic narrow white trailing edge to secondaries.

♦ Distinctive pale brown wader that hawks insects in graceful, dashing flight like a huge swallow ♦ Gregarious ♦ Frequents baked or sparsely vegetated fields adjacent to wetlands ♦ Harsh chattering calls, *kirrik-ek, kek kek...* suggest Little Tern.

94

Black-winged Stilt *Himantopus himantopus* 38cm (15")

Aptly-named wader with preference for saltpans, coastal marshes and saline lagoons. Strikingly black and white with sharply pointed wings, black needle bill and extraordinarily long pink legs. Calls ill-tempered, nasally and Coot-like, *kek, kek....*

▼ **Summer adult** Variable dark markings on head – from all white through to solid black cap and nape. Males are blackest above, with glossy green sheen; slightly smaller females duller, more sooty. Both sexes washed greyish on head in winter.

Status Locally common summer visitor to Mediterranean. Winters mostly in Africa. Rare visitor Britain (has bred).

Flight Fantastic legs trail behind like long pink ribbons. Black wings markedly triangular in shape. First-winters noticeably browner above with white trailing edge.

Avocet *Recurvirostra avosetta* 41cm (16")

Large, mainly white wader with bold black markings, long blue legs and a slender black bill with unmistakable upward sweep. Call equally distinctive, a loud, liquid *klüüt* (by which name Avocet is known in Holland).

Adult Black crown, nape and wing-markings, but looks all white at distance. Sexes similar but female has shorter, more strongly curved bill. Immature (not shown) easily recognised by brownish mottling on back and wings.

Fledgling Small, brown and fluffy; often confused with smaller waders. Note tiny upturned bill.

Status Increasing both as a summer and winter visitor, but very localised. **Population** 600+ breeding pairs; 2500+ winter.

Flight Slim and elegant, but broad-winged, with 'dipped in ink' primaries and pale legs trailing. Pied pattern gives shimmering effect from flighting flocks.

◆ Mainly coastal. Nests on muddy margins of shallow lagoons ◆ Winters in closely-packed flocks, chiefly in south-west Europe but increasingly at a few favoured estuaries in southern England and adjacent North Sea coasts ◆ Feeds in tight groups (difficult to count), characteristically sweeping bill from side-to-side on mud surface or in shallows ◆ Freely swims ◆ Highly aggressive in defence of nest territory ◆ Flocks generally fly close to water surface.

Little Ringed Plover *Charadrius dubius* 15cm (6")

Energetic small wader with large eyes, short bill and 'stop-start' action characteristic of all plovers. Superficially similar to larger Ringed Plover but with relatively smaller head and trimmer, more tapering, body. If close, the bright yellow eye-ring is diagnostic, and in flight it lacks the bold wing-bar of Ringed. Sexes similar.

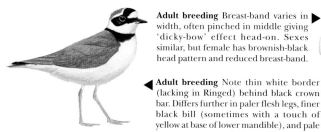

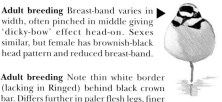

Adult breeding Breast-band varies in width, often pinched in middle giving 'dicky-bow' effect head-on. Sexes similar, but female has brownish-black head pattern and reduced breast-band.

Adult breeding Note thin white border (lacking in Ringed) behind black crown bar. Differs further in paler flesh legs, finer black bill (sometimes with a touch of yellow at base of lower mandible), and pale brown upperparts (colour of dry sand).

Juvenile Resembles adult, but blacks replaced by brown. Brownish breast-band often incomplete; the eye-ring is paler and narrower than in adults. Scaly brown upperparts and dark bill may cause confusion with juvenile Ringed, but note Little's plain brown cap without white eyebrow, and sandy smudge on forehead.

Flight Absence of wing-bar unique amongst 'ringed' plovers. Note narrow wings and white sides to tail.

Juvenile Ringed has whitish forehead and eyebrow, whereas these are strongly washed brown on Little Ringed Plover giving more hooded appearance.

Status Localised summer visitor (Mar-Sep). Scarce but increasing over most of England except SW; scarce migrant elsewhere. **Population** first bred 1938, now about 1000 pairs.

Ringed Plover juvenile

Little Ringed Plover juvenile

◆ Unlike Ringed confined to gravel pits, reservoirs and other freshwater habitats. Rare on estuaries ◆ In pairs or family parties (never in flocks) ◆ Call a high piping *pee-u*, just falling away at end ◆ Trilling song a repeated *tree-a, tree-a..*, given in wavering display flight like Ringed Plover ◆ Nervous, frequently wags tail (like Common Sandpiper).

More widespread of the two ringed plovers; mainly on coasts and estuaries, but also inland (can occur alongside Little Ringed Plover). In direct comparison with Little Ringed Plover, most appear robust, with a bigger head and distinctly bull-necked, but migrant Arctic race *tundrae* is smaller and trimmer. Leg colour and wingbar are key differences from Little Ringed Plover.

Adult breeding Orange legs and stubby ▶ orange bill with black tip are clear fieldmarks, even at distance. Note wider breast band, thicker white eyebrows and darker brown upperparts (colour of wet sand) than similar Little Ringed Plover. Sexes similar; male has faint orange eye-ring (but never so marked as Little Ringed Plover). Female's black head markings are mixed with brown.

◀

Juvenile Recalls winter adult but pale fringes to feathers of upperparts give a slightly scaly appearance. Yellowish-orange legs, whitish forehead and flared eyebrows are useful distinctions from Little Ringed Plover.

▶

Adult non-breeding Legs duller; bill mainly dark, orange only at base. Head and breast markings browner, less blackish, the breast band often broken in centre.

Status Resident breeder, numbers boosted on passage and in winter by birds from N Europe/Arctic. **Population** some 9,000 pairs; c35,000 in winter.

Flight Bold wing-bar makes flight identification easy. Note white sides to tail.

◆ Nests on shingle beaches and river banks, on coasts and increasingly inland; small parties occur on passage by inland waters but chiefly on estuaries after breeding ◆ Utters distinctive, liquid *too-eep* (rising on second note) in flight and on ground ◆ Yodelling *quitu-weeoo, quitu-weeoo...* during stiff-winged, slow-motion display as bird circles, tilts and banks low over nest site ◆ Striking breast pattern provides good camouflage on stony shores.

Paler than Ringed Plover (often as pale as winter Sanderling), with diagnostic blackish (not yellow/orange) legs and incomplete breast band in all plumages. Beware confusion with juvenile ringed plovers (which also have incomplete breast bands).

Breeding male Distinctive, with rufous or cinnamon ▶ cap and black head and breast patches. Note short black bar across forecrown not joined to black eye line (cf. Ringed and Little Ringed Plovers).

◀ **Juvenile** Shows weak chest patches and ill-defined whitish forehead and eyebrow. At close range, faint pale fringes to feathers of upperparts give weakly scalloped appearance.

Flight Suggests pallid Ringed Plover but shows even bolder wing-bar.

◀ **Breeding female** Plain grey-brown head and breast patches, with hint of brightness on ear-coverts and nape. Lacks black bar across forecrown present in male.

Status Formerly bred S England (ceased 1950s). Now rare annual visitor (Apr-Oct), chiefly to S & E coasts.

◀ **Non-breeding** Birds of both sexes resemble washed-out summer female; upperparts can bleach as pale as colour of dry white sand.

◆ Sandy beaches and intertidal flats ◆ Rare and local across most of Europe; more common on Mediterranean coasts◆ Most records in UK now are of lone birds, sometimes with Ringed Plovers ◆ Runs very fast ◆ Can often be picked out from other ringed plovers by its pallid and rather leggy appearance, with chunky head-end but decidedly truncated rear (line of belly seems to terminate abruptly at vent to give long-winged, tail-less impression) ◆ Flight call a short *kip-kip* like Sanderling, and quite unlike calls of Ringed and Little Ringed Plovers.

Scarce plover, possible as passage migrant on golf courses, airfields and open country, but nests in mountains. Recalls small Golden Plover in shape but yellowish legs and broad whitish supercilia meeting in a V on nape are unique in all plumages. Extremely tame (Dotterel means 'little fool').

Breeding female More brightly coloured ▶ than male, purer grey on breast and with darker cap and blacker belly patch.

◀ **Breeding male** White breast-band dividing grey chest from burnt orange and black of lower underparts is characteristic. Note whitish face.

◀ **Non-breeding** (autumn) Warm buff overall, with pale breast band; upperparts (especially of juvenile) heavily-scaled (like Ruff) with classic supercilia pattern evident.

Flight Typically fast plover flight but lacks wing-bar. Looks uniformly greyish above, but white shaft to outermost primary and narrow white rim to tail can be visible when alighting.

Status Scarce, highly localised, summer visitor to N Europe & Scottish highlands (May-Sep). Rare on passage elsewhere; in Britain, chiefly E England in May, W coast in September. **Population** <1000 pairs.

◆ Nests on barren montane plateaux; passage birds often in small parties ('trips'), stop off at traditional sites, favouring dry fields or short sward (not necessarily on coast) ◆ In hills scan ridges for distinctive profile of bird's head outlined against sky – narrow, waisted neck gives impression of a small bottle or skittle when viewed from behind ◆ If disturbed, rises with 'angry' rolling trill. Flight call a short turnstone-like rattle ◆ Female takes the lead in courtship and display; duller male incubates eggs and cares for young.

Golden Plover *Pluvialis apricaria* 27cm (11")

Highly gregarious. Forms dense flocks, often with Lapwings, in waterside or upland fields in winter. Despite name appears brownish overall unless close enough to see yellow spangling. Basic appearance (including black underparts of breeding plumage) shared by less sociable and more estuarine Grey Plover.

Male breeding Extensive black on underparts in breeding plumage, British breeders are more patchy with dusky face. ▶

◀ **Male breeding** Birds in north of range tend to have solid black on face and throat

Females of both northern and southern populations have less solid black below.

Non-breeding Plumages are similar. First-autumn birds are fresher than adults, with more spotted, less streaked, breasts and more finely barred flanks. ▶

Travels at height in dense, fast-moving flocks, the blunt body propelled by rapid, sharply pointed wings

Status Partial migrant, breeding widely in N & W. Numbers boosted in winter by immigration. **Population** 23,000 pairs. 500,000 birds winter.

Flight Shows weak wing-bar but is otherwise all dark above contrasting with white underwing. Lacks white rump and black armpits of Grey Plover, but compare with rare Dotterel.

◆ Nests on upland moors and bogs. After breeding moves to saltings, tidal flats and inland pastures ◆ On breeding moors male stands guard on hummock. Spangled back provides perfect camouflage, betrayed only by repeated, lonely whistle ◆ Evocative yodelling song given in aerial display ◆ Indulges in massive cold-weather movements, many perish during big freeze-ups ◆ Moves in typical jerky plover way, but stance rather upright ◆ Often lifts wings to reveal diagnostic white armpits ◆ Characteristic *too-ee* flight call, sounds sad but carries far.

100

Chunky, greyish wader of intertidal flats. Bigger nad bulkier than Golden Plover. Distant birds in winter plumage can be confused wth Knot but when bill and legs not appparent, trot-pause-bend feeding action distinguishes Grey Plover. First-summer birds do not acquire breeding plumage.

Non-breeding Birds are drab greyish, mottled darker, above; the plumage wears brownish by late winter inviting confusion with Golden Plover but rump and underwing pattern diagnostic. Note hefty black bill. ▶

Juvenile (autumn) Much brighter and more strongly marked than non-breeding adult, even tinged buffy-yellow above. Such birds suggest vagrant American Golden Plover (not treated here) but white rump and black 'arm-pits' provide most reliable distinctions.

Male breeding Unmistakable, with ▶ silver and black spangled upper-parts; lacks white flank stripe of Golden. Duller female has variable white flecking on black of face and underparts.

Flight Loose flocks or straggly lines, showing white rump and bold white stripe across blackish upperwing (cf. Golden). Black 'armpits' against white under-wing is a unique fieldmark.

Status Common winter visitor from High Arctic, and passage migrant (end July-May); some non-breeders over-summer. **Population** 45,000 winter.

◆ Unlike Golden, tied to estuaries and coasts, favouring muddy flats; uncommon inland ◆ Feeds by day or night, according to tides, its large eyes being adapted for night feeding ◆ Moves in typical plover way, but actions slower, more stealthy than Golden, with longish pauses then quick dash or bow to seize worms (latter sometimes washed before swallowing) ◆ Hauntingly plaintive 3-note whistle *tlee-oo-ee* (falling in middle) instantly identifies.

101

Well-known wader of meadows, marshes and fields. Recognised as a plover by its short bill and stop-go feeding action. Looks black and white at a distance and in flight, but when seen well long wispy crest and green upperparts glossed with purple, blue and bronze unique among waders. At all ages, white below with cinnamon undertail coverts.

Adult winter Retains dark breastband but throat ▶ becomes white and face tinged with buff. After late summer moult, green upperparts are broadly tipped buff. As buff tips abrade, adults difficult to tell from immatures in the field.

◀ **Adult summer male** All black throat and breast band, and very long crest. Female similar but has shorter crest, and is mottled whitish on face and throat.

◀ **Juvenile** Recognised by its shorter crest, dull brownish breastband and narrower buff fringes to upperparts. Large dark eye and rather plain buffy face gives younger birds a distinctive innocent look.

Flight Unmistakable in flappy, lolloping flight on unusually broad and rounded wings. Flocks seem to flicker black and white. Adults (especially males) can be picked out by their fuller, more bulging wingtips.

Status Common and wide-spread resident. Many N/E European birds winter in Britain. **Population** 200,000-260,000 pairs (declining); in winter, over one million birds.

In spring males display in dramatic rocking, rolling and diving song-flight on throbbing wings over nest site.

◆ Nests on open farmland, grassy moors and damp pasture ◆ More widespread in winter, forming flocks on grassland and fields – often with Golden Plovers (though the two species quickly split into separate flocks as they take wing) ◆ Onset of freezing weather causes huge diurnal movements to south and west ◆ Call is characteristic, a loud plaintive *pee-vit* (origin of country name, 'Peewit').

A stocky wader of tidal flats, bigger than Dunlin, with 'rugby ball' shape, straight black bill and short greenish legs. Essentially an estuary bird, feeds in dense packs over mud with hardly a space between them. Usually encountered in grey winter plumage.

Non-breeding adult Size and shape important; note also indistinct supercilium and eye-stripe and grey chevrons on flanks. Looks paler and greyer above than Dunlin.

Breeding adult The only medium-sized wader with rusty face and underparts. Returning adults in late summer have almost blackish upperparts through wear.

Juvenile More patterned and warmer than winter adult, with peachy wash across chest, and delicately scalloped upperparts – latter retained into first-winter plumage (feathers of mantle and wing coverts each with a thin black subterminal crescent).

Flight Pale grey rump and uppertail, chunky body and long-wings suggest Grey Plover, but latter shows stronger white rump and wing-bar and unique black 'armpits'.

Status Locally abundant winter and passage visitor (mid-July-Apr/May). British birds (race *islandica*) nest Greenland/E Canada. **Population** c300,000 birds, over 75% concentrated on estuaries of Wash, Alt, Ribble, Humber, Morecambe Bay, Thames and Dee.

◆ Highly gregarious, crowding together on favoured mudflats and high-tide roosts ◆ Feeds with slow 'plod and prod' technique, often in flocks that carpet the mud but which scarcely appear to be moving at first – a useful clue at long range ◆ Flight is swift, in lines or V formation. Vast flocks perform spectacular aerial manoeuvres – at a distance, resembling smoke swirling in the wind ◆ Call, a low *knut*, gives bird its name but almost inaudible unless birds close.

Typically encountered in small parties, scurrying over sandy beaches on black legs. Slightly larger than Dunlin, with shorter, straighter and altogether heavier black bill. Usually seen in winter plumage, when much the whitest wader.

Non-breeding adult Looks sparklingly clean grey above, with snow-white face and underparts emphasising prominent dark eye. Check for tell-tale black shoulder patch at bend of closed wing.

Juvenile Spangled appearance quite unlike winter adult. Look for black shoulders and yellow-buff half-collar at sides of breast.

Breeding adult Entire head, breast and upper-parts rufous, coarsely marked black. Belly gleaming white. In fresh spring plumage (May), looks paler, somewhat freckled or mealy above.

Status Widespread winter visitor and passage migrant. Nests high Arctic, winters S to S Africa. **Population** 12,000+ winter; more numerous on passage.

Flight Broad white wing-bar across blackish upperwing more marked than on any small wader except Grey Phalarope.

◆ Occurs in small, single species groups which fly fast and low across sand or surf ◆ Chases back and forth after waves, hurriedly picking off tidbits stranded by tide ◆ Odd birds occur inland, when quietly pottering action can be confusing (like outsized Little Stint); latter markedly smaller and more delicate, with shorter finer bill and spindly legs ◆ Call a soft *twick.* Parties utter quiet, conversational twitter ◆ Lack of hind toe unique amongst calidrids.

Broad-billed Sandpiper *Limicola falcinellus*   17cm (7")

Adult breeding Dark upperparts (marked by white V on mantle). Snipe-like head pattern distinctive, showing whitish supercilium and black crown split into three by narrow white lateral stripes. Belly white, with dark chevrons on flanks. Juvenile similar but warmer and brighter; flanks unmarked.

Status Localised summer visitor. Migrates SE, wintering on coasts from E Africa to Australia. Rare but annual vagrant Britain (May/Jul-Sep); mainly E coast.

Winter Pale and Dunlin-like. Rather short dark legs and bill shape, together with dark shoulders and ghost of head markings identify.

◆ Uncommon breeder on sedge bogs of Scandinavia ◆ Scarce on passage elsewhere. Most likely to be found amongst parties of Dunlin migrating north in May, differing in its slightly smaller size, appreciably shorter, greyish legs and long, thickish straight bill, clearly kinked down at tip ◆ Call suggests Dunlin's ◆ Looks dark in flight, with only a faint wing-bar.

Pectoral Sandpiper *Calidris melanotos*   21cm (8.5")

Adult At a glance, dull brownish and uninteresting – but yellowish legs diagnostic. Strongly streaked head/neck cut off sharply from white belly. Mainly dark bill, yellowish at base. Short pale supercilium. Juvenile has slightly warmer, brighter upperparts and shows more distinct white 'V' on mantle.

Flight Resembles Ruff in flight, having faint pale wing-bar and white ovals either side of dark rump. Executes erratic escape when flushed. Flight call resembles *dreeep* of Curlew Sandpiper, less hoarse than Dunlin.

◆ Most regular of a clutch of North American shorebirds that stray to Europe. Rare but annual visitor, especially Britain and Ireland (majority July-October) ◆ Bigger than a Dunlin; short, slightly decurved bill, small head and longish neck reminiscent of a Ruff, but tail more pointed ◆ All plumages similar (males larger than females) ◆ Prefers wet flashes and muddy shores with stubbly margins.

Little Stint *Calidris minuta*   13cm (5")

Tiny wader, even dwarfed by Dunlin, with relatively short straight bill. At all ages blackish legs, rotund appearance and relatively strongly marked upperparts are easiest distinctions from equally small Temminck's. Usually seen in juvenile plumage (cf. vagrant White-rumped Sandpiper.)

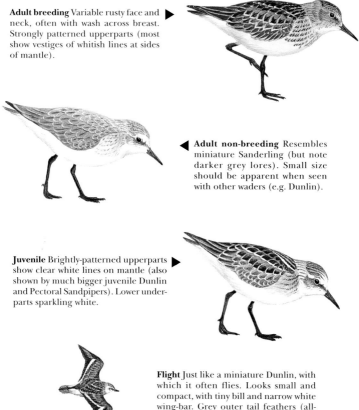

Adult breeding Variable rusty face and neck, often with wash across breast. Strongly patterned upperparts (most show vestiges of whitish lines at sides of mantle).

◀ **Adult non-breeding** Resembles miniature Sanderling (but note darker grey lores). Small size should be apparent when seen with other waders (e.g. Dunlin).

Juvenile Brightly-patterned upperparts show clear white lines on mantle (also shown by much bigger juvenile Dunlin and Pectoral Sandpipers). Lower underparts sparkling white.

Flight Just like a miniature Dunlin, with which it often flies. Looks small and compact, with tiny bill and narrow white wing-bar. Grey outer tail feathers (all-white on Temminck's Stint).

◆ Often tame ◆ Occurs in small groups, often with Dunlin, at estuarine wader roosts or muddy margins of inland lakes ◆ Animated feeder. Pecks at mud surface rather than wading, usually on less-exposed shores than Dunlin ◆ Some juveniles are duller and less rusty on upperparts than others ◆ Call a short *tip*, quite unlike Dunlin ◆ Breeds Lapland and Siberia. Migrates across north-west Europe, wintering south to South Africa. In Britain, small but variable numbers annually in autumn, chiefly eastern England. Rarer in winter and on spring passage.

Temminck's Stint *Calidris temminckii*   13cm (5")

Tiny wader of freshwater habitats. Relatively longer-bodied and shorter-legged than
Little Stint, with tail extending a little beyond wing-tip (most obvious in juveniles).
Typically virtually unmarked above and with paler (yellowish) legs than Little Stint.
With its subdued coloration and grey-brown breast bears a remarkable resemblance to
a miniature Common Sandpiper, but lacks white shoulder patch and never teeters and
bobs.

Adult breeding Usually only scattered dark-
centred feathers (with rusty-buff edges)
along scapulars, so upperparts generally
appear dull and rather patchy. Legs often
quite brownish-yellow.

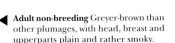

Adult non-breeding Greyer-brown than
other plumages, with head, breast and
upperparts plain and rather smoky.

Juvenile Head, breast and upperparts very
plain, but at close range shows narrow buff
scaling with fine, dark subterminal 'rings'.
Legs distinctly yellowish.

Status Breeds in mountains
and tundra shores in N; rare
breeder N Scotland. Scarce
migrant elsewhere in Britain,
chiefly in May and Sept, in E
England. **Population** 2-5 pairs.

Flight Towers like a minute snipe when
flushed, invariably giving very distinct
call: a tittering trill *titititititi*. Note that
diagnostic all-white (rather than grey)
outer tail feathers are only visible under
exceptional circumstances.

◆ Nests in upland bogs and lowland marshes ◆ On passage, favours
freshwater pools and muddy margins of lakes ◆ Mixes little with other
waders, but forms small groups (2-5 birds) ◆ Feeds quietly, slowly
and unobtrusively on shore, often amongst low waterside vegetation.
Looks short-legged and rather crouched ◆ Squats to rest or escape
notice, when all too easy to overlook.

Curlew Sandpiper *Calidris ferruginea*   20cm (8")

Rather elegant small wader. In red summer plumage needs only to be distinguished from larger, paler and much stockier Knot. Harder to pick out in other plumages, however, especially amongst flocks of similar Dunlin, but stands taller, with longer neck, longer black legs, and longer, more clearly decurved black bill.

Adult summer Dark chestnut-red head and underparts characteristic. Blackish back contrasts with pale grey wing-coverts and white vent. (Fresh whitish tips often give spring migrants a more pallid, frosted appearance.)

Moulting adult Tell-tale splotches of red on underparts when they first appear in late July/August (some still extensively red). In spring, however, northward migration to Arctic Siberian breeding grounds lies well to the east, so sightings in full breeding plumage in north-west Europe are few.

Juvenile Most birds seen in north-west Europe are juveniles. Often with Dunlin, but look for Curlew Sandpiper's longer bill, prominent whitish supercilium and more lightly streaked breast, washed cinnamon-buff. Confirm by checking for subtly marked dusky brown or greyish upperparts, each feather showing a fine pale fringe and dark subterminal 'anchor' which gives overall scaly effect, quite unlike Dunlin.

Flight Combination of clear white wing-bar and broad white rump patch eliminates all other small waders (except vagrant White-rumped Sandpiper from North America).

◆ Stops off on coastal marshes and muddy shores (fewer inland) ◆ In autumn, adults appear first, followed by juveniles a few weeks later, but numbers of both fluctuate greatly from year to year ◆ Extremely rare in winter ◆ Actions like Dunlin, but often wades up to its belly in deeper water to feed, head frequently pushed beneath surface in bouts of vigorous probing ◆ Gentle, rippling *chirrip* flight call is less grating than Dunlin's ◆ Passage migrant, chiefly late July–early October. Breeds Siberia, winters in tropical Africa.

Dunlin *Calidris alpina* 18cm (7")

Smaller than Starling. Our commonest shorebird, with a longish, slightly decurved black bill, black legs and hunched, round-shouldered posture. Familiarity with its various guises an important yardstick when confronted with 'something different'. Curlew Sandpiper and Little Stint are the most likely pitfalls.

Adult summer Isolated black belly patch unique amongst shorebirds. Notice bright chestnut upperparts, and streaked sides to paler face and hindneck creating distinctive cap and collar effect. (Brighter northern race shown). ▶

◀ **Adult winter** Typically appears neckless and rather dejected. Plain grey-brown upperparts match the sombre estuarine mud that is its winter home. Underparts white, suffused grey-brown and faintly streaked at sides of breast.

Juvenile/first-winter Bright upperparts reminiscent ▶ of summer adult, but rows of blackish spots on sides of belly and (usually) thin pale V on mantle identify. Head and breast washed warm brown, with brownish streaks. As autumn progresses, notice gradual invasion of plain grey feathers above and all white belly of winter plumage.

◀ **Juvenile Curlew Sandpiper** Differs in prominent white supercilium and longer, more decurved bill.

Flight Look for narrow white wing-bar and prominent white sides to dark rump and tail in flight. Flocks perform complex aerial ballet over mudflats, showing alternately dark and light as birds twist and turn as one.

Status Widespread but rather sparse breeder. Abundant winter visitor and passage migrant. **Population** c9,000 pairs. Winter: 500,000+ birds.

◆ Nests on moors and upland bogs ◆ Winters in large flocks on estuaries and coastal flats ◆ On passage, small parties also likely beside inland waters and floods ◆ Feeds busily in shallows or on muddy shores, with head down and delicate 'stitching' action ◆ Distinctive flight call, a shrill, nasal *treep* ◆ Listen for reedy trilling song on breeding grounds (like trills of a football-referee's whistle) ◆ Small race *schinzii* breeds in Britain/southern Scandinavia, replaced by brighter and larger-billed *alpina* further north.

Purple Sandpiper *Calidris maritima* — 21cm (8")

Dark slaty shorebird seen in winter on rocky coasts and groynes, often with slightly larger Turnstone. Tame but easily overlooked, its dark plumage difficult to spot amongst seaweedy rocks. Resembles a plump, sooty Dunlin but easily identified by its short yellow legs and variable orange-yellow base to slightly decurved blackish bill.

Adult winter No other shorebird is as dark but note dull white belly. Head, breast and upperparts uniform purplish-slate, with whitish chin but rather plain head. Pick out first-winter birds by their brighter and more obvious pale fringes to wing-coverts.

Adult summer Overall impression still dark but whitish supercilium and rusty fringes to crown and upperparts can suggest a 'funny Dunlin' – check for yellowish legs and bill base. Underparts whitish with untidy dark streaking across breast and flanks.

Juvenile Broad pale fringes to back and wings, and clean looking underparts with neatly streaked breast. Might be confused with juvenile Dunlin but again note yellowish legs and bill. (Seldom seen in this plumage in winter quarters).

Status Uncommon breeder in Scandinavia; 1-4 pairs Scotland. Localised winter visitor elsewhere, chiefly Oct-Apr. Rare inland away from breeding grounds. **Population** 25,000 birds winter (mainly in NE Britain).

Flight Blackish appearance relieved by narrow white wing-bar and white sides to rump.

◆ Nests on coastal tundra and mountain plateaux ◆ In winter occurs in parties of c5-20 birds on rocky shores ◆ Picks in unhurried manner at seaweed, mussels, crevices in rocks ◆ Look for at high-tide, resting on breakwaters and rocks, frequently within splash-zone. Reluctant to move, even with waves splashing at feet; typically scurries or flutters only a few yards before settling again ◆ Rather quiet in winter. Call is a soft *twit* or *twit-wit*.

110

Stocky seaside wader with short orange legs, a stubby, wedge-shaped, black bill and mellow rattle of a call. In breeding plumage, tortoiseshell back is eye-catching. Less obvious in piebald non-breeding plumages, which blend superbly with rocky and seaweed-strewn shores, its preferred habitat. Bustles about, poking at rocks and flipping over pebbles and beached seaweed in quest for small invertebrates.

Adult summer Complex black and ▼ white face pattern and variegated chestnut and black upperparts are unique. Male generally has whiter, less streaked crown than female.

Adult winter Sexes alike; blackish-brown above but still with black hoop across chest and semblance of facial markings. Often first noticed by its white underparts and orange legs. ▼

Juvenile Plainer brownish head than ▶ winter adult; neat pale fringes to mantle, tertials and wing-coverts give scalloped appearance. Legs duller, more yellowish.

Flight Summer left, winter right – bold white wing-bar and 'braces', white stripe down back and thick black tail band create unmistakable pied pattern at any season.

◆ Breeds on rocky Scandinavian coasts ◆ Unusual inland, even on passage ◆ European breeders migrate to West Africa, but birds from Canada and Greenland winter widely on coasts of western Europe ◆ Feeds in small, squabblesome groups on stony shores, seaweedy beaches and breakwaters (often with Purple Sandpipers); fewer on muddy shores ◆ Tame. If pressed, flies a short distance giving a quick, chuckling *tuk-a-tuk...* ◆ Some birds, mainly immatures, remain in British Isles throughout summer (but do not breed).

Ruff *Philomachus pugnax* — 20-30cm (8-12")

A variable wader of freshwater pools. The variation in size (male 25% larger), plumage and leg colour (typically orange or olive) is bewildering, but shape is always distinctive: relatively small headed with short decurved bill, slim neck, long legs and pot belly. Many suggest Redshank, but have strongly scaled upperparts and young birds have unmarked buffy underparts.

Adult winter More scaled above than Redshank, often with pale 'sheepskin noseband' on otherwise plain face, some are even white-headed. Bill usually has reddish base.

Breeding female ('Reeve') Lacks ruff. Breast and upperparts variegated, with bold, 'tiger-striped' tertials.

Breeding male Sports ear tufts and unique 'Elizabethan ruff' (above), latter worn only during May/June. Once moult commences, soon looks scruffy (right).

Juvenile Rich buff face and underparts, contrast with heavily-scaled upperparts; legs olive or yellowish-green.

Status Breeds N Eurasia; most winter Africa. A few breed in Britain (E Anglia) but chiefly passage migrant, with moderate numbers in winter (chiefly E England). **Population** 5-10 breeding females; 1500 on passage, with 300 in winter.

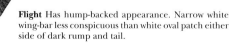

Flight Has hump-backed appearance. Narrow white wing-bar less conspicuous than white oval patch either side of dark rump and tail.

◆ Found singly or in small groups, beside freshwater pools, marshes and flood plains; in winter often on arable fields ◆ Picks at surface with random jabs, like domestic fowl ◆ Ritualised sparring of males at lek seldom seen in Britain, but females mate with selected males (thus no pair-bond) ◆ Flying flock often identifiable by variation in size of individuals ◆ Generally silent.

112

Plump woodland bird, usually seen in flight. Cryptic plumage gives impression of a small gamebird but very long bill (if visible) identifies it as a wader. All plumages are similar. Snipe, the only confusion species, has bold striping on crown and upperparts and is found in open country, not woods.

Adult 'Dead leaf' plumage lacks bold striping on mantle and crown of Snipe but shows short black transverse bars on crown.

◄ Freezes, squatting on ground to escape detection. Cryptic plumage renders it invisible, but watch for glint of large dark eye.

Look for at dusk, from late February to July, when territorial males fly over tree tops in unique roding display, uttering *twis-sick* call, accompanied by lower, frog-like croaks (as bird passes overhead). Long, hanging bill and curious flickering wing action provide instant identification, even in silhouette.

Rises suddenly like a gamebird from underfoot, with tell-tale clatter of wings and twisting escape flight through trees. Impression is of bulky, broad-winged shape with rusty 'back end'.

Status Widespread, but commonest in north. Absent as a breeding bird in SW England. **Population** 26,000 pairs. Influx from continent (Oct-Dec), boosts winter population to c800,000 birds.

◆ Breeds in extensive deciduous and coniferous forest with glades, rides and moist open areas in which to feed ◆ Feeds by day in summer, keeping to woodland ◆ More wide-ranging in winter, when feeds mainly at night; watch for twilight flights from woodland roosts to nearby damp fields. If ground frozen, may probe openly on sun-warmed lawns during the day ◆ Walks with bizarre rocking action, its short pinky legs hidden beneath low-slung belly ◆ Solitary.

113

Jack Snipe *Lymnocryptes minimus* 19cm (7.5")

Adult Markedly smaller than Snipe, with shorter bill and legs, and streaked flanks. Blackish mantle, glossed purple and velvet-green, with two pairs of burnished golden stripes diagnostic at rest. Legs brownish in winter.

Status In our region principally a winter visitor (Sept-Apr); widespread but overlooked.

Flight Dark, wedge tail unique among snipes. Escape flight low and brief.

◆ Seeks wet fields, boggy ditches and stubbly margins of reedbeds; likes watercress beds ◆ Plumage extremely cryptic and is rarely seen unless flushed ◆ On ground, betrayed only by bizarre 'trampolining' action of body on flexed legs – as if mounted on springs; inches forward and is virtually impossible to spot when still ◆ Occurs singly or in scattered twos and threes ◆ Breeds on vast quaking bogs in Lapland (outpost in southern Sweden), where peculiar aerial 'song' sounds like galloping horse! Otherwise usually silent.

Great Snipe *Gallinago media* 28cm (11")

Adult Bulkier than Snipe, with longer legs and heavier bill; differs in its extensively barred belly (adults have unbarred whitish belly centre), triple row of bold white tips to wing-coverts and bold white corners to tail (less so in juveniles).

Status Rare and extremely local summer visitor to Scandinavia and eastern Europe (May-September). Winters tropical Africa. Annual vagrant Britain.

Flight Unlike Snipe, flushes silently, flying off low and straight, flopping down after a short distance. Stout bill, full belly and broad wings reminiscent of Woodcock. Look for dark mid-wing panel framed by white.

◆ Bibbling song is like a symphony of icicles ◆ Except at lek, is quiet, rather solitary and seldom seen ◆ Breeds on uplands and drier bogs in Scandinavia and tussock marsh from Poland eastwards.

114

Tense, cautious marshbird that spends much of day hidden in swampy cover. Is often flushed when crossing wet fields. Easily recognised by its long straight bill, stripy head and cryptic plumage pattern with bold buff stripes forming obvious 'V' on back.

Adult All plumages similar. Appreciably larger and longer-billed than Jack Snipe, with barred flanks and different head pattern. Legs greenish. Long rapier bill. ▶

Sits tight when threatened. Unlike Jack, flushes explosively at a distance of about 10m, uttering harsh, scraping *scaap* – like quick tug of nylon zip. Zig-zags, pitches and climbs rapidly away, only dropping again at considerable distance. Narrow white trailing edge to innerwing. Differs from more ponderous Great Snipe in white belly and narrow white edges to cinnamon tail.

▼

In spring, stands proud on tussock, post or bush to 'sing' – a loud, rhythmic creaking, *chip-a, chip-a, chip-a...*

▲

Jack Snipe Broad golden supercilium enclosing dark 'raised eyebrow' and all dark crown; no neck and stout-based bicoloured bill.

Status Widespread breeder in N/W. Numbers have declined in Britain, though still a common winter visitor (from N Europe). **Population** >65,000 pairs; winter >100,000 birds.

Males dive steeply in switchback display ▶ flight. Air vibrating across splayed outer tail feathers produces unique drumming or loud thrumming sound; heard from afar, recalls bleating sheep.

◆ Common in marshes, wet meadows and boggy moors ◆ Active mostly early and late in day, probing shallow pools and muddy margins ◆ Often wades belly deep in water to feed. Picked out by its jerky movements and repeated thrusting of long bill deep into ooze, with vigorous 'sewing machine' action ◆ Occurs singly or in loose aggregations ('wisps').

Black-tailed Godwit *Limosa limosa* 38-44cm (15-17")

One of our largest waders. Elegant and long-legged, with very long, straight, rapier bill (pinkish-orange with dark tip). Stands tall, with as much leg visible above the knee as below – a useful aid in separating from stockier Bar-tailed.

Adult winter Head, breast and upperparts appear colder, greyer ▶ (colour of estuarine mud) and more uniform than Bar-tailed. Short white supercilium more or less stops above eye (cf. Bar-tailed).

Adult summer Both sexes acquire chestnut-orange head, neck and upper breast. ▶

▲ Differs from Bar-tailed in white belly with variable dark barring from breast to undertail. Upperparts black and chestnut, mixed with odd grey feathers. Female duller, but has longer bill.

Juvenile Strong orangy wash to neck and ▶ breast invites confusion with summer adult, but cinnamon fringes to neat, rounded coverts give wings a distinctly scaly look.

Status Localised breeder; rare in Britain (mainly in fens, also N Scotland; recolonised in 1950s). More numerous in coastal districts on passage. Winters mainly Africa, but Icelandic birds winter in west of our region. **Population** 30-60 pairs; winter c15,000 birds (esp. Ireland).

◀ **Flight** Black tail, dazzling white rump and broad white wingbars striking in flight – only Oystercatcher is similar. Long bill and legs, with toes clearly projecting beyond tail give rather stretched look. Seen overhead, shows gleaming white underwings with narrow dark trailing edge.

◆ Nests on damp grazing meadows ◆ Switches to coasts in winter, preferring muddier inner estuaries rather than seashores and tidal flats ◆ Often seen wading belly deep in shallow freshwater or coastal lagoons, thrusting head and bill beneath surface to feed ◆ Flight call a sharp *weeka weeka* ◆ In display, sounds like squeaky Lapwing ◆ Icelandic birds *islandica* have shorter bill and legs, and are darker and more extensively red in summer than nominate.

Bar-tailed Godwit *Limosa lapponica* 36-40cm (14-16")

Large, long-billed shorebird, most often seen in winter plumage. Stands head and shoulders above Redshank, Dunlin and Knot, with which it often occurs. Differs from rangier Black-tailed in shorter legs and slightly upcurved bill. Females have longer bills than males and can sometimes be mistaken for Black-tailed.

Male winter Recalls Black-tailed but has browner upperparts and breast, with streaks (lacking in Black-tailed). Key features include longer supercilium that extends well back behind eye and short thighs in comparison to length of leg visible below knee. Plain tertials with thin pale margins distinguish adults from similar first-winter birds.

Male summer Male underparts deep russet-red; upperparts blackish-brown with rich rusty fringes, giving overall darker impression than Black-tailed. Paler wing-coverts often stand out as a silvery panel.

Juvenile Resembles winter adult but has warm buff wash over chest, and buff notched tertials. Coarsely streaked brown and buff upperparts more reminiscent of a Curlew.

Female summer Typically much as winter plumage, but for warm flush to neck and chest. Note distinctly longer bill than male.

Flight Curlew-like in flight, with plain brown upperwing, closely barred tail and clear white wedge up back. Unlike Black-tailed toes scarcely project beyond tail.

Status Widespread winter visitor and passage migrant (end July-early May) **Population** 60,000+ winter.

◆ Keeps almost exclusively to sandy shores and mud-flats ◆ Found singly or in flocks, often dropping from sky in spectacular, goose-like whiffling descents ◆ Feeds in shallows or along shore, frequently just ahead of the tide ◆ Pushes long bill deep into mud between legs and works vigorously around to extract marine worms ◆ Flight-note a hurried *kuvik-kuvik* ◆ Breeds in the high Arctic.

117

Appreciably smaller than Curlew, with boldly striped crown, rather shorter legs (looks low-slung) and much shorter bill, which is more abruptly 'bent' at tip than the smooth, arcing bill of Curlew. Both are tricky to separate at distance and in flight but Whimbrel's loud, tittering whistle of about 7 notes: *pu-hu-hu-hu-hu-hu-hu* always diagnostic.

Adult Dark crown broken by pale central stripe is distinctive, but in profile Whimbrel's darker eye-stripe and pale supercilium distinguishes it from Curlew. Overall appearance is darker brown (less buff) than Curlew and bill often pinker over basal half of lower mandible. Female's bill longer but rarely exceeds 8.7cm.

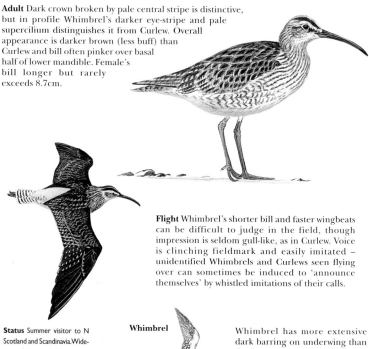

Flight Whimbrel's shorter bill and faster wingbeats can be difficult to judge in the field, though impression is seldom gull-like, as in Curlew. Voice is clinching fieldmark and easily imitated – unidentified Whimbrels and Curlews seen flying over can sometimes be induced to 'announce themselves' by whistled imitations of their calls.

Status Summer visitor to N Scotland and Scandinavia. Widespread in coastal areas on passage. **Population** <500 pairs breed, almost all in Shetland. A few winter in SW England & S Ireland.

Whimbrel

Whimbrel has more extensive dark barring on underwing than Curlew, giving overall darker impression.

Curlew

Underwing of Curlew is variably spotted and barred brown, but appears pale at long range.

◆ Breeds only in north, preferring dry, heathery moors, grassy hills and bogs ◆ Numerous and widespread on passage (April-May/July-September), stopping off to feed on rocky reefs, coastal fields and tidal flats. Winters mainly in coastal West Africa and is rare in northwest Europe October-March ◆ Passage birds often in flocks but also mingles freely with much larger Curlews at tidal roosts ◆ On breeding grounds, some calls easily confused with Curlews.

Our largest wader. Recognised by its streaked brown plumage, very long decurved bill and characteristic call, a haunting, drawn-out whistle, *cur-lee*. Whimbrel is main confusion species but Curlew is bigger with longer, more evenly decurved bill, streaky crown and different voice.

Adult Stands taller than Whimbrel, ▶ with longer grey legs and generally paler, more buff-brown appearance.

Some individuals show more distinct buffish supercilium and hint of pale 'parting' on crown, but never the clearly striped head of Whimbrel. Males have shorter bills (average 12cm; female 14.5cm).

Curlew

Whimbrel

Young Curlews, especially males, have shorter bills (9.5cm) than adults and can be mistaken for Whimbrel.

Flight Suggests a large gull. Long bill and far-carrying cry are easy field-marks but distant birds that refuse to call are tricky to separate from Whimbrel. Both species show broad white wedge on back and brownish-barred tail.

Status Widespread breeder, most numerous in N & W. Eastern populations migrate to winter in S & W Europe, especially British Isles. **Population** <50,000 pairs. Winter c200,000 birds.

◆ Evocative calls a familiar sound of boggy heaths, moors and upland rough grazing in summer ◆ Listen for bubbling song in fluttering and gliding display flight, on wings held up in shallow V ◆ When disturbed, circles over nest-site uttering incessant *qui-qui-qui...* until danger is past ◆ Common in winter on estuaries, tidal flats and coastal fields. Gathers in flocks, using long bill to probe mud and pasture for worms, crabs and molluscs ◆ Wary of approach, rising then peeling away with urgent cries, *cor-wee cor-wee!..* ◆ Non-breeding Bar-tailed Godwit similarly marked but has long, slightly upturned bill.

119

Taller and more elegant than Redshank, with longer legs and a longer, thinner bill that has hint of downward kink at tip (as though drop of water is hanging there). Note red in bill confined to lower mandible (cf. Redshank). Loud, sharp *chu-wit* or *chi-vi* is diagnostic and immediately betrays presence amongst other waders.

Adult summer Coal-black adult is darkest European wader (even the legs are blackish). At close range, upperparts liberally spotted and notched with white. Reveals startling white back and underwing in flight.

Adult winter Looks brighter and cleaner than Redshank, grey above and whiter below, with 'luminous' orange-red legs. Black lores and clear white brow generally create a more striking face pattern than Redshank (which has pale loral line and eye-ring).

Moulting adult Easily picked out by tell-tale black blotches of summer dress, but compare moulting male Ruff.

Juveniles (likely August/September) are easy to confuse with Redshank but have darker brown upperparts spotted white, and markedly smoky underparts with distinct brown barring.

Status Chiefly passage migrant. Some winter on estuaries in S/W, but most migrate to tropical Africa. **Population** Winter 100+ birds.

Flight All plumages distinguished from Redshank by plain wings (lacking broad white trailing edge). Note white back and feet trailing beyond tip of barred tail.

◆ Nests on bogs in far north ◆ Occurs widely on passage, beside inland floods and lakeshores, coastal marshes, muddy estuaries and lagoons ◆ Usually seen singly or in small groups, but parties of 30 or more may gather when passage peaks in August/September ◆ More energetic than Redshank, often dashing erratically through shallows in pursuit of small fish or wading belly-deep in water. Also swims, up-ending like a Mallard.

Noisy, excitable wader frequenting wetlands inland and on coast. Grey-brown plumage with bright orange-red legs and bill base distinguishes it from all other shorebirds except Spotted Redshank and some Ruff. Always alert – typical encounter is of bird bobbing nervously, then bursting into flight with a volley of frantic, ringing cries: *teu-hu, teu-huhu...*

Adult summer Upperparts brown, under-parts white, all variably streaked, spotted and barred dark brown. In poor light, sometimes appears deceptively dark, inviting confusion with summer Spotted.

◄ Adult winter Looks much more uniform; distinctly colder and greyer above, and pale below. Note strong smoky-grey wash to breast (finely streaked at close range). Bill is straight but shorter than Spotted's, and has more red at base.

◄ Juvenile Well-marked has warm brown upperparts extensively fringed buff, streaked buff-brown breast, brownish bill and orange-yellow legs. Might be mistaken for smaller Wood Sandpiper, but easily separated by voice and wing markings.

Stands sentinel on posts, monitoring intruders with anxious and incessant *kip-kip-kip*.

Status Breeds mainly in N and W of region. Abundant passage migrant and winter visitor, especially to British Isles and adjacent continental coasts. **Population** >35,000 pairs. Winter 100,000+ birds (many from Iceland).

No other wader combines broad white trailing edge to wing (visible from above and below) and white wedge up back.

◆ Nests on moors, marshes and wet meadows ◆ Winters mainly on estuaries and coasts ◆ Crowds together with other waders at high-tide roosts but usually feeds singly or in small groups – individuals rather evenly scattered across the mud ◆ Progresses mostly at a steady walk, picking and probing (Spotted feeds more urgently) ◆ Mournful *tyuuu* call epitomises our winter mud-flats ◆ On breeding grounds, listen for sustained yodelling song: *tudle-oodle-oodle...*

Greenshank *Tringa nebularia* 30cm (12")

Largest of the 'shanks', tall and rather angular in outline. Can often be picked out from a distance by its distinctly pallid grey and white appearance. Long, stout, slightly up-turned bill (with light greyish basal half, blackish tip), and pale olive-green or bluish (rarely yellowish) legs are key features. Powerful call is an easy fieldmark – a quick, triple whistle *tchu-tchu-tchu*; carries far and has characteristic ringing quality.

Adult summer Plumage unremarkable but distinctive. Notice variable mix of dull grey-brown and pale-fringed black feathers on back and wings. Head and neck whitish, with extensive dark streaks, becoming more spotted on breast; rest of underparts white.

Juvenile Resembles adult but mantle and wings darker and browner, with more buffish-white fringes .

Winter adult Paler and more uniform above. Head and neck especially pale – looking whitish on more distant views, but with dark streaking apparent when close.

Status Breeds N Scotland/ Scandinavia, eastwards. Common on passage across NW Europe. Winters mostly Africa but British birds rather sedentary, merely shifting slightly to S/W. **Population** c1,500 pairs. Winter 1,000-1,500 birds.

Flight Plain dark upperwing contrasts with gleaming white rump and wedge up back. Lightly barred tail usually appears pale too, adding to overall whiteness. Toes clearly project beyond tip of tail.

◆ Nests on remote pool-studded moorland and upland bogs, sometimes with trees ◆ On passage likely in almost any wetland habitat, from inland floods and lake shores to coastal marshes, estuaries and creeks (generally avoids open shores) ◆ Rather solitary, but migrants form small parties (seldom more than 15 or so) ◆ Active and erratic feeder; wades deeply but prone to almost comical dashes through shallows in pursuit of small fish ◆ In strong light, appears gleaming white below and very dark above.

Restless small wader of mainly freshwater margins and rocky streams, often seen perched on boulders and posts. Easily identified by its very distinctive voice, fluttery flight and incessant tail-wagging. Looks rather long in body and short in leg, with a long tail that clearly exceeds wingtips at rest. Legs pale olive to greyish-flesh.

Adult summer Pure white below, with olive-brown breast and upperparts (laced with fine black markings at close range). White 'comma' hooking up on to shoulder is an obvious fieldmark, even at distance. Shows clear white eye-ring, but less distinct whitish supercilium and dark stripe through eye. Duller in winter when wing-coverts are barred like juvenile, making ageing tricky.

Juvenile Similar to adult but juvenile has buff and dark brown barring on wing-coverts, and buff-fringes to tertials interrupted by dark brown spots. Vagrant Spotted Sandpiper from North America is similar but has slightly different call, paler legs and noticeably shorter tail.

Flight Takes flight readily, with much excited calling. Flight characteristically low across water, often describing a broad arc. Wing-action distinctive, alternating bursts of flickering wing-beats and short glides on stiff, down-bowed wings.

Note dark rump but clear white wing-bar and tail sides. Teeters nervously on touchdown.

Status Widespread summer visitor and passage migrant (Apr-Oct). Winters mainly in Africa; a few remain in milder S/W. **Population** c18,000 pairs.

◆ Nests beside stony rivers and lakes, especially common in uplands of north and west ◆ Widespread on passage, turning up at almost any inland water and on coast ◆ Always active, with tail-end constantly bouncing ◆ Often solitary, but loose parties of 3-5 gather on passage ◆ Calls impossible to miss – a clear, high-pitched, three-note whistle *swee-wee-wee...*, repeated often.

Contrasty freshwater wader with habit of flushing unexpectedly from ditches, slurry pools and marshy edges. Call is distinctive. Resembles Wood Sandpiper but appears black and white at any distance, with more prominent white eye-ring, shorter white supercilium (extends only to eye), longer straight bill and shorter, grey-green legs. Wags tail nervously.

Adult summer Not green but dark olive above, peppered with small white dots (compare bold chequering of Wood). Crown, foreneck and breast are strongly streaked but appears to cut off sharply at breast, as though smart white belly dipped in paint – the effect obvious at distance. Bill greenish, shading to blackish tip.

In winter head and breast paler and plainer, as though washed out (lacks heavy dark streaks of summer).

Juvenile Darker, with whitish throat and rich buff spotting above. Note short supercilium and narrow white eye-ring.

Flight Square white rump produces startling contrast with otherwise dark upperparts in flight, like an outsize House Martin. Note broad black tail bands.

Status Summer visitor to Scandinavia. Widespread passage migrant (Mar/May, with peak Jul/Aug).Winters mainly in Mediterranean basin and Africa. **Population** 500+ winter. (Has bred.)

Notice snowy underparts and contrasting blackish underwing, while feet barely protrude beyond tail. Flies fast with jerky, Snipe-like wing action.

◆ Breeds in old thrush nests in swampy northern forests and bogs ◆ Likely at any freshwater pool or ditch on passage ◆ In winter, often among watercress beds ◆ Always timid, usually solitary or in pairs ◆ Typical encounter is of striking black and white wader flushed and zig-zagging away with volley of almost hysterical calls. Towering escape flight finishes with sudden drop to water's edge ◆ Highly distinctive flight call, a loud, ringing *too-leet, weet-weet!*

Delicate, high-stepping wader of muddy freshwater margins, marshes and floods. Most likely to be confused with similar Green Sandpiper, but is more slightly built, with smaller head and bill, and longer, paler legs (greenish or yellowish). Distinctly browner upperparts and more prominent white supercilium (extending well back behind eye) are key plumage features.

Adult summer Differs from Green in dark brown upperparts with larger white spots. Neck and breast strongly streaked, with fine brown bars on flanks. Belly white.

In winter, adult is duller, less spotted above and greyer, less streaked below – breast looks more 'clouded'.

Juvenile Looks neater than adult, with yellower legs. Breast is more mottled than streaked and brown upperparts beautifully chequered with golden-buff (markings whitish in adult). Fresh juvenile Redshank can be mistaken for Wood Sandpiper; shows similar neat, buff-spotting above and washed-out orangey legs, but differences immediately obvious in flight.

Flight Shares square white rump and absence of wing-bar with Green Sandpiper, but Wood's overall appearance much less piebald.

Status Breeds N Europe. Migrates across Europe on broad front to winter in Africa. In Britain, few nest N Scotland; elsewhere regular on passage, especially S/E counties in May, with peak Jul-Sep. **Population** c10 pairs.

Notice pale underwing, and feet visibly protruding beyond more finely barred tail. Wood also shows clear white shaft to outer primary, lacking in Green.

◆ Nests in sedge swamps, marshes and bogs ◆ Occurs widely on passage, rarely in flocks but forming loose associations at favoured pools ◆ Often wades into deeper water than Green, stepping nimbly between emergent vegetation to pick food from the surface ◆ Flight note is distinctive: a short, dry *chiff-if-if* – quite unlike clear ringing volley of Green.

Red-necked Phalarope *Phalaropus lobatus* 18cm (7")

Dainty wader usually seen swimming buoyantly on water like a miniature Little Gull. Very tame. Spins this way and that, delicately picking titbits from surface – phalaropes are the only waders to do this. Needle-like black bill and black legs always distinguish Red-necked from bulkier Grey Phalarope.

Breeding female Unmistakable. Overall ▶ dark grey impression is relieved by golden 'tramlines' on mantle and diagnostic orange-red neck patch. White throat is best fieldmark at distance. Females brighter, more richly coloured than males.

◀ **Juvenile** Stray juveniles turn up during August/September (unlike Grey Phalarope, which mostly occurs late September-November). Rich golden stripes across dark back create much bolder pattern than juvenile Grey Phalarope, but underparts similarly white, with distinct 'scorching' on neck.

First-winter Moult into full grey-backed first-winter ▶ plumage delayed until arrival in winter quarters; therefore never as pale-backed as Grey in late autumn.

◀ Compare Red-necked's black needle bill with Grey's stouter, pale-based bill.

Red-necked

Adult winter Plumage partially-attained before leaving northern Europe, completed after birds have migrated south-east, to winter in Arabian Sea. Never so uniform pale grey above as Grey Phalarope. Some first-summer birds remain largely in winter plumage. ▶

Status Summer visitor, locally common on far northern breeding grounds, but very rare Scotland. Rare migrant elsewhere (esp. May and Aug/Sep). **Population** 20-30 pairs (mainly Shetland).

Flight Looks a little smaller than Dunlin in flight, but shows similar wing-bar. In breeding adults dark head and breast contrast strongly with white belly. Juvenile (shown) less chunky than Grey Phalarope, but basic pattern similar.

◆ Breeds on stagnant pools and bogs across northern Europe ◆ Feeds on mosquito larvae in summer and plankton in winter, stirred up by birds characteristic jerky, spinning action on water ◆ Call is low *twick*.

Essentially pelagic wader, breeding in the high Arctic but spending most of its life in flocks far out at sea. Feeds by swimming and spinning dizzily on water – a habit unique to phalaropes. Tricky to separate from Red-necked in winter plumage, but Grey is larger with a thicker bill (the most reliable field feature), and paler legs.

Breeding female Very rare in this ▶ plumage in region. Combination of chestnut underparts, white cheeks and black crown is unique but distant flying birds may appear dark with white underwings (cf. Knot). Bill yellow with black tip. As in all phalaropes, female more brightly coloured than male, which has pale spotted crown.

◀ **Juvenile** (September) Resembles juvenile Red-necked, but has thicker bill. Starts to moult into first-winter plumage earlier than juvenile Red-necked, so presence of plain, pale grey winter feathers on back during August/September points to Grey Phalarope.

First-winter (October/November) Much paler and ▶ more uniform above than equivalent Red-necked. Dark-centred tertials distinguish from winter adult.

Grey

Grey's bill is clearly thicker, usually with pale base, than Red-necked's all-black needle-like bill.

Adult winter Looks cleaner still, with uniform ▶ pale grey upperparts and tertials. (cf. stronger patterned Red-necked, rarely found in north-west Europe in winter).

Flight Looks very pale in flight and easily confused with winter Sanderling. Check for distinctive black eye patch and, if it settles on water, it's a phalarope!

◆ Nests on marshy tundra ◆ Pelagic for most of year, migrating exclusively at sea ◆ Winters off coast of West Africa ◆ Usually only seen in north-west Europe September-November, during seawatches or when storm driven inshore, then individuals can be scattered far inland ◆ Usually remarkably tame ◆ Call is a sharp *kip*.

Pomarine Skua *Stercorarius pomarinus* 46-50cm (18-20")

Similar to commoner Arctic Skua, but has heavier head and bill, broader body, wider wings and shallower, slower wing-beats. Juvenile less variable than Arctic; build and definition of underside primary pattern crucial to identity. All three small skuas have complex plumage stages, maturing after 3-5 years, making assessment tricky. Tail projection of 10cm (4").

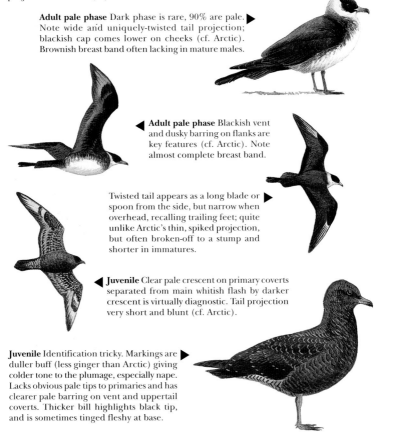

Adult pale phase Dark phase is rare, 90% are pale. Note wide and uniquely-twisted tail projection; blackish cap comes lower on cheeks (cf. Arctic). Brownish breast band often lacking in mature males.

Adult pale phase Blackish vent and dusky barring on flanks are key features (cf. Arctic). Note almost complete breast band.

Twisted tail appears as a long blade or spoon from the side, but narrow when overhead, recalling trailing feet; quite unlike Arctic's thin, spiked projection, but often broken-off to a stump and shorter in immatures.

Juvenile Clear pale crescent on primary coverts separated from main whitish flash by darker crescent is virtually diagnostic. Tail projection very short and blunt (cf. Arctic).

Juvenile Identification tricky. Markings are duller buff (less ginger than Arctic) giving colder tone to the plumage, especially nape. Lacks obvious pale tips to primaries and has clearer pale barring on vent and uppertail coverts. Thicker bill highlights black tip, and is sometimes tinged fleshy at base.

◆ Most likely to be encountered during seawatches or from offshore boats ◆ Usually migrates in small flocks, often flying high above the sea ◆ Rather shallow wing-beats of steady flight recall slower flight of Herring Gull (cf. Arctic) or even Great Skua ◆ More of a scavenger than Arctic, feeds on carrion as well as by chasing other seabirds ◆ Large, well-fed Arctics are all too easily misidentified as Pomarines but such birds usually appear small-headed relative to body bulk ◆ Scarce on passage offshore, breeding Arctic tundra, wintering southern oceans. Spring passage off western Britain in May; smaller numbers through English Channel. More scattered return August-November, when possible off all coasts – even inland after gales.

Blackish seabird with white flashes in wings and, in pale phase, white underparts. Piratical flight fast and falcon-like, the long, pointed wings allowing sudden, agile twists and turns. All three smaller skuas are similar, having complicated plumages, but most in western European waters will be either adults or juveniles (most immatures remain in winter quarters). Tail projection of 8cm (3").

Adults Occur in two colour phases (pale and dark) plus intermediates; dark phase predominant in south. Note especially tapered, pointed tail extension and smaller head and bill than Pomarine. Winter adults have barred body but blackish underwings.

Adult light phase

Adult dark phase

Juvenile Variable. Typically has warm, ginger-buff tones and bars; paler birds appear almost rufous-headed while darkest birds look blackish-brown with indistinct markings. All but darkest show warm buff marks at tips of fresh primaries (absent or weakly fringed in juvenile Pomarine and Long-tailed), which can be seen at rest. The short tail projections are pointed (blunt-tipped in the other two species).

Juvenile Has short tail, barred body and underwings. Lacks whitish underwing primary covert crescent shown by Pomarine. Attains adult plumage by third summer.

Status Summer visitor. Nests in loose colonies on coastal moors and islands, inc. locally in N/W Scotland. Winters S Atlantic. Frequent off all coasts, Apr-May and Aug-Oct; occasional in winter in SW approaches. Erratic inland. **Population** 3,350 pairs.

◆ The most likely skua to be seen chasing terns and gulls inshore ◆ Distant birds in steady flight are strangely curlew-like in build and flight action. In strong winds, progresses in bouts of swinging glides ('shearwatering'), unlike Pomarine ◆ Females larger than males in all three species – extreme examples can suggest larger Pomarine or smaller Long-tailed, which are both much rarer. Some distant skuas cannot be identified, even by experienced seawatchers.

Long-tailed Skua *Stercorarius longicaudus* 38-42cm (15-16")

Rarest, smallest and slimmest skua, about the size of Black-headed Gull. Breeding adults distinctive, but juveniles difficult to identify. At all times, relatively delicate head and bill, slim belly (but often full-chest) and long, almost tern-like wings important. Attains adult plumage at third summer. Tail projection of 18cm (7").

Adult breeding Separated from Arctic by greyish lower underparts (variable in extent) and stronger contrast above between blackish flight feathers and greyer forewing.

Adult breeding Longer, thinner tail streamers than Arctic are quite mobile in flight. Lacks white in wings (though narrow stripe detectable when close).

Juvenile Variable; tricky dark type shown. Always lacks Arctic's rufous tones, with paler buff and whitish barring and fringing giving plumage a colder, greyer tone. Lacks pale tips to primaries (cf. Arctic), and has more clearly pale barred vent and uppertail coverts (warmer buff and less contrasting in Arctic). Darkest birds of both species are very similar, but close views should reveal Long-tailed's whitish edging to wing feathers and ventral barring.

Juvenile dark type

Juvenile medium pale type

Status Breeds Arctic tundra, winters S oceans. Scarce passage pelagic, passing to west of Britain in May (when possible anywhere on Atlantic seaboard, esp. W Isles). Most inshore sightings occur North Sea Sept-Oct, when moribund juveniles occasionally 'wrecked' inland after storms.

Juvenile Slimmer, and generally much greyer than Arctic. Tail projections obvious, but blunt-tipped (pointed in Arctic). Virtually no white on upperwing (darkest Arctics usually show 3-4 white primary shafts, 2 in Long-tailed), but silvery band apparent on underside of primaries.

Palest birds distinctive, having almost white head and underparts, but usually a greyish breast band.

◆ Solitary or migrates in small flocks, with buoyant but deliberate wing action. Not given to bouts of gliding or shearing like Arctic ◆ Migrants seem to feed little, but sometimes chase terns ◆ From distance can suggest a dark grey Sandwich Tern ◆ Dark phase adults not known.

Our largest skua (about size of Herring Gull). A sturdily-built, dark seabird with striking white wing patches, most likely to be encountered during seawatches or from offshore boats. Stockier and more compact than dark juvenile gulls, with more determined, yet steady, flight action. When hunting, suddenly accelerates into a series of twists and turns, executed with remarkable agility. All plumages are similar, but juvenile separable at close range.

Adult Combination of sheer bulk, buff-freckled and ▶ dark-streaked plumage, and grey (not pinkish) legs prevent confusion with gulls. Dark immature Pomarine has fine wavy barring below, especially obvious on ventral area.

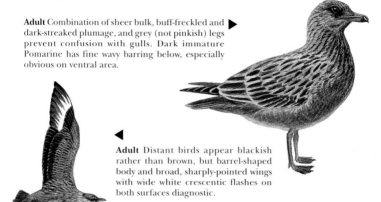

◀

Adult Distant birds appear blackish rather than brown, but barrel-shaped body and broad, sharply-pointed wings with wide white crescentic flashes on both surfaces diagnostic.

Shorter-bodied and more compact than dark young Pomarine, lacking ventral barring and with relatively broader wings and shorter tail.

Status Increasing but local summer visitor, breeding N. Scottish islands (and Iceland). Non-breeders or passage birds seen offshore round all coasts (Apr-Oct), least frequent SE England. Some winter in SW approaches. **Population** 7,900 pairs (majority in Shetland).

Juvenile At close range more uniform, less streaky than adult, with wing flashes slightly narrower and less obvious over long distances.

◆ Breeds in loose colonies on coastal moorland and islands ◆ Aggressive in defence of nest, pairs dive-bomb human intruders from behind (beware if standing near cliff edge on breeding islands); however (unlike Arctic) does not make physical contact ◆ A formidable avian pirate, readily chasing birds as large as Gannets in an effort to make them drop or disgorge food. Also feeds on carrion and scavenges behind trawlers ◆ Affectionately known by its Shetland name Bonxie to regular seawatchers.

131

Kittiwake *Rissa tridactyla* — 40cm (16")

Essentially marine, medium-sized gull. Dumpy and proud-breasted, with short black legs when standing; more at ease in flight, when agile and buoyant. Adult plumage attained by end of second winter, or earlier (many by end of first-summer moult).

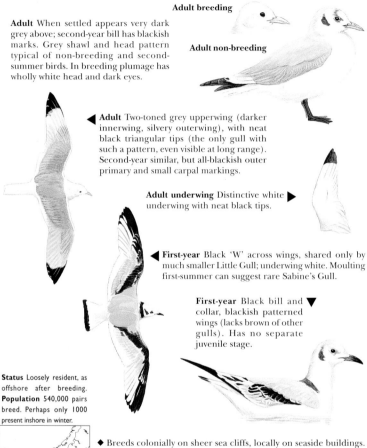

Adult breeding

Adult non-breeding

Adult When settled appears very dark grey above; second-year bill has blackish marks. Grey shawl and head pattern typical of non-breeding and second-summer birds. In breeding plumage has wholly white head and dark eyes.

◀ **Adult** Two-toned grey upperwing (darker innerwing, silvery outerwing), with neat black triangular tips (the only gull with such a pattern, even visible at long range). Second-year similar, but all-blackish outer primary and small carpal markings.

Adult underwing Distinctive white ▶ underwing with neat black tips.

◀ **First-year** Black 'W' across wings, shared only by much smaller Little Gull; underwing white. Moulting first-summer can suggest rare Sabine's Gull.

First-year Black bill and ▼ collar, blackish patterned wings (lacks brown of other gulls). Has no separate juvenile stage.

Status Loosely resident, as offshore after breeding.
Population 540,000 pairs breed. Perhaps only 1000 present inshore in winter.

◆ Breeds colonially on sheer sea cliffs, locally on seaside buildings. Largest, often immense, colonies in north of region. Moves out to sea after breeding ◆ Follows trawlers but otherwise mixes little with other gulls; increasingly present at fish-docks and sewage outfalls in winter. Occasional storm-driven birds turn-up at inland waters. Heavy inshore movements occur after winter storms, especially in the west ◆ Noisy at breeding colonies, which are dominated by piercing 'pieces-of-eight' or 'kitty-wake' cries ◆ Agile in flight; during strong head-winds parties fly through, rising and falling, flashing white undersides and swinging in like shearwaters.

Tiny, weak-billed gull, dwarfed by Black-headed. Adults have distinctly blunt wing-tips, whereas first-years are narrow-winged. When perched, pouting breast, dumpy shape and short legs give tern-like impression. Feeds with dipping flight action in manner of Black Tern. Adult plumage attained in third summer. Bill black and legs red or reddish in all plumages.

Adult breeding Full black hood and white wing tips suggest miniature Mediterranean, but blackish underwing and small size are easy distinctions. ▶

◀ **Adult non-breeding** Dark cap and ear-patch typical of all non-breeding stages. Note short bill and long wings.

Juvenile Blackish-brown mantle becomes grey and collar lost during first autumn. ▶

◀ **Adult non-breeding** Blackish underwing, with a narrow whitish border.

First-winter Dark outerwing and ▶ diagonal band shared by Kittiwake, but latter is size of Black-headed, lacks blackish cap, has a clear black collar and a thicker bill.

Adult breeding Broad wing-tip, without ▶ black marks; underwing blackish, with a narrow whitish border.

Second-year Resembles adult but has black marks on primaries and lighter, sometimes still whitish, ◀ underwing.

Status In Britain uncommon on passage and in winter. **Population** 150-350 in winter; odd pairs have bred.

◆ At passage times, especially August/September look for a small, tern-like gull dipping over freshwater lakes, or perching on waterside posts ◆ Frequent at inland waters on passage. Essentially marine in winter, keeping offshore unless storm-driven. Moult gatherings form in late summer, especially in Irish Sea and south-east Scotland. Sporadic breeding has occurred amongst Black-headed Gulls since 1975, but is not annual ◆ Small parties may be found flying through during sea-watches, but tiny size and narrow, patterned wings of immatures make them difficult to spot over a dappled sea ◆ Looks very dainty on water, riding on surface like a paper boat.

Ring-billed Gull *Larus delawarensis*   46-50cm (18-20")

Rare visitor to western Atlantic, favours freshwater pools by sea. Identification tricky. Bulkier than Common Gull, with thicker bill, flatter crown and paler grey upperparts.

Adult non-breeding Like Common but thicker, yellow bill has wide band (looks black-ended), iris pale (not obvious because of dark eye-ring) and has smaller mirrors in very pointed wing-tip. Second-year bill and legs often greyish-flesh, primaries without obvious spots and usually has some dark marks in tail. In flight dark tips to inner primaries and blacker underside outerwing useful in separating from small third-year Herring.

◄ **First-winter** Tail band less clean than Common; has dark spots on inner primaries and plain mid-wing panel (both lacking in second-year Herring). Underwing closer to Common.

◄ **First-winter** Striking pale pink bill with wide black band and tiny pale tip. Beware runt second-year Herring, but if not worn latter has more marbled tertial fringes (not neat pale edges) and barred (not plain) greater coverts, and shorter primary projection.

Sabine's Gull *Larus sabini*   33cm (13")

Rare migrant, August-October in North Sea and off western coasts. A small oceanic gull, occasional inshore after storms. Flight tern-like, showing piebald wing-pattern (beware distant young Kittiwake which can lack dark covert bar), but Sabine's has dark head and is daintier. In our waters nearly all are either dark-headed adults or juveniles (adults migrate before juveniles).

Adult Grey forewing and dark slate hood, even in autumn. Note yellow bill tip; legs black. First-summer (very rare in our region) has all dark bill and variable dark half-hood ◄ only on rear of head.

◄ **Juvenile** Wing pattern striking, recalls Redshank but has more white; brown head joined to back without a break. Note tail band.

Juvenile Brown, lightly scaled, upperparts, head and shawl. Legs greyish-pink. ►

Common Gull *Larus canus* — 40-43cm (16-17")

Wing pattern recalls Herring Gull, but Common is only a little larger than Black-headed. Relatively long wings, weak bill and small, domed head and dark eyes give an elegant appearance. Adult plumage attained in third summer.

Adult breeding Dark grey upperparts, dark eye and bright yellow bill and legs.

Adult non-breeding Bill and legs greyish or greenish, bill with dark subterminal mark. Head heavily-streaked in fresh plumage, wearing whiter.

First-winter Rounded head and small bill, latter dull flesh with blackish tip. Legs fleshy-pink. Mantle darker grey than most Herring Gulls. Juvenile has brown mantle and brown mottling extending to breast; bill and legs darker, fleshy-brown. Most as first-winter by autumn.

First-year underwing Darker underside to outer primaries and secondary bar than in young Herring.

Adult Relatively longer and narrower wings than Herring but tip blunter; larger white mirrors add to blobbed effect.

First-winter Dark grey saddle by late winter/spring, often contrasts with older, bleached, mid-wing panel; note cleaner tail pattern than immature Herring.

Status Resident, but few breed in S of region; massive winter influxes reach Britain from the continent. **Population** 70,000 pairs (mostly Scotland), swelling to 700,000 birds in winter.

Second-year Much as adult but has markings at wrist and smaller mirrrors at wing-tip. Tail normally all white.

◆ Likely almost anywhere, but favours farmland; after breeding, and especially in winter, also in towns, along coasts and on estuaries ◆ Breeds in colonies, chiefly on moorland ◆ Generally uncommon in south between May and July ◆ Gregarious; roosts in winter with Black-headed ◆ Most obvious call a distinctive, very high pitched, rising and falling wailing scream ◆ Much darker grey upperparts conspicuous when standing or swimming with Black-headed Gulls.

135

Mediterranean Gull *Larus melanocephalus* 38cm (15")

Recalls Black-headed, but chunkier head, with thicker, drooped bill gives very different expression, enhanced by a dusky mask in non-breeding plumages. Standing birds may be picked-out by taller, often blackish, legs and bulkier body. In flight ghostly whiteness of second-year and adult distinctive but first-year resembles Common Gull. Bill and leg colour variable. Attains adult plumage in third summer.

Adult breeding Blacker and more ▶ extensive hood than Black-headed. Legs and bill red; white primaries.

▲

Adult non-breeding Dusky mask of varying intensity. Legs red or blackish. Bill stout, red, brown or dusky; redder, with black sub-terminal band and pale tip in older birds.

◀ **Non-breeding Black-headed Gull** Spot or crescent behind eye, but transitional birds can show mask. Note relatively smaller, sleeker head and slimmer bill.

First-winter Dusky mask and drooped ▶ blackish bill. Legs usually blackish. Juvenile (not shown) has brown head and breast (lacks mask) and scaly brownish upperparts, but attains first-winter stage by August.

◀

First-winter Retained juvenile wing with dark primaries suggests Common Gull but stronger contrast (note very pale mantle and mid-wing panel). Underwing coverts whiter, unmottled. Note narrower tail band.

Adult Rather broad wings appear ▶ wholly white above and below.

Status Rare & local breeder. Mainly scarce but increasing migrant. **Population** 25 pairs at 14 sites in S England (1992).

Second-year Variable black marks in outer primaries like 'dirty fingernails'; otherwise wings appear wholly whitish on both surfaces. Wings broader with less black than Black-headed and lack 'blaze'. ▶

◆ Likely amongst flocks of Black-headed Gulls. Chiefly singles but small gatherings form in late-summer at a few sites ◆ More arrive amongst continental immigrations of Black-headed Gulls in late summer, winter and spring ◆ Locate by scrutinising flocks of Black-headed, checking for birds with a large hood in summer or a mask at other times ◆ Occasionally hybridises with Black-headed, producing offspring of mixed plumage and structural features.

Rather small, neatly-proportioned gull. Combination of either dark hood or ear-spot with slender red legs and bill distinctive. In flight relatively narrow, pointed wings show striking white blaze on both surfaces and narrow black trailing edge on outerwing. Highly gregarious. Adult plumage attained in second summer.

Adult breeding Wing-tip mostly black when closed. Dark hood attained in late winter, lost by mid-summer. Bill and legs dark wine-red in breeding season, bill black-tipped in winter. ▶

First-winter Dark ear-spot and juvenile-like wing and tail band. First-summer often attains dark hood. Bill and legs dull red, bill with black tip.

◀ **Juvenile** Strange, almost wader-like appearance with extensive dark brownish-ginger on crown and breast sides. Legs and bill dull orange, latter with black tip. First-winter stage is acquired during late summer.

First-winter Tail band and mottled upperwing retained throughout first year. Rest of plumage (including grey mantle) much as winter adult. Note white blaze and grey underwing. ▶

Juvenile Newly-fledged wings are short and rounded, compounding peculiar appearance, but note white blaze.

Adult winter Clean grey inner wing and ▶ wholly white tail acquired by most at one year of age (end of first summer). Underside of inner primaries very dark grey. Note pointed wing tip and blaze.

Status Abundant. Widespread resident and winter visitor. **Population** 220,000 pairs breed, swelling to 3 million birds in winter.

◆ Likely almost anywhere ◆ Breeds in dense colonies on both inland and estuarine marshes, birds rising in noisy cloud to chase off predators ◆ Many non-breeders spend summer at winter sites ◆ Highly gregarious at all times, forming enormous roosts outside breeding season ◆ Noisy squabbling gatherings form over food sources e.g. sewage outfalls, ploughing tractors and people feeding ducks ◆ Soars high, catching flying ants on wing in summer ◆ Typical calls include a high, excited *kak-ak-ak..*, a guttural rolled *kworrr* and a plaintive baby-like wail.

Great Black-backed Gull *Larus marinus* 65-75cm (25-30")

Largest and bulkiest gull, with stout hatchet bill, relatively long legs, thick neck, deep chest and short wing tip, which help in particular to identify small immatures. Fully adult plumage attained in third or fourth winter (see Herring Gull).

Adult Bulkier, less stream-lined than Lesser Black-backed with pale flesh-coloured (never yellow) legs. Note bulging profile to tertials and short wing-tip with large white markings. Blacker above than British race of Lesser but not as sooty black as Baltic race. Adults have white heads throughout the year.

Adult Wings blacker and relatively broader than in Lesser, with bold white trailing edge and larger white blob at tip. Underwing similar to Lesser, but larger white patch at very tip.

First-year Bulky build. Heavy blackish bill contrasts with paler head and underparts than other large gulls (but see Yellow-legged); lighter ground colour to plumage gives more chequered appearance than in Herring, with noticeably narrower and less solidly dark tail band. More extensive whitish uppertail-coverts extend in blunt wedge towards rump.

Inner primaries slightly paler than outer, but less than in Herring. Juveniles are browner on head and body than first-winter birds and can thus be particularly tricky.

Status common resident and winter visitor. **Population** c23,000 breeding pairs, increasing. Numbers swollen in winter with arrival of Norwegian birds.

Second-year Bill darker than in Herring until second summer by when blackish saddle becomes evident. Pay close attention to structure.

◆ Breeds as scattered pairs or in smallish colonies, typically on grassy cliff slopes ◆ Closely-attached to the coast but not uncommon inland at rubbish dumps and reservoirs, especially in winter ◆ Flight action is slow and ponderous on arched wings, especially when flying high but moves with remarkable agility when pursuing other gulls ◆ Gruff voice lower and more groaning than that of other large gulls ◆ Generally not gregarious but flocks do gather on favoured beaches.

Adults have slate (British race) or blackish (Scandinavian races) upperparts and yellow legs. Bulkier, bigger Great Black-backed is usually blacker, has relatively shorter primaries (with larger white spots), pale fleshy legs and is always white-headed (Lesser has brownish marks on head in autumn and winter). Immatures resemble Herring but are darker and best separated by wing pattern.

Adult breeding Danish race *intermedius* is darker backed than British *graellsii*. Baltic race *fuscus* is smaller, sleeker and longer-winged with sooty-black upper-parts. Legs bright yellow.

Adult breeding British race *graellsii* ▶ has slate upper-parts contrasting with black primaries.

Adult winter In fresh winter plumage *intermedius* and *graellsii* have brownish streaking on head, often forming a hood; feathers whiten with wear during winter. Race *fuscus* has weakly-streaked head (note Great Black-backed and Yellow-legged Gulls have whiter heads throughout winter). All races may show duller, fleshy-yellow legs in winter.

Adult winter *graellsii* Single white mirror (hidden at rest) ▶ sometimes joined to white spot at primary tip (Great Black-backed has more white in wing-tip). Dark grey upperparts contrast with black of primaries. Underside of primaries and secondaries shaded blackish-grey .

◀ **First-year** Much darker than other young gulls. Overall mottled dusky brown with lighter head. Blackish tail and flight feathers contrast with whitish uppertail-coverts. Lacks pale inner primaries of Herring and has dark greater covert bar.

Second-year Dark grey saddle ▶ contrasts with first-year wings; head and underparts whiter. By third winter many almost adult, except for pink legs and black near bill tip. Some have yellowish legs by end of second winter.

Status Breeds in W and N. Mainly winters in Africa. **Population** 89,000 breeding pairs. Winter numbers increased from 165 in 1953 to c70,000 by 1983.

◆ Formerly considered summer visitor to Britain but now also common in winter and on passage ◆ Breeds in colonies on low-lying islands, grassy cliff slopes and open moorland ◆ Forages in variety of open habitats from rubbish dumps and upland fields to reservoirs and estuaries. In winter, more abundant inland than in coastal areas ◆ Distant first-year birds over sea appear very dark and can be confused with skuas.

139

Herring Gull *Larus argentatus*　　53-66cm (21-26")

The familiar noisy gull of seaside towns. All large gulls attain adult plumage in their third or fourth winter. Immature plumages are confusing but age features are useful. Age summary: first-year – mottled brown, with dusky tail and blackish eyes and bill; second-year – paler body, greyish saddle, mottled wings, smudged tail, paler eyes and bill base; third-year – closer to adults but some brown in tail and wings (notably greater and primary coverts), bill largely pale with blackish tip; adult – yellow bill with red tip, legs pink.

Adult breeding British race *argenteus*. Grey above with pink legs. Nominate race (winter visitor from Scandinavia, shown opposite) mostly larger and slightly darker grey above. ▶

Adult winter In fresh autumn and winter plumage has brownish markings on head, but many birds in south of region remain mostly white headed in winter.

◀ **Adult winter** Note grey 'tongues' invading black wing tip (cf. Yellow-legged). From below, note white underside to primaries and secondaries (cf. Lesser Black-backed and Yellow-legged).

◀ **First-year** Shows obviously pale window on inner primaries. Note dark secondaries contrasting with paler, mottled greater coverts (contra Lesser Black-backed and Yellow-legged).

Second-year Paler, grey saddle than other large gulls of this age, bill extensively pale over at least basal half (cf. first-winter Ring-billed). ▼

Status Common breeding resident and winter visitor. Breeds all coasts. **Population** 205,000 breeding pairs. Numbers considerably swollen in winter with arrival of Scandinavian birds

Variant wing pattern Birds of nominate race have larger white marks in wing-tip, some (perhaps from the far north) have black restricted to wedges (with black almost invisible on the underside). These can suggest Glaucous Gull but have darker grey upperparts and at least some black. Beware: moulting adult Herring Gulls of British race in autumn show very little black in wing-tip and can appear strangely similar to Glaucous.

◆ Breeds in colonies on islands, cliffs and locally on coastal moorland; increasingly breeding on roof-tops ◆ More closely-attached to the coast than Lesser Black-backed, but common inland at rubbish dumps and reservoirs, especially in winter ◆ Noisy and quite aggressive, dive-bombs intruders near nest but rarely makes contact.

Relatively chunkier than Herring or Lesser Black-backed Gull. Grey of upperparts intermediate in shade between the two. Adults have yellow legs and red orbital ring (like Lesser Black-backed). Immatures recall those of Great Black-backed (see below). Formerly considered a race of Herring Gull but perhaps closer to Lesser Black-backed.

Adult Shade of grey close to Common Gull, clearly paler than ▶
graellsii Lesser Black-backed. Dark red orbital ring makes eye more prominent than in Herring. Weak head streaking in fresh autumn plumage abrades by mid-winter, giving snowy-headed look.

◀ **Adult** Trailing edge to wing more obvious than in Herring, with neater, squarer division between black and grey on primaries. Underside of primaries shaded light grey.

Adult Herring Gull of nominate race (breeds Scandinavia) ▶ Similarly bulky and almost as dark but has heavily streaked head, pink legs, more bulging tertials and more drooped wing-tip when standing. Most have larger white marks in primaries (sometimes extensive white wedges).

◀ **First-year** Suggests young Great Black-backed but has blacker tail and darker greater covert bar; white uppertail-coverts do not reach back. Shows paler brown inner primaries (but less so than in Herring).

Status Increasing visitor from Mediterranean/Black Sea. In Britain chiefly SE England (most abundant July/August). Has recently nested S England.

Second-year Shade of grey on saddle helpful. ▶ Bold blackish terminal tail band and tone of grey suggests giant first-winter Common Gull. Bill often darker than similar-aged Herring. Adult features more apparent by third-winter when almost adult except for pinkish (or pale yellow) legs and black near bill tip.

◆ Associates with Lesser Black-backed rather than Herring Gulls, foraging in fields and rubbish dumps, returning to roost on gravel pits and reservoirs ◆ Massive increase and northward spread in recent years from southern Europe indicate potential for future colonisation ◆ Interpreting shade of grey of large gulls requires caution due to tricks of the light; birds standing at different angles to the others in a flock can appear either darker or paler than they really are.

141

Iceland Gull *Larus glaucoides* 52-63cm (20-25")

Small version of Glaucous Gull (smaller than Herring), with a more domed crown, distinctly small bill (head and bill shape recalls Common Gull) and longer wings which project further beyond tail. Iceland is also relatively shorter-necked, more horizontal in stance and has distinctly larger eyes giving it a gentle expression.

Adult winter Extensive dirty brown streaking on head. Largest ▶ individuals (males) difficult to separate from smaller Glaucous (females) but if very close check for Iceland's red orbital ring which highlights eye (Glaucous has yellow or orange orbital ring when adult).

◀

Adult Wings relatively slimmer than in Glaucous, with relatively longer 'hand'. Looks slim-bodied from the rear but flying birds are tricky to separate with confidence.

◀**Adult** race *kumlieni* (Kumlien's Gull) has distinct grey wedges in primaries and can be confused with variant northern Herring but latter is bigger, darker grey above and has black, not grey, wedges.

First-year Extensively dusky bill pales over basal area during first-winter; some late first-winter birds (note dark eyes) and all second-winter birds (pale eyes) then have bill pattern similar to Glaucous.

▶

First-year Note relatively smaller ▶ head and bill but relatively larger eyes than Glaucous.

Status Scarce winter visitor; frequent N and W coasts. Non-breeders often summer here. **Population** Total of c75-150 scattered birds in most winters, but as many as 300 reported following exceptional influxes.

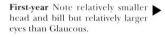

Second-year A typical small individual, showing long wing-tip, domed head and dainty bill, almost reminiscent of Common Gull in shape. In summer bleaches whitish, but such birds are patchy, not pure white (pure white birds are most likely albino Herring Gulls).

◆ As with Glaucous most occur in small influxes during January-March. Not infrequent at inland reservoir roosts ◆ Nominate race breeds only on Greenland; vagrant race *kumlieni* breeds on Baffin Island, north-east Canada, and is a vagrant to Britain and Ireland.

Large, sturdy buffy-brown or pale gull with ghostly white wings; larger, bulkier and deeper-chested than Herring, and close to Great Black-backed in size. Separating large Iceland from small Glaucous can be problematic (see Iceland).

Adult winter Has extensive dirty brown streaking on head. ▶ Paler grey above than Herring, with conspicuous all-white wing-tip. Bulkier, less stream-lined, than Iceland with bulging profile to tertials and shorter wing-tip.

◀ **Adult** Usually larger than Herring, but whiteness exaggerates size. Looks barrel-bodied from the rear.

First-year Massive, milky-tea coloured gull, always with whitish flight feathers. Close views reveal streaked (not spotted) markings and fine tail barring. Underwing can appear deceptively dark when overhead and contrasts with translucent flight feathers. ▼

▲ **First-year** Bill pink with neat black tip. Iceland can have similar pattern but bill of Glaucous is longer and more blade-like. Note rather small eyes; dark in first-winter, but pale from second-year onwards.

▲ **Second-year** Plumage paler, more patchy pale buff and whitish, and with pale eyes. Some pale grey feathers appear on mantle but not obviously until third winter when bill also yellowish with dusky subterminal marks.

Status Uncommon winter visitor from Arctic. **Population** 200-400 scattered in most winters. Most numerous Scotland and off-shore isles, but individuals likely all coasts. Non-breeders often summer here.

◆ Typically in small influxes during January-March, found singly with mixed gatherings of other large gulls, ghostly-white appearance making them obvious in a crowd, especially in flight . Odd individuals occur at inland reservoir roosts and rubbish dumps ◆ In summer the plumage of immature birds suffers from severe bleaching and can appear almost white at a distance, the primaries in particular become very ragged ◆ Beware occasional leucistic (diluted colour tones) or bleached immature Herring Gulls which can suggest both this species and Iceland; however, such birds lack the fine wavy barring of first year white-winged gulls and often show extensive brown in tail, on outer primaries or secondary bar, or have too much dark on the bill.

143

Slender-billed Gull *Larus genei*   42cm (16")

Rare, only likely southern France. Slightly larger than Black-headed Gull, with longer neck and pale eyes. Adults especially obvious if alert or in flight, but relaxed immature birds can be tricky. Saline lakes and coastal lagoons; nests colonially in brackish marshes.

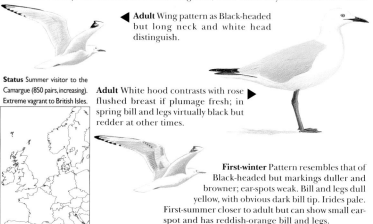

◀ **Adult** Wing pattern as Black-headed but long neck and white head distinguish.

Status Summer visitor to the Camargue (850 pairs, increasing). Extreme vagrant to British Isles.

Adult White hood contrasts with rose flushed breast if plumage fresh; in spring bill and legs virtually black but redder at other times. ▶

First-winter Pattern resembles that of Black-headed but markings duller and browner; ear-spots weak. Bill and legs dull yellow, with obvious dark bill tip. Irides pale. First-summer closer to adult but can show small ear-spot and has reddish-orange bill and legs.

Audouin's Gull *Larus audouinii*   48-53cm (19-21")

Rare, Mediterranean coasts. Distinctly smaller than Yellow-legged Gull, with long tapering wing-tip and dark bill and legs in all plumages. Long forehead slope exaggerates dark bill. Sandy beaches with rocky reefs. Adult plumage attained by third winter.

◀ **Adult** Wings more pointed than Yellow-legged, lacking obvious mirrors, also markedly paler grey, with obvious white trailing edge to secondaries.

Status Rare visitor, S France (but 100 breeding pairs Corsica); recent huge increase of Spanish population gives potential for vagrancy. Not yet recorded in UK or Ireland

Adult Blackish-red bill (often with small yellow tip) and dark grey or olive-grey legs are a unique combination. ▶

Second-winter Resembles that of first-winter Mediterranean, but larger, with mottling mostly on nape, lacks brownish bar on underside of secondaries and has darker primary undersides than Mediterranean. Juvenile is mottled brown, has wholly blackish tail suggesting Lesser Black-backed but underwing is less uniformly dark. First-winter birds attain pale grey feathering on mantle as bill becomes greyer.

144

Much the largest tern, almost the size of Herring Gull, with an impressive carrot-red, dusky-tipped bill. Steady flight action and blackish underside of primaries are strangely Gannet-like at a distance. Adult plumage attained in second winter. Feeds singly or in pairs along coasts and inland lakes. Loud, harsh heron-like *kraah* often draws attention to high-flying birds.

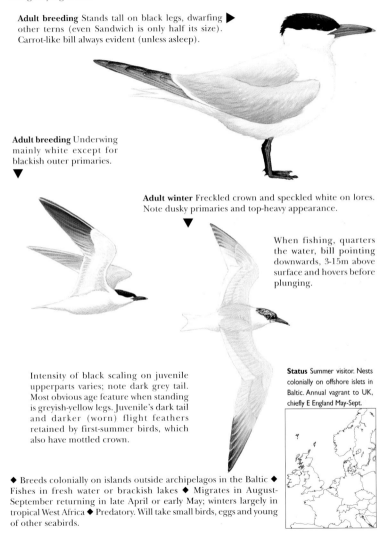

Adult breeding Stands tall on black legs, dwarfing ▶ other terns (even Sandwich is only half its size). Carrot-like bill always evident (unless asleep).

Adult breeding Underwing mainly white except for blackish outer primaries.
▼

Adult winter Freckled crown and speckled white on lores. Note dusky primaries and top-heavy appearance.
▼

When fishing, quarters the water, bill pointing downwards, 3-15m above surface and hovers before plunging.

Intensity of black scaling on juvenile upperparts varies; note dark grey tail. Most obvious age feature when standing is greyish-yellow legs. Juvenile's dark tail and darker (worn) flight feathers retained by first-summer birds, which also have mottled crown.

Status Summer visitor. Nests colonially on offshore islets in Baltic. Annual vagrant to UK, chiefly E England May-Sept.

◆ Breeds colonially on islands outside archipelagos in the Baltic ◆ Fishes in fresh water or brackish lakes ◆ Migrates in August-September returning in late April or early May; winters largely in tropical West Africa ◆ Predatory. Will take small birds, eggs and young of other seabirds.

145

Common Tern *Sterna hirundo* — 34cm (13")

Similar to Arctic, but slightly larger and longer legged, with bulkier head and neck, shorter tail streamers (not projecting beyond wing-tips) and longer red bill tipped black. In flight looks fuller-winged, body is more evenly proportioned fore and aft, and shows subtle differences in wing translucence and primary wear (see below).

Adult breeding In spring and autumn may have more extensive black of winter bill colour (suggesting rare Roseate). At rest, usually shows contrast between older (darker) and fresher (cleaner) primaries. Winter adults and first-summer birds have white forehead and black bill and legs.

Juvenile Duskier carpal bar, larger bill, and longer and redder legs than juvenile Arctic (legs blackish in late autumn). White cheeks reach bottom of eye (clouded or blackish immediately below eye in Arctic). Sandy-brown scaling varies. Recently-fledged birds have shorter bills.

Juvenile (flying) Recently fledged, autumn juveniles are greyer and have a longer bill and wings. Wings broader and carpal bar more pronounced than in Arctic. Has varyingly distinct grey bar across secondaries.

Adult (flying) primary moult staggered; thus old (darker) feathers normally evident as either outermost or central wedge on upperwing (less obvious in spring). First-summer have dark carpal bar and worn flight feathers retained from juvenile plumage, but tail like adult.

Status Common summer visitor, April to September; very rarely in winter on south coasts.
Population 16,000 breeding pairs.

Underwing Both Common (left) and Arctic (right), unlike Roseate, show a dark trailing edge, sharper and slightly narrower on Arctic and inconspicuous on juveniles. All primaries and secondaries appear translucent in Arctic against light, but only inner primaries on Common.

◆ Breeds locally on inshore islands, quiet beaches and increasingly inland by rivers, reservoirs and gravel pits ◆ Migrants gather on beaches and estuaries and to a lesser extent on inland waters, where it is the most likely member of its genus to be encountered ◆ Flight action steady and buoyant, with strong down-beat recalling Black-headed Gull, diving at varying angles from 5-10m; over freshwater lakes readily feeds by dipping to pick items from surface ◆ Typical call from migrants is a sharp *kip*; noisy at breeding colonies where predominate call is a full, rising *keee-arrr*.

146

Similar to Common Tern, but slightly smaller, with weaker bill, smaller, rounder head and very short legs (looks legless when standing, belly virtually resting on ground). Adults appear distinctly sleeker and longer-tailed than Common, whereas juveniles seem small and thin-winged.

Adult breeding Blood-red bill (rarely dark tipped in spring and autumn with vestiges of winter colour). Primaries appear uniformly silvery and streamers project a little beyond wing-tips. Winter adults and first-summer birds have white forehead and black bill and legs.

◀ **Juvenile** Smaller and smaller-billed than Common, with very short blackish legs (reddish when recently fledged). Appears more hooded, due to domed crown and blackish extending to just below eye.

Adult Primary moult complete, so upperwing always appears clean and evenly grey (cf. Common). Primaries narrower than in Common and wings appear to be set further forward due to smaller head, shorter neck. Long, whippy tail streamers often striking in spring. First summer birds have dark carpal bar, but tail more like adult.

◀ **Juvenile** Smaller and thinner-winged than Common, with whiter secondaries and weaker carpal bar, but latter variable. May even suggest Little rather than Common. Narrow dark tips to primary undersides often difficult to see, creating confusion with rarer Roseate.

Status Summer visitor, common in breeding ares from April to September. Normally winters in Antarctic waters, undertaking the longest migration of all birds. **Population** 40-70,000 breeding pairs, the majority in N Britain.

◆ Breeds in dense colonies on inshore islands and quiet beaches; locally by inland waters in N; exceptional in winter on south coasts ◆ Adults do not moult until arrival in winter quarters, thus even late autumn adults in breeding plumage ◆ Migrants occur on all coasts, but flocks migrate offshore or even high overland; small numbers on inland waters during adverse weather conditions ◆ Flight action more agile than Common, adults with longer, more mobile tail streamers ◆ Usually dives vertically, often pausing with short bursts of hovering (like Little Tern) but also executes sloping dives in shallow water ◆ All primaries and secondaries appear translucent when viewed against the sky from below (only inner primaries translucent in Common) ◆ Calls similar to Common, but higher in pitch and more nasal in quality.

147

Roseate Tern *Sterna dougallii* — 36cm (14")

Rare. Whiter than other terns, except Sandwich. Paler above and cleaner below than Common, with long streamers extending well beyond wing-tips when at rest. Smaller body, shorter wings, longer legs and longer bill than Common. Voice distinctive. Adult plumage attained in second winter.

Adult breeding Bill mainly black (red at base varies). Rosy flush on breast often evident. Winter adults/first-summers have white forehead and all black bill. Legs blackish in winter.

Juvenile Black scaling and blackish legs suggest Sandwich, but smaller, with white stripe along upperside of folded primaries. Recently fledged birds have shorter bills than adults. Dark tail corners and darker (worn) flight feathers retained by first-winter birds. First-summers retain darkish carpal bar, have white forehead but longish tail streamers.

Juvenile A recently fledged bird; older juveniles lack buff tone, have longer bill and whiter forehead. Dusky carpal bar usually evident but less than in Common. Secondaries typically light grey (like Common), rarely whiter (like Arctic).

Underwing Lacks dark trailing edge to underside of primaries shown by Common and Arctic (although very narrow on many juvenile Arctics).

Adult Outer primaries darken with wear. Very long streamers overlap when tail closed, appearing as single long thin ribbon. Lacks grey outerweb to outermost tail feather of both Arctic and Common.

White tips to primaries visible as white stripe along upperside, giving unique two-toned effect.

Status Extremely localised summer visitor, April-September. Winters in W Africa. **Population** 470 breeding pairs (78% at one Irish colony, but scattered pairs in tern colonies in N and W Britain).

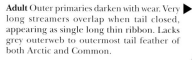

Roseate   Common

◆ Breeds on low, rocky islets or amongst other terns ◆ Migrants now very scarce, but should be searched for at favoured tern gatherings ◆ Very long tail streamers of adults give impression of a white Common Tern that has been stretched at the rear. Streamers often break-off; such birds then appear shorter-tailed than Common ◆ Distinctive nasal *chew-ick* (like Spotted Redshank) and a dry, rasping *aaack, aaack* (like Corncrake) ◆ Fast flight, with quick, shallow wing-beats; flowing streamers undulate ◆ Often forages further offshore than other terns ◆ Characteristically dives suddenly in mid-flight from 8-15m, briefly submerging.

148

Tiny; dwarfed by other terns when at rest and easily overlooked in mixed flocks but tends to keep slightly apart from them, often sitting amongst resting small waders. Hyperactive on the wing, with charactertistic pre-dive hovering. Non-breeding plumage stages invite confusion with those of similar-sized Black Tern, but Little is much paler above, has longer, slimmer bill and whiter forked tail. Potential for confusion in autumn with juvenile Arctic, which is smaller than adult and also often hovers before diving. Adult plumage attained by second winter.

Adult breeding Matchstick-like slender yellow bill, with variable dark tip, and short yellowish legs distinctive. Typical at-rest posture is more hunched, squat and neckless than shown.

Adult winter/first-summer Blackish bill and legs and narrow carpal bar give quite a different appearance, the white forehead becomes more diffuse. First-winter birds tends to have dusky yellow or yellowish-orange legs, but individual variation makes ageing difficult.

Juvenile Note blackish bill, dull yellowish-brown or orange-yellow legs. Upperparts washed buffy when recently fledged, fading to cleaner grey. Dark scaling makes forewing and primaries appear darker than whitish secondaries in flight, giving distant birds a strangely narrow-winged appearance. Scaling fades as autumn progresses.

Adult breeding Long, narrow wings; blackish outer primary webs form dark wedge on outerwing, even more obvious when feathers worn.

Status Local summer visitor, April to September. **Population** 2,800 breeding pairs on all coasts, chiefly SE and E England; declining through predation and disturbance.

◆ Breeds in small open colonies on shingle beaches, chiefly within reserves ◆ Migrants likely in very small numbers on all coasts, favouring sheltered beaches, lagoons and lower reaches of estuaries; occasional on inland waters ◆ Direct flight rapid and wader-like, on long, narrow wings – very distant birds even recall large white butterflies fluttering over the sea ◆ Habitually hovers on rapidly beating wings before plunging forcefully into water ◆ Typical call a sharp *kit, kit*. At breeding sites executes a slow, deliberate territorial flight whilst uttering a loud, repeated *kirri-virri* – reminiscent of a car engine turning over but failing to start.

The largest of our regular terns. Long black bill with 'buttered' yellow tip, and strident grating call diagnostic. Longer-billed and whiter overall than Common or Arctic, but compare with rare Roseate. Wing tips project well beyond short tail at rest.

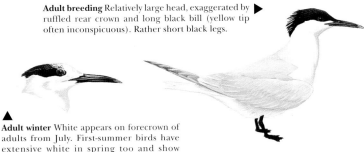

Adult breeding Relatively large head, exaggerated by ►
ruffled rear crown and long black bill (yellow tip
often inconspicuous). Rather short black legs.

▲
Adult winter White appears on forecrown of
adults from July. First-summer birds have
extensive white in spring too and show
abraded (dark) outer primaries.

Adult Long bill and short tail give front-heavy impression in
flight. Older primaries appear dark (either outer or inner
depending on state of moult and contrast strongly with
fresh pure grey of newer feathers); spring adults
mostly fresh. Underside of primaries shows dark subterminal
marks, appearing dark-tipped when worn.

◄

►
Juvenile Recently
fledged birds have dusky
forehead and short bills, at
first lacking yellow tip. Black scaling on upperparts
only shared by rare Roseate. Dark tail corners and
darker (worn) flight feathers retained by first-year
birds, which also have almost whole crown white (dark
only behind eye) in comparison to winter adult.

Status Summer visitor, late
March to early October.
Winters W Africa. **Population**
18,600 breeding pairs (90% are
in 29 colonies). Very rarely in
winter along south coast.

◆ Breeds in densely packed colonies on low inshore islets and quiet
beaches (most sites are within reserves). Freely mixes with other terns
and small gulls, even when breeding ◆ Migrants travel in family
parties along coastline, gathering together with others at favoured
stop-over sites on sandy beaches and estuary mouths ◆ Characteristic
far-carrying raucous *kirr-rick* attracts attention; in late summer adult's
harsh calls are mixed with penetrating squeaking cry of accompanying juveniles ◆ Flight action buoyant yet positive, on slender,
pointed wings; quarters inshore waters when fishing, peering
downwards, pausing to plunge from 5-10m with visible splash.

Gull-billed Tern *Gelochelidon nilotica* 38cm (15")

Easily confused with Sandwich Tern, but has stouter bill and relatively longer legs. In flight chunkier head and neck, slightly broader wings with clean-looking upperwing and steadier wing-action. Winter adults have dusky mask like Mediterranean Gull. Grey rump and tail uniform with rest of upperparts (slightly whiter than mantle in Sandwich). Call distinctive, godwit-like *kay-vek*. Does not plunge-dive but dips like a Marsh Tern.

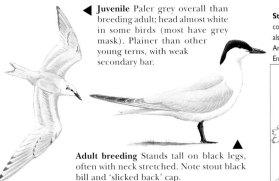

Juvenile Paler grey overall than breeding adult; head almost white in some birds (most have grey mask). Plainer than other young terns, with weak secondary bar.

Adult breeding Stands tall on black legs, often with neck stretched. Note stout black bill and 'slicked back' cap.

Status Summer visitor. Favours coastal marshes and lagoons; also inland on freshwater lakes. Annual vagrant to UK, chiefly E England May-Sept. Winters Africa.

Whiskered Tern *Chlidonias hybrida* 25cm (10")

A robust marsh tern of lakes and marshes in C and S Europe. Distinctly larger than the other two marsh terns, with bigger bill and longer legs. Non-breeders lack bold carpal band of similar first-summer Common Tern and have greyer tail only shallowly notched (with outerweb pale, not dark). Call is a short, nasal, Corncrake-like rasp *naakh, naahk*.

Adult breeding Dark grey underparts contrast with white cheeks and ventral area; upperparts grey.

Adult breeding Chunkier than Black, with head pattern of a 'sea tern' and white underwings.

Adult winter From White-winged Black by different structure and absence of dark marks on underwing-coverts. First-summer underparts patchy.

Status Locally common summer visitor. Winters tropical Africa (a few winter in Camargue). Rare vagrant to Britain, April-Sept.

Juvenile Like White-winged Black but structure, especially the sturdier bill, important. Note saddle is also browner.

151

Black Tern *Chlidonias niger*   23cm (9")

Small dark grey marsh tern, with almost square tail, relatively small bill and short legs. Unmistakable in breeding plumage. Other plumages may be confused with juvenile White-winged Black, Common and Arctic Terns and Little Gull, all of which feed by dipping when over freshwater. Non-breeding Black Tern easily identified by combination of dusky breast smudges and obviously grey rump and tail.

Adult breeding Blackish-grey, darkest on head, with white ventral area; longer bill, blackish (rarely red) legs, and greyer body and wings distinguish from White-winged Black when perched. ▶

Adult breeding Whitish (not black) underwing coverts distingush from White-winged Black. ◀

Juvenile Dark brown scaling on mantle and scapulars ages as juvenile; note conspicuous smudges at sides of breast. Legs dingy orange (blacker in adults). ▶

Adult winter Purer and paler grey than juvenile. Tail appears almost rounded if spread. First-summer birds similar but retain old (dark) outer primaries, vestiges of dark carpal bar and may show scattered dark feathers on underbody (but not underwing). ◀

▲
Juvenile Note dark 'thumb-marks' at sides of breast.

Status Breeds by freshwater lakes and marshes in continental Europe, winters at sea off African coasts. Passage migrant in small numbers, chiefly S & E England but generally uncommon. Has very rarely nested E England.

Juvenile Darker and browner grey than adult ▶ winter, with darker saddle and carpal bar. Saddle less contrasting than in White-winged Black, which lacks breast smudges and has whiter rump. Tail shallowly forked when closed.

◆ Migrants occur, often in small flocks, at both inland waters and during coastal sea-watches, chiefly May-June and August-September ◆ Sociable but mixes with Little Gulls (which have similar lifestyle) rather than with other terns ◆ Usually seen swooping and dipping over inland waters, wheeling round like a clumsy swallow ◆ Perches on tops of submerged posts and on shoreline ◆ Flight rapid and direct; when migrating over the sea, the darkness of upperparts renders them difficult to pick-up unless close, but look for flashing white undersides ◆ Typical call a sharp *kik*.

Vagrant marsh tern. Unmistakable in stunning breeding plumage, but otherwise resembles Black Tern though has slightly smaller bill and longer legs (stands a little taller if perched with Blacks). Non-breeding plumages require more care.

Adult breeding Much blacker body than Black, contrasting strongly with whitish forewing; legs redder. Late summer adults show mixed winter and breeding plumage features.

Adult breeding Striking black (not whitish) underwing-coverts contrast with whitish upperside forewing and silvery underside to secondaries.

Juvenile Very dark saddle. Slight or no indication of dark mark at breast sides. More white at sides of head than Black, with white supercilium often dividing cap from ear-patch (has 'ear-phone' appearance).

First-summer birds similar to adult winter but are very pale and worn, retain old (dark) outer primaries, vestiges of narrow carpal bar and may show dark markings on scapulars (but not underwing). Has less black on head than Black.

Adult winter Lacks breast smudges of Black and is paler grey above, has whiter rump and outer tail feathers. Underwing white (like Black) but some black feathers of breeding plumage retained as lines of spots until early winter.

Juvenile Blackish saddle contrasts with pale wings (darker leading and trailing edges) and almost white rump. Lacks prominent breast smudges of Black.

◆ Breeds in eastern Europe through Russia and Asia ◆ Scarce in our region, typically encountered as single juveniles on gravel pits, lakes and reservoirs during August and September; adults less frequent in May-June ◆ Often with Black Terns (in Britain mostly likely E and SE England) ◆ Winters on inland lakes and rivers in Africa and South Asia to Australia.

Guillemot *Uria aalge* 40cm (16")

Our commonest auk. Normally comes ashore only to breed, crowding together in noisy, smelly colonies on sheer sea-cliffs and rocky stacks. A degree paler and browner than Razorbill, with a more slender, sharply pointed bill, thinner neck and shorter tail. Messy grey-brown streaking on flanks diagnostic.

Breeding adult. Southern race (*albionis*) is chocolate-brown ▶ above, palest on head. Northern race *aalge* (nests northern Scotland/northern Europe) blacker above, like Razorbill. Both races have short white wing-bar.

Some individuals – known as 'bridled' ▶ Guillemots – have a narrow white eye ring, drawn out into furrow behind, like spectacles; such birds are commonest in north.

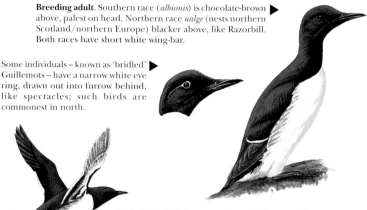

Flight Spiky bill gives more elongated front end than Razorbill, balanced by feet protruding at rear.

Flight Has typical auk flight – swift, low and direct, on rapid wingbeats. Differs from Razorbill in its dirtier-looking armpits and underwing, and more extensively dark rump.

Status Highly gregarious sea-bird. In British Isles nests mainly in N/W, but widespread off all coasts in winter. **Population** 1,200,000 birds.

Winter Foreneck and sides of face white. Differs from similar Razorbill in thin dark streak running back from eye across cheek, narrow broken collar, and dirty flanks. Guillemot's more pointed head and blunter tail can be useful distinction. Immatures retain this plumage well into summer.

◆ Size can be difficult to judge at sea – might be mistaken for grebe or even Red-throated Diver ◆ Impossible to miss on breeding ledges from late April–mid-August, where prolonged rumbling *aarrr* creates sustained, cacophonous din ◆ Young birds put to sea when only a third grown; flanks are unstreaked at first, but face is whiter with dark eye line than similar young Razorbill.

154

Razorbill *Alca torda* 38cm (15")

Differs from similar Guillemot in its blacker 'tuxedo', clean white flanks and deeper, blade-like bill. Has longer, more pointed tail than other auks (often cocked when swimming); can be useful fieldmark at sea.

Breeding adult Combination of heavy bill scored by vertical white band and white line running from bill to eye (like pince-nez) gives fierce expression.

Flight Looks more contrasty than Guillemot with clean underwing-coverts and clear white sides to rump.

Winter Tricky to separate from Guillemot at distance; check for Razorbill's blunter head, unmarked flanks and more extensive, smudgier black cap (in lieu of Guillemot's dark eye line). First-year birds in early winter have more black on side of head and smaller bill than adults.

Status Gregarious seabird; comes ashore only to breed (end Apr–mid Aug). In British Isles nests mainly in N/W but likely off all coasts in winter. **Population** c180,000 birds.

◆ Often forms mixed flocks with Guillemot; both frequently observed travelling in fast-flying, wave-hugging lines or as distant white blips hurtling by offshore, too far out to identify ◆ Breeds colonially in crevices on sea-cliffs and offshore stacks, usually vastly outnumbered by Guillemots ◆ Viewed from clifftop vantage, birds can often be watched 'flying' underwater in pursuit of fish ◆ Often flies from cliff in curious slow-motion display ◆ Voice a deep, growling *urrr* ◆ Young birds jump from ledges in July, when barely a third grown; their tiny size and stubby bill suggest Little Auk, but latter never occurs in North Sea before late October.

Brünnich's Guillemot *Uria lomvia* 39-43cm (16")

An Arctic species, though small numbers thought to winter in North Sea. Blacker above than Guillemot, with unstreaked white flanks and a thicker bill, which shows narrow whitish streak at gape (most obvious in summer).

Status Extreme vagrant to Britain.

Winter Full dark cap extends below eye like juvenile Razorbill (but latter has longer pointed tail). Resembles Razorbill in flight, showing much white at sides of rump but underwing is less contrasting.

Black Guillemot *Cepphus grylle*   30-32cm (12")

Small, rotund auk with a slender bill. Nests singly or in small groups beneath rocks and in crevices at base of cliffs. Summer and winter plumages differ greatly but both highly distinctive. Adult's bright red feet and gape, together with bold white oval patch on otherwise black upperwing, diagnostic at all seasons.

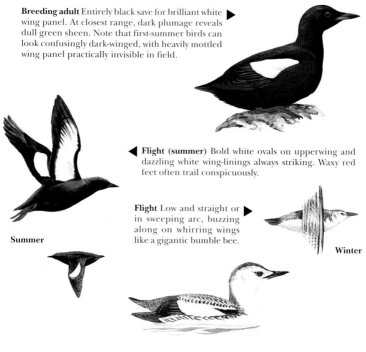

Breeding adult Entirely black save for brilliant white wing panel. At closest range, dark plumage reveals dull green sheen. Note that first-summer birds can look confusingly dark-winged, with heavily mottled wing panel practically invisible in field. ▶

◀ **Flight (summer)** Bold white ovals on upperwing and dazzling white wing-linings always striking. Waxy red feet often trail conspicuously.

Flight Low and straight or in sweeping arc, buzzing along on whirring wings like a gigantic bumble bee. ▶

Summer

Winter

Non-breeding adult (August-April) Retains characteristic clear white wing panel but crown, upperparts and flanks are uniquely dappled black and white; face and underparts white, with small dark eye-patch. First-winter birds look similar but have white wing panels obscured by dark mottling, and brownish legs.

Status Uncommon and thinly spread resident, confined to N and W. Largely sedentary. **Population** 40,000 birds.

◆ Found mainly in scattered ones and twos on sheltered coastal waters, sea lochs and bays ◆ Floats buoyantly like a cork, but can be hard to spot in hoar-frosted winter plumage. At a distance, might then be mistaken for a small grebe or even drake Smew (latter found mostly on inland freshwater) ◆ Periodically raises itself in water and flaps wings, revealing tell-tale wing markings ◆ Comes ashore to loaf on rocks and jetties beside sea (never found on high cliff ledges). Stance less upright, more squatting than Guillemot ◆ Calls include Rock Pipit-like squeaks and an irritating, high-pitched whistle (suggests Kingfisher), but are often hard to pinpoint.

Puffin *Fratercula arctica* 28cm (11")

Dumpy, black and white auk that nests colonially in burrows on grassy sea-cliffs and islands; extraordinarily tame. Pelagic in winter when rarely seen inshore. Smaller, chunkier and with darker underwing than larger auks – check for orange feet on alighting.

Adult winter Face dirtier, with narrower, duller bill (sheds brightly coloured bill-sheath of summer). Legs yellowish.

First-winter (August-March) Like winter adult, but bill smaller still.

Status Summer visitor to coasts of N/W (esp. Scotland). **Population** c1,000,000 birds.

Adult breeding Whitish 'clown's face' with large, multi-coloured triangular bill unmistakable. Legs bright orange.

Flight Rapid, on whirring wings. No white in wing.

◆ Trips to colonies are most rewarding from end June-July when adults ferrying beakfulls of fish, which droop like silver whiskers. Evening visits are best, as birds assemble on clifftop and in rafts on sea below ◆ Rides skilfully on updraughts at cliff edge ◆ Looks compact on water, with no neck and short tail. Bobs on water like bath-tub toy.

Little Auk *Alle alle* 19cm (7.5")

Winter Tiny black and white seabird that would fit snugly into cupped hands. Chubby neckless form (frog-like), stubby bill and untidy white streaks on scapulars diagnostic.

Status Scarce winter visitor. Most winter well to N of Britain, but occurs annually (storm-driven in unpredictable numbers), mainly along North Sea coasts from Shetland to Norfolk during Nov-Feb.

Flight Looks about Starling size, showing characteristic black underwings with white trailing edge and no bill.

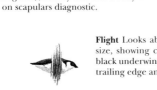

Breeding adult Full black hood. ▶

◆ Breeds in vast high Arctic colonies. Winters at sea, occasionally on coastal and inland waters after gales ◆ Usually seen flying past exposed coasts during severe on-shore storms ◆ Scuds rapidly by, frequently tagging on to flocks of waders, ducks – even migrating Starlings ◆ Often swims very low, trailing wings forlornly in water. But healthier birds are much more buoyant.

Collared Dove *Streptopelia decaocto* 32cm (12.5")

A slender, long-tailed dove of mainly pale coloration, originating from Asia. Reached western Europe from the Balkans c.1930 and first bred in Britain in 1955. Is now familiar in towns and villages everywhere. Perches freely on television aerials, street lamps and wires uttering its endlessly repeated, trisyllabic song.

Adult Uniform grey-buff appearance with narrow ▶ black half-collar across hindneck diagnostic. Pinkish tinge to face and chest. At rest, dusky brown primaries look short in relation to long, pale tail (cf. Turtle Dove). Sexes alike.

◀ **Juvenile** Duller, with narrow pale fringes to feathers of upperparts. Lacks black necklace.

▼ Takes off in a flurry of wingbeats, tail fully fanned. Uppertail shows broad whitish corners but lacks Turtle's crisp black and white pattern.

Collared

Flight Quick, spurting along with clipped beats of angled wings.

Note Collared's paler underwings and broad white tip to black undertail, latter very conspicuous when braking to land. Compare generally dark underside of Turtle.

Turtle

Status Hugely successful colonist, now resident and firmly established across most of region. **Population** 230,000 pairs.

◆ Lives in close association with man and invariably confiding ◆ Common in parks, gardens and farmyards, coming freely to take grain from bird-tables, chicken runs, etc. ◆ Alights with distinctive nasal *kwurr* (almost gull-like), then habitually raises its tail ◆ In display flight, rises steeply from perch, then sails back down on spread wings exhibiting striking black and white undertail ◆ Nest a flimsy platform of twigs in conifer, tall hedge, etc. (breeds February-October) ◆ Gregarious; flocks wherever food is plentiful.

Europe's smallest dove (size of Mistle Thrush). Usually detected, and easily identified, by its soft, purring song. Slim, compact form and dark, patterned back distinguish it from more elongated and pallid-looking Collared Dove. Blackish tail with clear white rim diagnostic at all ages.

Adult Black and white neck-patch and scaly back (created ▶ by broad rusty fringes to dark centred wing-coverts) unique amongst Europe's pigeons. Longish wings often held loosely to reveal blue-grey rump. Note orange eye with naked red surround, blue-grey cap, vinous breast and white belly. Sexes similar.

◀ **Juvenile** More uniform, sandy juvenile looks washed out by comparison. Lacks adult's distinctive neck patch and scalloped wings (feathers have thin, pale fringes but lack bold, dark centres).

Flight Fast and direct, but characteristically tilts from side to side. Combination of small size, narrow pointed wings and quick, jerky beats reminiscent of Green Sandpiper, an impression heightened by the contrast between dark breast, dark underwings and pale belly (cf. Collared Dove).

Distinctive tail pattern shows best on take-off and landing, as tail is fanned. Note blue-grey midwing panel.

Status Declining summer visitor (end Apr-Sep). Winters in tropical Africa. **Population** c75,000 pairs, confined mainly to lowlands in S and E England.

◆ Rather timid, frequenting open arable land with hedgerows, copses and woodland edge. Typically seen in pairs or small groups dotted along telephone wires strung out across cultivated land ◆ Song epitomises lazy summer days; a repeated deep, dreamy, soporific crooning (full of 'r's): *rroorr-rr-rr, rroorr-rr-rr....* ◆ Builds flimsy twig nest in thick hedge, bush or tree ◆ Feeds on ground, taking weed seeds and grain ◆ Forms flocks prior to autumn migration.

Rock Dove *Columba livia* 33cm (13")

The wild ancestor of all domestic pigeons. Now a scarce resident, confined to cliff coasts and islands of north and west. White lower back (rump) and two thick black bars across the folded wing diagnostic.

Adult Light grey back contrasts sharply with slate-blue head and body, and a beautiful iridescence on neck, shading from emerald across nape to purple on upper breast. Eyes orange, legs red. To eliminate Feral Pigeons, look especially for pureness of plumage, narrower black bill and small white cere. ▶

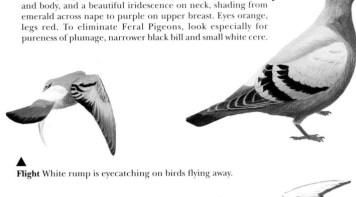

▲

Flight White rump is eyecatching on birds flying away.

Flight Fast, dashing by on rapid, pointed wings. Striking white underwings an excellent field-mark against dark body and undertail.

Feral Pigeon Domesticated form of Rock Dove, originally reared in dovecotes for the table. Now common in towns and villages everywhere, nesting in buildings, beneath bridges, cliffs, etc. Plumage immensely variable, some identical to pure Rock Doves (save for often thicker bill and puffy white cere). Most however betray mixed ancestry, with variegated plumages of white, red, grey or black. Unlike wild cousin, often perches in trees.

Population c100,000 pairs
(Rock/Feral Pigeon combined).

◆ Sociable; nests colonially on ledges in cliffs and sea-caves, where threatened by interbreeding with feral stock. Usually seen in small parties but flocks of 100+ occur in winter on clifftops, dunes and coastal fields ◆ Rarely seeks trees but in all other respects identical to Feral Pigeon, with same familiar, crooning voice, a rather hurried: *oor-roo-coo*, repeated ◆ Explosive take-off on clattering wings. Sails back into land, alighting with characteristic audible flutter, as though wings starched ◆ Walks briskly, with nodding head ◆ Watch for slow-flapping display flight, interspersed with glides on raised wings.

Stock Dove *Columba oenas* — 33cm (13")

Appreciably smaller and more delicate than Woodpigeon, with no white markings and a shorter tail which projects less beyond wing-tips at rest.

Adult Gentle-looking dove, with attractive lavender plumage. Has violet and green iridescence on neck, but no collar. Two short, broken black bands on innerwing are a useful fieldmark, though sometimes tricky to see. Juvenile duller, without neck sheen. ▶

◀ The only dove to nest in tree holes (occasionally also in nestboxes, cliffs, derelict buildings). Compare dark gentle eyes with Woodpigeon's pale, staring eyes. Bright pink, yellow-tipped bill sometimes striking.

Flight Pale midwing panel framed by darker grey forewing and blackish trailing edge is diagnostic. When passing overhead, appears predominantly grey (cf. Woodpigeon's paler belly and ruddier chest).

Stock Doves (centre and right) are easily overlooked amongst feeding Woodpigeons. Best picked out by their darker, more uniformly blue appearance and quicker walk, with constantly nodding head. Compare the obese waddle, dull grey upperparts and whitish belly of heavier Woodpigeon (left).

Status Widespread resident (shuns higher hills). Sedentary.
Population 270,000 pairs; scarcer in Ireland.

◆ Usually seen in pairs or small flocks of 10-50 birds in woods, parkland and farms with mature timber ◆ Rather timid, rising with soft flutter of wings ◆ In flight, short neck and square tail give compact outline – actually looks more stocky than Woodpigeon, its smaller size and quicker wingbeats more reminiscent of a Jackdaw ◆ Has slow, deep wingbeats in display, followed by a glide on wings raised in shallow V; beware possible confusion with displaying Rock Doves/Feral Pigeons (latter have silvery underwings), or even distant raptor ◆ Song easily overlooked but very distinctive, a rising series of deep, gruff notes: *ooo-wu, ooo-wu...*, repeated 4-12 times.

161

Woodpigeon *Columba palumbus*   41cm (16")

Our largest pigeon. Looks mainly grey, with a plump, chesty outline and small 'pigeon head'. Striking white armbands a unique field mark at all ages, visible at long range in flight and (usually) as a white flash at bend of wing at rest. Sexes alike (as in all pigeons and doves).

Adult The only pigeon with a broad ▶ white collar and pale yellow eyes – looks startled. Sides of neck glossed purple and green.

◀ **Adult** Heavy, waddling walk on short pink legs exaggerates overweight appearance. Has prodigious appetite, gulping food wholesale.

◀ **Juvenile** Has dark eyes and no white collar. Differs from similar Stock Dove and other grey pigeons by white wing flash and longer tail, which extends well beyond wingtips at rest.

Flight White band divides dark outer-wing from grey innerwing. Pale bluish rump contrasts with blackish tail band. Seen overhead, plain grey underwing, vinous breast and thick black tip to tail are useful pointers.

Status Mainly resident in west; northern and eastern populations migrate (Sept-Apr), some reaching British Isles in winter. **Population** 3,500,000 pairs (one of the ten most abundant British birds).

◆ Common in woods, fields, cities, parks, gardens (absent only bleakest uplands). Generally wary of man, but bolder in towns ◆ Highly gregarious, forming huge winter flocks that often festoon bare hedgerow trees ◆ Bursts into air with a loud clatter of wings or crashes noisily away through treetops ◆ Quick, direct flight can be surprisingly like Peregrine at times; veers noticeably away if surprised by man ◆ Settles fussily in trees, as though seeking just the right perch. Alights with flurry of wingbeats, habitually raising then lowering tail on touchdown ◆ In diagnostic display flight, climbs steeply with quick beats, clapping wings at apex, then pitching down on stiffly bowed wings ◆ Well-known cooing song, a lazy, muffled phrase: *who Cooks for-you, oh...*, repeated 3-5 times, before ending with an abrupt *who*.

Pin-tailed Sandgrouse *Pterocles alchata* 31-39cm (12-15")

Male Pea-green above with golden drops. Glowing orange face, black throat and pale brick chest-band. ▶

Female More marbled above; white throat and double black collar identify.

Status Resident in S France (c160 pairs). Not in UK or Ireland.

Flight Fast on rapidly moving wings – very like Golden Plover, with similar chunky body and sharply pointed wings. Both sexes show clean, snowy belly and white underwing sharply edged black, but pintail is invisible at distance.

◆ In our region confined to the arid, stony plain of La Crau (east of Camargue) ◆ Forms flocks but always elusive ◆ Usually seen in flight, after being flushed ◆ Far-carrying flight call a repeated guttural bubbling *qatarr- quarr...* ◆ Creeps furtively along with belly hugging ground, feeding on seeds.

Great Spotted Cuckoo *Clamator glandarius* 40cm (15.5")

Adult Grey crest and creamy underparts with pale yellow wash on throat. ▶

▼ **Juvenile** Differs in its neater, black cap and warm buff flush across chest.

Status Localised summer visitor to SW Europe (adults Mar-Aug; juvs linger until autumn). Winters tropical Africa. Rare vagrant Britain.

◆ Mediterranean species breeding in olive groves, dry brush and open country with scattered trees ◆ Parasitises nests of crows, especially Magpies ◆ Typical cuckoo features of slightly decurved bill, long graduated tail and hurried flight with shallow wing action ◆ Often perches openly on wires and fences ◆ Noisy during breeding season, uttering a loud, irritated, rattling chatter *che-che-che-che-che.... kee-ow, kee-ow, kee-ow.*

Common Cuckoo *Cuculus canorus*   33cm (13")

Male's far-carrying *cuc-koo* (or more excited *cuc-cuc-koo*) is instantly recognised, but female's loud, 'bubbling' liquid trill less well-known. Occurs in all types of countryside, mid-April/end June, but rather shy and most likely to be seen in flight, when its small head, long pointed wings and long graduated tail appear distinctly falcon-like. Alights in ragged manner with tail splayed and raised, and wings drooped loosely in classic cuckoo-pose.

Adult Combination of blue-grey head, breast and upperparts, ▶
white underparts barred blackish, and yellow eyes and feet can
suggest Sparrowhawk. Look for Cuckoo's slender decurved
bill, long wings and white tail spotting, conspicuous in
flight. Sexes similar, but some females
separable by brownish
wash across more barred
breast.

◀ **Female rufous phase** Uncommon; has chestnut
upperparts, heavily barred black. Easily confused
with female Common Kestrel – check bill shape.

Juvenile Upperparts either dark
slaty-brown, finely edged white (as
shown) or as rufous adult. Both
types aged by conspicuous white
patch on nape. Incessant begging
cries grab attention: *tsip... tsip...*;
sound is irritating, insistent, but
hard to locate. In flight, note more
rounded wings and shorter tail than
adult.

Status Widespread summer
visitor (mid Apr-Sep). Winters
southern Africa. **Population**
c16,000-32,000 pairs.

Flight Flies low with hurried,
shallow beats (wings not raised
above horizontal); holds head up
and makes frequent shifts of body,
as though uncertain where to go.
Regularly pursued by small birds.

◆ Solitary, but occasionally seen chasing in twos or threes, giving
gruff coughing calls ◆ Well-known brood parasite; lays eggs
principally in the nests of Meadow Pipit, Dunnock and Reed Warbler
◆ Young Cuckoos soon dwarf foster parents, soliciting food with
gaping red mouth ◆ Insectivorous, with liking for hairy caterpillars
ignored by other birds, which are gleaned from vegetation or in
awkward shuffle on ground ◆ Adults depart in July; young follow
independently August – September.

Barn Owl *Tyto alba* — 33-39cm (c13-15")

The familiar white owl, often caught in car headlights when driving at night. Pale, ghostly appearance with unmarked white underwings characteristic (cf. Short-eared Owl). Haunts open country and farmland with patchwork of rough fields, ditches, rank verges, young plantations and marshes. Mainly nocturnal, but sometimes seen hunting during the day, especially on winter afternoons.

Adult Heart-shaped face and small black eyes ▶ diagnostic. Golden-buff upperparts reveal soft grey shading with black and white spangles when close. Birds found in Britain and south-west Europe (of nominate race, *alba*) are white below. Birds with palest primaries often males and those with copious spotting on underparts female, but sexing by plumage characteristics is unreliable.

Nests in holes in old trees, buildings, nestboxes. Young resemble fuzzy adults, betraying nest-site with loud hissing and snoring hunger cries.

Hunting flight low and halting – action recalls gull following tractor and plough. Often glides, legs dangling. Pounces on small rodents with lightning drop or back-flip to ground.

Status Still widespread now greatly reduced in numbers. Scarce, patchy resident in Britain. **Population** c5,000-6,000 pairs.

◆ Solitary ◆ Forages widely. Waits, watches and listens for prey from low perch or quarters rough fields on moth-like wings ◆ Usually silent but voice unmistakable; utters a short shriek if surprised in flight and unearthly screams at night ◆ Dark-breasted race *guttata* (north-east Europe) strays to east coast of Britain; has white-face and underwing, but darker above and rich buff below.

165

Snowy Owl *Nyctea scandiaca* — 53-66cm (21-26")

Female/Immature Predominantly white, heavily spotted and barred brown. Young females much more heavily barred.

Adult male Smaller than female. Appears entirely white at distance. At close range, small black marks visible on coverts and primary tips.

Status An Arctic species, sporadic breeder in Scandinavian mountains. Nomadic, wanders further south in winter. 1-3 birds resident in N Scotland in recent years (bred Shetland 1967-75); exceptional vagrant elsewhere in Britain.

◆ Huge, partly diurnal owl of the arctic tundra, islands and coasts ◆ Flight Buzzard-like, but Snowy is substantially heavier ◆ At rest on ground looks like a big, white cat with piercing, yellow eyes ◆ Hard to find on the broken rocky terrain and upland moors it inhabits ◆ Often sits in lee of ridge, its presence betrayed only by repeated stoops of mobbing skuas, gulls or crows ◆ Mainly silent ◆ Feeds chiefly on lemmings and voles.

Eagle Owl *Bubo bubo* — 60-75cm (24-30")

Much bigger than a Buzzard. Long erectile feather ear-tufts and burning orange eyes always identify - only Long-eared Owl looks similar, but Eagle Owl weighs upto10 times as much. When sitting on cliff ledge, looks like huge domestic tabby cat.

Status Rare, localised resident across Europe. Not in UK or Ireland, but popularity in wildlife parks ensures occasional escapes.

◆ Huge. Largest of Europe's owls, with feet size of a man's hand ◆ Nests in broad range of habitats, from quarries and rocky, scrub-covered hills to mountains and boreal forests ◆ Shy; usually only noticed at dusk, as it leaves its daytime roost ◆ Is most vocal at dawn and dusk, especially in late winter. Powerful, low booming *HOO-o* (as if blown across neck of empty bottle) is unmistakable; repeated every 8-10secs and carries up to 5km ◆ Captures prey up to size of hares, ducks, Capercaillie – swallows rats whole.

Hawk Owl *Surnia ulula*   36-41cm (c15")

Adult Size and general appearance suggests female Sparrowhawk, but notice bigger, characteristically marked head – as though wearing a fur trapper's hat. Fierce yellow eyes glare from white face thickly bordered black. Otherwise mainly grey, with hawk-like barring below and prominent pale scapulars.

Status Nomadic and difficult to find (numbers fluctuate widely between years). Most likely to be encountered in S Scandinavia in winter, especially during infrequent irruption years, when vole populations crash. Extremely rare vagrant to Britain.

Flight Fast and direct like Sparrowhawk or bounding like Little Owl, with steep upward swoop to treetop perch.

◆ Distinctive long-tailed owl nesting in tree holes in boreal taiga ◆ Partly diurnal ◆ Perches conspicuously on tall broken stumps in open forest, clearings and bogs, where fearless of man ◆ Male has sonorous bubbling song, *hu hu hu uüüüüüüüüü* (can suggest distant drumming of Snipe) ◆ Alarm hawk-like, *ki ki ki ki...* ◆ Voles are staple diet.

Tengmalm's Owl *Aegolius funereus*   24-26cm (10")

Adult Pale scapulars and yellow ► eyes set in black-trimmed whitish face suggestive of Hawk Owl. But Tengmalm's has blotchy (not barred) underparts, shorter tail and quite different expression – eyes wide-open, eyebrows raised, as if taken by surprise.

Juvenile is chocolate-brown with white spotting on wings – like no other European owl.

Status Mainly resident, but population fluctuates in response to abundance of food. Extreme vagrant to British Isles.

◆ Small, square-faced owl of northern taiga and upland conifer forests in south ◆ Predominantly nocturnal, so much more often heard than seen ◆ Song distinctive, a series of hollow, sometimes quavering, hoots: *po po po po po*. The number of hoots per bout varies but in January-April song may be repeated every few seconds. Carries over 2km ◆ Characteristic call is a loud, lip-smacking *yiak!* ◆ Breeds mostly in Black Woodpecker holes and owl-boxes ◆ Preys mainly on small rodents.

167

Scops Owl *Otus scops* — 19-20cm (7.5")

Adult The only small owl with ear tufts and delicately streaked and vermiculated plumage (like bark of tree).

Overall colour rufous or grey, with row of white spots along scapulars. Lacks prominent eyebrows and fierce gaze of more rotund Little Owl.

Is mostly seen when surprised at its daytime roost in leafy tree or copse; then draws itself up tall, ears erect and yellow eyes half-open in characteristic 'can't see me' squint.

Status Summer visitor only, north to the Loire (Mar-Oct). Winters tropical Africa, rarely in Europe. Vagrant UK & Ireland.

◆ Small, slimline owl with 'ears' ◆ Breeds in lightly wooded cultivations, orchards, parks and gardens ◆ Occurs alongside Little Owl and might be confused, but Scops is strictly nocturnal ◆ Voice, a familiar sound on balmy Mediterranean nights, is monotonous 'asdic' whistle, *tyuu*; repeated every 2-3 secs, but hard to pinpoint. Females duet in slightly higher voice ◆ Eats insects.

Pygmy Owl *Glaucidium passerinum* — 16-17cm (6.5")

Adult Size alone is distinctive. Severe expression, yellow eyes and grey-brown upperparts barred and spotted with white suggest miniature Little Owl. But breast and sides of chest are barred with brown, and white underparts sparsely streaked brown.

Status Mainly resident. Not uncommon, but easily overlooked. Not in UK or Ireland.

Habitually jerks and waves its longish, barred tail. Flies off fast, bounding along with rapid pulses of wing-beats, like a finch.

◆ Tiny owl, size of Hawfinch ◆ Fierce predator of tall coniferous and mixed forests in north and mountains of central Europe ◆ Hunts by day, mostly early and late, for small rodents and birds ◆ Best sought at dusk (especially March-April), when male is most vocal ◆ Monotonous song a rapid, Bullfinch-like pipe, repeated 40-50 times per minute: *dhü, ü-ü-ü dhü, dhü, dhü..* ◆ Hard to locate; often sounds low down but check tops of nearby tall spruces ◆ Nests in woodpecker holes and nest-boxes.

The only small owl in Britain and north-west Europe, but range overlaps with migratory Scops Owl in south of region. Scarcely bigger than a Starling. Usually spotted on a favoured telegraph pole, fence, barn roof or other prominent look-out, early or late in the day. First impression is invariably of a squat, grey-brown blob with a distinctly flat-topped head. On close inspection, fixed yellow eyes glaring from beneath heavy pale eyebrows characteristic.

Adult Size and scowling expression identify. Upperparts grey-brown, peppered white on crown and with bold white spots on back and wings. Underparts white, heavily smudged grey-brown. Note long pale legs and short grey-brown tail, barred white. ▶

◀ **Juvenile** Differs from adult in its unspotted, fuzzy grey ('crew-cut') crown, noticeably fluffy flank feathers, and more diffuse streaking below.

Flight Blunt rounded wings obvious in indulating flight.

When disturbed, pitches forward from perch and flies quickly away with strong bursts of wingbeats then a pause on closed wings – this bounding, woodpecker-like action is characteristic. Often looks surprisingly big.

Status Common in Europe. Introduced into England from continental Europe in 1800s. Now a widespread resident in England/Wales, north to S Scotland. Absent Ireland. **Population** c6,000-12,000 pairs.

◆ Active by day and night ◆ Occurs mainly in lowlands, preferring farmland, orchards, hedgerows and parks with scattered old trees, buildings, ruins and stone walls in which to perch, roost and nest ◆ Found singly or in pairs, often tied to a particular spot ◆ Bobs or crouches in alarm on close approach, then ducks from sight into ivy or hole ◆ Subsists on worms, insects, mice, birds ◆ Drops on to prey from perch, sometimes running on ground. Returns to same or nearby post ◆ Monotonous song carries well: a mellow, drawn-out *cooo-ek*, rising at end (not unlike call of Curlew) ◆ Other calls mostly variations of sharp yelping or miaowing *kyow*.

169

The commonest owl in north-west Europe. Frequents woods, parks, churchyards and large gardens (even in built-up areas), anywhere with mature trees. Strictly nocturnal so seldom seen, but loud quavering hoot heard mainly from November-March familiar to all: *WHOOOO...* (pause) ... *hu WHOOoooo.* Female answers with sharp *ke-VICK*, but also hoots.

Adult Occurs in rufous or grey colour phases (some intermediate). In Britain, most are rufous. Big head and soft, loose wings cloaking short tail give stout appearance. Distinguished from other owls by benevolent dark eyes set in rounded rufous or grey face. Note broad dark stripe over crown and white shoulder marks. Upperparts rufous, barred and mottled brown; underparts whitish, with tan splotches and bold dark streaks. At roost, eyes half-closed in cat-like squint. Sexes alike. ▶

◀

Fledgling Nests in hole in large deciduous tree (or nestbox). Fluffy grey fledglings leave nest in May and clamber in nearby trees. Dark eyes, copious wavy brown barring and *shi-ii* begging call, like child's squeaky toy, identify.

Flight Silent (as all owls); rather quick, on broad, rounded wings. Seldom flies far.

Status Widespread resident. Sedentary. Absent Ireland and most islands. **Population** >20,000 pairs.

◆ Solitary or in pairs all year ◆ Rarely seen by day, unless discovered at roost in canopy of lofty tree when betrayed by persistent angry mobbing of other birds. Listen for (e.g.) Blackbird's *chink-chink* and Jay's harsh squawks – always worth following up such clues ◆ At night, sits watching for rodents, frogs, worms, beetles, pouncing after short glide from perch; also takes birds. Disgorges indigestible fur, feathers etc. in large pellets ◆ Hoots mainly during November-March (occasionally during day) ◆ May respond to imitation hoot made by blowing across knuckle of thumbs into hollow of clasped hands.

Ural Owl *Strix uralensis* 61cm (24")

Adult Typical view is of a creamy nun-like face peering intently from leafy canopy, or glimpse of a big brown shape disappearing through the tree-tops.

With its dark eyes and pale plumage, resembles a huge, washed out Tawny Owl. Yellow bill is an unusual feature on otherwise bland face. Pale buff chest boldly streaked.

Buzzard-like flight, with long, banded, wedge-shaped tail and banded flight feathers.

Status Resident; scarce and very local. Not in UK or Ireland.

◆ Very large ◆ Inhabits deciduous hill forests of eastern Europe and mixed and coniferous forests in Scandinavia ◆ Exceedingly aggressive in defence of nest-site ◆ Wary of approach at other times; whereabouts often betrayed by angry screeching of Jays and chinking Blackbirds ◆ Nests mainly in holes in trees and stumps; some populations have recently been boosted through provision of special nest-boxes ◆ Deep, powerful hoot: *WOOhoo...* (4 second pause) *hu-WOOho,* can be heard all year ◆ Hunts rodents and birds.

Great Grey Owl *Strix nebulosa* 65-70cm (26-28")

Adult Huge grey owl with an unmistakable face – uniquely marked by concentric rings, aptly likened to the annual growth rings visible when a tree is felled. Penetrating gaze of yellow eyes seems hypnotic. Huge wings envelop most of tail length (cf. Ural Owl).

Slow flight, with long glides. Flattened face, massive wings with pale rufous primary patch and ample tail with broad dark tip diagnostic.

◆ Magnificent owl confined in region to the mature boreal forests of northern and eastern Scandinavia ◆ Usually seen early and late in day, in clearings, forest bogs and burnt areas ◆ Perches on roadside pole or bush top waiting to drop on voles ◆ Looks as big as Eagle Owl, but bulk is mainly feathers and weighs only half as much ◆ Fearless of man ◆ Large round head swivels smoothly and eerily, like turret of tank ◆ Breeds in broken stumps and disused hawk's nests ◆ Deep, booming song (like 8-12 muffled beats on electronic drum synthesiser), suggests heavy, bouncing ball coming to rest ◆ Rare in region, not in UK or Ireland.

171

Long-eared Owl *Asio otus* 35-37cm (14-15")

Similar to the very much larger Eagle Owl, and the only British owl with bright orange eyes and long erectile ear tufts (sometimes invisible at rest). Superbly camouflaged; sits tight if approached with care, but retreats smartly and silently if startled. Posture more upright than Short-eared Owl, but the two easily confused in flight.

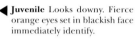 

Adult At roost, hunches like a fat cat, ears relaxed. When disturbed, draws itself up, ears erect and eyes glaring. Rich tawny face distinctive but expression changes with mood. Upperparts buff-brown, beautifully mottled and barred. Underparts buffy, with more uniform and extensive streaking than Short-eared Owl.

Juvenile Looks downy. Fierce orange eyes set in blackish face immediately identify.

Most likely to be encountered at its winter roost in thick conifers or hawthorn scrub; gathers in loose groups that sit 2-4 metres up.

Flight Rarely flies by day, except on passage or at dusk when feeding young. Quarters the ground with stiff, jerky beats like Short-eared Owl but glides on flatter wings. Dis-tinguished from latter by (usually) darker appearance and absence of white band along trailing edge of wing and at tip of more finely barred tail. Orangy roundels on darkish upperwing, together with broken dusky barring across tip of pale under-wings are key fieldmarks. Approaching bird some-times shows white 'spotlight' at shoulder.

Status Sparsely distributed resident across most of region. In Br. Isles, occurs mainly in N/E; the common owl in Ireland. Periodic large influxes from continent in winter. **Population** c2,000-7,000 pairs.

◆ Inhabits coniferous woods and stands of trees amidst open country. Hunts over rough fields, plantations, clearfell, scrubby heath and fringes of moorland and marsh ◆ Mainly silent. Song a short, deep, far-carrying *ooh....* (like sound produced by blowing briefly across top of empty bottle), repeated at 2-3 second intervals ◆ Young beg with monotonous tell-tale *zee-ü* (heard May–July) – suggests gentle swing of a squeaky pub sign or the sound of a party blower!

172

Day-flying owl, characterised by yellow eyes glaring out from dark recesses of pasty-white face. Most active early and late in day. Can look strikingly pale in wavering, harrier-like flight, but dark wing markings separate from more ghostly Barn Owl. Regularly alights on posts and on ground. If startled, typically departs with penetrating glance over shoulder.

Adult Ear-tufts inconspicuous and ▶ seldom seen. Upperparts more biscuit-coloured in tone than Long-eared Owl and more coarsely blotched dark brown and white. Underparts also paler, creamy-buff; note heavy dark streaks largely restricted to upper breast (pale belly scarcely marked).

◀ **Juvenile** Shares blackish face with young Long-eared Owl, but yellow eyes distinguish it.

Flight Flies with slow, stiff beats of long wings, as though rowing through the air. During frequent banks and glides, wings often upheld in shallow V. Distinguished from Long-eared Owl by whiter belly and underwings, with primaries 'dipped in ink'.

Status Scarce and patchy resident, nesting chiefly in N Europe. In Britain, breeds chiefly on uplands in N and coastal districts in E; sporadic in Ireland. **Population** c1,000-3,500 pairs. Periodic influxes from continent in winter (up to 50,000 birds).

Flight Pale tip to more clearly banded, wedge-shaped tail, narrow white trailing edge to upperwing and paler, yellower patches on base of primaries contrasting with obvious dark carpal patch.

◆ Nests on ground in open country, especially heather moorland, tracts of recently planted conifers in hills, and lowland marshes ◆ Forages widely in winter, over saltmarshes, coastal dunes, rough ground, etc. ◆ Roosts on ground, often communally in winter. Assembles in some numbers at prey-rich localities, taking small rodents and birds ◆ Usually silent. Song is a repeated, hollow *boo-boo-boo....* typically given in high-circling display flight, during which male claps wings rapidly together beneath body and drops.

173

Common Swift *Apus apus* 16-17cm (6.5")

Dark, scythe-winged aerial feeder seen careering through sky in characteristic noisy, screaming parties. Flies in lower airspace early and late in day, and in wet weather. Spends virtually entire life (even mating and sleeping) on the wing, coming to land only to nest. Larger than Barn Swallow, unlike which it never perches on wires or vegetation.

Adult Uniform blackish-brown plumage relieved only by whitish chin. Very long, narrow, swept-back wings and fat, cigar-shaped body give illusion that bird is bigger than it really is. Clearly forked tail lacks Swallow's streamers and is often held tightly closed. Bill tiny. Sexes alike; similar juvenile has narrow pale feather edgings. ▶

Status Widespread summer visitor, common everywhere except in far N and W. Vanguard arrives Britain from end April; most depart by end August, but odd birds linger until October. Winters southern Africa. **Population** c100,000 pairs.

Nests colonially beneath eaves of buildings, less often in caves or hollow trees. Enters nest site at breakneck speed and is only rarely seen perched below, clinging to walls with tiny legs and feet (unusually, all four toes face forwards).

◆ Breeds commonly in built-up areas, but travels huge distances to feed ◆ Typically seen in parties of 10-100 birds, but congregates in massive swarms on spring and autumn migration, especially over wetlands and reservoirs ◆ Flight action varied: either very fast with twinkling wingbeats or slower, with sudden flurries of wingbeats and glides on wings stiffly outstretched and slightly bowed down. Jinks, rises and falls with quick flick of wings and briefly spread tail as it gulps insect prey in huge, gaping mouth ◆ Shrill, piercing screaming call, *sree*, is the essence of warm summer evenings.

Alpine Swift *Apus melba*   20-22cm (8-9")

Europe's largest swift, with a wingspan of 60cm (2ft). Size not always easy to gauge when flying high overhead, when shape can be mistaken for Hobby.

Adult Appears all dark at distance but white belly often seems to 'twinkle' as birds sweep about sky. (Beware occasional partial albino Common Swifts).

Pattern suggests gigantic long-winged Sand Martin: white belly and throat divided by brown breast band. However white of throat often obscured; unlike Sand Martin, vent is dark.

Status Summer visitor to S Europe (Apr-Sep). Winters tropical Africa. Rare annual visitor to Britain.

◆ Wing-beats visibly slower than Common Swift, but flight even more powerful, faster ◆ Locally common in mountainous country and some towns ◆ Breeds in noisy colonies in cliffs, tall buildings and bridges ◆ Rapid, bibbling call suggests Little Grebe's titter rather than Common Swift; heard mainly at nest-site, also from flocks ◆ Covers huge distances to feed, often straying well beyond usual range.

Pallid Swift *Apus pallidus*   16-17cm (6.5")

Almost identical to Swift, with which it mixes; but is slightly broader-headed, and has marginally blunter wing-tips and tail corners

Adult In good light and when viewed against dark background, flight feathers and rump look distinctly paler and browner than Common Swift's (approaching colour of Sand Martin).

Looks paler and browner below than Common Swift. Flight feathers especially paler, contrasting with darker leading forewing and outer primaries. More extensive whitish forehead and throat than Common Swift, divided by dark eye-band. Stronger pale scaling on belly.

Status Very localised summer visitor to region (Apr-Nov). Winters tropical Africa. Vagrant to Britain.

◆ Breeds in S Europe, but few colonies away from Mediterranean (however easily overlooked, e.g. colonies recently found Switzerland) ◆ Nests on cliffs and buildings ◆ Call like Common Swift's but slightly slower, more truncated (can suggest distant male Wigeon).

175

Nightjar *Caprimulgus europaeus*   25-28cm (10-11")

Mysterious ground-nesting bird of dry lowland heath, young coniferous plantations and clear felled areas, more often heard than seen. Nocturnal, seldom stirring from roost until daylight all but gone, when male's eerie churring begins.

▼ **Adult** Size of Mistle Thrush, but long wings and tail make it seem much larger. Both sexes have remarkably cryptic plumage of greys, browns and buffs like flaky bark that provides near perfect camouflage at daytime roost on ground or along branch. Seldom seen in sufficient daylight to appreciate subtlety of markings, but pale flashes across shoulder, throat and below eye sometimes discernible on perched bird in half-light. Tiny bill and legs.

Male

Male Shows clear white spots ▶ in wingtip and corners of tail, lacking in female.

Female

Flight Flies softly and silently. Progress quick, with stiff, jerky beats or glides on wings uplifted in shallow V. Silhouette remarkably Kestrel-like but actions distinctive, characterised by sudden twists, bouts of hovering and erratic, bat-like swoops, mostly between ground level and tree-top height.

Status Scarce and local summer visitor (mid/late May-Sep), restricted by habitat choice. Absent from mountainous regions and in north. Winters tropical Africa. **Population** c3,000 pairs (<30prs Ireland).

◆ Suitable habitat often supports several pairs ◆ Listen from dusk onwards on warm, still evenings May-August, when sustained, far-carrying 'churring': rrrrrrurrrrrrrurrrrrrurrr... discloses presence ◆ Look for singing bird perched on bushtop or prominent dead limb ◆ Sound rises and falls; may last many minutes before sudden collapse into gurgling trickle, as though power unexpectedly switched off ◆ Male claps wings in courtship flight (sounds like snapping twigs) ◆ Liquid *gu-ick* flight note given by both sexes as they trawl for moths and other night-flying insects with their enormous, gaping, bristly mouths ◆ Strangely inquisitive; can sometimes be lured in by waving a white handkerchief tied to the end of a long stick.

Kingfisher *Alcedo atthis* — 16-17cm (6.5")

Unmistakable jewel of still or slow-moving freshwater. Dazzling plumage can look unexpectedly dark in shadow. Long dagger-like bill, large head and stubby tail identify, but often merely glimpsed as bird races past. Sexes similar, juvenile duller.

Male Brilliant turquoise-blue above and orange-red below, with bold white chin and neck patch. Tiny, coral-red legs. Bill entirely black. ▶

Female As male, but lower mandible extensively red. Nests in burrow excavated by both sexes in river bank. ▼

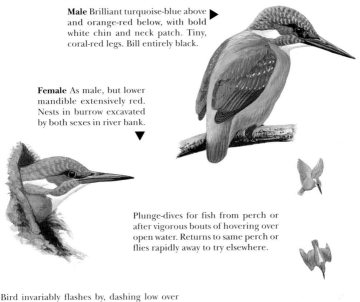

Plunge-dives for fish from perch or after vigorous bouts of hovering over open water. Returns to same perch or flies rapidly away to try elsewhere.

Bird invariably flashes by, dashing low over water on whirring wings. Shining electric blue flash on back is the most striking fieldmark.

Status Decreasing but widespread resident (virtually absent Scandinavia). Mainly sedentary, but young disperse during Jul-Oct, when may be seen in suburban parks and gardens. **Population** 4,500-7,500 pairs.

◆ Look on lakes, gravel pits, rivers and streams with overhanging vegetation and branches; sometimes on coasts in winter ◆ Nervously bobs head and jerks tail, then streaks away. Typically follows contours of river, but flight path frequently creates a wide arc over more open water, before coming to an incredibly abrupt stop on perch. May surprise observer by flying over land (even through trees) ◆ Will sit openly on boat or post, but often disappears in dappled shade at waterside. Scan banks carefully, checking likely perches 1-5m above water. Watch for tell-tale white flash on neck, but sometimes easier to spot reflection of sitting bird in water ◆ Solitary. Rivals meet with furious whistled exchanges ◆ Timid and more often heard than seen. Highly distinctive call, a shrill penetrating whistle *chee* or *chi-kee*, carries well and forewarns of approach.

177

Bee-eater *Merops apiaster* 28cm (11")

Flight Note adult's elongated central tail feathers and black border to pale chestnut underwing in flight.

Status Common summer visitor to Mediterranean, but scarce and local in our region (May-early Sep). Winters in tropical Africa. Annual vagrant Britain (has bred).

Adult Rainbow of colours unique among European birds. Note chestnut back with golden shoulders.

◆ Stunning multi-coloured bird, much sought after by birders in the Mediterranean area ◆ Juvenile is drabber with green back and wings, and lacks tail projections ◆ Breeds in small colonies in open country, tunnelling nest-holes into sandy banks ◆ Perches openly on wires, fences and dead branches ◆ Hawks bees, wasps and other flying insects in supremely graceful swooping and sailing flight ◆ Migrates in flocks (often too high to be seen) betrayed by constant, highly characteristic calls: *quilp, quilp...*; voice has delightful, far-carrying, liquid quality.

Roller *Coracias garrulus* 32cm (13")

Adult Silhouette crow-like with stout black bill. But plumage predominantly blue, with bright chestnut back. Juvenile duller with whitish face and streaking on breast.

Flight Even more dazzling, with purplish rump and electric blue flashes in broad wings.

Status Summer visitor (Apr-Sep), but very scarce in our region. Winters in tropical Africa. Rare vagrant to Britain.

◆ Colourful migrant to Mediterranean region ◆ Prefers lightly wooded open country, nesting in tree holes and ruins ◆ Usually seen sitting on telegraph poles and overhead cables ◆ Drops frequently to ground to pick off large insects and lizards, then shifts to another prominent lookout ◆ Unmistakable when close; but often appears dark at distance, especially in flight, when surprisingly easy to confuse with a Jackdaw ◆ In spring, spectacular tumbling display flights are accompanied by harsh, croaking calls, *rack-ack...*; sometimes in series, like short burst of automatic gun-fire.

Hoopoe *Upupa epops* 26-28cm (10.5")

Adult Boldly pied and cinnamon-pink plumage, large crest and long, decurved bill unmistakable. Sexes alike.

▲ Fans crest briefly on landing and when alarmed.

Flight About size of Mistle Thrush but full rounded make it look larger in flight. Jerky, bouncing butterfly-like flight on dazzling black and white wings.

◆ Summer visitor to south and east Europe. Breeds in open woodland, cultivations and village edge, with mix of meadows, groves and gardens ◆ A scarce but regular spring and autumn migrant elsewhere frequenting coastal dunes and pastures ◆ Has bred south-east England ◆ Perches on trees, buildings and wires, but feeds on ground ◆ Characteristic far-carrying song, a hollow *poo-poo-poo*, gives bird its name ◆ Solitary ◆ Winters mainly in Africa.

Ring-necked Parakeet *Psittacula krameri* 38-42cm (15-16.5")

Pale green parrot with a coral-red hooked bill, dusky flight feathers and long, slender blue-green tail.

Female Shows only an indistinct ▶ emerald collar. Juvenile as female but flight feathers yellower.

Flight Very fast, with shallow beats of narrow, pointed wings. Prone to erratic yawing and sudden dives.

Population Up to 5,000 birds.

▲ **Male** Black throat and necklace, thin rose-pink collar and bluish wash to nape.

◆ Native of India, introduced into Europe (first noted Kent 1969). Scarce but firmly established in south-east England (especially London area) and the Low Countries. May occur elsewhere ◆ Frequents towns, parks and gardens, often raiding bird feeders ◆ Solitary or in small parties ◆ Very noisy. Loud screeching *kee-ak, kee-ak*.

Wryneck *Jynx torquilla*   16-17cm (6.5")

Often suggests a big warbler. Slim and sinuous brown relative of the woodpeckers, but with distinctive Nightjar-like coloration and a long grey tail, finely barred black. Not shy but unobtrusive, making observation difficult. Name derives from habit of twisting and craning neck into quite bizarre poses.

Adult Buff-white underparts, delicately barred brown. Bold dark stripe running down centre of nape and back is most striking feature, characteristically 'snaking' as bird looks about. Grey sides to neck and mantle form obvious pale braces, most conspicuous from behind. Juvenile similar.

Flight Looks rather large and long-tailed in gently undulating flight. Easily mistaken for similarly-sized immature Barred Warbler or Red-backed Shrike (all three species may occur together during migrant falls, especially along North Sea coasts in autumn).

Head Note short, pointed bill. Crown feathers habitually raised in excitement or alarm.

Status Widespread summer visitor, much decreased during 20th century. Once common in S Britain, now extinct. although still a very scarce breeder in Scotland. Passage migrant Apr-Oct (chiefly to coastal districts).
Population 0-10 pairs.

Feeds mainly on ground, probing for ants with its long tongue. Hops jerkily along, with tail raised.

◆ Breeds in holes in trees, walls and nestboxes, in open woods, orchards, parks and gardens ◆ Far-carrying song is generally first clue to presence in spring, comprising a dozen or so high-pitched notes: *kew-kew-kew....* Sounds very like call of Lesser Spotted Woodpecker or Hobby, but with a strangely distant, ventriloquial quality that can be hard to pinpoint. Try looking for calling bird amongst topmost branches of taller trees ◆ Clings to trees, but does not behave in true woodpecker fashion ◆ Migrants silent and solitary, making detection doubly difficult.

Lesser Spotted Woodpecker *Dendropos minor*   15cm (6")

A sparrow-sized woodpecker found in mature deciduous and mixed woods, parklands, old hedgerow trees, and stands of waterside willows and alders. Combination of laddered back (look for close white bars across a black background) and absence of any red on underparts separates from all other European woodpeckers.

Adult male Tiny size, red crown and entirely ▶ buff-white underparts (save for a few streaks on flanks) diagnostic amongst pied woodpeckers. Unlike larger and more frequently seen Great Spotted, black bar across white cheek not joined to black of nape.

◀ **Adult female** No red on head. Instead shows a pale mushroom fore-crown (less extensive than male's red cap).

Juvenile Resembles adult ▶ female but duller, and more spotted and streaked below. Presence of red flecks in crown signify juvenile male.

Flight Undulating flight less exaggerated, less bouncing than other woodpeckers. Lacks conspicuous white ovals on shoulder shown by other pied woodpeckers.

Status Widespread resident. Absent from Scotland and Ireland; scarce and sparsely distributed breeder in most of England and Wales. Badly affected by loss of elm trees. **Population** 3,000-6,000 pairs.

◆ Smallest and one of the most elusive of European woodpeckers ◆ Keeps mainly to treetops, where easily overlooked as it flits quietly but acrobatically amongst the upper branches and outermost twigs ◆ Best looked for in Feb-April, when birds are most vocal and before trees in leaf. Try checking through roving flocks of tits and nuthatches during winter ◆ Announces itself with a distinctive high, but rather flat and feeble call: *pee-pee-pee-pee-pee-pee-pee...* or by frequent drumming (both sexes) ◆ Drumming is more prolonged (lasting 1-1.5secs) but quieter, with a more tinny, rattling quality than Great Spotted's powerful 'machine-gunning'. May pause only briefly before next burst ◆ *Chik* call-note sounds like great Spotted's, but is always fainter.

Grey-headed Woodpecker *Picus canus*   25-26cm (10")

◀ Similar to Green in flight but slightly smaller and stockier, with duller, less contrasting, yellow rump.

Male Resembles Green but face and underparts grey with markings restricted to narrow black whiskers on cheek and lores, and red 'rose petal' on forecrown. Pale brown eye. Female, crown entirely grey. ▶

Status Widespread resident, nowhere numerous. Not in UK or Ireland.

◆ Shy and often elusive woodpecker, smaller than similar Green ◆ Inhabits mixed and deciduous woods, riverine stands, parks and avenues in lowlands and hill country ◆ 'Yaffling' song (an easily imitated whistle), comprises 5-20 *kiu* notes which characteristically slow to a petering conclusion ◆ Unlike Green, drums frequently, in loud, steady bursts of 1-2 seconds duration ◆ Feeds on ground and in trees.

Black Woodpecker *Dryocopus martius*   45-47cm (18")

Male Entirely black but for white ▶ eye, pale bill and all red crown.

◀ **Female** Red confined to rear of crown only.

Markedly pinched neck; floppy Jay-like flight. Sweeps upward to alight on tree.

Status Increasing resident. Northern populations partially migratory in autumn. Not (yet) recorded in Britain.

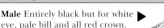

◆ Largest woodpecker (size of crow) ◆ Fairly common in all types of mature forest, but ranges widely over large territory ◆ Swooshing of wings clearly audible as bird sweeps past ◆ Often lands high on trunk, where difficult to see ◆ Can be found in winter as it returns to roost in large and oval former nest hole ◆ Loud, far-carrying calls include piercing *klee-aa* when perched and throaty *krük, krük...* in flight. Song a wild, Green Woodpecker-like 'yaffle', *kwik-wik-wik....* ◆ Powerful drumming a 2-3 second burst.

Size of Jackdaw. Largest British woodpecker and the only one that is green, but needs to be distinguished from similar Grey-headed elsewhere in Europe. Adult's manic white eyes, crimson crown and black face unique. Has the stiff spiky tail, strong dagger bill and long tongue characteristic of most woodpeckers, but rarely drums.

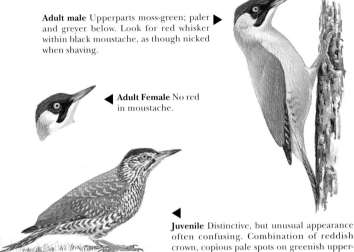

Adult male Upperparts moss-green; paler and greyer below. Look for red whisker within black moustache, as though nicked when shaving. ▶

◀ **Adult Female** No red in moustache.

◀

Juvenile Distinctive, but unusual appearance often confusing. Combination of reddish crown, copious pale spots on greenish upperparts, and rash of abundant dark streaks and bars over whitish face and underparts, identify. Patchy red moustache signifies young male.

Flight Easily disturbed, flying off with startled outburst of ringing cries: *kyu-kyu-kyuk...* Brilliant yellow rump and barred flight feathers obvious fieldmarks at all ages. Heavy, bounding action, with short bursts of noisy wingbeats punctuated by pronounced closures of wings. Retreats to tree cover, where adept at hiding behind trunk.

Status Common and widespread resident. Mainly sedentary. In Britain, most numerous in area to south of Aberystwyth-Norwich; patchily distributed further north (colonised Scotland from 1940's). Absent Ireland.
Population 15,000 pairs.

◆ Wary bird of deciduous and mixed woods, heaths, parks and farmland; also occurs coastal swards, well away from cover ◆ Loud ringing laugh or 'yaffle': *klue-klue-klue-klue...*, (upto 20 notes) invariably gives bird away. Often calls from favoured song post, such as dead limb poking through woodland canopy ◆ Forages extensively on ground for ants, alternating bouts of vigorous probing with frequent pauses to look around. Progresses with heavy upright hops, dragging tail ◆ Climbs or spirals up treetrunks with jerky hops, pausing to chip at bark or peep over shoulder.

Great Spotted Woodpecker *Dendrocopos major* 22-23cm (9")

Most abundant of the ten European woodpeckers. Thrush-sized, but with boldly pied plumage, strong pointed bill and an excitable, aggressive manner. Unbroken black bar running from bill to nape is diagnostic. In Britain, the only woodpecker with a red vent, but shares this feature with a further three species elsewhere in north-west Europe.

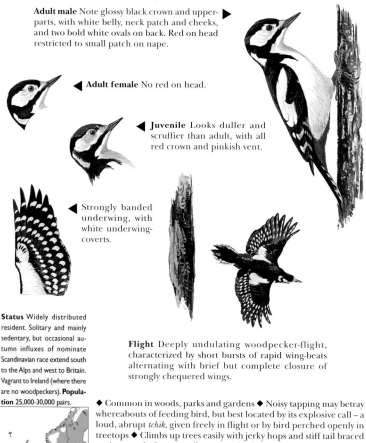

Adult male Note glossy black crown and upper-parts, with white belly, neck patch and cheeks, and two bold white ovals on back. Red on head restricted to small patch on nape.

Adult female No red on head.

Juvenile Looks duller and scruffier than adult, with all red crown and pinkish vent.

Strongly banded underwing, with white underwing-coverts.

Flight Deeply undulating woodpecker-flight, characterized by short bursts of rapid wing-beats alternating with brief but complete closure of strongly chequered wings.

Status Widely distributed resident. Solitary and mainly sedentary, but occasional autumn influxes of nominate Scandinavian race extend south to the Alps and west to Britain. Vagrant to Ireland (where there are no woodpeckers). **Population** 25,000-30,000 pairs.

◆ Common in woods, parks and gardens ◆ Noisy tapping may betray whereabouts of feeding bird, but best located by its explosive call – a loud, abrupt *tchik*, given freely in flight or by bird perched openly in treetops ◆ Climbs up trees easily with jerky hops and stiff tail braced against trunk. Occasionally reverses back down in same jerky fashion (only Nuthatches able to descend headfirst) ◆ Drums frequently, chiefly January-July, both sexes vibrating their bills on dead wood to produce the well-known rapid, hollow and far-carrying burst. Drumming is much louder but briefer than Lesser Spotted's, lasting only half a second; heard at distance, can suggest a creaking tree ◆ In spring, harsh, excited chattering draws attention to courtship chases through treetops ◆ Raids bird-feeders in winter.

Syrian Woodpecker *Dendrocopos syriacus* 22-23cm (9")

Female As male, but nape entirely black. Juvenile has red crown; very like young Great Spotted, which can sometimes lack black cheek bar. ▶

◀ **Male** At a glance, easily confused with Great Spotted. Best distinguished by whiter face (no black bar linking moustache to nape), more extensive red patch on nape, little white in mainly black tail, and paler, Bullfinch-pink vent. On some, flanks faintly streaked.

Status Resident. Range steadily expanding north and west to include E Austria and Poland. Not in UK or Ireland.

◆ Invader from south-east Europe, successfully colonising region since 1940s ◆ Occurs alongside very similar Great Spotted but keeps mainly to lowlands, with marked preference for town parks, villages, orchards and vineyards, rather than forest ◆ Often located by its call; initially suggests Great Spotted's familiar *tchik* note but Syrian's discernably softer, less explosive *djük* (like dripping tap) ◆ Drumburst typically longer than Great Spotted's.

Middle Spotted Woodpecker *Dendrocopos medius* 20cm (8")

Adult White ovals on back give rise to confusion with larger Great Spotted and Syrian Woodpeckers, juveniles of which have red crowns like Middle Spotted. Brilliant red crown often raised in excitement.

Quickly distinguished by its delicate rose-pink vent, pale face with isolated black bar on cheek (not reaching bill) and clear streaking on buff-washed underparts. Sexes similar, juvenile duller.

Status Declining resident. Patchily distributed but locally quite common. Not in UK or Ireland.

◆ Most attractive of the spotted woodpeckers ◆ Found in mature deciduous forest, principally oak, but also in well-wooded suburbs and parks ◆ Always on the move ◆ Voice is distinctive but spends much time quietly exploring upper branches and trunk, and is often overlooked ◆ Call more chattering than other woodpeckers, *kikekekek...* ◆ Seldom drums but has unusual mewing song in spring: *quah, quah, quah, quah...*; sound is strangled and distinctly hawk-like.

185

White-backed Woodpecker *Dendrocopos leucotos*   24-26cm (9.5-10.5")

Largest, quietest and most elusive of the pied woodpeckers, especially after nesting (April-May).

◀ **Female** No red on head.

Male Uniquely combines all red ▶ crown and laddered back (lacks conspicuous white ovals shown by Syrian, Great and Middle Spotted Woodpeckers), with streaked underparts showing pinkish flush and vent. Notice broken cheek bar. Bill often appears strikingly long.

Status Rare and declining resident (lost to many former haunts through felling of old timber). Confined to N/E of region, with isolated outpost in Pyrenees. Not in UK or Ireland.

◆ Restricted to older forests, particularly beech and birch, in hill country and mountains ◆ Despite name, white back seldom obvious at rest, and back largely blackish in rare Pyrenean population (ssp. *lilfordi*) ◆ Feeds from ground level to canopy, but quiet tapping in trees is often only clue to its presence ◆ Call is weaker than Great Spotted's, a soft, Blackbird-like *kyuk*. But drumming is louder and lasts longer (c2 seconds); note the pace quickens but volume fades at end.

Three-toed Woodpecker *Picoides tridactylus*   21-22cm (8.5")

Adult Differs from all other woodpeckers in its black ▶ and white striped face, and mainly black wings with broad white patch down back (even more marked than on larger White-backed Woodpecker). Underparts white, heavily barred black on flanks. Male has sprinkling of golden on crown. (Race *alpinus* of central Europe is darker).

Status Resident, most numerous in North. Not in UK or Ireland.

◀ **Female** Black crown, speckled with white (no yellow).

◆ Unobtrusive woodpecker of the Scandinavian taiga and more locally in montane pinewoods of central/eastern Europe ◆ Often exploits areas of burned and dying timber ◆ Tame but rather quiet and invariably difficult to find ◆ Forages slowly, low on trunk ◆ 'Machine-gun' drumburst, longer and slower than Great Spotted's ◆ Call a soft *ptük* ◆ Three-toed feet unique amongst European woodpeckers.

186

Most likely to be seen along North Sea coasts in winter. Frequents dunes, shorelines, saltmarshes and rough coastal fields, feeding on ground, often with other larks, finches and especially Snow Buntings. Invariably difficult to locate – typical first encounter is when inadvertently flushed. In flight, tail pattern and voice are best fieldmarks. At rest, black and pale yellow face unmistakable.

Winter male Lacks 'horns' in winter plumage. Face pattern obscured by fresh pale fringes, which gradually abrade to give brighter appearance by spring (below). When face hidden, separated from Skylark by more uniform or weakly streaked pinkish-brown upperparts and flanks, pinkish nape, unstreaked breast and black legs. ▶

Breeding male Characteristic 'viking horns' adorn head in breeding plumage. ◀

Female Distinguished from male ▶
by duller face and more streaked back.

Flight Swift and low in close formation, parties frequently swinging about and dashing back past observer before vanishing some distance away. Tail is most striking feature: shows a pale centre bordered either side by broad dark triangle. Narrow white tail-sides less obvious than pale belly as birds skim by.

Status Declining. Nests on moors and mountain plateaux in Scandinavia. Scarce passage migrant and winter visitor (Oct-Apr) elsewhere, mainly to North Sea coasts. **Population** In recent years, <100 birds wintering in Britain, where now regular at only a few traditional sites. Sporadic breeder in Scottish highlands.

◆ Found in parties of 3-15 birds ◆ Hugs ground, moving with crouching walk and short scurrying runs ◆ Feeds on insects and seeds of small plants, such as *Salicornia* ◆ Flight call has high, crystal ring: *tsee-ee-it*; clarity may approach sound produced by running wet finger around the rim of a wine glass ◆ Jingling song unlikely to be heard away from breeding grounds.

Short-toed Lark *Calandrella brachydactyla* 14cm (5.75")

Adult Smaller and paler than Skylark, with broad pale supercilium, virtually unmarked whitish underparts and longer tertials that cloak primaries. Look for small dusky patches at sides of breast; often obscured by pale feather tips when plumage fresh. Many appear distinctively rusty-capped. Overall pallid appearance and dark centred median coverts forming band across wing shared by elegant, leggy Tawny Pipit, but Short-toed Lark is dumpy and shuffling with stouter bill.

Status Summer visitor, principally to Mediterranean basin. Scarce migrant to Britain and Ireland, chiefly Sept-Oct.

◆ Small, finch-like lark of dry, open country with scant vegetation ◆ Song comes in characterisitic spluttering one-second bursts punctuated by one-second pauses – watch for slim, pale-bellied bird drifting high overhead in 'yo-yo' display ◆ Typically passes unnoticed on ground until flushed; flocks rise suddenly as a close-knit group, like Linnets ◆ Flight call suggests House Martin or a dry Skylark: a short dry *tchirrup* ◆ Greyer Asiatic race is vagrant in autumn.

Calandra Lark *Melanocorypha calandra* 19cm (7.5")

Flight Black underwing with clear white trailing edge diagnostic – obvious in song-fight, suspended on high like Skylark or flying lower down on long, broad wings with slow, deliberate beats. Short tail has conspicuous white outers.

Adult Big, bulky lark recognised by its heavy pale bill and large black neck patches. Latter shown to full effect against unmarked whitish underparts as bird stands tall on rock or fence post to survey its territory. Breast patches most obvious on spring males, being often obscured in fresh-plumaged autumn birds.

Status Resident in south-east France. Accidental in Britain and Ireland.

◆ Breeds commonly in open grasslands and crops in southern Europe, but rare and extremely vocal in north-west ◆ Song and flight-call suggest Skylark's, but louder – as though notes are being squirted out: a continuous stream of sound incorporating 'squabbling starlings' and expert mimicry of other bird calls.

Crested Lark *Galerida cristata* 17cm (6.75")

Adult Stouter than Skylark, with a longer, stronger bill and rather tired, dusty looking plumage. Very like Thekla, but longer bill appears distinctly decurved (culmen curving, lower mandible straight) and has rather softer, browner streaks across buffier chest.

Flight Looks plump and short-tailed, with conspicuous rusty-buff sides to tail. Lacks Thekla's obviously contrasting rump.

Status Patchy resident, most common in S/E. Highly sedentary. Britain & Ireland: accidental, most April-May, coastal southern England.

◆ Tame lark of dry open country, favouring lowland villages, roadsides, industrial areas, fields and allotments ◆ Readily distinguished from all other larks but Thekla by its long, spiky, frequently upstanding crest ◆ Clear, sweet fluting call is characteristic, *tee-tee-wheeoo* ◆ Song suggests slow, halting Skylark, with typical lark trills and snatches of fluty call.

Thekla Lark *Galerida theklae* 17cm (6.75")

Adult Separated with difficulty from Crested by its shorter, stubbier bill (both mandibles slightly convex), sharper, blacker streaking over cleaner chest and more obvious pale 'goggles' around eye.

Flight Cinnamon-pink rump contrasting with noticeably grey back is best distinction most obvious as birds fly directly away or in fluttering touchdown.

Status Rare resident SE France. Not recorded Britain or Ireland.

◆ Frustratingly like Crested Lark, but with a shorter, rather untidy crest and blunter bill ◆ Prefers wilder, rockier terrain (especially uncultivated scrubby hill country ◆ Song confusingly like Crested's, but tends to mix more chortling phrases with notes a little like wash leather squeaking on window; often given from top of bush rather than ground ◆ Call softer than Crested's, *tu ti weeer...*

189

Woodlark *Lullula arborea* 15cm (6")

Smaller than Skylark, with a shorter crest and distinctly sawn-off tail. Most often detected by its remarkably beautiful song or when a pair or family group is unexpectedly flushed from ground at close quarters. Black-and-white wrist patch is a unique fieldmark, visible at rest and in flight.

Adult Differs from other larks by its conspicuously ▶ long, whitish supercilia more or less meeting in V on nape, and foxy ear-coverts with pale tear-drop on cheek below eye. Clean belly, with clear-cut band of fine dark streaks across warm buff breast.

Unless raised in excitement, crest barely perceptible.

Flight Distinctive, with broad wings and very short tail. Jerky, bouncing action may suggest Lesser Spotted Woodpecker. Lacks white sides to tail and white trailing edge to wings always shown by Skylark. Check for black and white wing patch.

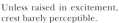

Status Mainly resident in S/W; N/E populations shift south in winter. In Britain, local but increasing, confined to south and east; largely sedentary but deserts East Anglian strongholds Sep-Feb. **Population** c500-1,000 pairs.

Rises to c50-100m in wide-circling song-flight (Skylark is often so high that it is lost to sight). Also sings from ground, overhead wires, piles of brush-wood. Song outstanding for its clarity and sweetness, comprises short fluty phrases: *dilee-dilee-dilee, lu-lu-lu...*; may last several minutes but sound seems to come and go, making location difficult.

◆ Rather elusive in Britain where restricted to dry heaths and sandy brecks with scattered trees, extensive forestry clearfell and young coniferous plantations; on continent, also in vineyards, alpine meadows. In autumn and winter parties gather in sheltered stubble fields ◆ Seldom observed away from established haunts, where starts to sing on bright days from February onwards ◆ Unlike Skylark, perches freely on wires and trees ◆ Feeds quietly on ground – listen for tell-tale soft call: *lit-loo-eet*. Sound difficult to pinpoint but watch for birds to pop-up on stump or raised furrow to check if coast is clear.

Streaky aerial songster, common in all kinds of open country. Larger than Woodlark, with a noticeably longer tail and more conspicuous crest.

Adult Typically buff-brown above, streaked blackish. Buff-white below, with neat gorget of streaks across breast. Superficially pipit-like but is stouter with a thickish bill, short crest (often raised) and long primaries which extend well beyond tertials at rest. Weak buffish supercilium fades behind eye (cf. Woodlark).

Juvenile Spotty-looking, has short tail at first and might be confused with juvenile Woodlark (check for latter's diagnostic wrist patch and V-shaped eyebrows). As adult after August moult.

Hangs high overhead (often lost to sight) in familiar song-flight or rises vertically from ground on fluttering wings, as though drawn skyward by invisible thread. Well-known song a loud, continuous and spirited outpouring (may last 5 minutes or more); continues during gradual descent, but ceases abruptly at low altitude, whereupon bird drops like stone to ground. Sings throughout year.

Flight Looks deceptively big – at times, thrush-like. Distinguished from Crested and Woodlarks by conspicuous white-sides to tail and narrow white trailing edge to wings (latter also eliminates pipits). Flight undulating, with brief pauses between bursts of rather floppy wingbeats. Alights with a characteristic brief hover just above ground.

Status Abundant and wide spread resident in NW Europe. Deserts inhospitable uplands in winter, when massive numbers also arrive from N/E Europe. **Population** c2,500,000 pairs but has decreased alarmingly since 1990. Winter: c25 million birds.

◆ Terrestrial ◆ Shuffles quietly about (seldom hops like most streaky buntings), and is difficult to spot on the ground ◆ In winter, forms large flocks in stubble and ploughed fields ◆ Sits tight, crouching in furrow or grass to escape notice. Flocks rise suddenly with easily recognised, cheerful rippling *chirrup* calls, twisting and turning as they flee, before melting back to earth at safe distance.

Sand Martin *Riparia riparia* 12cm (4.75")

Smallest of Europe's swallows and one of only two species that are brown above (cf. Crag Martin). Tail is only slightly forked. An early summer migrant, the first arrivals reaching our region early in March. Closely associated with water, especially lakes, gravel pits and wider stretches of rivers, beside which it usually nests.

Adult Dull earth-brown above, white below with distinctive brown band across chest (a pattern only shared by much larger, scythe-winged Alpine Swift). Sexes alike. Dark underwing-coverts are an easy distinction from Barn Swallow and House Martin.

Juvenile As adult, but separable at close range by neat pale fringes to upperparts, especially on rump and wings (looks scaly).

Status Common and widespread summer visitor, Mar/Apr-Aug; few remain by end Sept. Winters tropical Africa. Prone to periodic population crashes associated with drought in Sahel winter quarters. **Population** c130,000-400,000 pairs.

Flight Zippy, flickering low over surface of open water. Erratic, jinking action somewhat reminiscent of a small bat. Constant, busy movement lacks the grace and glides of larger Barn Swallow or House Martin. Rump is brown.

◆ Breeds colonially (mostly fewer than 50 pairs, sometimes more), tunnelling into sandy banks, cliffs and quarry spoil heaps – a habit unique among European swallows ◆ Colonies prone to sudden panics when nests are left en masse in a swirling, chirruping cloud, frequently in response to a passing hawk ◆ Cheerful call has a hard, rippling quality: *tschr* or *tchrrrp* ◆ Same notes also form the basis of the simple twittering song ◆ Gregarious at all times ◆ On passage, roosts in reedbeds with Barn Swallows.

Crag Martin *Ptyonoprogne rupestris*   14.5cm (5.75")

Chunky brown swallow inhabiting cliffs, gorges and mountainous areas in south of region. Typically seen in small groups patrolling to and fro along the face of a sun-warmed cliff or bridge. Not very vocal; call is an abrupt *chrrit*. Cements its half-cup mud nest beneath rocky overhangs and structures such as road tunnels, bridges and buildings.

Shallow notched tail becomes square when spread to reveal row of clear white spots near tip (lacking in Sand Martin).

Status Partially migratory. Rarely strays north of breeding range. Accidental Britain.

Adult Most likely to be confused with Sand Martin, but Crag is larger, greyer above and dirty whitish to smoky-brown below, with no breast band. Very dark underwing-coverts contrasting with brown flight feathers and body the best fieldmark. Juvenile has warmer rufous tone and yellowish gape (dark in adult).

Red-rumped Swallow *Hirundo daurica*   17cm (6.5")

Mediterranean species that just creeps into extreme south of region. Pale rump patch and relaxed gliding and soaring flight suggest House Martin, but Red-rumped has the classic swallow's tail. Attaches distinctive mud cup nest with short tunnel entrance to roof of cave or ruin, under bridge or culvert. Call a short, sparrow-like *djweit*. Song is nasal, twanging.

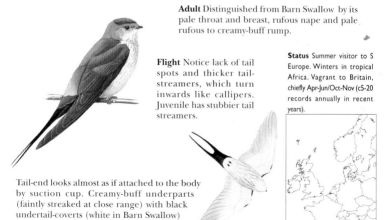

Adult Distinguished from Barn Swallow by its pale throat and breast, rufous nape and pale rufous to creamy-buff rump.

Flight Notice lack of tail spots and thicker tail-streamers, which turn inwards like callipers. Juvenile has stubbier tail streamers.

Status Summer visitor to S Europe. Winters in tropical Africa. Vagrant to Britain, chiefly Apr-Jun/Oct-Nov (c5-20 records annually in recent years).

Tail-end looks almost as if attached to the body by suction cup. Creamy-buff underparts (faintly streaked at close range) with black undertail-coverts (white in Barn Swallow) are diagnostic.

Barn Swallow *Hirundo rustica* 17-19cm (6.5-7.5")

The most common and familiar swallow (or hirundine) across north-west Europe, usually seen swooping low over ground or water in pursuit of flying insects. Distinguished from martins and larger but unrelated Swift by combination of all-dark upperparts and throat, pale belly and greatly elongated outer tail feathers – the classic swallow-tail. Confusion most likely with scarce Red-rumped Swallow.

Adult Chestnut-red forehead and ▶ throat framed by dark, metallic-blue breast-band and upperparts. Belly and under-wing-coverts pinkish-cream. Male (shown) averages longer tail streamers than female.

▲ **Juvenile** Duller than adult, with pale rusty face, patchy breast-band and yellow gape flange. Forked tail lacks streamers and clearly falls short of wingtips at rest.

◀ Breeds in isolated pairs or small loose colonies on ledges or rafters within outbuildings, beneath bridges, etc. Watch for conspicuous white spots across spread tail as birds brake on approach to nest – an open half-cup of mud, straw and feathers, cemented to beam.

Status Widespread summer visitor (chiefly Apr-Oct) and passage migrant (stragglers into Nov/Dec). British birds winter S.Africa. **Population** c820,000 pairs.

Flight Dashing low level flight characterised by sudden jinks. Light, elegant wing action interrupted by pause with wings pulled well back. Rather short tail gives juvenile somewhat bat-like impression on wing.

◆ Earliest arrivals reach Mediterranean in February, and southern Britain mid-March onwards. Look for them flickering low over freshwater ◆ Nests in villages and farms, but likely to be seen over any habitat ◆ Cheerful *vit vit* call becomes a more urgent, rapidly repeated *si-vlit* in alarm ◆ Song a rapid, twittering or lively warble, punctuated at intervals by a low rattle and sneeze ◆ On migration, forms large swarms with Swifts and martins over wetlands, and roosts in reedbeds ◆ Unlike Swift, lands freely on vegetation and ground, shuffling awkwardly along on tiny legs.

House Martin *Delichon urbica* 12.5cm (5")

Seldom arrives before mid-April, when new arrivals typically seen hawking low over freshwater with other hirundines. Chunkier than Sand Martin, looking strikingly black and white at any distance. Tail is clearly forked, but lacks Swallow's streamers. Call, and snow white rump on otherwise dark upperparts diagnostic.

Adult Easily told from Swallow by glossy blue-black upperparts contrasting with snow white underparts and rump. No breast-band. On ground, short white feathered legs are conspicuous. Sexes alike. Similar juvenile more brownish above, with dingy wash across chest that can sometimes suggest Sand Martin.

Breeds colonially in towns and villages, where clusters of 4-6 hemispherical mud-nests cemented beneath the eaves, jutting window ledge or bridge are a familiar sight. Can still have young in the nest into October.

Highly sociable. Seen strung out in long lines along fences and overhead wires with other hirundines prior to southward migration in autumn.

Flight Hawks aerial insects with characteristic brief, rapid flurries of wingbeats between bouts of gliding on open wings. Swoops and wheels like a paper plane, with sudden twists to capture prey. Regularly flies higher in sky than Barn Swallow or Sand Martin. Might be mistaken for stray Red-rumped Swallow, which also shows pale rump and has similarly relaxed flight, but House Martin has white undertail-coverts.

Status Common and widespread summer visitor, chiefly Apr-Oct. Frequently lingers into Nov, with odd birds seen midwinter. Winters tropical Africa. **Population** c320,000-690,000 pairs.

◆ Repeated flight call, a hard *pr-prt* is excellent fieldmark. Blends into more conversational chorus from birds milling about nest-site ◆ Song largely a spluttering composition of calls ◆ Lands beside puddles or ponds to collect gobbets of mud for nest.

Superficially lark-like in plumage and habits, but with relatively long, slender tails, pipits are sprightly birds, walking or running while larks shuffle. When flushed they rise suddenly, invariably calling, and fly-off with bouncing undulations. Identification on plumage alone is often tricky and calls are important. Tree Pipit is very like Meadow, but season and whereabouts (Tree found usually in woods or clearings) offer useful clues, backed-up by voice, subtle plumage differences and incessant slow pumping of tail.

Adult Bulkier and cleaner below than Meadow. Differs in marked contrast between snowy belly and warm buff throat, breast, flanks; bolder, more evenly-spaced streaks on breast and weaker, finer streaking on flanks. The upperparts are also more boldly streaked than Meadow.

Shorter, more arched hind-claw is diagnostic (visible if perched on wires). By midsummer, underparts become whiter and bold mantle streaks become fainter, through wear.

Note slightly stouter bill, more obvious buffy supercilium and less conspicuous eye-ring than Meadow.

Status Widespread summer visitor, Apr-Sept. Scarce migrant Ireland. Winters in Africa. **Population** 120,000 territories.

Flight Sings from tree-top, prominent branch or in song-flight, gliding down with raised wings and tail (like a paper plane) – much as other pipits, but only Tree habitually does so in woodland. Cheery song is much stronger than Meadow's; opens like a Chaffinch and concludes with characteristic terminal flourish: *seeurr-seeurr-seeurr-seeurr*.

◆ Breeds in open woodland, clearings, plantations and bushy or sparsely-wooded hillsides ◆ Feeds quietly on ground under trees and bushes; also in nearby field edges ◆ Usually first noticed when flushed, when it rises giving diagnostic hoarse *treeezz* (quite unlike other pipits) ◆ Looks plumper than Meadow as it flies up, often from amongst low cover rather than open grassland ◆ Often solitary, but forms groups of 4-5 on passage; migrants readily picked up on call as they pass overhead.

Meadow Pipit *Anthus pratensis*

Most widespread and abundant of our pipits, even coming into towns in wintry weather. Equally at home on open moorland as it is in grassy fields, by lakesides and on beaches (where it mingles with Rock Pipits). Very gregarious; forms large flocks in coastal fields at migration times.

Adult Slightly smaller and shorter-bodied than Tree Pipit, with bold black streaking forming long coarse lines right down flanks. Underparts lack the contrast between breast and belly shown by Tree. Worn birds are off-whitish below and greyish-olive above, but the streaking remains evident (unlike Tree which can become quite plain on mantle). At close range, note longer, less curved hind claw.

Fresh-plumaged birds are very bright buffy-olive above, and warm buff below, showing bold blackish streaking both above and below. The pink legs are very bright in juveniles.

Has slightly rounder crown and weaker bill than Tree Pipit; sports only a hint of a supercilium, but bolder eye-ring makes eye seem more conspicuous.

Flight Smaller, more pointed at the front than any lark. Like most pipits, shows white outer tail feathers if tail spread (greyish in Rock however). Lacks white trailing edge to wings shown by Skylark.

Status Abundant resident and partial migrant, with winter influxes. **Population** 2,800,000 territories.

◆ Rises suddenly from grass, giving a nervous, lisped *sep-seep* (or *pi-pit*), which may be repeated in a stronger 4 or 5 note version; struggles to gain height in weak, jerky flight ◆ Call *pseet* (very similar to calls of Rock and Water Pipits) ◆ Weak song is simpler than Tree Pipit's and lacks terminal flourish; has a faintly 'ringing' quality. Given from low perch or in parachute song-flight from slope or bush top ◆ Largely terrestrial, but will perch on tree tops.

Red-throated Pipit *Anthus cervinus*   14.5cm (5.5")

Adult Distinctive brick red face/throat ▶ (brightest, most extensive in males). Upperparts warmer brown and with bolder black striping than other pipits; in fresh plumage shows clear pale 'tramlines' on mantle.

▲
First-year Resemble dark, boldly-streaked Meadow Pipits. Underparts whiter than other pipits with bold black streaks forming stripes along flanks. Boldly streaked rump is diagnostic, but difficult to see.

◆ Breeds arctic Scandinavia eastwards; winters mostly in Africa ◆ Migrants favour lakesides and wet grassland ◆ When flushed, appears slightly plumper and shorter-tailed than Meadow; gives characteristic call – a thin, shrill, penetrating *pseeee*, like short blast of dog whistle (lacks Trees rasping quality) ◆ Annual vagrant Britain and W Europe, mainly coasts April-June/Sept-Oct.

Water Pipit *Anthus spinoletta*   16.5cm (6.5")

Non-breeding adult Whitish below (lacking other pipits' buffy tones), with dark brown streaks across breast and flanks. Drab grey-brown upperparts indistinctly streaked darker. Whitish wing-bars, tertial edges and supercilium are key features. ▶

Fresh spring adult Blue-grey head, white supercilium and virtually unstreaked pinkish chest identify. White wing-bars and rosy flush disappear with wear, becoming drab greyish above and dingy whitish below. ▼

Status Altitudunal and dispersive migrant, breeds alpine zone; winters by lowland streams, cress-beds, pools and marshes. Britain & Ireland: scattered birds in winter, chiefly over southern England, with distinct passage in April.

▲ Pure white outer tail feathers show if tail spread (greyish in similar Scandinavian race of Rock Pipit).

◆ Dark legs shared only by Rock Pipit (both formerly lumped) ◆ Song-flight from rock outcrops and grassy slopes recalls that of Meadow ◆ Call a single loud *wheest*, rather stronger than Meadow ◆ Rather nervous, often flying considerable distance when flushed.

198

Rock Pipit *Anthus petrosus* — 16.5cm (6.5")

A plump, dark pipit of rocky coasts and islands. Spiky black bill, weak supercilium and dark, reddish-brown legs distinctive. Distinctly chunkier than other small pipits, with drab light grey or brownish outer tail feathers (may bleach whiter at tail corners). Formerly considered conspecific with Water Pipit.

Adult nominate race (Britain/western Europe) Dusky-olive above and ▶ buffy-toned olive-yellow below in fresh plumage, becoming greyer with wear. Diffuse streaking hardly contrasts on upperparts but forms long lines of smoky streaks on underparts – quite unlike clear black streaking of Meadow.

▲ **Meadow Pipit** (shown for comparison) Forages on beaches with Rock Pipits, especially in winter; has clear-cut black streaking above and below, and is much warmer olive-brown and buff with bright pink legs.

◀ **Flight** Distinctly wider-winged and rather shorter-tailed than Meadow. Check for greyish outer tail feathers (Meadow and Water have clean white outer tails).

Song-flights in typical pipit-fashion from rocky outcrop or cliff face.

▼

Race *littoralis* (Scandinavian Rock Pipit) Falls between Rock and Water in plumage, but is typical of Rock in behaviour and its drab greyish outer tail feathers. In spring this race is variable, but most become greyer on crown and nape and are almost unstreaked above; underparts become paler, with a rosy flush developing on the breast, but streaking typically remains on flanks. Indistinguishable from race *petrosus* in non-breeding plumage.

Status Locally common resident and partial migrant. **Population** 46,500 pairs.

◆ Forages in pairs or alone on seaweed covered rocks, investigating rock pools and tide-line debris ◆ In winter also on estuaries and even by inland freshwater lakes (these perhaps *littoralis* in the main) ◆ Generally very approachable (unlike Water Pipit) ◆ Flies up with single or repeated lazy *wheest* (slower and lower in pitch than Meadow's call), less shrill than call of Water Pipit.

Richard's Pipit *Anthus richardi* 18cm (7")

Scarce migrant. Typically met in coastal rough grassland, during migrations. A very big, pot-bellied, long-legged, long-tailed pipit, often first noticed when flushed; rises with loud sparrow-like *schreep*. Size suggests long-tailed Skylark. Struts about in grass, with long legs like a well-groomed racehorse, pausing to stretch and peer over top of grass. All plumages similar. Regular vagrant September-November at coastal watch points. Breeds Siberian steppe, winters in South Asia.

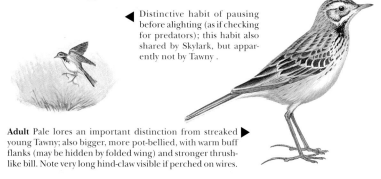

◀ Distinctive habit of pausing before alighting (as if checking for predators); this habit also shared by Skylark, but apparently not by Tawny .

Adult Pale lores an important distinction from streaked ▶ young Tawny; also bigger, more pot-bellied, with warm buff flanks (may be hidden by folded wing) and stronger thrush-like bill. Note very long hind-claw visible if perched on wires.

Tawny Pipit *Anthus campestris* 16.5cm (6.5")

Local in dry, sandy country. An almost uniformly pale sandy pipit with long pinkish legs and long tail. Furtively runs and darts as it feeds, tail wagging like a big pale wagtail. Call is a sparrow-like throw-away *schilip*, much weaker than the full-bodied *schreep* of Richard's; also has a low *chup*. Undertakes undulating song-flight, from hillside or outcrop, a slowly repeating *z'deee-z'deee-z'deee...*

Juvenile Scale-streaked above and ▶ has breast band of irregular spots.

Distinguished from Richard's by dark loral line, flanks being the same colour as the rest of the underparts. Attains adult plumage by late autumn.

Status Local summer visitor, wintering in Africa. Dry fields, sandy heath and even bare mountainsides. Annual vagrant to Britain and Ireland, chiefly August-October at coastal watch points.

Adult Distinctive in ▶ its almost uniform sandy appearance; breast markings may be scattered or entirely absent. The median covert spots are often striking.

Slim black and white bird with a long, constantly wagging tail. Frequently seen beside water but equally in fields, farmyards, parks, playing fields, roadsides, rooftops. The Pied Wagtail (race *yarrellii*) is resident Britsh Isles, although a very few nest on adjacent continental coasts. Nominate White (race *alba*) nests throughout rest of Europe, and is scarce but regular passage migrant to Britain (March-May/August-October).

Pied male summer Black back and rump, and sooty flanks identify. Note white face, broad white fringes to wing feathers, and conspicuous white outer-tail feathers. Black chin extends as prominent black bib across chest. Legs black.

Pied adult winter Chin becomes white, but retains black breast band.

Pied juvenile Olive-grey above, dirty white below. Has smoky-buff face, smudgy dark malar and breast band. Indistinguishable from juvenile White. First-winter plumage like winter adult from September onwards, but face washed pale lemon. Presence of sooty crown, rump and flanks rules out immature White.

Pied female summer As male but back is slate-grey.

White Wagtail At all seasons, separable from Pied by clean grey back, rump and flanks.

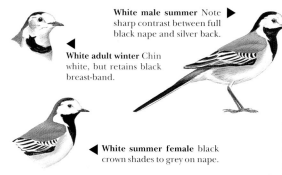

White male summer Note sharp contrast between full black nape and silver back.

White adult winter Chin white, but retains black breast-band.

Status Common resident. Both races gravitate south in winter; some Pieds leave Britain for Iberia and Whites from North. Europe winter south to Mediterranean. **Population** c430,000 pairs.

White summer female black crown shades to grey on nape.

◆ Walks or runs with nodding head, sudden lunges and flycatching leaps ◆ In flight, can be picked out at distance by long tail and conspicuously dipping action, with distinct bursts of wingbeats ◆ Flight call characteristic: a loud *tchiz-ick*; also utters an emphatic *tsu-wee* ◆ Lively, twittering song ◆ In winter, forms large roosts in reedbeds, towns, etc.

Relatively shorter tailed than other wagtails; winters in Africa. Five distinct races regularly breed in our region, all having yellow underparts, and black tail with conspicuous white sides. Females of all races alike, but males separable by different head patterns. Differ markedly from Grey Wagtail in greenish back and rump, shorter tail, black legs, voice and habitat preferences.

Male *flavissima*. This race nests Britain and ▶ locally in coastal districts of adjacent continent. Supercilium and entire underparts vivid yellow; cheeks and upperparts greenish. Variable in winter plumage (Sept. onwards); more like female, but underparts richer yellow.

▲
Female *flavissima*. Like male but paler below and duller, more brownish above.

◀ **Juvenile** Drab; earthy-brown above, dirty buff-white below. Smudgy dark malar stripe and necklace suggest juvenile Pied Wagtail, but upperparts are brownish rather than grey. Acquires first-winter plumage from August; most are buff-yellow below like female, but some birds are confusingly pale – always look for yellow vent.

Other races Ranges overlap and hybrids not infrequent.

◀ Nominate *flava* (Blue-headed) occupies most of region: blue-grey head, white chin, yellow throat. Strong white supercilium.

Status Declining. Summer visitor (Apr-Sep/Oct). In British Isles, chiefly found in lowland eastern & central England; scarce-absent in N/W. Rarely nests Ireland. More widespread on passage. **Population** c50,000 pairs.

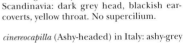

◀ *thunbergi* (Grey-headed) in northern Scandinavia: dark grey head, blackish ear-coverts, yellow throat. No supercilium.

◀ *cinereocapilla* (Ashy-headed) in Italy: ashy-grey head, blackish ear-coverts, white throat. Usually no supercilium

◀ *iberiae* (Spanish) in Iberia/south-west France: ashy-blue head, blackish ear-coverts, white throat. White supercilium often confined to dash behind eye.

◆ Breeds by lowland meadows, fringes of wetlands (including salt-marshes); fewer on cultivated land ◆ Forms large flocks in late summer, especially at communal roosts and on passage ◆ Follows grazing livestock, darting to and fro after insects ◆ Announces presence with loud *tsweep* or shriller *tsree-ree* ◆ Simple song a twittering mix of call-notes ◆ Typical bouncing, wagtail flight. Lacks white wing-stripe shown by Grey Wagtail.

Grey Wagtail *Motacilla cinerea* — 18-20cm (7-8")

Longest-tailed of the wagtails. Elegant and vivacious. During breeding season prefers rocky, fast-flowing rivers and streams (especially those lined with deciduous trees), so is most often seen in hill country. In winter, disperses to slower waters, lake-shores, watercress beds, even city centres and coasts. Degree of yellow on body varies according to age, sex and season, but yellow rump, slate-grey upperparts and pinkish legs (black in other wagtails) diagnostic.

Male summer Combination of lemon yellow underparts (palest on flank, brightest on vent), white moustache and black bib identifies. Narrow white supercilium. Wings mainly black, with bold white fringes to tertials.

Female summer As male but throat buff-white, with or without variable amount of black mottling.

Adult winter Both sexes have pale throat and buff-yellow chest, like washed-out summer female. Juvenile differs from non-breeding adult by softer expression, more uniform peachy-buff underparts and buff-yellow vent. Tail considerably shorter.

Note broad translucent band across wings as bird passes overhead. ▼

Grey

Pied

Flight Markedly bouncing. Readily distinguished from Pied by yellow rump and long tail, which shows white at sides even when closed.

Status Widespread resident, but absent most of Scandinavia. In British Isles, occurs mainly in hilly north & west, and chiefly as winter visitor in east England.
Population c55,000 pairs.

◆ Thin metallic *tiz-zit* draws attention. Is clearly audible above babble of rushing water or hubbub in town. Suggests Pied's familiar *chis-sick*, but is sharper and readily distinguished with practice ◆ Generally solitary ◆ Watch out for bird flying, perched on boulder mid-stream or on branch overhanging water ◆ Walks sedately, slowly pumping tail or teeters excitedly, flirting flashy white outer-tails ◆ Rather flighty. Skips noisily away or takes refuge in tree, tail bouncing ◆ Unimpressive song a medley of calls and brief, Wren-like warbling.

203

Exotic-looking winter visitor that raids berry-laden shrubs and trees in hedgerows and suburban gardens. Plump, crested form and silky appearance is like no other European bird, but beware confusion with Starling in flight – shape and size surprisingly similar in silhouette.

Adult Long crest and sleek pinkish-brown plumage unmistakable. Notice black throat and mask, rusty vent, long grey rump and blackish tail with bold yellow tip. Name derives from bright red tips to secondaries (most obvious in males), like dabs of sealing wax. ▶

Both sexes show yellow and white V-shaped edges to primary-tips. Females usually duller with less contrasting bib and tail tip.

Flight On the wing, looks remarkably like Starling. Listen for distinctive call-note, a sibilant, trilling *sirrr* that builds to ringing chorus from departing flock.

Status Winter visitor from remote taiga forests of north Eurasia. Nomadic, occurring in unpredictable numbers and prone to periodic large invasions. Annual in N/E Britain, with first arrivals from late Oct/Nov, often lingering into April. **Population** Varies from 100+ to many thousands.

Juvenile is drabber and lacks V-shaped primary tips. Instead shows straight white line across length of folded primaries. Red waxy tips reduced or lacking.

◆ Always tame ◆ Perches freely on wires, TV aerials, treetops ◆ Typically seen in parties of 3-10 birds, but flocks of 100+ not uncommon in irruption years ◆ Agile and acrobatic when feeding. Shape is one moment long and thin, the next puffed-up and rounded ◆ Often surprises observers in fine weather by making short fly-catching sallies in graceful manner very reminiscent of a Bee-eater.

Dipper *Cinclus cinclus* 18cm (7")

Unique chunky blackish bird with stunning white breast, invariably by fast-flowing rivers and streams chiefly in hill country. Usually seen bobbing and curtsying on rocks in midstream, before plunging beneath torrent to hunt aquatic invertebrates, small fish etc. Pot-bellied form, short cocked tail and rapid whirring flight suggest giant amphibious wren.

Adult Resembles a small, dark thrush but chocolate cap and snow white bib unique. British birds (race *gularis*) have chestnut belt below white (narrower on darker *hibernicus* found in west Scotland/Ireland). Rest of plumage blackish. Legs dark. Sexes alike.

Juvenile Scaly, looks scruffy; dark grey above, dirty whitish below but same distinctive shape and actions as adult. Legs paler than adults.

Blends superbly amongst rocks and splashing water. Easily overlooked, especially when seen from behind. Notice white eyelids, conspicuous when bird blinks.

Flight Often inadvertently flushed. Typical view is of dark blur scudding low over water on whirring wings, only to vanish around the next bend.

Status Widespread resident. Locally not uncommon in hilly north and west Britain and Ireland. May descend to lowland streams and lakesides in winter. **Population** c9,000-26,000 pairs, decreasing.

◆ Best found by watching up and downstream from bridges over suitable waterways ◆ Penetrating, strident *zrit-zrit*, clearly audible above rushing water, warns of approaching bird ◆ Sometimes pitches into river in mid-flight. Swims well ◆ Occasionally darts across dry-land, when dark body and white gorget can lead to momentary confusion with Ring Ouzel ◆ Breeds February onwards, constructing domed mossy nest beneath bridges and banks ◆ Scandinavian race *cinclus* (Black-bellied Dipper) has wholly blackish belly (no chestnut belt) and is an occasional visitor to eastern Britain in winter.

Dunnock (Hedge Accentor) *Prunella modularis*   14.5cm (5.75")

Unobtrusive garden bird, seldom venturing far from cover. Typically seen feeding quietly on shady lawn or beneath hedge. Streaked brown upperparts superfically sparrow-like, but note thin spiky bill, distinctive actions and voice. Never in flocks like sparrows.

Adult Easily recognised by blue-grey face and underparts (brownish on crown and ear-coverts), and warm flanks streaked rufous-brown. ▶

Status Widespread resident (north European birds migrate south, Sep-Apr). **Population** >2,800,000 territories.

Juvenile Differs in whitish throat, faint pale eyebrows, and buffish underparts with copious dark streaks.

◆ Common in hedgerows, parks, gardens, heaths and in scrubby woodland and hills (up to treeline) ◆ Hops in unhurried, shuffling manner (as if feet tied together), incessantly flicking its wings. Pecks delicately for insects and tiny seeds ◆ Shrill, piping *tseek* demands attention ◆ Year-round song, characteristically given from top of bramble, a hurried, jingling ditty: *weed, sissi-weed, sissi-weed...*◆ Becomes curiously restive in autumn, circling high in air, calling excitedly.

Alpine Accentor *Prunella collaris*   18cm (7")

Adult Like a large Dunnock, with distinctive wing pattern: a black panel bordered with white wing-bars and a cinnamon secondary panel, both visible at great distance. Legs reddish, bill with yellow base. Duller juvenile lacks barred bib of adult. ▶

Flight Look for white tips to tail. Often flies up onto rocks or walls, unlike Dunnock.

Status Breeds C & S Europe. Very rare vagrant to Britain.

◆ Locally common on high alpine plateaux of central and southern Europe ◆ Breeds above tree-line, on rocky grassland and scree ◆ Tame but unobtrusive ◆ Regularly feeds beside snow patches ◆ Rippling *tchurrupp* call recalls Skylark ◆ Song, somewhat Dunnock-like, is interrupted by rolling calls ◆ After breeding, seen in small flocks ◆ Descends to lower slopes in winter (takes scraps at ski centres).

Wren *Troglodytes troglodytes* 9-10cm (3.75")

Adult Tiny size and short, frequently cocked tail unmistakable. Is rufous-brown above, with pale eyebrow (from behind eye) and finely barred wings and tail. Grey-buff below, barred on flanks.Juvenile similar.

Flight Brief and low, whirring wings all a-blur.

Status Resident. One of the most abundant of British birds. **Population** c10 million pairs.

◆ Common in low, dense cover almost everywhere, from woods and gardens to marshes, moors and sea-cliffs ◆ Hops, creeps, climbs or scurries mouse-like amongst brushwood, ivy, tangled growth, even beached seaweed ◆ Walks along branches with revolving spread wings and cocked tail to confront intruders ◆ Pops-up at close quarters to chastise with repeated, stony *tit tit it* or rolling, scolding *churr*. Looks irritated, bobbing this way, then that ◆ Year-round song is an astonishingly loud, explosive, 5-second outburst of clear high notes and rattling trills.

Robin *Erithacus rubecula* 14cm (5.5")

Flight Flits quickly away. Curtseys on landing, flicking wings and tail in characteristic manner

Adult Instantly recognised by its red face and breast, attractively edged blue-grey. Upperparts plain olive-brown; belly white. Sexes identical.

Status Common resident. In Britain, one of ten most abundant birds; falls of shyer continental birds occur, especially on east coast/Northern Isles in autumn. **Population** c6 million pairs.

Juvenile Lacks red at first. Heavily spotted buff above, scaled buff below. Soon acquires red splotches on breast. As adult after moult July-September. Variable buff wing-bar boldest on first-winters.

◆ Familiar bird of woods, parks and gardens ◆ Jaunty, plump outline distinctive ◆ British birds confiding; European birds less so ◆ Hops on ground with wings drooped, dips, then pauses alert and upright ◆ Sings all year. Well-known song comprises soulful, rippling, crystal-clear cascades of 2-3 seconds duration; sounds sadder in autumn ◆ Both sexes sing and are pugnacious in defence of own individual territory ◆ Commonest call a tutting *tic tic ic*, given from low perch.

Nightingale *Luscinia megarhynchos*   16.5cm (6.5")

Flight Rounded, rusty tail usually all that is seen as bird dives for cover.

▲
Juvenile Scaly; resembles juvenile Robin, but has characteristic rusty tail.

Status Summer visitor (Apr-Sep). Declining in Britain (confined to SE England). Winters tropical Africa. **Population** c5000 pairs.

Adult Warm brown above with bright chestnut tail. Big dark eye and pulsating white throat conspicuous on singing bird, contrasting with duller grey-buff underparts. Stands tall, on long pale legs. Sexes alike.

◆ Shy bird, famous for its remarkable song ◆ Locally common in drier forests, thickets, wooded heaths and groves, often near streams ◆ Mostly skulks in undergrowth, so seldom seen ◆ Sings night and day, usually from thick cover but sometimes from exposed perch. Fabulously rich, with rapid sequences of *chook* notes, liquid and vibrating trills, and a slower *piu piu...* ending in characteristic crescendo ◆ Calls a low, creaking *krrrk* and penetrating *hueet*.

Thrush Nightingale *Luscinia luscinia*   16.5cm (6.5")

Adult Very similar to Nightingale but upperparts are darker and greyer (lacking rufous tone), contrasting more strongly with dull rufous tail.

Duller, less clean white and buff below, with diffuse grey mottling on breast, and dusky malar smudge (usually lacking in Nightingale).

Status Summer visitor (May-Sep). Winters in East Africa. Vagrant Britain.

◆ Eastern counterpart of Nightingale, which it replaces in southern Scandinavia ◆ Calls and behaviour as Nightingale, but prefers riverine woodland and marshy thickets ◆ Best distinguished by slower but even louder and more powerful song, often with 1-3 clear, introductory *pew* notes, characteristic stammering and galloping '*jok*' phrases, and rapid teeth-chattering noise. Lacks climax of Nightingale.

Bluethroat *Luscinia svecica* 14cm (5.5")

Like a slim, long-legged Robin, with a bold pale supercilium. Characteristic throat markings vary with age, sex and season, but rufous wedges at base of tail always diagnostic. Two distinct races nest in north-west Europe; only males wearing intense blue throat and upper breast of breeding plumage separable:

Scandinavian race *svecica* Breeding male has glossy blue ▶ bib separated from white belly by bands of black, white and rust. Red spot in centre of throat. Nests in willow scrub and birch woods, favouring streamsides and bogs.

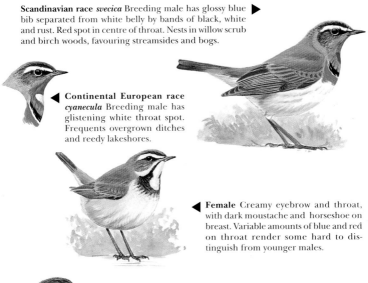

◀ **Continental European race** *cyanecula* Breeding male has glistening white throat spot. Frequents overgrown ditches and reedy lakeshores.

◀ **Female** Creamy eyebrow and throat, with dark moustache and horseshoe on breast. Variable amounts of blue and red on throat render some hard to distinguish from younger males.

◀ **Adult male autumn/first-winter male** Colourful bib partly obscured by fresh pale tips. First-years (both sexes) recognised by buff tips to greater coverts.

Status Summer visitor (Mar-Oct). Winters Mediterranean basin and tropical Africa. Britain & Ireland: scarce passage migrant (most in May), Northern Isles & North Sea coasts; fewer Sep/Oct and much rarer in west. Has bred Scotland & England.

Flight Flits low like a Robin, but rusty tail patches identify.

◆ Generally unobtrusive, keeping close to scrubby cover ◆ Hops quickly in upright manner, frequently cocking tail ◆ More showy when singing, either from low perch or in pipit-like display-flight, tail spread in gliding descent to reveal red panels ◆ Loud, varied song (in parts suggests Sedge Warbler) typically builds from hesitant start, *jip jip jip...* into rapid cascade of repeated phrases, some harsh, some sweet, mixed with mimicry and attention grabbing, drawn-out *zweep* notes ◆ Call, a soft *chak* ◆ Alarm, *heet* ◆ Buff speckled juvenile resembles young Robin, but has distinctive red tail patches.

209

Black Redstart *Phoenicurus ochruros* 14.5cm (5.75")

In all plumages darker than Redstart, but with same conspicuous and constantly quivering rusty-red tail. In north-west Europe, associated mainly with towns, industrial sites, derelict and waste land, quarries and cliffs. Its gargling song emanating from a rooftop, television aerial or some other lofty perch is often the first indications of its presence.

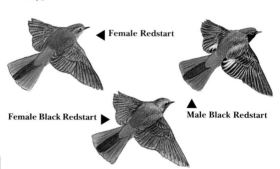

Breeding male Slaty-black above, with coal-black face and chest, and rust-red rump and tail. Variable white flash in wing more marked on some than others. Like Redstart, shows pale rusty vent and dark brown central tail-feathers. In autumn, resembles female but has more blackish face, white on belly and in wing.

Female (and similar first-year males) Drabber, sooty grey-brown without white in wing. Distinguished from female Redstart by overall darker appearance, indistinct eye-ring and dull sooty throat and underparts.

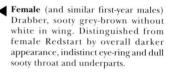

◀ **Female Redstart**

Female Black Redstart ▶

▲ **Male Black Redstart**

Status Common summer visitor, resident in south. Winters mainly in Mediterranean basin. Has bred annually in SE Britain since 1920s, but occurs mostly on passage (especially E/S coasts), with peak numbers Oct/Nov. **Population** 70-120 pairs; c500 winter, mainly on coasts in milder south-west.

◆ Nests mainly in urban environments; in southern Europe, also in mountains ◆ Perches freely on cliffs, walls, fences and rooftops, but feeds quietly and can easily be missed ◆ Characteristic song is a short (sometimes Robin-like) warble punctuated by a tell-tale wheezy sneeze or series of distinctly gravelly notes – as if rubbing a handful of ball-bearings together ◆ Calls quieter than Redstart's: *tsip* or *tsip-tsip-tsip*. Alarm a tutting *tit-it-ic* ◆ Juvenile is like female, but browner and faintly barred. Lacks bold pale mottling of juvenile Redstart, but shares shivering orange tail.

Redstart *Phoenicurus phoenicurus* 14cm (c5.5")

Robin-like, but trimmer. Distinguished from all other European birds except similar Black Redstart by its incessantly quivering rust-red tail. Both species drop repeatedly from low perch to feed on ground, but Redstart occurs mainly where there are trees. Only females likely to confuse.

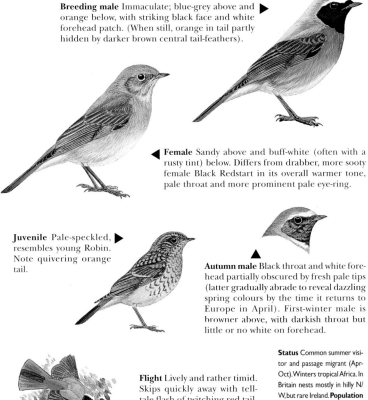

Breeding male Immaculate; blue-grey above and orange below, with striking black face and white forehead patch. (When still, orange in tail partly hidden by darker brown central tail-feathers).

Female Sandy above and buff-white (often with a rusty tint) below. Differs from drabber, more sooty female Black Redstart in its overall warmer tone, pale throat and more prominent pale eye-ring.

Juvenile Pale-speckled, resembles young Robin. Note quivering orange tail.

Autumn male Black throat and white forehead partially obscured by fresh pale tips (latter gradually abrade to reveal dazzling spring colours by the time it returns to Europe in April). First-winter male is browner above, with darkish throat but little or no white on forehead.

Status Common summer visitor and passage migrant (Apr-Oct). Winters tropical Africa. In Britain nests mostly in hilly N/W, but rare Ireland. **Population** >100,000 pairs.

Flight Lively and rather timid. Skips quickly away with tell-tale flash of twitching red tail. May dive for cover or perch openly on wire, post or sprig.

◆ Breeds in open forest, parkland and heaths with scattered trees; also in gardens in continental Europe ◆ Short, clear song starts with promise: *see, you you you...* but fizzles out into a brief, hurried warble ◆ Tall sprigs poking through woodland canopy favoured as song-posts – male's snowy forehead often catches the eye ◆ Call is a loud, plaintive *hueet* (very like Willow Warbler's) or longer *hueet-tic-tic* ◆ Likely almost anywhere on passage, sometimes in large falls on coasts.

211

Whinchat *Saxicola rubetra* 12-13cm (5")

Restless, short-tailed chat that perches openly on bush-tops, tall weeds and fences, flicking its wings and tail. Males in summer distinctive. Females and autumn birds can be confused with female Stonechat, but Whinchat's conspicuous creamy eyebrow, boldly streaked rump and white wedges at base of tail (often noticed as birds flick tail to balance in the wind) are reliable fieldmarks.

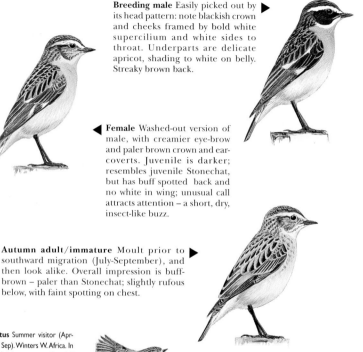

Breeding male Easily picked out by its head pattern: note blackish crown and cheeks framed by bold white supercilium and white sides to throat. Underparts are delicate apricot, shading to white on belly. Streaky brown back.

Female Washed-out version of male, with creamier eye-brow and paler brown crown and ear-coverts. Juvenile is darker; resembles juvenile Stonechat, but has buff spotted back and no white in wing; unusual call attracts attention – a short, dry, insect-like buzz.

Autumn adult/immature Moult prior to southward migration (July-September), and then look alike. Overall impression is buff-brown – paler than Stonechat; slightly rufous below, with faint spotting on chest.

Status Summer visitor (Apr-end Sep). Winters W. Africa. In British Isles, nests mostly to N/W of Humber/Severn divide.
Population <30,000 pairs, declining.

Flight Shows white flash across shoulder like Stonechat, but only Whinchat has white triangle at either side of short dark tail and uniformly boldly streaked rump.

◆ Nests on heaths, grassy moors, rough fields, damp rushy meadows and young coniferous plantations ◆ Like Stonechat, pounces to the ground for insects, returning to same slightly elevated perch or flying quickly to another sprig nearby ◆ Broken song mixes short musical phrases with dry *churrs* and distinct pauses ◆ Call an agitated *tu-tek, tu-tek-tek* ◆ Widespread on migration, often in some numbers in coastal bushes and fields.

Perky, round-headed chat of bushy marginal land, coasts, heaths and other rough ground. Often seen in pairs, perched upright on topmost spray of gorse. Objects to close approach with persistent, stony *tsak-tsak* – like two pebbles knocked together. Differs principally from Whinchat in lack of pale eyebrow, usually dark throat, and longer, all-dark tail with more rounded tip.

Male Distinctive. Has all-black head with broad white ▶ half-collar, rufous-orange underparts, and clear white flash in wing (often concealed at rest). In winter colours dulled by brownish fresh feather tips but basic pattern remains. (British/Irish birds, race *hibernans*, typically darker than *rubicola* of Continent)

◀ **Female** Paler, more streaky above. Head is grey-brown, throat mottled. Shows small and indistinct whitish flash in neck and wing.

▲

Autumn female Can have pale throat, even hint of pale brow – but never shows Whinchat's conspicuous buffy supercilium.

Juvenile Recalls young Robin but is ▶ much darker; note abundant pale flecks above, untidily streaked chest, bright rufous wing-edges and white flash in wing.

Flight Look for pale rufous or streaked whitish rump, and white shoulder flash as bird flies. Tail is always dark, lacking white triangles at base shown by Whinchat.

Status Resident in west, making local movements in winter. In British Isles, breeds chiefly along N/W coasts. **Population** 20,000-40,000 pairs.

◆ Flies rapidly on whirring wings from one prominent low lookout to another ◆ At rest, flicks wings and tail ◆ 'Stone-chatting' call often preceded by plaintive *hweet* note ◆ Brief, jangling song is easily mistaken for a Dunnock's. Sometimes given in dancing song-flight, in which male rises vertically to about 6m, with tail fanned and wings held down ◆ Eastern form or 'Siberian Stonechat' is rare vagrant in late autumn; its pale throat and eyebrow suggest Whinchat, but shows unmarked buffy-white rump and black tail.

Northern Wheatear *Oenanthe oenanthe* 15-16cm (6")

Familiar bird of open country. Breeds commonly on rocky moors, hilly pasture, sandy brecks and coasts, especially where grass is close-cropped by rabbits or sheep. Plumage varies widely between individuals, but flashing white rump and inverted black 'T' on tail always identifies.

Breeding male Blue-grey above with white ▶ supercilium, black mask and wings. Orange-buff chest wears to white as season progresses. First-summer birds have (worn) brownish-black wings.

Female Drabber, brownish-grey above and may have either pale or dusky-brown cheeks. Note pale supercilium fades to buff in front of eye.
▶

◀ **Autumn adult/first-winter** All warm buff below, with conspicuous bright fringes to wings. Adult males often recognisable by contrasting face (black lores and white supercilium).

Juvenile Looks scaly; splotched ▶ buff-white above, with distinct rusty margins to wings. Tail as adult.

Status Summer visitor and passage migrant (Mar-end Oct). Winters tropical Africa. Britain & Ireland: breeds mainly in N/W, mostly above 300m. **Population >67,000 pairs.**

Flight Bobbing white rump and tail obvious in low, dashing flight. Pattern of black and white tail and greyish underwing helps separate this from Black-eared and other rarer wheatears.

◆ One of our earliest summer migrants, likely on almost any short grass. Arrive early March but passage continues through May, when larger Greenland race *leucorrhoa* (males typically darker, more extensively orange below) also seen ◆ Stands erect on boulders, fences and walls ◆ Feeds on ground, running rapidly; pauses and bobs tail constantly in motion ◆ Song (often opens with sharp whistled *weet*) a brief warble mixed with harsh creaky notes – sometimes given in dancing flight ◆ Alarm *chak*, like pebbles knocked together.

Black-eared Wheatear *Oenanthe hispanica*   14.5cm (5.75")

Sandy wheatear breeding only in south of region. Slighter than Northern Wheatear and plumage even more variable, both sexes having either pale or wholly dark throat. Rump white. In autumn, females/first-winters can be tricky to distinguish from Northern Wheatear. Close attention to tail pattern important.

Breeding male Distinctive; sparkling sandy-buff with whiter crown (mantle also whitens with wear), jet black wings and either all black face or black mask with white throat. First-summer male differs in browner wings. ▶

First-winter More grey-buff above and warm honey-buff below. Distinguished with care from Northern by tail pattern and weaker supercilium.

Breeding female Not so clean or con-trasting as male. Differs from female Northern in warmer sandy-brown back and chest contrasting with whiter lower underparts, darker wings and scapulars. ▶

Flight Typically more white on rump and tail than Northern; note more extensive black in tail-sides but narrower, often broken and rather jagged black band at tip.

Status Summer visitor to Mediterranean (Mar-Sep). Winters tropical Africa. Rare vagrant Britain.

◆ Haunts stony, maquis-covered slopes and other dry, open country with scattered scrub (including vineyards) ◆ Habitually perches up on low sprig or bush, from where makes dashing sallies to ground after insects (Northern more inclined to run about and feed on ground) ◆ Often hovers momentarily before alighting, when inky-black underwing-coverts may catch one's eye ◆ Song comprises short, regularly spaced phrases (some scratchy, others recalling Skylark or buzzy like Sand Martin); may be given from prominent perch or in fluttery song-flight ◆ Call a short rasping *chek* (like filing of finger nail).

Ring Ouzel *Turdus torquatus* 24cm (9.5")

The 'mountain Blackbird'. In Britain and Scandinavia breeds in wild, sparsely wooded fell country and scree; on continent, also in montane coniferous forest. Watch for migrants on downland and in coastal fields and scrub. Crescent-shaped white bib, long primaries, and wide pale margins to wing feathers separate from superficially similar Blackbird.

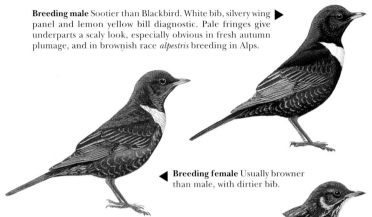

Breeding male Sootier than Blackbird. White bib, silvery wing panel and lemon yellow bill diagnostic. Pale fringes give underparts a scaly look, especially obvious in fresh autumn plumage, and in brownish race *alpestris* breeding in Alps.

◀ **Breeding female** Usually browner than male, with dirtier bib.

Juvenile No gorget. Sounds like young Blackbird, but heavy ▶ chocolate and cream barring over entire underparts unique. (Unlikely to be seen in this plumage outside breeding grounds).

◀ **Autumn/winter** White bib obscured by fresh smoky fringes, and scarcely detectable on some first-winter females. Silvery wings readily identify, but is frequently tricky to sex.

Status Principally summer visitor. Winters S Europe/N Africa. Has declined in some haunts. **Population** c6,000-11,000 pairs.

Flight Flies swiftly on long wings, typically at some height across valleys or headlong down slope. Seen overhead, the white gorget and dark underwing-coverts contrasting with decidedly silvery flight feathers identify.

◆ Actions Blackbird-like, but wary. Retreats quickly with characteristic winding, clacking rattle *tchuk-uk-uk-uk* (stonier, more metallic than Blackbird's rattling alarm) ◆ Song composed of brief, quiet Fieldfare-like chuckles and hoarse thrush-like phrases (audible only at close range), but broken by regular repetition of 2-4 penetratingly clear, ringing notes – latter far-carrying and often first clue that birds are about (at first, sounds not unlike distant Song Thrush). Scan carefully for singing bird perched on treetop, crag or skyline ◆ Migrants often associate with flocks of winter thrushes or skulk in cover, flushing suddenly and noisily from bushes. Look for them March-May and September-November.

216

Familiar thrush, common in towns, villages, fields and woods. Watch for distinctive habit of raising tail on landing. Highly territorial, devotes much time to seeing off rivals; more gregarious in winter.

Adult male Entirely jet black plumage, with crocus yellow bill and eye-ring. Larger and longer-tailed than all-black Starling with dark legs and different jizz.

Female Dark brown with whitish throat and mottled rufous-brown breast. Bill orange or dark. Some birds more clearly spotted on breast – might be confused with Song Thrush, but latter has pink legs and is much paler, with clear dark spotting below.

Juvenile Most like female, but head and body ginger, heavily mottled below and with rufous flecks on mantle. Moults to first-winter plumage July-October.

First-year male Differs from adult in blackish bill, and distinctly brown wings contrasting with dull black body.

Partial albinism not uncommon. Beware possible confusion of some examples with Ring Ouzel, but Blackbird has visibly short primaries at rest and lacks silvery wings.

Flight Flies quickly, with bursts of flicking wingbeats and tendency to yaw (not rising and falling like Mistle Thrush and Fieldfare). Swerves unhesitatingly into cover.

◆ Feeds on ground and berry-laden hedges. Hops or runs, sometimes with wings drooped and tail up, then pauses to look and listen in classic thrush fashion. Forages noisily in leaf litter ◆ Excitable. When disturbed (e.g. by cat or roosting owl), repeatedly flicks wings and cocks tail, uttering nervy *took* or more agitated *chink-chink-chink*. If pressed, flies in panic, fast and low to cover, giving well-known hysterical rattle ◆ Sings openly from fence, rooftop, tree. Song a rich, relaxed, mellow fluting, often ending in a quiet chuckle; lacks repetition that is hallmark of Song Thrush.

Status Largely resident. N/E European birds migrate S/W in winter. In Britain, one of 10 most abundant birds; marked influx from continent in autumn. **Population** >6 million pairs.

217

Robust and gregarious thrush, slightly bigger than a Blackbird, easily identified by its striking plumage and aggressive, chattering calls. In west of region, occurs only as winter visitor. Against frosty winter backdrop contrast between dark breast and white belly is a striking fieldmark – like a waistcoat.

Adult The only thrush with blue-grey head, chestnut-brown back, and grey rump. Note heavy black speckling on rich ochre breast, and white belly with bold dark shields along flanks. At close range, shows short pale brow and dark lores. Yellow bill has dusky tip in winter. Sexes similar. First-winter birds duller than adult; in fresh plumage, recognised by small white tips to greater coverts.

◀ **Adult** Grey rump and black tail conspicuous when flying away – unique amongst our thrushes.

Flight Unhurried, rising and falling on short bursts of wingbeats interrupted by a brief pause. Seen from below, flashing white wing linings are an excellent fieldmark. Only pot-bellied Mistle Thrush is similar – but notice Fieldfare's trimmer outline and distinctly darker waistcoat and under-tail.

Fieldfare

Mistle Thrush

Status Common breeder in Scandinavia; range expanding westwards elsewhere in Europe. In Britain, a handful (<15prs) have bred most years since 1967. **Population** About one million birds in winter.

◆ Breeds across N/E Europe, occupying a range of wooded habitats, from gardens and parks to upland forest ◆ In winter, frequents berried hedgerows and open country; typically seen in large, loose flocks spread across fields, often in company with smaller Redwing. In hard weather, visits birdtables for apples and scraps ◆ Hops with confident air and Blackbird-like pauses, wings drooped beside tail ◆ Flocks wary of close approach, rising with Lapwing-like *weeip* or loud and chiding *chacker-chack-chack*, before peeling away to safety of hedgerow trees ◆ Song (seldom heard in Britain) a disappointing jumble of unmusical squeaks and chuckles, like under-rehearsed Blackbird. Alarm call a harsh grating rattle like Mistle Thrush.

218

Most resembles Song Thrush, but slightly smaller and darker with distinctively marked face that gives angrier expression. Breeds only in north of region (favours upland birch forest), but migrates south and west to rest of Europe in autumn. Highly gregarious in winter, with marked preference for hedgerows and open country, roaming widely, often in mixed flocks with larger Fieldfare or in fields with Lapwings and Golden Plovers.

Adult Rust-red flanks, bold creamy eyebrow and ▶ angled moustache framing ear-coverts diagnostic. Underparts more silvery than those of Song Thrush, with spots on breast arranged more as long, dark streaks. Presence of buffy tips to tertials and greater coverts, as shown here, indicative of fresh first-winter birds (lacking on adults). Sexes alike.

◀ **Adult** Bill mainly dark with yellow base. Pale eyebrow quickly rules out Song Thrush.

Adult Upperparts darker, more chocolaty than ▶ Song Thrush, wings typically distinctly paler.

Flight Fast and direct, on rapid wings – suggests cross between Song Thrush and Starling. Rusty armpits identify (underwing coverts warm buff on Song Thrush).

Status Breeds Scandinavia; common winter visitor elsewhere. c40-80pairs have nested annually since 1960s in NorthernScotland (especially in upland pine/birch plantations near water). **Population** About one million birds in winter.

◆ Leaves breeding grounds September-October, migrating mainly at night. Waves of new arrivals tumble from morning sky in steep, undulating descent to perch warily atop hedgerow trees – berry-laden hawthorns a particular favourite ◆ Takes fright readily, with birds exploding from bushes in all directions. Listen for thin *steeih* call (frequently heard from migrants passing over at night) ◆ In hard weather, joins Fieldfares in gardens for apples and scraps ◆ Winter flocks sometimes indulge in babbling chorus of subsong ◆ Full song, usually delivered from top of birch, is rather variable; typically starts strongly with 5-7 loud fluty notes *chiree-chiree-chiree, chiru-chri*, but then peters out into an extended weak, scratchy warbling.

219

Song Thrush *Turdus philomelos* 23cm (9")

Slightly bigger than a Starling. The commonest spotted thrush, nesting widely in parks, gardens and all kinds of woodland. Most likely to be confused with appreciably larger Mistle Thrush; always lacks the dark breast patches, pale wing-edgings and white corners to tail that are key features of Mistle.

Adult Distinguished from Mistle by smaller size, ▶ shorter tail and warmer olive-brown upperparts. Underparts white with rich buff wash across chest and profuse V-shaped spots, softly olive-blurred on flanks. Legs pinkish. Sexes alike.

◀ **Juvenile** Aged by copious buff flecks on mantle and wing-coverts. As adult after moult July-September.

Feeds mainly on ground. Runs or hops quickly – stance is more upright than Blackbird's. Pauses frequently to listen for worms, head typically cocked to one side.

Status Common resident, though birds nesting especially Scandinavia and E. Europe migrate S/W in winter. In British Isles largely sedentary; resident Hebridean race is darker. Paler, greyer continental race occurs on passage and as winter visitor.
Population c1.4 million pairs.

Flight Fast and direct. Golden-buff underwing-coverts eliminate all other thrushes. Listen for quiet *tsip* call-note (quite unlike Mistle's dry, wooden rattle).

◆ Forages alone or in loose association with other thrushes. Eats a wide range of insects, worms and fruit, but prefers snails – can sometimes be heard smashing shells against a favourite stone or 'anvil' ◆ Woodland breeder, often timid. Generally keeps within short flight of cover, retreating swiftly to bushes with rapid, chattering Blackbird-like alarm rattle (though similar, the two calls are separable with practice) ◆ Loud, clear song carries up to 1km. Sings from high in tree, wire or other prominent song-post. Characterized by short varied phrases, each repeated 2-5 times: e.g. *cherry-tea cherry-tea cherry-tea, wake-me-up wake-me-up wake-me-up, quick quick quick quick....*

Our largest thrush, easily identified by harsh rattling call. Distinctive white corners to tail show best on take-off and landing. Frequents mature gardens, parkland and open forest; also open country and hills with copses and plantations. Compare Song Thrush and flying Fieldfare.

Adult Distinguished from Song Thrush by its much ▶ greater size, longer tail and colder, greyer upperparts with paler, ochre rump and conspicuous light edges to wings. Also in creamy-white underparts with heavier, more rounded spots that coalesce to form characteristic dark smudge at sides of breast – most obvious in head-on view. Legs yellowish. Sexes alike.

◀**Juvenile** Regularly misidentified as 'something rare'. Has extremely pallid grey head, pale-fringed wings, and abundant black and white droplets over upperparts.

Flight Strong, generally at treetop height. Bursts of powerful beats interrupted by periodic closure of long wings give un-dulating progress.

Notice pot-belly and striking white underwing-coverts – latter shared only with Fieldfare (which differs in marked contrast between dark waistcoat and unmarked white belly).

Status Common but thinly distributed resident. Scandinavian population winters mainly France/Iberia. In British Isles, largely sedentary but Scottish birds migrate S/W in winter. **Population** 340,000 pairs.

◆ Bold, noisy and aggressive ◆ Forages in open situations, making confident, bounding hops. Looks barrel-chested, head held high◆ Flushes with unmistakable dry *trrr-rrr-rrr* (like sound produced by old-fashioned wooden football rattle). Flies for considerable distance or makes for safety of tallest trees (Song Thrush shoots low into cover) ◆ Breeds early, singing in all weathers (country name is 'Stormcock') ◆ Loud, ringing song delivered from tops of loftiest trees, carries over 2kms. Sounds Blackbird-like but phrases more broken, comprising peals of 3-6 short, clear notes, then a pause ◆ Usually seen in pairs or small, loose parties; seldom in big flocks.

Rock Thrush *Monticola saxatilis*   19cm (7.5")

Flighty, short-tailed thrush of boulder-strewn mountainsides, usually over 1,000m. When perched, long bill and shortish tail catch the eye. Clear, fluting song is like Blue Rock's, but phrases longer, more cascading. Feeds on invertebrates, lizards, berries.

Breeding male Strikingly colourful; blue above with darker wings and snowy patch on back. Tail and underparts orange-red. In autumn, strongly scaled and barred with hint of whitish saddle and rustier vent.

Female Grey-brown, is pale spotted above, dark barred below with warm rusty tint.

Status Breeds S Europe (Apr-Sep), winters tropical Africa. Extreme vagrant to Britain.

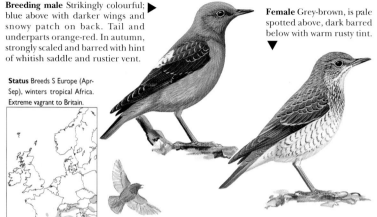

In song-flight male ascends, then parachutes down.

Blue Rock Thrush *Monticola solitarius*   20cm (8")

Haunts ruins, cliffs and gorges, from sea level to about 800m. Shape similar to Rock Thrush but longer bill and tail make it appear bigger, and tail is dark. Watches quietly from old buildings, rocky outcrops. Song combines elements of Mistle Thrush and Blackbird, but its short, fluting phrases seem more rushed.

Breeding male Slate-blue, but colour and intensity changes with the light, and at distance often looks black. At a glance might easily be taken for a Blackbird, but long bill is striking – even in silhouette. In autumn, faintly scaled.

Female Dark brown, but strongly scaled and barred buff below. Lacks red tail of Rock Thrush.

Status Resident in Mediterranean region, but winters at lower levels; many migrate to North Africa. Accidental in Britain (possible escapes).

Retiring and invariably difficult to catch sight of; usually only glimpsed foraging in low, dense vegetation beside overgrown waterways and swampy wetlands. Instantly identified by its explosive song (heard throughout the year) – often shouted at passers-by when bird is unwittingly disturbed in pathside thicket.

Adult Unstreaked, rich chestnut-brown above and greyish-white below. Broad rounded tail often flicked, fanned and cocked (note mottled undertail-coverts). Distinctly Wren-like impression of head, whereas grey breast and habit of lurking in tangles can suggest Dunnock. Legs pinkish. All plumages similar.

Generally goes unnoticed but for song – a variable, but once heard, never forgotten *chut-chewitchoo! cheti-cheti-cheti*! – delivered like sudden volley of machine-gun fire. Usually sings from thick cover, occasionally from top of low bush. Most vocal in early morning.

Flight Short rounded wings give rapid, whirring flight, as it flies low from one bush to the next.

Status Essentially Mediterranean. Rare but increasing resident in S Britain (first bred 1972). **Population** Under 400 pairs.

◆ Vulnerable to severe winters particularly at the edge of its range when numbers can be drastically reduced. Recovers rapidly ◆ Frequents thick vegetation and damp, bramble tangles along the margins of slow-moving rivers and canals, ditches and scrubby fringes of swamps, usually with a substantial element of reed (*Phragmites*) and sallow (*Salix*) ◆ Can sometimes be enticed into the open by gentle 'pishing' noises ◆ Call an explosive *chik*. Also a stuttering, Wren-like scold ◆ Loose tail comprises 10 feathers (all other passerines in the region have 12) ◆ If seen briefly, could be confused with equally retiring nightingales, but Cetti's is smaller, darker above and below, and without rufous in tail.

223

Icterine Warbler *Hippolais icterina*   13.5cm (5.25")

Degree of primary projection is most reliable difference between Icterine and Melodious Warblers; recalls washed-out or yellowish arboreal Reed Warbler but square tail tip and short undertail-coverts are distinctive. Overall angular crown shape, with prominent fleshy-orange spike of a bill and plain faced appearance (without dark eyeline) are crucial *Hippolais* features.

Beautiful varied song, delivered within tree canopy. Suggests Marsh Warbler but much richer, based chiefly on mimicry of other songbirds. Freely given, nasal *geea* phrase diagnostic.

Status Scarce migrants most likely to be encountered August-mid October in coastal districts but also possible May-June. Breeds E & C Europe. Most regular E & SE England.

Adult Combination of pale yellow underparts, blue-grey legs and conspicuous pale panel on wing (fading with wear) characteristic. Juvenile often lacks obvious yellow, being brown and whitish, with whitish wing panel. Long wings (length of exposed primaries = length of longest tertial).

◆ Can be confused with migrant Reed Warblers, which readily feed in bushes and trees, and Garden Warblers (much stubbier bill) ◆ Fresh-plumaged Willow Warblers are conspicuously yellow but have weak bills and dark eyestripe ◆ Keeps mainly to leafy cover of hedgerows, thickets and trees, where difficult to observe.

Melodious Warbler *Hippolais polyglotta*   13cm (5")

Status Scarce migrants most likely to be encountered August-mid October in coastal districts. Breeds SW Europe; occurs chiefly in S Ireland, SW England and W Wales.

Adult Marginally shorter-billed; shorter wings (wing point scarcely half length of tertials), browner legs and lack of obvious wing panel.

◆ Song variable but generally less powerful and repetitive than Icterine ◆ Sparrow-like call characteristic (sometimes given in song) ◆ Some lack yellowish plumage tones and can be confusing but facial, bill and tail tip features are critical field marks.

Zitting Cisticola (Fan-tailed Warbler) *Cisticola juncidis* 10cm (4")

Flight Fans tail during pulses of wingbeats in unique bouncing song-flight, uttering distinctive rasping *zip* at rise of each bound.

Status Locally common resident. Range periodically expands north but contracts after cold winters. Very rare vagrant UK and Ireland.

Adult Small size and boldly-striped mantle distinctive but check also for black and pale spots at tip of graduated tail.

◆ Tiny pale buff, but well-streaked, warbler of open grassy habitats ◆ Instantly recognised as it circles in characteristic jerky, bouncing song-flight above cornfields, meadows, lakesides, waste ground, etc. ◆ Otherwise keeps low in grasses but will sing from perch, when relatively big eye and large pinkish feet often striking ◆ When flushed look for tail-rim of dark and pale spots ◆ Walks on ground like miniature pipit.

River Warbler *Locustella fluviatilis* 14cm (5.5")

Adult Resembles Savi's but is olive-brown rather than rufous-brown in coloration, has bolder pale scaling on undertail-coverts and indistinct mottling or diffuse greyish streaking across breast (and sometimes throat).

Locally common summer visitor to E Europe, wintering in Africa. Very rare but increasingly frequent vagrant to UK, chiefly May-June.

◆ Rarely seen unless in song ◆ Closely resembles Savi's in size and plumage but habitat and song differs ◆ Attracts attention with its remarkable song, usually delivered from canopy of bush or low tree: a pulsating rhythmic *eeez-eeez-eeez-eeez.....*, not unlike a sewing machine. Starts-up suddenly, can continue for long spells but hard to pinpoint ◆ Favours woodland-edge and thickets by meandering rivers (whereas Savi's invariably haunts expansive reed-beds).

225

Grasshopper Warbler *Locustella naevia*   13cm (5")

Secretive warbler which attracts attention through its remarkable song – sounds like fishing line being continually reeled in. Sings mainly at dawn and dusk (also at night), often for minutes on end. Otherwise seldom encountered unless flushed from underfoot. Creeps mouse-like through dense ground cover. Adults and juveniles alike.

Adult Overall appearance rather dowdy. Soft dark streaks on olive-brown upperparts often hard to detect (unless close). Note narrow pale eye-ring, weak supercilium and dull white throat and belly. Rest of underparts buffy-white (some yellowish); variably weakly streaked but usually unmarked except for streaks on undertail-coverts visible at close range. Legs pale.

Often sings from concealment in low vegetation. Sometimes perches more openly to sing from low bush.

Broad, rounded tail hangs rather heavily, almost concealed from below by long, wide tail coverts (typical of *Locustella*). Bill is held permanently open whilst singing (another feature of *Locustellas*), the short wings and long tail vibrating continuously.

Flight Full tail seems to drag behind in flight.

Status Summer visitor, mid-April to Sep. Widely but thinly distributed throughout British Isles. Winters W. Africa. **Population** 16,000 pairs.

◆ Breeds in rank grass, weeds and tangled low scrub of young forestry plantations, heathland and brambly edges of marshes and coastal hollows ◆ Reeling song not especially loud but carries well (c500m); can be lost in blustery conditions so best listened for when still ◆ Singing birds have characteristic *Locustella* trait of rotating head hence sound seems to come and go, making it hard to pin-point – try checking likely song-posts 1-5ft above ground ◆ High-pitched, tinny, insect-like nature of song makes it difficult for some to hear ◆ Call is a sharp *cht* ◆ Much more extrovert Sedge Warbler is cleaner below, with ginger rump and bold creamy eyebrow.

Furtive *Locustella* warbler only likely to be seen when in song: a far-carrying, buzzing trill (sounds more like an insect than a bird). Otherwise creeps unnoticed through tangled vegetation at the base of dense reedbeds. All plumages similar.

Adult Closely resembles Reed Warbler in coloration but long broad, slightly scaled, undertail-coverts almost conceal tail underside, and narrow whitish curved edge to outerwing sometimes visible. More extensively brownish-buff below than Reed, with whitish only obvious on throat. Lacks grey tones of breast of Cetti's Warbler. On ground cocks broad tail high, hopping about on large pale feet (Reed Warbler's legs are greyish). ▶

Usually sings from a reed stem, typically perching just below the reed tops.

Very full, rounded tail seems to hang like a pendulum from singing bird. Like other *Locustellas*, habitually sings with head turning and bill wide open; all *Acrocephalus* warblers sing with bill constantly opening and closing revealing a vivid orange or red gape, whereas Savi's mouth is dull, pinkish.

Status Summer visitor (end April/May-August) to extensive reedbeds in S and E England (especially E Anglia and Kent). Winters tropical Africa. **Population** 5-20 pairs.

Flight Very full graduated tail is obvious.

◆ Favours extensive reedbeds ◆ Sings mainly in early morning and evening ◆ Song diagnostic; starts off slowly but soon speeds-up, then faster, lower in pitch and much more buzzing than Grasshopper Warbler – like the crackle of overhead power lines in fog. ◆ Typically utters c5-30 second bursts of song, often in quick succession ◆ Sharp *tchink-tchink* (like Cetti's) or Blackbird-like alarm chatter sometimes gives reedbed skulkers away.

Moustached Warbler *Acrocephalus melanopogon*   13cm (5")

Adult Richly-coloured, recalling Sedge but with bolder, blunter, chalky-white super-cilium (Sedge has more tapered creamy supercilium) contrasting with blackish crown and eye-stripe (beware worn Sedge can appear to have dusky crown, but Sedge has longer primary projection).

Status Extremely local resident and partial migrant (inland populations migratory). Accidental Britain.

Rufous-washed vent, flanks and breast sides contrast with greyish-white throat and central underparts.

◆ Overall russet colour and short-winged, full-tailed impresssion of flushed birds suggests Cetti's rather than Sedge Warbler ◆ Skulks in wetland vegetation, especially *Typha* (reedmace) beds ◆ Prone to prominent tail cocking as it hops through cover ◆ Song is characteristic; resembles Sedge Warbler's but less frantic, interspersed with diagnostic rising series of notes: *lu-lu-lu-lu lu...* ◆ Call a low, soft *chak*.

Aquatic Warbler *Acrocephalus paludicola*   13cm (5")

Adult Bold head pattern diagnostic in spring (when Sedge fully dark-crowned); note clear fine streaking on sides of breast and flanks. Lores can be dark in adults.

Status Exceedingly local summer visitor to eastern Europe. Winters in Africa, but passage route mysterious, seemingly regular migrant on autumn passage to S England, N France in August (almost all are juveniles).

◆ Very local breeder in tussocky meadows in open country ◆ Most likely to be seen on passage, typically in swampy vegetation at fringes of reed-beds ◆ A boldy-streaked little warbler (an impression not imparted by Sedge at all) ◆ Crown shows bold black sides with unstreaked, creamy-yellow central stripe and supercilium (juvenile Sedge can be similar but has weak streaking in central crown stripe) ◆ Bold straw-coloured stripes at sides of mantle are often obvious, contrasting with almost blackish mantle centre; the rump is clearly but more weakly streaked ◆ Extremely skulking, this is one of the most difficult of birds to see in the field ◆ Song resembles Sedge Warbler, but more sustained, less suddenly changing in content; is frequently punctuated by distinctive, flat trills *trrrrr......* (like twanging a wooden school ruler on edge of desk).

A dark-capped, white-browed warbler of wetland habitats. More extrovert than plain-backed Reed Warbler, with a livelier song, sometimes given in a characteristic excited display flight. Sexes similar.

Adult Quickly distinguished from other reed warblers by bold creamy ▶ eyebrow contrasting with blackish crown sides. Mantle clearly streaked in fresh plumage (but almost plain in many worn spring birds). Unstreaked gingery rump often catches the eye – especially in flight. Underparts creamy-white, washed olive-buff on flanks.

Juvenile Markedly brighter, buffier and more cleanly streaked than adult, with paler central crown stripe and weak spotting on breast visible when close (suggesting rare Aquatic Warbler). ▶

▼ **Aquatic Warbler juvenile** Paler, yellower or straw coloured, with more contrasting striping than adult and more sparse streaking on flanks (note juvenile Sedge has weak spots on breast sides). Note pale lores (dark in Sedge).

Flight Like Reed Warbler, flight low, jerky and seldom very far, before pitching into cover.

Status Common and widespread summer visitor and passage migrant (mid April-Sept). In Britain breeding N to Orkney. Winters in tropical Africa. **Population** c350,000 pairs.

◆ Breeds in wide range of marshy habitats, including overgrown ditches, wet meadows, bushy canal-banks, reedbeds and marshy edges of lakes, rivers, etc. ◆ Passage birds may be found in drier, bushier habitats ◆ Song not unlike Reed Warbler but the tempo is faster, more frantic and varied: a busier, more cheerful mix of musical phrases, harsh chattering and random squeaky whistled notes – as though constantly cursing and swearing under its breath ◆ Sings from reed or bush, often culminating in short, fluttering song flight (which Reed never does) – climbs steeply for 3-5m, then glides back to perch in slow, spiralling descent ◆ Call a hard *tuk, tuk* (scolding, Wren-like) ◆ Comes readily to investigate 'pishing', giving creaking *trrrr*.

229

Marsh Warbler *Acrocephalus palustris*   13cm (5")

Reed and Marsh Warblers are best separated by their very different songs and abundance (Marsh in the western part of its range is rare and localised). Separation by sight alone unreliable.

Adult Upperparts olive-brown; generally looks pale (especially rump), lacking Reed's rufous tones. Underparts, washed yellow-buff on chest and flanks. Also look for, slightly longer wings and paler edges to more contrasting tertials and primary tips.

Status Summer visitor. Rare breeder in S England, arriving late May. Rare on passage (end May-Oct). Winters SE Africa. **Population** c10-60prs.

Legs usually paler, pinkish-straw, at least in first-winter birds (adults often darker-legged, but claws paler than in Reed). Call a short *chet*.

◆ The key field mark to identify is voice ◆ Marsh vigorous, recalling Sedge; a supreme mimic, a lively chattering imitating a stream of different species mixed with characteristic Goldfinch twittering and *zi-chay* notes ◆ Prefers more varied damp habitats such as streamsides and coastal landslips, with nettlebeds, stands of tall herbs and osiers.

Reed Warbler *Acrocephalus scirpaceus*   13cm (5")

Adult Warmer than adult Marsh, tinged rufous with rusty rump; flanks darker, more rusty-buff and legs normally darker, grey-brown (but variable). Responds well to pishing; can often be coaxed into giving close views. Call a low *djerrr*.

On passage, both species can occur in hedges, coastal scrub, etc. Rather long under-tail coverts and graduated tail tip are useful pointers for eliminating *Hippolais* when faced with migrant Reed in atypical habitats.

Status Common summer visitor (late Apr-Oct). Rare Ireland (c50prs in SE). Widespread on passage. Winters tropical Africa. **Population** 40,000-80,000prs.

◆ Grumpy, monotonous: *churr churr churr, jag jag, chirruc chirruc chirruc...* as if just ticking over. Tied mainly to reedbeds (*Phragmites*), or fringing vegetation ◆ Usually sings from reed stem, gradually sidling up into view.

Great Reed Warbler *Acrocephalus arundinaceus* 18cm (7")

Adult Has more prominent supercilium (extending well beyond eye), stouter bill and stronger greyish legs than Reed Warbler. (Young birds in autumn are in fresh rufous and buff plumage, contrasting with greyer worn adults.)

Lumbers heavily through cover and clambers up reed stems to sing loud song from near or at top of reeds.

Status Locally common summer visitor (Apr-Sep). Winters tropical Africa. Annual vagrant Britain, chiefly S & SE England (in spring and autumn).

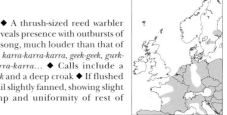

◆ A thrush-sized reed warbler ◆ Reveals presence with outbursts of powerful song, much louder than that of Reed Warbler: *karra-karra-karra, geek-geek, gurk-gurk, seep-seep, karra-karra...* ◆ Calls include a growled *gurrg*, a low *chak* and a deep croak ◆ If flushed from bank flies heavily with tail slightly fanned, showing slight contrast between rufous-buff rump and uniformity of rest of upperparts.

Blyth's Reed Warbler *Acrocephalus dumetorum* 13cm (5")

Adult Spring birds generally olive or greyish-brown above, with dark grey legs; first-autumn birds more variable, many quite warm brown above with paler fleshy-grey legs. Most reliable field mark is short primary projection, and relatively uniform tertials; the bill often appears more spiked and is darker than Reed or Marsh (bill of Marsh is the palest).

◆ An Asiatic species, gradually spreading west into north-east Europe ◆ Very similar to both Marsh and Reed Warblers ◆ Favours woodland edges, riverine thickets and parkland; Blyth's avoids reed-beds, but migrant Reed may be found in woods ◆ Hops about in low to mid level of tree canopy with tail slightly cocked, calling with a dry *tack* and the occasional *churrg* ◆ Song distinctive; varied but sweet and slow, with steady, plodding delivery; includes some mimicry and repetition (like Song Thrush), incorporates a characteristic liquid *sweedledoo* ◆ Overlaps with Marsh; Blyth's prefers larger trees. ◆ Local summer visitor to Baltic region (May-September); winters in south-east Asia. Rare vagrant to Britain late August and September, North Sea coasts.

Spectacled Warbler *Sylvia conspicillata*   13cm (5")

Spring male Suggests tiny Whitethroat but has blackish lores, broken white eye ring and whole wing appears sandy-rufous with blackish centres only on tertials and bend of wing (not on greater coverts).

Status Locally common summer visitor; some present in winter in Camargue. Accidental Britain.

Juvenile/fresh female Can ▶ appear almost uniform dull mousy or buffish-brown with sandy-rufous wings.

◆ Perches on bush tops with tail half-cocked before diving into dense cover or flitting quickly low between bushes ◆ Song a hurried chattering, recalling Whitethroat but faster and somewhat higher in pitch, often given in flight ◆ Calls include a short *taktak* and a distinctive rasping rattled *tcharrr*.

Subalpine Warbler *Sylvia cantillans*   13cm (5")

Female Dull brown above and dull pinky-buff below, with strikingly white undertail-coverts. First-autumn birds often have rufous fringes to wing feathers (cf. Spectacled) and lack obvious white in outer tail. ▶

◀ **Male** Distinctive in having bluish-grey upperparts and pinkish to rusty-orange throat and breast with conspicuous white malar stripe.

◆ A small *Sylvia* of wooded and bushy Mediterranean hills and mountainsides ◆ Skulking when not in song, keeping to cover of bushes and small trees, feeding both low down and up into canopy; often hopping into view on bushtops with tail cocked like a Dartford ◆ Song recalls a hurried Whitethroat song but slightly thinner and more musical; often given in flight ◆ Calls include a soft *chat chat chat chat*, the notes often running into a chatter ◆ Locally common summer visitor. Winters in Africa ◆ Annual vagrant Britain.

Sardinian Warbler *Sylvia melanocephala*   13cm (5")

Female Suggests drab, stocky Whitethroat but lacks rufous in wing and has red orbital ring (lacking in first-autumn birds) and brownish-buff underparts.

◀ **Male** Black hood, pure white throat, greyish underparts and red eyes are distinctive.

Juveniles show no white in tail.

Status Chiefly resident. Rare vagrant Britain.

◆ Locally common in bushy scrub with scattered trees, especially in coastal areas ◆ Machine-gun-like, loud, stuttering, rattled chatter of a call betrays bird's presence ◆ Often first glimpsed jerkily flying over low scrub, showing narrow white outers and corners to spread tail as it dives back into cover ◆ Keeps to cover of dense scrub, feeding near ground, popping up to give bursts of song – a sustained musical chattering, Whitethroat-like but with bursts of rattling call included.

Orphean Warbler *Sylvia hortensis*   15.5cm (6")

Male Dusky hood, contrasting with white throat. Eyes are pale in adults, brown in younger birds, but iris colour surprisingly difficult to see in the field. ▶

Female and immature Like giant Lesser Whitethroat.

Status Locally numerous summer visitor. Winters in Africa. Accidental Britain.

◆ Large grey warbler of wooded southern hillsides, gardens and olive groves ◆ Keeps well hidden in foliage of shrubbery and trees ◆ Best located by its song: a slow, thrush-like warble, repeated with slight variations and brief pauses ◆ White tail sides seem to extend round tail corners when alighting with tail spread ◆ Call a hard Blackcap-like *tak-tak* and a coarse *churrrr*.

233

Barred Warbler *Sylvia nisoria*   15.5cm (6")

Juvenile Sandy-grey above and whitish below. Resembles Garden Warbler but heavier, with stronger bill and noticeably longer tail. Weak barring on flanks, pale margins to flight feathers (especially tertials) and faint double wing-bar confirm identity.

Status Summer visitor (May-Sep). Winters E Africa. In Britain, scarce autumn migrant, mainly east coast (Aug-Oct).

Adult Grey with crescentic barring below and a staring yellow eye – like a pint-sized Cuckoo.

◆ Big, lethargic warbler ◆ Breeds in eastern part of region, frequenting open bushy country ◆ Skulks for hours in thick scrub, betrayed only by distinctive slowing rattle, like scolding sparrow ◆ Song recalls Garden Warbler's, and is sometimes delivered in brief display flight.

Garden Warbler *Sylvia borin*   14cm (5.5")

Voice and apparent lack of fieldmarks is key to identification of Garden Warbler. Plumper than Blackcap, with stubbier bill and more rounded crown. Prominent dark eye gives gentle expression.

Adult and juvenile Alike; uniformly grey-brown above (no cap) and buff-white below (warmest on breast and flanks).

Status Widespread summer visitor and passage migrant, mid Apr-Oct (reaches Britain in May). Winters c/s Africa. **Population** 200,000 territories.

At close range, thin white eye ring, hint of a pale supercilium, grey shading on sides of neck and pale tips to tertials and primaries, are important characters.

◆ Breeds commonly in thick scrub and open mixed woodland with rich undergrowth, tangled young plantations and clearings with bushy regrowth ◆ Mostly skulks in thick cover, but periodically emerges in crown of trees when singing ◆ Song like Blackcap's, but softer and more sustained, without latter's high, fluted peaks. Has more the character of a babbling brook – a brisk, even warble that may flow almost unbroken for several minutes ◆ Call a harsh *tchek* (softer than Blackcap's stony *tac*).

Blackcap *Sylvia atricapilla* 14cm (5.5")

Grey woodland warbler with a distinctive capped appearance. Forms a species pair with Garden Warbler; both more often heard than seen. Songs sound confusingly similar at first, but the two species can be separated with practice.

Adult male Grey-brown above and greyish-white below, with silver-grey face and nape. Diagnostic black cap finishes neatly at eye level. (Never has black bib shown by superficially similar Marsh and Willow Tits).

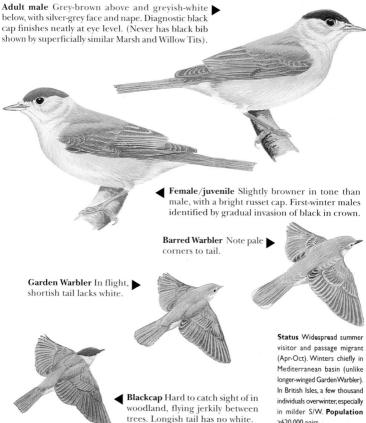

Female/juvenile Slightly browner in tone than male, with a bright russet cap. First-winter males identified by gradual invasion of black in crown.

Barred Warbler Note pale corners to tail.

Garden Warbler In flight, shortish tail lacks white.

Blackcap Hard to catch sight of in woodland, flying jerkily between trees. Longish tail has no white.

Status Widespread summer visitor and passage migrant (Apr-Oct). Winters chiefly in Mediterranean basin (unlike longer-winged Garden Warbler). In British Isles, a few thousand individuals overwinter, especially in milder S/W. **Population** >620,000 pairs.

◆ Common in open mixed and deciduous woods, parks and gardens with tall trees and lush understorey ◆ Sings vigorously from cover, occasionally from crown of tree; generally less skulking than Garden Warbler ◆ Full song is sweeter, more powerful and varied than Garden Warbler's, delivered in shorter, snappier phrases – a rich, melodious warbling with tell-tale clear, fluting notes hitting high sweet peaks ◆ Occurs more widely on passage (sometimes numerous on coasts) ◆ In autumn, frequently seen feeding on berry-laden elders in warm, sunny spots ◆ Hard *tac* note (used throughout year) can be imitated by striking two small pebbles together.

235

Lesser Whitethroat *Sylvia curruca*   13.5cm (5.25")

Slim, subtly attractive warbler with knack of slipping unseen through leafy hedgerows and scrub. Often betrays whereabouts by its dull rattling song or hard, Blackcap-like *tac* – like sound produced by knocking two pebbles together. Periodically works its way to top or edge of cover, when pale silky-white throat catches the eye. Grey head with darker grey ear-coverts gives characteristic (if somewhat variable) masked appearance.

Adult breeding Slightly smaller and shorter-tailed than Whitethroat. Distinguished from latter by its duller, more grey-brown upperparts, darker eyes, steel-grey legs and absence of rufous in wings. Bill blackish. ▶

First-winter In fresh autumn plumage (from late August) adults and first-winters look much alike, some displaying a narrow pale supercilium and eye-ring. First-winter separable at close range by bluish base to lower mandible and paler greyer eyes.

▶

Status Fairly common summer visitor (mid Apr-Sep), but scarce or absent as breeding bird over most of N/W Britain. Some passage birds linger into Oct. Migrates through E Mediterranean to winter in E Africa.
Population 80,000 territories.

Flight Birds darting from cover look silvery below, with white outertails.

◆ Generally prefers areas of taller scrub than Whitethroat – bushy commons, hawthorn and blackthorn thickets, tall hedgerows and woodland edge ◆ Distinctive song a loud, rather flat rattle (much like opening half-dozen notes of Yellowhammer's song), sometimes preceded by a subdued musical warbling, audible only at close quarters ◆ Voice usually emanates from thick scrubby cover; occasionally sings in short flights between bushes but never in dancing song-flight like Whitethroat ◆ Seems less secretive in autumn (certainly call is heard more), when attracted to ripe elderberries.

236

About size of Robin, but slimmer and stance much less upright. At a glance, looks ginger above and buff-white below, with a clear white throat. Differs from similar Lesser Whitethroat in its bright rusty wing margins, darker and more contrasting tertial centres, pale legs and light brown iris. Sexes differ (in Lesser Whitethroat, sexes are alike).

Breeding male Ash-grey head and pinkish tinge ▶ to breast. White throat puffs in song, giving a ragged or bearded appearance. Pale iris gives distinctly agitated look.

◀ **Juvenile and first-winter** Resemble female but have softer, more evenly buff coloration and dark brown eyes.

◀ **Adult female** Generally browner than male. Duller eyes give less intense expression.

Flight When pressed, flits low and rather jerkily away, showing longish tail with prominent white sides; soon dives into cover again.

Status Common and widespread summer visitor, subject to periodic population crashes associated with drought in its African wintering grounds. In British Isles arrives from second half April (later in north), most departing again in Aug-Sept; a few linger into October. **Population** 700,000-800,000 territories.

◆ Excitable and rather leggy *Sylvia* frequenting nettlebeds and brambles, bushy heaths and commons, hedgerows and scrubby banks ◆ Habitually raises its crown feathers in excitement or alarm ◆ Suddenly pops up atop brambles or low scrub, bobbing and curtsying nervously on approach ◆ Remains hidden, scolding intruder with distinctive low *jerr* or faster *vet, vet* calls until danger is past ◆ Song a short, scratchy warble, frequently repeated. Usually delivered from an open perch (bushtop, post or wire) or in characteristic short, dancing song-flight before returning to perch or dropping back to cover.

Dartford Warbler *Sylvia undata*   13cm (5")

Tiny long-tailed warbler of dry lowland heath and Mediterranean scrub. At a glance appears wholly dark – almost as if silhouetted – and markedly long, thin tail (accounts for half of total length) is cocked over back in characteristic pose.

Adult male Upperparts dark grey to slaty-brown; underparts dull vinous-red, with a whitish belly. At close range, fine white spotting visible on throat giving suggestion of a dull moustache. Male has orange or red eyes and eye-ring. Legs yellowish or reddish.

Adult female Usually slightly browner above and paler, more pinkish or rufous-buff below. Eyes and eye-ring generally duller and browner. Juvenile even paler and buffier below.

Status Mainly resident, not uncommon in SW Europe. In Britain rare and localised in S England. Dispersive or locally migratory outside breeding season. **Population** Increasing, >1000 pairs, but hard weather causes declines.

Flight Flies weakly on whirring wings, bobbing tail. Rarely travels far, skimming ground vegetation before diving into next bush.

◆ Restless and elusive (though can be quite tame), usually seen singly or in pairs in coastal thickets or inland heaths with plenty of gorse and tall heather ◆ Best located by its rather weak song: a short, scratching warble, most reminiscent of a distant Whitethroat ◆ Rises to about 6m in brief hovering song flight but sings mainly from topmost spray of low bush, with tail and crown feathers raised. After a few moments, typically drops back down into cover ◆ Frustratingly, can remain hidden in the scantiest cover or scampers along ground, objecting to close approach with a low, drawn-out *djarr* or rattling *trtrtutuk.*

Least numerous of the three *Phylloscopus* or leaf warblers nesting in Britain; more common in Europe, especially in forested east. Larger and generally more vivid than Willow Warbler, though occasional dull individuals occur. Reaches Europe in mid April and slips away, almost unnoticed, from late July (remarkably few seen on passage).

Adult Contrast between primrose yellow ▶ face and breast and snow-white belly identifies. Upperparts beech leaf green, with clean yellow supercilium. Pale legs and bright pink lower mandible. Notice strongly-patterned wings: very dark-centred tertials and yellow edgings to flight feathers.

Whole bird quivers in song and when seen overhead, the markedly long drooping wings and short tail create an unmistakable image – recognisable even in silhouette.

Forages high in woodland canopy, where easily overlooked but for distinctive voice. Has various favoured song-posts (frequently returning to same), but also performs characteristic 'fluttering parachute' song-flights from one branch to another.

Status Widespread summer visitor (mid Apr-Sep). In Britain, main centre of population lies in west, but surprisingly rare in Ireland (c30 pairs). Winters central Africa. **Population** 17,000 territories.

◆ Breeds in mature deciduous or mixed woods, usually with a sparse understorey; particularly fond of oak, birch and beech ◆ Has two distinct songs: most frequent type begins with stuttering note and accelerates into a beautiful shivering trill, *stip stip stitititititipp shrreee* – like the sound of a coin spinning to rest on a plate. Each song lasts c3 secs, but may be repeated up to 8 times a minute ◆ Second song type is performed less often, a series of 4-20 clear piping notes, *pew pew pew....* Is sometimes given as prelude to trilling song ◆ Call is a soft, melancholy *pew*, easily mistaken for the familiar piping note of a Bullfinch (but quite unlike the anxious *hooeet* call of Willow Warbler).

Chiffchaff *Phylloscopus collybita* 10-11cm (4.25")

Named after its distinctive song. One of the earliest summer migrants (first arrivals often frequent waterside bushes and trees). Also tends to linger later in autumn. Warblers seen in north-west Europe during November-March are usually this species. Drabber than Willow Warbler with more rounded crown, shorter primary projection, indistinct supercilium, dark legs and different voice.

Spring adult Differs from Willow Warbler in its dowdy brownish- ▶ olive upperparts, buff-white underparts, and darker legs and bill. Thin, broken eye ring generally appears brighter and more distinct than supercilium.

◀ **Autumn adult** From September, adults and first-winters alike; much fresher, more olive above and buff below.

Siberian race *tristis* (rare but annual in late autumn) Lacks any olive ▶ or yellow, with quite noticeable pale wing-bar in fresh plumage (bar longer and more diffuse than in Greenish, which has fleshy lower mandible and different call). Scandinavian race *abietinus* (occurs on passage) is greyer above, whiter below than nominate.

Sings from crown of large trees. Characteristically jerks tail with each note, as though pumping sound out.

Status Common summer visitor and passage migrant (Mar-Nov). Winters chiefly Mediterranean basin, also sparsely in milder regions of Britain/Ireland. **Population** 930,000 territories.

Primary projection is shorter than on Willow Warbler (length A barely half of B), reflecting Chiffchaff's shorter annual migrations.

◆ Monotonous song (heard on fine days at any season) frequently runs out of sequence: *chiff-chaff., chaff-chiff, chiff-chaff....*; low, stuttering *terr terr...* notes audible at close range, as if song struggling to get going ◆ Fidgets about foliage, with flicking wings. Distinctive habit of twitching tail downwards is useful characteristic ◆ Call louder, more forceful and monosyllabic than that of Willow Warbler: *wheet.*; also a more plaintive *peeep* and a loose *sweeo* are given by autumn and winter birds (many of which show features of eastern races) ◆ Breeds in open woodland and copses with scrubby undergrowth, preferring more mature timber than Willow Warbler.

240

Common summer migrant. Has the slim form, fine bill and dull greenish appearance characteristic of all *Phylloscopus*. Closely resembles Chiffchaff, from which best distinguished by voice, longer primary projection and (usually) pale legs. Many northern birds however lack yellow tones in plumage and are very brown and white.

Spring adult Differs from Chiffchaff in its lighter upperparts with ▶ fresher, olive tone and cleaner underparts, most with a delicate yellow tint to face and upper breast. Sharper, yellower supercilium, more obvious orangey bill base and pinky-brown legs are important features. A few have dark legs but (unlike Chiffchaff) toes are usually still pale.

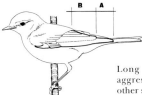

◀ First-winter More brightly coloured, extensively yellow or yellow-buff below, with a strong yellow eyebrow (more vivid than any Chiffchaff). Freshly moulted adults similar, but whiter on belly.

Willow Warbler is a long-winged, long-distance migrant and primary projection is correspondingly long, especially in males (lengths A and B about equal). Females are smaller and relatively shorter-winged and easily confused with Chifffchaff.

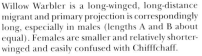

Long wings evident in often aggressive, dashing pursuit of other small birds from its patch.

Status Ubiquitous summer visitor (Apr-Sep/Oct). Winters tropical Africa. **Population** >3,000,000 territories.

◆ Breeds in most open wooded habitats (including heaths with scattered trees, forest edge, young plantations, clearings with bushy regrowth) ◆ Likely almost anywhere on passage, sometimes in big falls on coasts ◆ Actions quick and restless, but without habitual tail twitch of foraging Chiffchaff. Hovers and flycatches, but feeds mainly by gleaning insects from foliage ◆ Song immediately identifies: a lovely, mellow scale of 3-5 seconds duration, which drops gently like a falling leaf and ends in a flourish ◆ Disyllabic *hoo-eet* call is plaintive and has an enquiring quality; separable with care from the more emphatic single *wheet* of Chiffchaff.

241

Western Bonelli's Warbler *Phylloscopus bonelli*   11cm (4.5")

Adult Brighter white underparts and dull grey-brown upperparts suggest a washed-out Chiffchaff, but yellowish-green wings are more boldly patterned, with particularly dark centres to tertials.

Status Common summer visitor, wintering in tropical Africa. Annual vagrant Britain, chiefly May/Sept.

The yellowish rump and uppertail-coverts are usually hard to see unless bird hovers briefly whilst feeding.

◆ A very pale, lively little woodland warbler ◆ Breeds in broad-leaved, mixed and pure coniferous forests, especially in hilly country ◆ Distinctive song (not unlike twittering Greenfinch): a dry stuttering trill, lower and more even in pitch, and shorter, than trill of Wood Warbler. Typical call a rising sweet *pr'eee* or *doo-eee* ◆ Has a plainer head pattern than most other leaf-warblers, obvious very dark eye and fleshy lower mandible. Legs are often quite pale ◆ Chiffchaff of race *tristis* similarly dull and whitish but has blackish bill and legs, shorter primaries, stronger supercilium and less patterned wings ◆ An arboreal warbler, very active, readily hovering and fly-catching in short bursts as it works its way through the canopy.

Greenish Warbler *Phylloscopus trochiloides*   11cm (4.5")

Adult In fresh plumage olive-brown above, tinged greyish on mantle, contrasting with creamy-white underparts, supercilium and wing-bar.

Abraded birds (first-summer in spring and adults in late summer and autumn) are drab grey-brown overall with wing-bar reduced to a series of spots, a fine line, or even absent.

Status Uncommon summer visitor to Baltic region. Winters in SE Asia. Regular vagrant Britain, occasional in June, chiefly late August and September, mostly E England.

At all ages fleshy-orange lower mandible, often exaggerated by habit of carrying bill angled upwards makes bill appear stouter and fleshier than that of Chiffchaff or Willow Warbler.

◆ An Asiatic species, gradually spreading west into north-east Europe ◆ Favours broad-leaved woodlands, parks and large gardens ◆ Sings and forages in upper tree canopy ◆ Song distinctive: a cheery *si ti twee, si ti twe, si ti twe, si twe, sitwesitisitisti* ◆ Call a sweet, sparrow-like, rising *ch'wee* or *tselee*.

Pallas's Warbler *Phylloscopus proregulus*   9cm (3.5")

Yellow crown-stripe often apparent as bird peers under leaves for invertebrates – but may be concealed as bird flits about tree-tops.

The paler, cleaner cheeks, blacker eye-stripe and darker-looking lower mandible of Pallas's are then helpful distinctions from below.

Tell-tale yellow rump patch may be glimpsed in flight, but is obvious if bird hovers whilst foraging.

◆ Smallest leaf-warbler ◆ Closely resembles Yellow-browed, but has diagnostic clear yellow central crown-stripe and rump patch. In addition, is usually brighter green above, with yellower wing-bars and broader, yellower supercilium ◆ Prone to bouts of repeated hovering whilst foraging (Yellow-browed only occasionally hovers, and does not do so habitually) ◆ Call a thin *weest* or *tsee*, flatter and less piercing than Yellow-browed ◆ Increasingly frequent vagrant from Siberia ◆ In Britain most likely at eastern and southern coast migration points, late October.

Yellow-browed Warbler *Phylloscopus inornatus*   10cm (4")

Bold ribbon-like bar crosses full width of wing but pattern is shared by rarer Pallas's which can be very similar if viewed in dull-light from below.

Though may show hint of a paler crown centre, this is never clear yellow like a Pallas's, and rump is always olive.

◆ Lively little leaf warbler with striking long, creamy supercilium and double wing-bars ◆ Often feeds in willows and sycamores, sometimes accompanying parties of Goldcrests, Firecrests and tits – but flits actively about canopy ◆ Slightly longer-bodied than Firecrest, from which quickly distinguished by wide bar across width of wing ◆ Call a distinctive rising *t'sweeet*, very similar to that of Coal Tit ◆ Regular vagrant from Siberia, winters south-east Asia. Annual visitor to Britain, most likely on eastern and southern coasts September/October. Rarely overwinters in sheltered south-western valleys.

Goldcrest *Regulus regulus* 9cm (3.5")

Europe's smallest bird. Prefers conifers, foraging in treetops where its persistent, *si-si-si* draws attention. Typical view is of dull buffy belly and short, notched tail, or of restless, wing-flicking silhouette. Tiny, rounded form, needle-like bill and golden central-parting of crown edged with black quickly eliminates all but similar Firecrest.

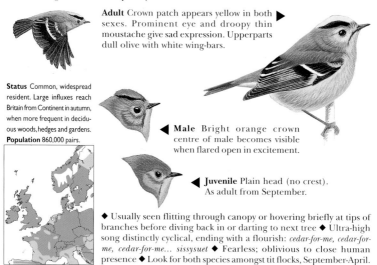

Adult Crown patch appears yellow in both sexes. Prominent eye and droopy thin moustache give sad expression. Upperparts dull olive with white wing-bars.

Status Common, widespread resident. Large influxes reach Britain from Continent in autumn, when more frequent in deciduous woods, hedges and gardens. **Population** 860,000 pairs.

Male Bright orange crown centre of male becomes visible when flared open in excitement.

Juvenile Plain head (no crest). As adult from September.

◆ Usually seen flitting through canopy or hovering briefly at tips of branches before diving back in or darting to next tree ◆ Ultra-high song distinctly cyclical, ending with a flourish: *cedar-for-me, cedar-for-me, cedar-for-me... sissysuet* ◆ Fearless; oblivious to close human presence ◆ Look for both species amongst tit flocks, September-April.

Firecrest *Regulus ignicapillus* 9cm (3.5")

Female

Status Resident (summer visitor C/E Europe. In Britain scarce breeder in S England. Uncommon on passage in coastal S England and Wales, small numbers wintering. **Population** 50-100 pairs.

Brighter than Goldcrest, whiter below and greener above. Stunning head pattern: wide chalky supercilium, clashing with the dusky eyestripe and grey cheeks. Male (right) has flaming orange crown-stripe when flared (yellow in female, left).

Male

Juvenile Ephemeral juvenile stage, lacks crest but has whitish supercilium.

◆ Has a passion for ivy and holm oaks; watch out for wintering birds in sheltered waterside willows ◆ Spends less time in each tree, moving on after furtive search of the foliage (Goldcrest is more thorough in its leaf-searching) ◆ Call less shrill (lower and slower) *ze-ze-zeep* or a single *zeep*. Song similar, accelerates but lacks terminal flourish: *zizizizizitt.*

244

Spotted Flycatcher *Muscicapa striata* — 14cm (5.5")

Robin-sized bird of tree canopy. Long slim form, faintly streaked crown, softly streaked breast, and absence of white in wing and tail distinguishes adult from other flycatchers. Only juvenile is truly spotted. Sits upright on fences, exposed snags or at sunlit edge of cover, where gleam of silky white underparts often first catches the eye. Watches for insects which it captures in flight with an audible snap of bill.

Adult Unspotted. Mouse-brown upper-parts with pale fringes to wing feathers, big dark eye, spiky black bill (noticeably broad at base when viewed from below) and short dark legs always characteristic. ▶

◀ **Juvenile** Boldly marked with pale buff spots on head and especially mantle and scapulars. Resembles adult after moult (July-September) into first-winter plumage, but broader buff margins to flight feathers often create distinct impression of a pale wing-bar. (Never so bold as white wing and tail flashes of similar juvenile Pied.)

Flight Long wings evident in elegant, dashing flight. Twists and turns with great agility in pursuit of flying insects before returning to same or nearby perch, with much nervous flicking and flirting of wings. Seconds later, darts out again.

Status Widespread summer visitor and passage migrant. Rarely arrives Britain before beginning of May; departs Sep/Oct. Winters tropical Africa. **Population** c150,000 pairs; declining.

◆ Nests in open forest, woodland edge, mature parks and gardens ◆ High-pitched squeaky *tzee*, like rotation of a rusty wheelbarrow wheel, often first sign of presence (easily dismissed as call of Robin or fledgling bird) ◆ Poor song easily overlooked – merely an extension of the call, a short series of faint squeaks with a brief pause between each note ◆ Alarm call, *tzee-tzucc* ◆ Usually solitary or in pairs.

Red-breasted Flycatcher *Ficedula parva*   11.5cm (4.5")

Adult male Red bib and big eye suggest ▶ diminutive Robin, but eye-ring, tail markings, grey head and fly-catching behaviour identify.

Status Summer visitor. Scarce annual migrant to E/SW Britain (Aug-Nov); very rarely in spring.

◀

Female and first-year Brown head and creamy chest. First-years differ slightly in variable buffish tips to tertials and wing-coverts; some males have rosy flush to chest.

◆ Smallest and most secretive of Europe's flycatchers, recognised in all plumages by its distinct pale eye-ring and bold white wedges at base of dark, frequently cocked tail ◆ Breeds only in east of region ◆ Darts restlessly about shady canopy of dank mixed and deciduous forest ◆ Dry, Wren-like rattle, *zrrrrt* often betrays migrants ◆ Fluty, falling song suggests sad Willow Warbler.

Collared Flycatcher *Ficedula albicollis*   13cm (5")

Breeding male Distinguished from Pied by ▶ large white forehead patch, broad white collar, pale rump and extensive white patch at base of primaries.

Female Upperparts typically more grey-brown than similar female Pied, often with ghost of male's collar and rump patch. ▶

Status Summer visitor (May-Sep). Vagrant Britain.

Note bigger, club-shaped white patch at base of primaries (lacking or much narrower in female Pied).

◆ More contrasting than Pied Flycatcher, which breeds alongside in mature deciduous woods across middle Europe, with outpost in Baltic ◆ Habits as Pied, but song and clear, penetrating *seep* call (quite unlike Pied) diagnostic ◆ Uninspired song a mix of slow, squeaky notes, *seep* calls and occasional musical phrases ◆ Males indistinguishable from females after summer moult, both closely resembling Pied.

Pied Flycatcher *Ficedula hypoleuca* 13cm (5")

Always distinguished from larger Spotted Flycatcher by its dumpier shape and conspicuous white markings in wing and tail. Male unmistakably pied in spring but virtually identical to drabber female after moult July/August. Only Collared Flycatcher of eastern Europe is closely similar, but compare Pied Wagtail and female Chaffinch, both of which fly-catch at times.

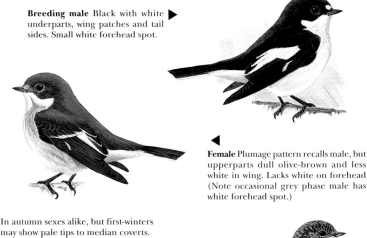

Breeding male Black with white ▶ underparts, wing patches and tail sides. Small white forehead spot.

◀ **Female** Plumage pattern recalls male, but upperparts dull olive-brown and less white in wing. Lacks white on forehead (Note occasional grey phase male has white forehead spot.)

In autumn sexes alike, but first-winters may show pale tips to median coverts.

Juvenile Mottled, like juvenile ▶ Spotted Flycatcher. Check for bold white wing and tail markings.

Status Widespread summer visitor and passage migrant (Apr-Oct). **Population** 35,000-40,000 pairs (Remarkably, 1-2 pairs only in Ireland).

Flight White in wings and tail show best in flight, and on alighting when tail is cocked and wings flicked in nervy, Dunnock-like fashion.

◆ Breeds in tree holes and nestboxes, mainly in deciduous woods. In Britain, locally abundant in hill oak and birch in west ◆ Short, sweet but rather variable and insignificant song based on sequence of double notes *zeecha* or *tseeplee* (can suggest Reed Bunting, Great Tit and Common Redstart) ◆ Will perch openly but prefers cover of leafy canopy, passing unnoticed but for sudden sally after fly or to pluck insect from bark ◆ Listen for persistent sharp *pik, pik...* calls ◆ Frequently returns to different perch (unlike Spotted) ◆ During midsummer moult is quiet and difficult to find ◆ Common migrant in Britain, especially on east and south coasts late August-early October.

247

Bearded Tit *Panurus biarmicus* 16.5cm (6.5")

Acrobatic bird of tawny colour and very long tail. Restricted to reedbeds, where more often heard than seen. Call a loud, twanging *pting*, like two coins flicked together (virtually diagnostic, but can be copied precisely by Reed Warbler). Typically sidles up reed-stem to perch briefly in view, then whizzes away.

Adult male Strikingly handsome with bright tawny body ▶ and uniquely patterned blue-grey head, showing long, droopy black moustaches, orange eyes and bright yellow-orange bill. Wings attractively banded in black, white and tawny. Pale below; black undertail-coverts diagnostic.

Juvenile female

◀ **Juvenile** Both sexes resemble adult female but are deeper orange-buff, with bold black saddle and edges to tail. Male (left) has black lores and yellow bill; female (top left) has greyish lores and dark bill.

Juvenile male

Adult female Plain brown head and duller bill, ▶ but overall pale buff colour and long tail always distinctive. Undertail-coverts buff.

Status Largely resident, but periodically dispersive; patchily distributed in larger reedbeds across region. In winter, sometimes appears in small reedy stands beside reservoirs. **Population** c400 pairs (England).

Flight Fast and low across reed tops, with whirring wings and long, wobbly tail streaming behind. Concludes with abrupt dive into reeds.

◆ Prolific breeder but populations fluctuate greatly due to cold weather losses and irruptive dispersals in autumn. Such movements preceded by groups flying high above reeds ◆ Tame but restless ◆ Best looked for on calm, bright days – watch for birds hopping along muddy margins of reedbeds or creeping through broken stems at waterline, gleaning insects and seeds ◆ Gentle pishing encourages them to show ◆ Despite name, is actually related to the Asian babblers.

Long-tailed Tit *Aegithalos caudatus*   14cm (5.5")

Restless small bird of deciduous and mixed woods, hedgerows and bushy heaths, usually encountered in pairs or extended family units of up to 20. Looks black and white at any distance, with a tiny black bill and inquiring pin head eyes. The extraordinarily long tail – accounts for over half total length – is unique among small woodland birds.

Adult Rosy-pink scapulars, rump and vent ▶ and a white crown bordered by thick black stripe over eye.

◀

Juvenile Tail markedly shorter than adult's at first (and frequently bent like a spoon owing to the contours of the nest). Plumage darker and fluffier than adult's, without any pink; broad chocolate mask and white flash across chocolate wings distinctive. As adult after moult (August-September).

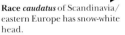

Race *caudatus* of Scandinavia/ ▶ eastern Europe has snow-white head.

Flight Weak, wobbly and bouncing, with long tail trailing like the stick of a fluffy lollipop.

Status Common resident. Widely distributed but scarce or absent in far N/W. **Population** 250,000 pairs.

◆ Not a true tit, but equally acrobatic ◆ Commonly joins roving tit flocks – its constant calls often first indication that a feeding party is approaching (if you miss them first time, they often come by again) ◆ Listen for characteristic dry, rippling *tsyrupp* and quieter, tongue-clicking *tupp, tupp* notes ◆ Chorus of excited, high Goldcrest-like *tsee-tsee-tsee* calls signals flock is on the move. Watch then for follow-my-leader procession of birds from one stand of trees to next ◆ Feeds from highest treetops to lowest shrubs, oblivious to close approach ◆ Constructs remarkable domed nest of cobwebs, moss, lichen and feathers in low thorny scrub or fork of tree.

Marsh Tit *Parus palustris*   11.5cm (4.5")

Marsh and Willow Tits are difficult to separate and can confuse even experienced birdwatchers (Willow passed completely unnoticed in Britain until 1900). Subtle differences in plumage discernible only when close – first check wings, then head. Location and habitat sometimes help, but most reliable distinguishing feature is voice. Smaller Coal Tit displays obvious white wing-bars and nape patch.

Race *palustris* (Northern Britain/North-west Europe) Lacks ▶ pale panel on wing. Appears grey-brown above with white cheeks; rest of underparts grey-white. Looks well-groomed, sleeker than Willow Tit, with glossier black cap and smaller black bib, neatly trimmed like Charlie Chaplin moustache. At close range, neat black cap reveals blue sheen, most obvious on forecrown.

◀ Race *dresseri* (Southern Britain/ North-west France) Distinctly warm brown above, with an even buff wash below. (Beware hint of wing panel in fresh plumage).

Prefers dry, open deciduous and mixed woodlands and parkland, especially oak and beech in spite of name. Seldom in conifers.

Status Sedentary resident. In Britain, patchily distributed north to south-east Scotland.
Population 60,000 pairs.

◆ Forages alone or in pairs, but (in Britain at least) more inclined than Willow Tit to join roving tit flocks ◆ Often seeks seeds and berries beneath trees and in undergrowth ◆ Seems more volatile than Willow, with diagnostic loud, sneezing call, *sit-choo!* (often followed by a repeated, harsh scolding note) ◆ Various songs include a rapid, monotonous series of notes, *chip-chip-chip-chip-chip-chip-chip*, unlike any other tit ◆ Nests in ready-made tree-hole or nestbox ◆ Juveniles have dull cap, separable from Willow Tit only by voice.

Willow Tit *Parus montanus*   11.5cm (4.5")

Unlike Marsh Tit, whitish fringes to secondaries create characteristic pale panel on closed wing. Large head with matt black cap, slightly longer black bib with tattier edges (like stubbly growth), and fluffier flank feathers sometimes a suggestion of paler outer-tail feathers, but best distinguished from Marsh Tit by voice.

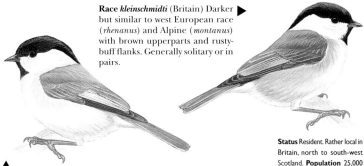

Race *kleinschmidti* (Britain) Darker ▶ but similar to west European race (*rhenanus*) and Alpine (*montanus*) with brown upperparts and rusty-buff flanks. Generally solitary or in pairs.

Status Resident. Rather local in Britain, north to south-west Scotland. **Population** 25,000 pairs.

▲
Race *borealis* (Scandinavia) Palest and most distinctive race; greyer above and whiter below, with pure white cheeks and frostier wing panel. Forms social groups and joins other tits in winter.

◆ Prefers damp woodland, waterside thickets of birch, willow and alder. In Scandinavia and mountains of central Europe, however, associated with coniferous and mixed forest ◆ Usually found by its diagnostic call: a harsh, drawn-out, nasal, *si-si-TCHAY TCHAY...* (the two introductory notes faint and high) ◆ Infrequent song a clear, descending *tiu tiu tiu....*, like piping song of Wood Warbler ◆ Song of Alpine race *montanus* quite different: a pure, soft, melancholy whistle, *ü ü ü ü....* ◆ Excavates own nest hole in rotten trunk.

Siberian Tit *Parus cinctus*   13.5cm (5.25")

Adult Larger than northern Willow Tit, with a longer tail, dull brown cap and bigger, scruffier black bib.

◆ Untidy looking tit confined to northernmost boreal forests ◆ Cinnamon-brown mantle and pale rusty flanks (faded in summer) distinctive ◆ Hoarse calls include repeated *chee chee chee* ◆ Tame but sparsely distributed resident ◆ Not in UK and Ireland.

The only small woodland bird with a prominent spiky crest. Closely tied to mature coniferous forest (especially pine and spruce), often with a heathery understorey and a scattering of deciduous trees. Most easily found by walking quiet forest trail and listening out for characteristic trilling call, a dry, rolling *tchirr-r-r-r...* (suggests an indignant Blue Tit).

Adult The pointed, black-and-white chequered crest, isolated black 'C' shape on ear-coverts and broad black bib extending around neck as narrow halter to nape are unique fieldmarks. Sexes similar but juvenile has shorter crest and broken halter.

Feeds mainly in conifers but sometimes in heather and on ground. Notice plain brown upperparts (no wing-bars) and dull white belly, with buffy flanks.

Scottish birds can be elusive – in winter, try checking bird feeders at known haunts.

Flight Has typical weak, flitting flight of all tits.

◆ Often travels in pairs, sometimes within mixed tit flocks ◆ Forages extensively in crowns of old conifers, but gives itself away by frequent use of trilling note or high trisyllabic call, *tsee-tsee-tsee* (beware dismissing latter as call of Long-tailed Tit) ◆ Can be infuriatingly difficult to see well – typical view is of a restless small shape silhouetted against sky in dimly lit canopy of tall pine. With patience, will eventually hop into view at tips of outer branches, when one's first impression is often of a distinctly faded Blue Tit ◆ Song is an extension of the trilling call ◆ Will excavate own nest hole in decaying tree stump.

Coal Tit *Parus ater*   11.5cm (4.5")

Smallest of the tits. Common in mixed and especially coniferous woodlands, including maturing plantations. Comes freely to garden bird tables (invariably outnumbered by Blue and Great Tits), but typically darts quickly away again, carrying food in bill. Voice distinctive.

Adult Bold white nape patch and double ▶ white wing-bars immediately distinguish Coal from all other tits.

◀ **Adult** Both sexes have a grey back (rather drabber in British race *britannicus*) and buff-white underparts, with smart glossy-black head and white cheeks. Sedentary Irish subspecies *hibernicus* differs in its slightly paler rump and yellowish tint to cheeks and nape (becoming whiter with wear); underparts pale yellow, flanks and undertail-coverts cinnamon-buff.

Generally dowdy appearance may cause momentary confusion ▶ with Marsh and Willow Tits, but note Coal Tit's black bib is much larger, broader and distinctly triangular in shape – latter a useful fieldmark on birds feeding overhead in treetops.

◀ **Juvenile** Drabber than adult; cheeks, nape, wing-bars and underparts washed dirty-yellowish.

Status Widespread resident, locally abundant in coniferous forests. Absent as breeding bird only from treeless uplands and outlying islands of far N and W. **Population** c900,000 pairs.

◆ Quick, restless and agile tit, with a rather fine bill adapted to probing amongst pine needles and cones ◆ Usually seen feeding busily in treetops where its repetitive, sprightly, piping song *see-too, see-too, see-too* (sounds like a speeded-up Great Tit) or thin, Goldcrest-like squeaks give birds away ◆ Associates freely with 'crests, treecreepers and other tits in winter, foraging in mixed flocks through woodland canopy and on ground ◆ Often sings from topmost spray of conifer or announces itself with a clear, penetrating *tsui* or *tseet* ◆ Breeds in holes in tree roots, stumps, walls, nestboxes and even in ground.

253

Blue Tit *Parus caeruleus*   12cm (4.75")

The commonest tit, frequenting deciduous or mixed woodland, hedgerows, parks and gardens everywhere. A familiar visitor to bird tables. Pale blue cap and all-blue tail unique.

Adult White face with narrow black eye-stripe, and neat black bib and bridle. Green back and blue wings with single white wingbar recall distinctly larger, longer-tailed Great Tit, but Blue has stubbier bill and short dark streak confined to centre of yellow breast (cf. Great's bold belly stripe).

Female

Sexes much alike; in direct comparison, male (below) has broader, deeper blue necklace and darker wing-coverts than female (right). ▼

Male

Juvenile Looks glum. Dull version of adult, with pale yellow face and greyish-green cap.

▼

Flight Typical tit flight, quick and undulating with bursts of flicking wingbeats. Seldom flies very far, preferring to work its passage from tree to tree. No white in tail (cf. Great Tit).

Status Resident and mainly sedentary. One of the 10 most abundant British birds. Absent only from barren uplands and outlying islands of far N/W.
Population 4,500,000 pairs.

In spring, watch for characteristic fluttering butterfly display flight, as male floats down between trees.

◆ Colourful, compact woodland tit that accompanies mixed feeding flocks in winter; can become very tame in gardens ◆ Hangs acrobatically to work at tips of branches or picks at food between feet ◆ Repertoire of calls largely a variation of same basic theme: *tsee-tsee-tsee du* (or similar) ◆ Song typically 2 or 3 hurried notes, followed by a longer trill: *see-see t-t-t-t-t* or *tsee-tsee-tsee trrrrrr* ◆ Gives rapid, scolding *churr-rr-rr* in alarm, crown feathers raised ◆ Hole-nester (quickly takes to nestboxes), raising a single brood of 7-16 young.

254

Largest and most striking tit, common in woods, parks and gardens almost everywhere.
Familiar at bird-tables, easily recognised by its bold plumage and loud and varied calls.

Adult Glossy blue-black head with snow-white cheek ▶
patches and thick black stripe down centre of bright
yellow underparts diagnostic. From behind, yellowish
patch on nape suggests Coal Tit, but note green back
and steel-blue wings crossed by single white wing-bar.

Male

Sexes similar but males (right) have wider black belly stripe
(especially between legs); stripe is narrower on rather duller
female (below), breaking-up or fading between legs.
▼

Female

Juvenile Much duller, has
sootier head and belly stripe,
and pale yellow wash to cheeks
with broken black surround.
◀

Flight Undulating, stronger than other
tits, with audible bursts of whirring
wings when close. Steel-blue tail shows
conspicuous white edges.

Status Widespread and abundant resident. Absent as breeding
bird only from barren uplands
and outlying islands of far N/W.
Population Over 2,000,000
pairs.

◆ Noisy, bold and assertive tit, coming quickly to investigate pishing
◆ Hole-nester, taking readily to nestboxes ◆ Outside breeding season,
roves woodlands with other tits and nuthatches, foraging in treetops
or rummaging on ground ◆ Often draws attention by hammering
noisily at seed (held adroitly in feet) or plant stem with spiky bill ◆
Wide range of calls (over 60 recorded) ◆ Spring song (heard from
January onwards) is characteristic, a ringing *tee-cha, tee-cha, tee-cha*.
Other commonly heard calls include Chaffinch-like *tsink, tsink*, a sad
tee tu-tuh and an agitated chatter in alarm.

Nuthatch *Sitta europaea* 14cm (5.5")

Agile, extrovert tree-climber that gives itself away by hammering noisily at acorns wedged in bark or by its sudden and unmistakable outbursts of loud excited calls, *tweet, tweet, tweet...* Blue-grey upperparts with pale throat and black mask unique among birds in our region.

Scandinavian race *europaea*
Male is white below, female washed rufous-buff.

British and west European race *caesia*
Orange-buff below, chestnut on flanks with white-spotted vent. Females and juveniles more washed-out.

Status Widespread resident. In Britain, locally common N to Scottish border. Absent Ireland.
Population c130,000 pairs.

Flight Short square tail and strong chisel bill contribute to a stubby, front-heavy look in flight. Listen for sharp *tseet* calls as birds flit jerkily between trees.

◆ Favours older deciduous and mixed woods, parks and gardens, especially oaks ◆ Various loud songs include a rapid, trilling *chi-chi-chi-chi...* and a clear, whistled *peeu, peeu...* ◆ Nests in a tree-hole, the entrance plastered with mud to precise fit ◆ Extremely active; hops jerkily up, down and around branches and trunks – the only woodpecker-like bird able to descend headfirst ◆ Bold and inquisitive – entice closer by pishing ◆ Look for within tit-flocks and at bird tables in winter.

Treecreeper *Certhia familiaris*   12.5cm (5")

Restless but unobtrusive woodland bird seen creeping mouse-like up trees. Slender decurved bill and bark-like plumage diagnostic of both treecreeper species. Adults/juvenile similar.

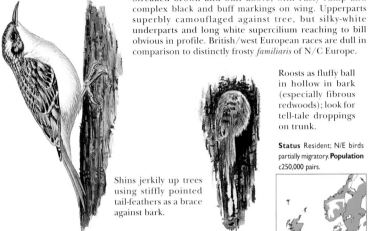

Streaked brown and buff above, with rusty rump and complex black and buff markings on wing. Upperparts superbly camouflaged against tree, but silky-white underparts and long white supercilium reaching to bill obvious in profile. British/west European races are dull in comparison to distinctly frosty *familiaris* of N/C Europe.

Roosts as fluffy ball in hollow in bark (especially fibrous redwoods); look for tell-tale droppings on trunk.

Status Resident; N/E birds partially migratory. **Population** c250,000 pairs.

Shins jerkily up trees using stiffly pointed tail-feathers as a brace against bark.

◆ Common in all types of mature woodland, parks ◆ Where range overlaps with Short-toed Treecreeper, tends to prefer coniferous forest at higher elevations ◆ Thin, sibilant, slightly tremulous call, *tsrree* ◆ Short, high-pitched song begins *tsee-tsee-tsee...* then ends in a hurried flourish ◆ Often travels with tit flocks.

Short-toed Treecreeper *Certhia brachydactyla*   12.5cm (5")

Looks plainer than Tree-creeper. Duller supercilium fades in front of eye, and dirtier underparts sullied buffish on flanks.

Subtle differences in wing markings, longer, more curved bill and shorter hindclaw of doubtful use in the field.

Status Resident; sedentary. Vagrant to Britain.

Virtually identical to Treecreeper but for voice ◆ Diagnostic call is a strong, clear *zeet* given at intervals or in series with crystal ring (as if struck on tiny anvil) ◆ Song a louder, more emphatic ditty *look.. for.. me.. be-hind-this-big.. tree* ◆ Prefers deciduous woods, parks and avenues below c1,000m ◆ The only treecreeper in the Channel Islands.

Wallcreeper *Tichodroma muraria*   16cm (6.5")

Adult Grey-bodied and exceedingly hard to find as it creeps jerkily about rock faces, probing for insects with slender, decurved bill. Watch for quick flash of red (and bold white spots) in restlessly flicking wings. Male in summer has black throat; pale in winter, like female's.

Non-breeding male   **Breeding male**

Status Scarce resident. Rare vagrant to Britain.

◆ Alpine cliff-climber, usually only seen as it floats from one crag to next like a big, crimson-winged butterfly ◆ Breeds in high mountains. Moves lower in winter to explore valley bluffs, quarries and old buildings.

Penduline Tit *Remiz pendulinus*   11cm (4.25")

Adult Plumage pattern similar to that of male Red-backed Shrike. ▼ Male has pale grey crown and nape, with black mask, maroon back and blotching on breast, with silvery fringes to black wing and tail feathers.

Male constructs characteristic flask-shaped nest of plant fibres, suspended from twigs of tree, frequently overhanging water.

Status Mainly summer visitor. Range has expanded to N & W, to Netherlands and Belgium (has even recently bred Norway). Increasingly frequent vagrant to Britain.

◀ **Juvenile** Pallid appearance can be confusing, warbler-like with plain head, prominent dark eye and thin bill. Note semblance of adult wing pattern.

◆ Found in riverbanks, tangled backwaters and other wetland habitats fringed with poplar, willow, *Typha* and reed ◆ Smaller than a Blue Tit, with a sharp, silvery bill ◆ Usually detected by its distinctive call, a high, drawn-out, wheezy *seeoo*, heard from birds flying over, feeding in treetops or reedbed ◆ Inquisitive; can be enticed very close by pishing.

A slim, thrush-sized bird with noticeably long wings, crimson eyes and stout reddish bill. Golden and black male unmistakable. Beware misidentifying bright yellow rump of larger Green Woodpecker for tail-end of similarly coloured female/immature oriole.

Adult male Brilliant yellow head and body set off by glossy black wings and lores. Conspicuous yellow flash on primary coverts is visible both at rest and in flight.

Adult female Rather variable. Typically bright yellowish-green above with dark wings, and whitish below, with fine dark streaks across breast and yellow flanks. Confusingly, some older females extensively yellow like adult male, though wings not so black.

Juvenile and first-year Like adult female, but whiter below with variable dark streaking. Bill brownish.

Flight Easy, elegant, quick and gently undulating, often concluding with a graceful upward sweep into canopy. All birds show dark tail with golden corners, plus vivid yellow rump and underwing-coverts.

Status Widespread summer visitor (May-Sep) from tropical Africa. Has toe-hold only in S Scandinavia. In British Isles, rare passage migrant. Has bred annually E Anglia since 1967, showing marked preference for hybrid poplars near water. **Population** c30-40 pairs.

◆ Secretive arboreal bird, much more often heard than seen ◆ Frequents broad-leaved woods, parks, copses, avenues and shelter-belts. Keeps mainly to treetops, with uncanny ability to slip unnoticed through foliage ◆ Watching patiently along woodland edge or glade for bird to fly across from one stand of trees to another offers perhaps best chance of seeing one. Sometimes ventures out in pursuit of passing crow or raptor ◆ Male's beautiful, far-carrying song a short, fluting whistle *weela-weeo* – or even *or-i-ole*. Easily confused with Blackbird's mellow whistling at a distance ◆ Harsh Jay-like calls equally characteristic, but often overlooked.

259

Great Grey Shrike *Lanius excubitor* — 24-25cm (9.5")

Adult Paler than Lesser Grey, with longer bill, narrower black band through eye, grey forehead, thin white supercilium and prominent white shoulders. Lacks pink breast of other grey shrikes. (Juvenile faintly barred above and below).

Preys on insects, small mammals and birds, seizing latter in flight. Often interrupts bounding flight to hover, like a miniature Kestrel.

Status Uncommon. Nests patchily across NW Europe, south to central France. Winter visitor elsewhere (scarce Britain), often returning in successive years to favoured spots.

Flight White wing patch forms narrower but conspicuously longer band across wing than other grey shrikes.

◆ Large, pale shrike ◆ Perches openly on tops of small trees, its shining white breast obvious from a distance ◆ Has longer tail than Lesser Grey, but appreciably shorter primaries ◆ Frequents open country with trees and scrub, including heaths, marshes, bogs and plantations ◆ Various calls include a repeated hiccuping, *quick-ick* ◆ Harsh Jay-like squawks in alarm.

Southern Grey Shrike *Lanius meridionalis* — 24-25cm (9.5")

Adult Looks dark and sturdy, with discernibly heavy bill. Resembles Lesser Grey but darker, ash-pink below and storm-grey above, and shoulders narrowly trimmed white. Other features recall Great Grey, having short primaries, narrow black mask and thin white supercilium (unlike Great Grey, latter ceases above eye).

White wing patch narrower than in Lesser Grey, but similarly confined to primaries (not extending onto bases of secondaries as in Great Grey).

Status Resident. Not in UK.

◆ Formerly considered a race of Great Grey ◆ In many respects like a cross between Lesser and Great Grey Shrikes, replacing latter in dry, open habitats in southernmost France, Iberia and North Africa ◆ Song a monotonously repeated bleeping, *shek-shek*.

Lesser Grey Shrike *Lanius minor*   20cm (8")

Adult Plump, compact shrike. Distinguished from other grey shrikes by stubbier bill, broad black mask extending over forecrown (no white supercilium), mainly grey shoulders and long primary projection. Variable pink flush below (less marked in female).

Immature Finely scaled above. Grey forehead invites confusion with other grey shrikes, but thick bill and long wings (conveniently highlighted by pale feather margins) identify.

Status Localised summer visitor. Rare vagrant Britain.

Flight Conspicuous bold white primary patch, shorter (but relatively wider) than in other grey shrikes.

◆ An eastern species, all but lost as a breeding bird in north-west Europe ◆ Frequents open, grassy country with bushy clumps and scattered groups of tall trees ◆ Prolonged, chattering jumble of a song (like strangled thrush), includes much mimicry ◆ Hops in upright manner on ground, looking surprisingly like wheatear.

Woodchat Shrike *Lanius senator*   19cm (7.5")

Adult Unmistakable; boldly pied with unique chestnut crown. Male has solid black mask; female (usually) differs in more mottled forehead and browner mantle.

Flight White shoulders, wing patch, rump and outertail create striking pattern.

Status Summer visitor. Winters tropical Africa. Vagrant Britain.

Juvenile Easily confused with young Red-backed Shrike but ghost of white rump and shoulder patch, and white flash in primaries (obvious in flight).

◆ Common around Mediterranean, rather patchy elsewhere ◆ Breeds in dry, open terrain with well-spaced trees and scrub, olive groves and old orchards ◆ Loud, somewhat scratchy song can be hard to pin down; is sustained and chattering, with much mimicry ◆ Perches on exposed perch or skulks in cover, often betrayed by gleaming white underparts.

Red-backed Shrike *Lanius collurio*   17cm (6.75")

Smallest of the region's shrikes, with the dark mask, stout hooked bill, long tail and predatory nature characteristic of the genus. Sexes differ, though both distinctive. Juvenile easily confused with juvenile Woodchat but is rustier above, with warm brown tail (dark brown in Woodchat), and lacks pale markings on shoulder, rump and wing.

Adult male Easily recognised by pale ▶ grey crown and rump, black mask, chestnut-red back and breast white with pinkish blush.

◀ **Adult female** Rather variable. A few like adult male, but most have brownish to grey crown, ill-defined brownish mask and duller red back. Underparts creamy, always showing distinctive brown scaling when close. Tail predominately brown with hint of white at sides.

Juvenile Resembles female, but ▶ upperparts finely barred black giving markedly scalloped appearance (hard to detect at distance). The effect is most pronounced on the wings, where emphasised by broad pale tips.

Status Widespread but declining summer visitor. Once common in Britain, now scarce passage migrant (mid-May-Sep) rarely nests. Winters in tropical Africa.
Population 0-8 pairs.

Male Black tail with much white at base, seen best in dashing sallies or bounding flight.

◆ Breeds in open bushy country, rough ground, heaths and clearings; likes patches of bramble and hawthorn ◆ Arrives rather late (May onwards) ◆ Declares its presence with harsh *tchev, tchev....* or chattering alarm ◆ Song a varied mix of quiet, jerky warbling and accomplished mimicry ◆ In eastern Europe, often found alongside Barred Warbler (surprisingly, the two can look similar in flight) ◆ Sits openly to watch for prey, swooping down on insects, small mammals, lizards and birds.

Starling *Sturnus vulgaris* 21cm (8.25")

Widespread throughout the region, a noisy and irascible bird, with blackish plumage glossed purple and green. Smaller than male Blackbird, with a spikier bill, shorter tail, reddish legs and bustling, waddling walk.

Summer Iridescent plumage, etched and spangled in gold. Male ▶ has shaggy 'beard', dark brown eyes and bluish base to bill. 'Spottier' female has paler brown eyes and pale flesh bill base.

Juvenile Drab grey-brown, ▼ with whitish throat and margins to wings.

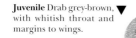

◀ **Winter** Both sexes have black bill and copious white speckling, densest on head. Pale tips gradually abrade to reveal smart summer gloss.

Status Resident. Millions emigrate to Britain from N/E Europe in winter. **Population** >1.5 million 'pairs'.

◆ Common in towns, villages and open country ◆ Utters constant whistling, clicking and gurgling noises from rooftops; an expert mimic ◆ In spring, males perform unique wing-waving song-display, as though struggling for balance ◆ Large, noisy post-breeding flocks compete frantically for food ◆ In winter, roosts in huge numbers in cities, reedbeds and woods. Disperses in successive waves at dawn.

Spotless Starling *Sturnus unicolor* 21cm (8.25")

Adult Oily, purplish plumage has characteristic 'wet-combed' hackles, lacking Starling's green sheen, bright spangling and wing edgings. Legs bubblegum-pink

Status Resident S Europe. Not in UK or Ireland.

◆ Replaces Starling as a breeding bird in Iberia ◆ Since 1985, has colonised south-east France (50+ pairs) ◆ In winter, only faint pale spotting ◆ Juvenile darker than Starling ◆ Noisier than Starling, song includes distinctive sudden, shuddering *see-oooo*.

263

Jay *Garrulus glandarius* 34cm (13")

Pigeon-sized. Colourful woodland corvid, notoriously shy and wary – generally glimpsed as a coloured bird with black tail and white rump flashes through the trees, screeching its harsh warning. Typical call is a dry, rasping *skaaak*; a familiar woodland sound.

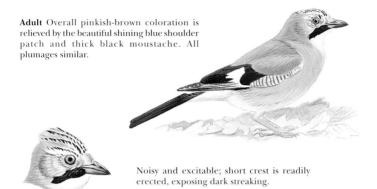

Adult Overall pinkish-brown coloration is relieved by the beautiful shining blue shoulder patch and thick black moustache. All plumages similar.

Noisy and excitable; short crest is readily erected, exposing dark streaking.

Flight Action is hesitantly undulating on broad, blunt wings; rising birds initially show black tail contrasting with white rump and wing flashes, and bright blue shoulder patches. Unlikely to be confused, but compare similar-sized Hoopoe.

Status Resident, but subject to periodic irruptions in years of poor acorn harvest, taking birds far from wooded cover. **Population** 170,000 territories.

From below, the black tail contrasts with pinkish-brown body.

◆ Common woodland bird, but especially associated with oaks – acorns a favourite food ◆ In recent decades, has moved increasingly into towns; in many city parks, has become bold and fearless ◆ Feeds on ground, jauntily hopping sideways as it searches for acorns ◆ Their long persecution by gamekeepers as an egg-thief belies their importance as a planter of forests; Jays bury acorns throughout the autumn – indeed a single Jay can plant 3,000 acorns in a month ◆ Rarely seen far from the shelter of trees, a party usually breaks cover one at a time, hurriedly flapping across a clearing or valley ◆ As well as its angry screeches, wide repertoire of calls includes a buzzard-like mewing note.

Magpie *Pica pica*

46cm (18")

Unmistakable and familiar sight in both town and country. Just as easily recognised by its noisy, machine-gun chattering, *chak-chak-chak-chak*..... Over recent decades has become as much a garden bird, taking advantage of the extra protection afforded by suburbia. All plumages similar.

Flight The short, broad wings and long, trailing graduated tail are distinctive, even in silhouette. Flight consists of burst of rapid beats, interspersed with glides.

Adult A handsome bird, with its very long green and bronze-purple tail and black and white wings and body. Juveniles have shorter tails and duller black plumage areas, with little gloss.

The tall, thorny domed nest, with side entrance is as familiar a sight in winter hedgerows as the bird itself. Usually a fresh nest is built each year.

Status Resident, widespread and increasing. **Population** 910,000 territories.

◆ Occurs in variety of open country from farmland with hedges, to city parks and inshore islands, but avoids large tracts of treeless country and dense forest ◆ In spring it takes eggs and chicks of hedgerow and garden birds and receives a disproportionate amount of blame for the demise of our songbird populations ◆ Calls include an enquiring *ch'chak* and an affirmative *che-uk*, but best known for its staccato chattering – used persistently in mobbing cats, owls and other potential predators ◆ Often in pairs; non-breeders form loose groups of 20 or more, whilst winter roosts can number over 100 birds ◆ Feeds chiefly on ground, often clearing up the remains of road casualties ◆ In southern Europe, nest is parasitised by the Great Spotted Cuckoo.

Nutcracker *Nucifraga caryocatactes*   33cm (13")

Flight Action and size recalls a short-tailed Jay; white undertail-coverts and chiefly white tail underside contrast with the dark plumage.

Status Local resident, but subject to sporadic movements. Rare vagrant to Britain during periodic irruptions.

Adult All plumages similar. White spotting can give the impression of a grey-bodied bird, with dark brown crown and black wings.

◆ Unmistakable inhabitant of coniferous forests (especially in mountains) ◆ Usually solitary ◆ Perches on tree-tops giving short-tailed, sharp-billed, big-headed silhouette ◆ Harsh, far-carrying call, *kraaaak* ◆ Feeds on pine seeds and nuts ◆ Siberian populations subject to periodic irruptions at times of food shortages ◆ Resident population in Alps northward to Germany and Belgium.

Siberian Jay *Perisoreus infaustus*   31cm (12")

Flight Often first noticed swooping through the trees, when the rusty-orange rump, outer tail feathers and wing patches attract attention.

Status Resident, locally common. Not in Britain.

Adult All plumages similar. Soft fluffy plumage, big head and short bill give a strange impression when bird is perched, the darker hood being the most obvious feature.

◆ A drab brown jay of Scandinavian coniferous and birch forests ◆ Often very tame, but difficult to find during the breeding season ◆ Attracted by smoke of camp-fires ◆ Usually in small parties, swooping down to ground revealing rusty tail. Also sits like a large flycatcher on tops of tall trees ◆ Disappears as suddenly as it appeared, melting back into the dark forest gloom ◆ Various calls, including a buzzard-like mewing and Jay-like screeches.

Chough *Pyrrhocorax pyrrhocorax*   40cm (16")

Adult Scarlet legs and curved bill. Wing and tail tips virtually equal when perched.

Flight Rectangular wings. Tail very square at tip.

Status Local resident. Now extinct England, but locally numerous Wales, Isle of Man, Islay and Ireland. **Population** 1145 prs.

◆ Lively, buoyant corvid of coastal and inland cliffs, and alpine zone of mountains ◆ Nests in caves, old buildings and mine shafts ◆ Chiefly insectivorous; particularly fond of ants and beetles, obtained by digging with slender bill. At long range, vigorous digging and probing actions helpful in separation from similar-sized Jackdaw ◆ Flicks wings and bows as it calls ◆ Typical call, given freely in flight, an excited, hoarse *chee-aw*, often repeated.

Alpine Chough *Pyrrhocorax graculus*   38cm (15")

Adult Small yellow bill diagnostic. Juvenile has dusky legs and bill, latter becoming yellowish soon after fledging.

Flight Tail longer and more rounded than Chough.

Wing-tip narrower, with fingered primaries less even in length.

Status Resident. Not in Britain.

◆ Frequents high mountains, alpine pastures and scree slopes; tame at some alpine tourist resorts ◆ Largely replaces Chough in central Europe, but both occur in the Pyrenees ◆ More of a scavenger than Chough, and found in large flocks ◆ Calls include a sweet rippling *preeep* and thin whistled *sweeeoo* – quite unlike other corvids.

Jackdaw *Corvus monedula* 33-34cm (13")

Small, sociable crow (about size of Feral Pigeon), seen in pairs on rooftops, church towers and old buildings or in flocks in arable fields with larger, more staid Rook. Walks in a jaunty, bustling manner, head held high. Voice distinctive.

Adult Immediately recognised by its grey nape (duller in female), small bill and pale, glassy eye. Looks all black at distance, but close inspection reveals faint blue gloss above and greyish tone below. ▶

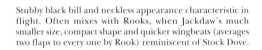

Stubby black bill and neckless appearance characteristic in flight. Often mixes with Rooks, when Jackdaw's much smaller size, compact shape and quicker wingbeats (averages two flaps to every one by Rook) reminiscent of Stock Dove.

Juvenile Lacks grey cowl ▶
and has duller eyes.

Jackdaw

Status Widespread and increasing resident. British birds largely sedentary (some winter in Ireland, where especially numerous). Continental immigrants reach Britain Oct-Apr, often migrating with Rooks.
Population 600,000 territories.

Flight Flocks soar and wheel in unison, or tumble playfully. Easy then to confuse with rarer Chough (lower); note Jackdaw's rather narrow, pointed wings and more rounded tail.

Chough

◆ Bright-eyed and inquisitive opportunist, adept at raiding litter bins ◆ Common in farmland (especially sheep and cattle pastures), parks, woods, towns, ruins and cliffs; generally shuns highest ground ◆ Breeds colonially in holes in cliff crevices, old trees, quarries, buildings, chimney pots ◆ Forms large winter roosts, usually with Rooks, passing over in noisy flights at dawn and dusk ◆ Listen for sharp, resounding calls, *kya!* or *jyack-jyack!* (lone birds have uncanny ability to sound like a flock) ◆ Caution: certain calls remarkably like those of Chough, *chyow*.

Much larger than Crow (size of Buzzard), with a 4-5ft wingspan. Announces itself with loud, far-carrying croaks. Most often seen in flight, typically in pairs or small groups patrolling skyline of a distant ridge or riding on updraughts high overhead. Huge bill, large diamond-shaped tail and long fingered wings are key fieldmarks. Wingtips often appear narrow and swept-back (even more so during spring and summer months when gradual moult of flight feathers leaves gaps in outerwing).

Adult Massive arched bill and shaggy beard diagnostic. Entirely black plumage shows distinct purple gloss when close.

Flight Masterful, acrobatic. Dives, rolls and tumbles through the air as if for fun. Soars and glides on flat wings, looking raptor-like at times.

Carrion Crow

Raven

Juvenile Similar but sooty-brown plumage lacks gloss.

Status Resident; increasing. In Britain sparsely distributed, mainly in N/W (exceptionally rare winter visitor in S/E); widespread in Ireland. **Population** 10,000+ pairs.

Flight Longer, more boldly-fingered, wings longer, wedge-shaped tail useful in separation form Carrion Crow (right). Beware possible confusion with other corvids – especially Rook, which has similar outline.

◆ Wary of people ◆ In north-west Europe found mainly on rugged cliff coasts and wild uplands, especially those grazed by sheep and deer ◆ Breeds early (February-May), placing bulky stick nest on high crag, cliff crevice or tree in wooded glen ◆ Calls unmistakable: a deep, hollow *pruk pruk* or resonant, throaty *kronk*, audible at very long range ◆ Feeds mainly on sheep and deer carrion; also kills small mammals, birds. Flocks may gather to pick over rubbish tips or carcass, and to roost.

269

Rook *Corvus frugilegus* 44-46cm (18")

Highly gregarious crow seen in flocks on farmland, sometimes accompanied by smaller Jackdaw. A familiar scavenger on motorway hard shoulders. Appears all dark at distance and thus tricky to separate from Carrion Crow, but differs in its unusual triangular outline with rather loose (ill-fitting) plumage, shaggy 'trousers', steep forehead and longer, more tapering bill.

Adult Bare whitish face and bill unique ▶ among crows. At close range, plumage extensively glossed blue/purple.

▲
Immature During their first twelve months, young Rooks have a dark bill and face, and bristly nasal patch – exactly like Carrion Crow. But Rook has lumpier head and more pointed bill, with a bump on peaked crown and distinctive cowled appearance.

Flight Though difficult to distinguish from Crow in flight, Rook is a more accomplished flier – quicker, more agile, often playful. Check for longer, pointed head, almost wedge-shaped tail and more fingered wing tips (can suggest Raven). When swollen with food, pouch bulging visibly beneath bill is a useful feature (not shown by Crow).

Status Widespread resident. Continental immigrants swell numbers in E Britain in winter. Abundant Ireland. **Population** 1,400,000 pairs.

Breeds colonially, in rookeries – clusters of bulky stick nests placed conspicuously in tops of tall stands of trees. (Crow is a solitary nester).

◆ Common in patchwork of lowland arable, pasture, woodland and copse. Absent only from major uplands and conurbations ◆ Walks with an upright strut or rolling waddle; also hops ◆ Like all crows, has a varied vocabulary; usual call is a gruff, pleasing *kaargh*. Juvenile's voice is higher ◆ Forms huge winter roosts, often with Jackdaws.

Carrion and Hooded Crows *Corvus corone* 47cm (18.5")

The familiar crow. Two distinct races occur (see maps); in British Isles and western Europe, Carrion Crow (*corone*) is common everywhere except north and west Scotland, Ireland, Isle of Man and Europe east of Denmark, where it is replaced by Hooded (*cornix*). Where breeding ranges overlap hybrids are frequent.

Carrion Adult entirely black (juvenile often separable when close by duller, almost brown, tone of head and upperparts). Some recently-fledged juveniles show whitish band along full length of wing (remnants of waxy feather sheaths). Easily confused with Rook, especially at a distance when latter's characteristic bare face not evident.

Status Common and widespread resident. In England small numbers of 'Hoodies' turn up in winter along the east coast. **Population** (Carrion) 790,000 pairs.

Note too that first-year Rook has an all-dark face/bill crow-like. Check for crow's blunter black bill, smoother crown, tighter plumage and neatly trimmed thigh (cf. Rook's tapering bill, lumpy crown, and baggy leggings).

Flight Typically slower than playful Rook. Crow's squarer tail and wings not always apparent, but can be a useful distinction; cf. wedge tail and more pointed wings of Rook, and much larger Raven.

Carrion   **Hooded**

Hooded Unmistakable. Head, wings and tail black, but body grey (can show pinkish cast in fresh plumage).

Population (Hooded) 450,000 pairs; (hybrid) 20,000 pairs.

◆ Wary, aggressive scavenger found in all habitats from city centre to tideline, forest to mountain top ◆ Generally seen in ones and twos, but the adage 'crows alone, Rooks in a flock' unreliable; often accompanies other crows, and hundreds may gather at favoured feeding spots and roosts ◆ Watch for crow's frequent nervy wing flicks whenever on ground or perched ◆ Calls varied. Typically a loud, angry *kraa*, usually given in series of 2-6 calls ◆ Unlike Rook, pairs nest alone (usually in tree).

271

House Sparrow *Passer domesticus*   14.5cm (5.75")

One of Europe's most familiar and widespread birds – a sociable, cheeky and aggressive opportunist, closely associated with man. Robustly built, with a stout conical bill for cracking seeds. Hops on ground, cocking and flicking tail, but also seen clinging awkwardly to seed-heads and bird feeders.

Breeding male Black bill contrasts with whitish ▶ cheeks. Distinguished from Tree Sparrow by its much larger black bib fanning out across upper breast, liver-brown nape, grey crown and single white wing-bar.

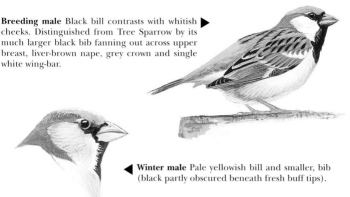

◀ **Winter male** Pale yellowish bill and smaller, bib (black partly obscured beneath fresh buff tips).

Female and juvenile Dowdy, with pale ▶ band behind eye, weak buffy wing-bars and yellowish bill throughout the year. Absence of streaking on plain, dusty-looking underparts eliminates most other seedeaters, but compare females of Greenfinch and Chaffinch.

Status Abundant resident. Perhaps surprisingly, is ranked only fifth most common bird in Britain & Ireland. **Population** 3,500,000-6,000,000 pairs.

Flight Mixes freely with other seedeaters in winter. Pick out sparrows in flight by their more square-ended tails (markedly forked or cleft in finches and buntings). Note male's distinctive grey rump.

◆ Ubiquitous inhabitant of towns, villages and adjacent countryside, absent only from highest uplands remote of human habitation ◆ Often nests colonially, breeding in roofs and holes in buildings; sometimes constructs its untidy domed grass nest in tree crevice or more openly in bush ◆ Gathers in large noisy flocks at harvest time, and to roost in ivy, thickets or beneath eaves ◆ Always garrulous, its well-known *chirrup* and *chissip* calls also given in flight ◆ Unmusical song is merely a random series of same notes. Develops into scolding chatter or anxious *teu, teu* in alarm.

Tree Sparrow *Passer montanus* — 14cm (5.5")

Unusual among true sparrows (*Passer*) in that sexes alike. Like male House Sparrow but has wholly chocolate brown cap, black ear muffs and white collar (not quite meeting on nape).

Breeding adult Black bill. Trimmer than male ▶ House Sparrow, with a more rounded crown, two narrow white wing-bars and yellowish-brown (not grey) rump. White collar is conspicuous fieldmark, even at distance.

Juvenile Lacks smart appearance of adult, ▶ having a paler crown, dingier collar and dull grey bib and ear muffs.

◀ **Winter** Yellowish bill base. Differs from winter male House Sparrow (lower) in its all-brown crown, whiter cheeks and smaller black bib (virtually confined to chin).

Tree Sparrow

Clean, bright underparts catch the eye as flock pops into view on top of hedge.

House Sparrow

Flight Faster than House Sparrow, often zipping over at considerable height. Flight note is characteristic, a hard *tek, tek...*

Status Common and widespread resident. Greatly declined in Britain (seems prone to periodic peaks and troughs, with apparently well-established colonies suddenly ceasing to exist); chiefly coastal in Ireland. **Population** 110,000 territories.

◆ A bird of the countryside in our region, preferring cultivated land, woodland edge, parks and village gardens ◆ Takes readily to nestboxes, but breeds mainly in tree holes ◆ Although gregarious, tends to form small localised communities and so can prove elusive ◆ More wide ranging in winter, feeding in stubble and weedy fields with other seedeaters or in gangs of up to 50 or so. Occasionally visits suburban bird tables ◆ Feeds quietly on ground, and is generally rather flighty ◆ Call a short, sharp *chik* or *chup*, clearer and more metallic than House Sparrow's.

273

Rock Sparrow *Petronia petronia* — 14cm (5.5")

Adult Broad creamy supercilium, dark lateral crown stripes and brown stripes on breast and flanks are clear fieldmarks. Small yellow patch on lower throat is hard to see in field.

Flight Relatively big head and short tail gives solid look in flight. Look for white tail spots as birds alight.

◆ Resembles a female House Sparrow, but chunkier with a large yellowish bill, boldly striped head and distinct streaking on chest ◆ White spots in tail diagnostic ◆ Breeds in rocky hills, gorges and ruins ◆ Sociable. Feeds on stony ground and sits about on old buildings, wires and rocks ◆ Hops and shuffles on ground, when brown streaked appearance and clear eyebrow can be confused with Woodlark ◆ Utters various sparrow-like chirps, but peculiar nasal *zwey-i* (or longer *zwey-ee-i*) is characteristic.

Snow Finch *Montifringilla nivalis* — 18cm (7")

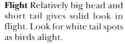

Breeding female Differs in mottled ▶ bib and yellowish bill.

Flight Only bird within its range to show such extensive white in wing and tail.

Breeding male Grey head and rich brown back separates ▲ from Snow Bunting. Note black bib and bill.

◆ Large, sturdy finch confined to the highest alpine peaks, above tree-line and seldom below 1,800m ◆ Only Snow Bunting looks similar, but ranges never overlap ◆ Tame. Often seen at mountain ski resorts and beside alpine roads, but can be elusive on extensive upland plateaux ◆ Usually in small flocks, which sweep in on flickering pied wings like flurry of giant snowflakes ◆ Call, a hoarse *tsweek* ◆ Jerkily repeated song, *sit-ti-cher, sit-ti-cher....*

Shy and elusive finch of broad-leaved and mixed woods, parkland, orchards and large gardens, especially those with hornbeam, poplar or cherry. Substantially larger than Chaffinch, with a big head, bull neck, and massive conical bill that is steel-blue in summer, pale yellowish in winter. Both sexes recognised by neat black bib, grey collar, bold white wing flash and short, square tail dipped in white (brightest in male).

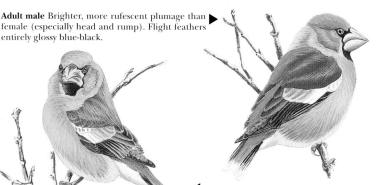

Adult male Brighter, more rufescent plumage than female (especially head and rump). Flight feathers entirely glossy blue-black.

Adult female Washed-out version of male (paler and greyer overall). Ash-grey secondaries form distinct pale panel on folded wing.

Juvenile Outsize pale bill and buffy underparts scalloped with black unique. Sex by wing colour (as adults).

Flight Looks weighty in fast, bounding flight above treetops. Bold white wingstripe shows as translucent band – an excellent fieldmark as birds pass overhead.

Status Thinly spread resident, rather easier to see in eastern Europe. In Britain, scarce and local (absent Ireland and most of Scotland). **Population** 3,000-6,500 pairs.

◆ Best found by searching likely habitat January-April (often gathers in small flocks at traditional haunts), when trees are bare and birds most vocal ◆ Stop frequently to listen for unobtrusive but characteristic call – an abrupt, explosive *ptik,* usually given from treetops or in flight (sound suggests Robin's familiar ticking call but has more edge and, unlike Robin, is never given in series from low cover) ◆ Often sits high in canopy but also hops quietly on woodland floor. Easily overlooked amongst leaf litter – watch for white-tipped tail as birds fly up ◆ Weak song seldom noticed, a mix of *ptik* calls, wheezes, and shrill *ts-zee* notes like swing of unoiled garden gate.

Chaffinch *Fringilla coelebs* 15cm (6")

One of Europe's most abundant birds. Colourful male is easy to identify, but brownish female is sparrow-like. However, double white wing-bar, greenish rump and prominent white outer tail feathers are constant fieldmarks, both at rest and in flight.

Breeding male The only finch with blue-grey crown and nape and pinkish-red face and underparts. Bill blue with black tip. ▶

◀ **Non-breeding male** After autumn moult, fresh buff tips give rise to more subdued appearance; tips gradually wear to reveal full colours by spring. Bill pale brown.

Female Unstreaked brownish above and below. ▶ Head shows hint of nape patch but never the bold stripes of female Brambling. Bill pale brown all year. Juvenile similar, but young males show pinkish patches by August/September.

All Chaffinches have white-sided tail, greenish rump and white underwings. Compare dark tail, white rump and yellow armpits of closely related Brambling. Both have typical undulating finch flight, but Chaffinch's call is softer – *chup*, like quietly dripping tap.

Brambling   **Chaffinch**

Status Abundant resident, but N/E populations migrate. Many winter in British Isles, where total may exceed 30 million.
Population 7.5 million pairs.

◆ Breeds in almost any habitat with trees ◆ In winter, roams farmland in flocks, often with other finches, sparrows and buntings. All suddenly fly up into hedges, then trickle back down to feed ◆ Trips quietly along with characteristically nodding head ◆ Loud, cheerful song ends in a flourish: *chip chip chip cherry-erry-erry tissy-choo-weeoo*. On Continent many finish with a sharp *tchik* – confusingly like Great Spotted Woodpecker ◆ Usual call is a loud Great Tit-like *chink*. Sometimes a monotonous and extremely penetrating *hreet*.

Robust northern counterpart of Chaffinch. Breeds in Scandinavia but winters widely across rest of Europe, where usually seen in winter plumage. Long white rump, and white belly contrasting with orange chest and shoulders, are key fieldmarks.

Winter Both sexes have scaly black and buff back, yellow bill with dark tip, and dark stripe either side of pale grey nape. Contrast between orange vest and shoulders and white belly a useful fieldmark. Male (shown here) is more brightly coloured with blackish (patchy) face. ▼

Breeding male Combination of ► glossy black hood and cape, tangerine breast and epaulets unique. Bill blue-black.

◄ **Female** Has winter-type plumage all year. Note cleaner face, drabber bill, and less extensive, more washed out orange breast and shoulders than male.

Chaffinch Differs in greenish rump, double white wing-bar and obvious white sides to tail. ▼

Compare **female Chaffinch's** much plainer head.

Status Winter visitor from Scandinavia/northern Europe (September-May). Nomadic; in Britain (as elsewhere), much more numerous some years than others. **Population** c50,000 - 2,000,000 birds winter. (Has bred).

Flight Brambling bulkier than Chaffinch, with clear white rump and all-dark, more deeply forked tail.

◆ Common in northern birchwoods and taiga, where its dull, repetitive Greenfinch-like *dzweee* is characteristic summer sound ◆ Distinctive flight calls betray birds passing over – listen for soft *juk-juk* and harsh, nasal *way-eek* ◆ Feeds mostly on ground, hopping jerkily like Chaffinch ◆ In winter, sometimes occurs in big flocks (roosts can run into thousands). Mixes freely with other finches, feeding beneath trees (especially beech) or in ploughed and weedy fields (above) ◆ Infrequent at bird tables.

Serin *Serinus serinus* 11cm (4.25")

Male Streaked upperparts with bright ▶ lemon face and chest unmistakable. Belly white, with heavy streaks (not extending on to breast, as in female).

Flight Combination of yellow rump but plain brown wings and tail eliminates all other green finches.

Status Summer visitor in north, resident around Mediterranean. Scarce annual visitor to Britain (odd pairs nest).

◀

Female Dull, coarsely streaked appearance with yellow rump and stubby bill identifies. Note weak yellow wash to face and upper breast (almost lacking in similar brown juvenile).

◆ Tiny, well-streaked finch with a bouncy character and yellow rump ◆ Common in parks, gardens and lightly wooded countryside ◆ Stumpy grey bill and absence of yellow markings in wing and tail diagnostic (compare Siskin) ◆ Male's prolonged wheezy jingle-jangle song is characteristic – suggests Goldcrest or a speeded up Corn Bunting. Often given in erratic, twisting display-flight on slow-flapping wings, like large butterfly ◆ Flight call distinctive liquid, *tri-lil-lit.*

Citril Finch *Serinus citrinella* 11.5cm (4.5")

Male Recalls miniature Greenfinch, but softly coloured with characteristic grey wash to nape and broad yellow wing-bars. (Unlike Serin, is wholly yellow-green below; lacks yellow tail flashes of Siskin). ▶

◀ **Female** Duller than male, with faintly streaked back. Juvenile brownish, heavily streaked; creamy wing-bars.

Status Localised resident. Not in UK or Ireland.

◆ Slim alpine cousin of Serin (both can occur together) ◆ Restricted to tree-line conifers and alpine meadows, generally above 1,000m (lower in winter) ◆ Differs from Serin in its longer bill, twin yellow wing-bars and unstreaked plumage with soft grey shading ◆ Goldfinch-like song and flight-call have unusual liquid, nasal quality – as though mixing glass splinters ◆ Usually seen in small parties, often feeding on ground ◆ Flits up into trees when approached.

Tiny, spiky-billed finch (scarcely bigger than a Blue Tit) with characteristic pattern of black and yellow in wings and tail. Brightly coloured male is easily identified; duller female can be tricky to separate from Redpoll when feeding in treetops, but Siskin's wing-bars are broader. Compare also Serin. Clear, penetrating flight-note *tea-yu* often signals approach.

Male Europe's only green finch to show neat black crown and bib. Note streaked, greenish upperparts and yellow breast with black streaking on flanks. Bright yellow double wing-bar and feather edgings are important fieldmarks.

Female Drabber, lacks black cap and bib, and is much more coarsely streaked. Wide wing-bars (can look almost white) and pale lemon wash across chest help distinguish from Redpoll. Juvenile is browner, more heavily spotted and streaked, but wing-bars quickly identify.

Frequent at bird tables in winter, drawn especially to red peanut bags.

Flight Rapid and bouncing. Bold yellow wing-bars, rump and tail sides are eye-catching, but outerwing is dark (cf. Greenfinch).

Status Widespread resident and winter visitor. Locally common in Britain/Ireland, where dramatic increase and spread since 1960s as coniferous plantations mature. **Population** >350,000 pairs.

◆ Breeds in forests of spruce, fir and pine ◆ In winter, prefers waterside alders and birch ◆ Typical encounter is of previously unnoticed party of birds suddenly exiting treetops as a dancing, chattering cloud ◆ Flocks with Redpolls and Goldfinches ◆ Acrobatic and tit-like, hanging upside-down to extract seeds of alder and spruce ◆ Fast, chattering song interrupted by unexpected mechanical wheeze – like camera part rewinding at end of film ◆ Males perform Greenfinch-like song-flight in spring.

Chunky, sparrow-sized finch with a stout pale bill and fierce expression. Bright yellow wing and tail patches are obvious fieldmarks, especially striking in flight. Male's overall greenish impression can be confused with smaller Siskin, Serin and Citril Finch, while drabber female and juvenile are sparrow-like – but only Greenfinch has such a bold yellow margin to wing (less obvious in juveniles).

Male Olive-green above, with an attractive grey area in wings; paler and more yellowish-green below. Extensive yellow wing and tail flashes. Colours become brighter in spring through wear. ▶

◀ Female Duller and more brownish. At close range, chest and mantle appear faintly mottled or streaked.

Juvenile Drabbest of all; distinctly streaked above and below, with dusky mark across cheek. Yellow edges to primaries can be inconspicuous. Noisy *jip, jip...* sometimes heard from family groups in summer months is easily mistaken for sound of Crossbills. ▶

Flight Looks dumpy and quite sparrow-like, but tail is clearly forked (sparrows have square-cut tails). Yellow sides to tail suggest similar Siskin, but only Greenfinch shows yellow on primaries. Flight call is a bouncy *dju-rur-rur-rut*.

Status Common and widespread resident. **Population** 690,000 pairs.

◆ Nests widely in shrubby gardens and parks, hedgerows and woodland edge ◆ In winter, flocks with sparrows and finches in stubble, weedy fields and saltmarsh. Frequent at bird-tables, where a bit of a bully ◆ Simple song a drawn-out, nasal *dzhwee* (very like Brambling), repeated at intervals from top of tree. Often interwoven with a more varied Canary-like twittering ◆ In spring, males perform their 'bat-like' song-flight, flying a shimmying circuit around treetops on slow, stiff-wings (which look surprisingly long).

Small, dainty finch with a sharply pointed bill adapted to extracting seeds of dandelion, teasel and thistle. Adult's striking red, white and black head pattern impossible to confuse, but absent in more pallid, mealy-headed juvenile. All ages identified by broad, golden-yellow band across black wings, conspicuous at rest and especially in flight. Voice distinctive.

Adult Colourful mask unique. Upperparts tawny-brown; underparts paper-white, with rich buff flanks. Buffy marks at either side of breast resemble an open waistcoat when viewed from the front. Bill pinkish-white with dark tip. Sexes similar. ▶

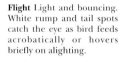

◀ **Juvenile** Differs from adult in plain face, lightly spotted chest and buff spots (snow white in adult) at tips of tertials and primaries. Best identified by yellow wing flashes. Acquires characteristic face markings during moult (August-October).

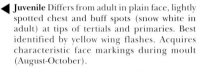

Flight Light and bouncing. White rump and tail spots catch the eye as bird feeds acrobatically or hovers briefly on alighting.

Status Common and widespread resident (range has expanded in northern Britain). 80% of British population migrates to winter SW Europe (Sept-May); Irish birds more sedentary. **Population** c275,000 pairs.

◆ Usually seen in pairs or small parties (charms), occasionally in larger flocks, flitting over rough fields, roadside verges and neglected land with an abundance of thistles, etc. ◆ Mixes with other finches in winter, sometimes feeding in trees (especially birch and alder) with Redpolls and Siskins ◆ Hangs tit-like to tease out seeds ◆ Breeds in parks, gardens, small roadside trees, orchards ◆ Frequently repeated call swiftly identifies: a cheerful, bouncy, liquid tinkling *tickeLIT tickeLIT*..., as though walking on splinters of broken glass ◆ Song an extension of call, mixed with brief Wren-like trills and rasping notes; often delivered from a prominent tree or wire.

Twite *Carduelis flavirostris* 14cm (5.5")

Sleek, tawny-brown streaky finch of open country (uplands in summer, coasts in winter), most likely to be confused with Linnet but with some aspects of Redpoll. Slightly longer-tailed than Linnet, with more streaked head, warm buff face and throat and buff wing-bar (like Redpoll).

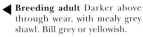

Winter adult Tawny-brown above, coarsely streaked blackish. Legs dark. Buffy wing-bar often striking (Linnet has similar bar only when juvenile). Males have pink rump (very difficult to detect); females and juveniles have streaked buffish rumps, but juvenile has pink legs.

Breeding adult Darker above through wear, with mealy grey shawl. Bill grey or yellowish.

At first glance, lacks obvious field-marks but face is the key: stubby yellow bill, warm buffy eyebrow and 'glowing' honey-buff face and throat always identify.

Winter Linnet Compare weaker streaking, greyish head and bill, and whitish chin. Streaky young Redpoll has yellow bill, but mainly frequents woodland; lacks Twite's warm face and white flashes in wings and tail.

Status Locally not uncommon resident in N Britain and W Ireland, breeding on moors, upland pastures, and islands; in winter locally widespread in coastal E England but scarce in S England & Wales. **Population** <70,000 breeding pairs.

◆ Gregarious. In winter resorts to low-lying coasts in rough fields and saltings with other finches and buntings. 'Splinter groups' regularly visit nearby pools of standing freshwater (e.g. puddles in fields, car parks) to drink and bathe ◆ Tucks down in weedy ground cover where difficult to see until flushed, flocks rising as a busy, twittering, dancing cloud, turning this way and that, or bouncing far away before wheeling around and vanishing to earth again ◆ Listen for characteristic nasal *TWA-it* (hence name) or *tchoo-eek* calls amidst flock's Linnet-like (but slightly harder) twittering ◆ Flocks gather on wires 'like clothes-pegs', endlessly swapping places with brief, dancing flits ◆ From Linnet in flight by cleaner belly, less white in wings and slightly longer tail, latter giving a slimmer 'torpedo-shape'.

282

Small, streaky brown finch with a dinky yellow bill and deeply notched tail. Combination of red forecrown and tiny black bib diagnostic on adults. Strongly arboreal with penchant for birch and alder woods (also young conifers). Usually detected by its distinctive reedy trills interspersed with bursts of staccato flight calls, *chut-ut-ut-ut* (like tapping of keys on manual typewriter). Buff and brown British race *cabaret* known as Lesser Redpoll.

Breeding male Rosy-pink breast and rump. ▶
Buff wing-bars often wear narrow and whitish.
Coarse brown streaking on buffy flanks.

◀ **Juvenile** Lacks red forecrown and black
chin (normally attained during moult July-
October). Pale bill and tit-like acrobatics
eliminate confusion species.

◀ **Female/first-year male** Streaked brownish
rump; no (or scarcely any) pink on chest.

◀ **Non-breeding** In fresher winter plumage, upperparts (including rump) paler and buffier and
wing-bars broader and buffer; breast washed
pink.

Flight No obvious fieldmarks. Voice
and exaggerated 'bouncing' action
offer best clues.

▶
Scandinavian race *flammea* **(Mealy
Redpoll)** Slightly larger. Regular winter
visitor to Britain on northern and eastern
coasts, sometimes in big numbers. Paler and
greyer, with clearer and whiter wing-bars and
more contrasting dark streaking on whiter flanks.
Rump is streaked but often looks whitish in flight.

Status Widespread resident
and partial migrant, patchy in
SW England & Scottish islands.
Population c230,000 pairs;
now decreasing after marked
expansion.

◆ Usually seen in pairs during summer. In flocks of 10-100 birds at
other times, feeding mostly in trees, where often passes unnoticed
until sudden departure as a busy, swirling cloud – listen for
characteristic 'buzzing' chorus ◆ Agile; hangs like Christmas
ornament from the tiniest twigs ◆ In winter, often with Siskins ◆
Draws attention with rising *djuee* call ◆ Sings from tree or in bouncy
display flight.

Linnet *Carduelis cannabina* 14cm (5.5")

Small finch characteristic of lowland heath, hedgerows and rough ground. Male in spring has pale grey head with splashes of red on forecrown and chest. Buff-chested female and winter male are easily overlooked, but subtle facial markings give greyish head a character all of its own. Linnet's grey bill rules out similar Redpoll and Twite.

Male In summer, unstreaked russet back is unlike any other ▶ European finch. In winter (when red markings hidden beneath fresh buffy tips) very like female, but browns are noticeably warmer.

◀ **Female** Darker, more brownish and streaked (always lacks red), but shows contrast between greyish head and browner mantle. Softly-patterned face is distinctive, with pale mark above and below eye, pale cheek spot and pale, lightly streaked throat.

Spring males perch openly on low ▶ bushes to sing. Song is a lively, sweet, musical twitter that once made Linnet a popular cage-bird.

◀ **Juvenile** Paler, buff-brown with rather plain face. Body is more spotted than streaked.

Linnet

Status Common resident. Some birds, especially northern populations, migrate south in winter (Sep-Apr). **Population** 680,000 pairs; declining.

Flight Fast and bouncy, with constant twittering calls. Both sexes show white flashes in dark primaries and tail (less obvious at rest).

Twite

Twite Darker, has more of a ▶ 'torpedo-shape'.

◆ Highly gregarious in winter, frequenting weedy fields, rough pasture and coastal saltmarsh ◆ Flocks periodically rise from the ground as a dense twittering cloud that wheels to and fro before settling again ◆ Often feeds with Twite on coasts; latter is most likely pitfall, but has yellow bill and is much more heavily streaked.

284

Bullfinch *Pyrrhula pyrrhula* 15cm (5.75")

A plump, bull-necked finch with a distinct black cap and stubby black bill. Almost always seen in pairs or (during late summer) in family groups but rarely more than c10 birds together, even in winter. Pink males invariably spotted first.

Male Easily identified by its bright salmon-pink underparts and blue-grey back. ▶

Female Similarly patterned, but duller; ash-pink ◀ below and grey-brown above, palest on nape. Both sexes have glossy blue-black wings and tail, broad white wing-bar and a conspicuous square white rump.

Juvenile Lacks black cap and has dark, ◀ beady-eye. Otherwise resembles adult female but buffier, with a buffish wingbar and vent. (As respective adults after moult July-October).

Seldom flies far; typical encounter is of pair breaking from shrubby cover – one partner moments behind the other – and bounding away low before plunging into depths of next bushy thicket.

Flight Bobbing white rump (more prominent than on any other finch) is most striking feature and aids swift identification, even on briefest of views.

Status Widespread resident. In British Isles, fairly common but declining. Native birds very sedentary, but northern race occurs as scarce winter visitor, chiefly to northern Isles. **Population** c290,000 pairs.

◆ Shy and retiring ◆ Frequents hedgerows, scrubby plantations, woodland edge, Blackthorn thickets, large gardens and orchards; has a particular liking for fruit tree buds (sometimes causing extensive damage) ◆ Feeds quietly in bushes and tall weeds, nibbling at buds, berries and seeds ◆ Most easily found by listening for characteristic sad, softly piping calls, *peu* or *hew-hew*. Partners often answer one another in gentle, reassuring tones ◆ Subdued song (seldom noticed) a curious disjointed warbling, as if in need of oiling ◆ Scandinavian race *pyrrhula* (Northern Bullfinch) slightly larger, paler grey above and brighter below.

Common Crossbill *Loxia curvirostra*   16.5cm (6.5")

Crossbills – chunky, stout-billed finches with mandibles uniquely crossed at tip. Long dark wings frequently droop beside short, deeply forked tail to reveal brightly coloured rump. Bill size varies individually, but in Common Crossbill typically appears longer than it is deep, with tip of lower mandible often clearly visible above culmen in profile.

Adult male Brick-red with fiery rump. ▶

◀ **Adult female** Grey-green, somewhat yellower below. Rump bright greenish-yellow. (Lacks yellow in wings and tail shown by superficially similar Greenfinch.)

First-year male Extremely variable. Some resemble female, ▶ others more golden in colour or splotched yellow and red.

◀ **Juvenile** Coarse dark streaking above and below diagnostic. Twin buffy wing-bars, more pronounced on some. (Smaller Siskin has obvious yellow in wings and tail).

Status Resident. Numbers vary enormously between years as birds roam widely in search of fruiting pines. **Population** Unknown, swollen by irregular (sometimes huge) irruptions from northern Eurasia.

Flight Calls frequently in strongly undulating flight, often well above trees. Heavy head and short tail gives characteristic top-heavy appearance.

◆ Nomadic bird of mature coniferous forests and plantations. Usually seen in noisy family groups or troops of 10-50 birds, sometimes hundreds ◆ Loud, clipping calls highly distinctive, *jip, jip* (at times, lone birds can sound like flock). Watch then for birds flying over or perched openly atop trees ◆ Rather tame ◆ Clambers parrot-like among branches or hangs acrobatically like a tit ◆ Feeds almost exclusively on seeds of cones (constant rain of debris can betray birds feeding quietly overhead) ◆ Thirsty birds; staking out a likely watering hole often rewarding ◆ Song a varied, jerky composition of chipping calls and clear, Great Tit-like notes.

Parrot Crossbill *Loxia pytyopsittacus*   17.5cm (7")

Bill shape diagnostic: thick lower mandible with prominent bulge below. Bill looks square with rather blunt tips; tip of lower mandible not normally visible above culmen in profile (unlike many, but not all Commons).

Male

Female

Two-barred Crossbill Double, broad white wing-bars and tips to tertials distinguish Two-barred from Common. Rare vagrant.

Status Confined to Scandinavian pine forests. Vagrant elsewhere, infrequently irrupting S and W as far as Britain (odd pairs have bred Scotland, N/E England).

◆ Largest crossbill ◆ Differs chiefly in its more massive head and parrot-like bill, and especially call ◆ Bulkier than Common with thicker neck and bigger, squarer head. Bill often appears more as an extension of flattened forehead and crown ◆ Similar to Scottish (though some Parrots at least may be recognised by their exceptionally large head and bill) ◆ Call is best fieldmark, a rather lower, deeper *tyoop, tyoop*... (can suggest a Blackbird).

Scottish Crossbill *Loxia scotica*   16.5cm (6.5")

Status Rare resident. Nomadic, but movements (apparently?) restricted to north-central Scotland. **Population** c1500 individuals.

Male All plumages match Crossbill; but slightly bigger head, puffier cheeks and deeper, blunter bill than most Commons (more bulging mandibles can make bill of Scottish seem quite square, though head and bill still smaller than typical Parrot).

◆ Britain's only endemic bird, confined to old Caledonian forest with well-spaced, mature Scot's Pine ◆ Looks and sounds intermediate between Common and Parrot Crossbills (of which variously regarded as a race until 1975) ◆ Frequently impossible to separate with certainty; location and choice of habitat provide useful starting point, but Common (and more rarely Parrot) can occur in same woods ◆ Seldom forms flocks of more than 15-20 birds.

Scarlet Rosefinch *Carpodacus erythrinus* 14.5cm (5.75")

Adult male Scarlet on head, breast and rump contrasts with whitish belly. Rest of upperparts brown, rinsed red. Drab first summer males resemble female but sing. ▶

Status Summer visitor. Winters in Asia. Range expanding westwards (now breeds Holland and France). Scarce migrant Britain; has bred (may colonise). 0-10 pairs

Female Dull grey-brown, faintly streaked above; whiter below, with soft grey streaks. First autumn birds have olive tone to upperparts, stronger streaking and good wing-bars.

◆ Sparrow-sized finch with a pale bulbous bill ◆ Prefers thickets and woodland next to water ◆ Far-carrying song distinctive: a clear, mellow whistle: *pleased to meet-you* ◆ Call is a clear, rising nasal, *hew-eek* ◆ Juvenile Greenfinch has much shorter tail, larger head and green wing edges.

Pine Grosbeak *Pinicola enucleator* 20cm (8")

Female As male, but red replaced by beautiful golden-yellow. ▶

Male Raspberry-red with patches of soft grey shading, and grey vent. ▼

Status Resident in far north; some southward dispersal in winter. Accidental Britain.

◆ Largest finch (size of Redwing), always with conspicuous white double wingbars and tertial fringes ◆ Restricted to boreal forests, where thinly spread and often elusive ◆ Quite fearless of humans ◆ At first glance, suggests Crossbill but has much longer tail and stout (but surprisingly small), uncrossed bill ◆ Fluting song strongly reminiscent of Mistle Thrush's, but sounds a little rushed ◆ Call a soft *tew-tew* ◆ Feeds quietly on buds, berries and seeds in trees and on ground ◆ Bulky, thrush-like in flight, but progress more undulating.

Our largest bunting. In general size and coloration resembles a Skylark but lacks any white in wings and tail. In summer, males perch conspicuously on roadside wires and hedgetops to sing, head tossed back in classic bunting fashion. Its unmistakable jangling ditty can be heard well into August.

Adult Streaked, lark-like plumage is grey-brown above and buff-white below, with no obvious field marks. Best clues are stout pale bill and coarse streaks on underparts which seem to coalesce to form a large, dark 'spot' in centre of breast. Sexes alike.

Winter plumage is similar but more buffy, with heavier streaking below.

If disturbed, often flies out in a wide arc before landing again on a bush or wire some distance away. Curious habit of touching down with a tell-tale flutter or momentary hover is a useful character.

Perched birds look big and plump, with a heavy head and powerful seed-cracking bill. Pink legs can be strikingly pale.

Status Widespread but now patchy and fast declining resident, inexplicably absent from large tracts of seemingly suitable habitat. **Population** <20,000 territories.

◆ Locally common bird of downland, extensive arable cultivations and marginal land ◆ Gregarious in winter (often with Yellowhammers); sometimes gathers to roost in numbers in reed-beds and scrubby saltmarsh ◆ Brief but monotonously repeated song comprises an accelerating series of *tuk* notes and culminates in a spluttering, discordant jangle, like the vigorous rattling of a bunch of keys ◆ Occasionally sings in flight, moving between song posts on rapid, fluttery wings with legs dangling ◆ Looks heavy but rather sparrow-like on the ground and in flight, which is strong and undulating over distance ◆ Distinctive *quit-it-it* flight call has 'softly popping' quality.

Lapland Bunting *Calcarius lapponicus* 15.5cm (6")

Bulky, ground-loving bunting most likely to be seen in winter on rough pasture, stubble and saltmarsh. Might be confused with female Reed Bunting, but differs in its pale bill, rusty wing panel, long primary projection and much less white in tail. Call diagnostic in flight.

Breeding male Combination of black head and chest, with fox-red nape, bold white flash running from eye to shoulder and dark-tipped yellow bill unmistakable.

◀ **Female** Differs from female Reed Bunting in clear buff supercilium, pale central crown stripe (variable), foxy nape and yellow bill.

Winter male Rufous greater coverts sandwiched between double white wing-bar (forms an obvious rusty panel on closed wing), together with pale pinkish-yellow bill are the key field-marks. Males can usually be picked out by their blotchy dark chest markings (distinctive summer markings being obscured by fresh buffy tips).

◀ **Female and first-winter** Paler, more streaky nape and broad buff central crown stripe (not shown by Reed Bunting or adult male Lapland). ▼

Status In Britain scarce on autumn passage (west coasts) and in winter (east coasts) from Greenland and Scandinavia (Sep–Apr/May). **Population** 250–500 birds; occasional larger influxes. Has bred Scotland.

◆ Breeds on hummocky Scandinavian tundra, where male performs clear, musical song from low perch or in circular display-flight ◆ Odd migrants may be seen at coastal headlands but in winter small parties appear, often with other buntings, finches and larks ◆ Keeps low, hugging ground in crouching walk or scurries mouse-like in manner of a lark or Snow Bunting (most other seedeaters *hop*) ◆ Frequently escapes notice until flushed at close quarters; rises quickly and flies off strongly (cf. Reed Bunting) ◆ Looks chunky in flight (like a Corn Bunting), but characteristic dry, rattling *ticky-tik* call identifies.

Bulky, ground-loving bunting with conspicuous white panels on wings and tail. Familiar winter visitor to sand and shingle shores with short, sparse vegetation. Plumage variable but always distinctive, both as flocks scurry on ground and in flight, when like shreds of white paper blowing in wind. Bill orange in winter, black in summer.

Winter male Shows extensive white in wing. Head, back and breast softly marked rich buff, black and white. As buff tips wear develops progressively whiter face, than boldly pied appearance of summer.

Winter female Buffier on face and chest, with much less white in wings. First-winters look similar but more buffy, often without obvious white in wing.

Breeding female Unlike male, has greyish head and dark streaked mantle.

Breeding male White, with either strikingly black or frosted saddle. Black eye and bill recall coals stuck on to face of tiny snowman.

Status Summer visitor to stony mountains and tundra in north. Nests on highest tops in Scotland. Winters mainly along coasts. **Population** <100 pairs; 10,000+ birds in winter.

Flight Long black and white wings characteristic, flickering in markedly bouncing flight.

◆ Approachable, but in dappled winter plumage is easily overlooked on ground ◆ Feeds in busy flocks, bustling along with belly pressed low. Birds continually leap-frog one another as if trying to be first ◆ Distinctive calls draw attention to birds passing over. Rippling *tir-rrr-ipp* diagnostic, but soft clear *teeu* sounds like Lapland Bunting (look for Snow's white wings) ◆ In summer, male performs delightful song-flight, with crystal timbre ◆ Though grey-headed juvenile resembles Snow Finch, ranges never overlap.

Slender yellow bunting with a stout grey bill, long cleft tail and bright chestnut rump. A familiar sight and sound in all kinds of open country, though with some variation in plumage and song. Metallic *tzik* call often draws attention to bird perched openly, nervously flicking tail to reveal prominent white outer feathers.

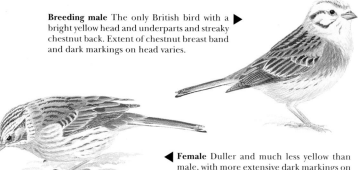

Breeding male The only British bird with a ▶ bright yellow head and underparts and streaky chestnut back. Extent of chestnut breast band and dark markings on head varies.

◀ **Female** Duller and much less yellow than male, with more extensive dark markings on head and streakier underparts.

Non-breeding male Resembles female (yellow of head ▶ and underparts largely concealed by dull olive feather fringes), but has brighter yellow belly. Some first-winter females are confusingly nondescript – greyish-buff below with extensive streaks and scarcely any yellow, but chestnut rump identifies.

Flight Quick and direct or undulating flight, showing obvious white in outer tail. Flight call distinctive, a liquid *tillip*.

Status Abundant and wide-spread resident. **Population** 1,400,000 territories.

◆ A common breeding bird of fields and hedgerows, heathland, bushy clearings and young plantations ◆ Nests late (often into August), its characteristic if monotonous song may be heard when most other bird song has ceased ◆ Song, delivered from top of bush, post or roadside wire, is traditionally rendered as *'a-little-bit-of-bread-and-no....cheese'* (though some versions lack the final note). More accurately, a series of 6 or 7 brief scraping notes, followed by a short pause for breath before a final drawn-out wheeze: *tze-tze-tze-tze-tze-tze-tze......tzuuh* ◆ Flocks in winter, often with other buntings, finches and sparrows, to feed in stubble, fields and farmyards ◆ Forages on ground with sparrow-like hop.

Cirl Bunting *Emberiza cirlus* 16.5cm (6.5")

Southern counterpart of Yellowhammer. Male unmistakable. Female and immatures only safely distinguished from Yellowhammer by greyish or olive-brown (not bright rusty) rumps. Voice distinctive, but calls are weak.

Adult male Boldly striped yellow, black ▶ and olive head with broad black bib unique.

Female and immature Colour of rump important field-mark. Head markings more contrasting and striped than those of female Yellowhammer, looking paler-cheeked between the dark eye and moustachial stripes, and with a brighter supercilium – reflecting pattern of male. Notice olive-grey wash across chest and a weak chestnut patch at sides of breast – again mirroring pattern of male.

▲ Underparts pale, buffish-yellow with fine dark streaking. Female Yellowhammer has yellower underparts and more coarsely streaked breast and flanks, but young females are dull and can confuse.

Winter male Appearance more ▶ subdued, but the basic pattern remains.

Flight Dull rump separates from similar Yellowhammer in flight.

Typical view is of singing male's banded head peeping out from crown of tree.

Status Resident, mainly sedentar quite widespread in southern England. Now very local and almost confined to coastal valleys in south Devon, with few remaining in adjacent counties. **Population** 380 pairs.

◆ Frequents lightly wooded slopes and cultivated land with bushes, mature hedgerows and trees. In Britain favours tall hedgerows in sheltered coastal valleys. Weed-rich stubble is important in winter, when mixes with other seedeaters ◆ Unobtrusive; shuffles quietly about on ground ◆ Usually detected by its song – a brief, monotone rattle, most likely to be confused with Lesser Whitethroat but can suggest song of Yellowhammer, but without the long drawn out note at the end ◆ Calls include a rather irritating, high-pitched, bat-like *sit* (unlike Yellowhammer's metallic *tzik*) and a weak, plaintive *seea*.

293

Rock Bunting *Emberiza cia*   16cm (6.25")

Male Bright cinnamon-rufous body
with black streaks on back. Head and
upper breast silver-grey, marked by
distinctive black frame to ear-
coverts and lateral crown
stripes. Bill grey. ▶

Female Duller, colourless version
of male; finely streaked on breast.
(Dowdier juvenile has messy
streaking on unstriped buffish
head and breast.)
▼

Status Mainly resident, descending to lower levels in winter.
Accidental Britain.

◆ Long-tailed bunting with a boldly striped head ◆ Confined to rocky
mountains in south, frequenting wooded and scrubby slopes ◆ Often
sits quietly but for occasional thin calls, *seea* (as though announcing
its Latin name, *cia*). Also an irritatingly high *sit*, indistinguishable
from Cirl Bunting ◆ Picks trackside grit and seeds, flying up with
bright rusty rump and flashing white tail-sides when disturbed – only
Yellowhammer similar ◆ Song suggests Dunnock; 7-10 quick, jerky
notes delivered from outcrop or tree.

Ortolan Bunting *Emberiza hortulana*   16.5cm (6.5")

Adult Pinkish body suggests Rock ▶
Bunting but grey-green hood with
pale yellow moustache and throat
diagnostic. Female is similar to
male but head more olive
with streaking on
crown.

First-year Duller than female,
more streaked on head and
breast. ▼

Status Summer visitor, much
declined in region. Winters
tropical Africa. Scarce migrant to
coasts E/S Britain (especially
August-October).

◆ Plump, dome-headed bunting with characteristic but softly
patterned face ◆ Pink bill and yellowy eye-ring unique among
buntings in north-west Europe ◆ Breeds on bushy hills, shrubby
alpine slopes and meadows, and cultivated land with scattered trees
◆ Lovely song typically 4-7 clear, ringing notes with melancholy finale,
see-see-see drü-drü-drü (or variation) ◆ Feeds unobtrusively on ground
◆ Rather plain in flight, showing dull brown rump and usually little
white in tail ◆ Utters a clipped *plitt*.

294

Rustic Bunting *Emberiza rustica* — 14.5-15.5cm (6")

Breeding male Unmistakable; silky-white below, with black and white striped head, white nape patch, and liver-brown shawl, breast band and flank streaks. Duller female has browner, less contrasting head.

Status Increasing summer visitor. Winters in Far East. Britain & Ireland: rare migrant, chiefly coastal, September-October.

Non-breeding Plumage resembles female Reed Bunting but differs in its pale ear-spot and upper wing-bar, coarse rufous splotching over breast and flanks (more marked on males), and rufous rump.

◆ Handsome northern bunting now breeding in southern Scandinavia (though more common further north and east) ◆ Favours the boggier fringes of taiga forest ◆ Restless and rather timid; peaked and slightly ragged crown, raised in excitement, can be useful pointer ◆ Flies direct to cover if disturbed, uttering distinctive high *tsip* (like flight call of Song Thrush) ◆ Song short and clear, suggestive of both Dunnock and, in parts, Blackcap.

Little Bunting *Emberiza pusilla* — 13-14cm (5.25")

Breeding Distinguished from Reed by rich chestnut face/crown, bold black lateral crown stripes, and dark frame to ear-coverts not reaching bill. Thin, creamy eye ring, white upper wing-bar and finely-streaked breast/flanks all good supporting field-marks. Male has chestnut chin (female's white).

Non-breeding is generally with duller; chestnut face less extensive and wing-bar buffy.

◆ Breeds sparsely in damp taiga woods, and only rarely within our region. A stray elsewhere, especially to coastal fields in autumn ◆ Resembles female Reed Bunting, but smaller and trimmer with rather fine pointed bill, red-faced appearance and different voice ◆ Furtive but flighty ground feeder. Often escapes notice until flushed, retreating quickly to bushy cover with Robin-like ticking calls, *tzik...*; appears nervy, flicking tail that shows little white in outers (*contra* Reed Bunting) ◆ Song brief, somewhat like a Wren's, but more musical. Rare summer visitor. Winters South-east Asia ◆ In Britain scarce migrant, chiefly coastal, September-October; occasional inland in winter.

Reed Bunting *Emberiza schoeniclus* 15.5cm (6")

Fidgety wetland bunting with a streaky brown, sparrow-like back, dark stubby bill and longish tail, habitually flicked and fanned to reveal conspicuous white edges. Attention often drawn by characteristic call, a sad *seeoo* (falling in pitch), given when perched and in flight. Compare also rarer Little and Rustic Buntings.

Breeding male Black head with bold white ▶ collar and moustache unique among European birds – a striking pattern, visible at long range and in flight.

◀ **Breeding female** Superficially sparrow-like but differs in strongly marked face and dark streaks over breast and flanks. Head brown with pale supercilium and distinct dark malar stripe bordering whitish throat. Similar juvenile has buffer underparts, more neatly streaked.

Winter male By late winter, male's black and white ▶ head pattern increasingly evident through combination of wear and partial moult.

Reed Bunting

Lapland Bunting

Status Common resident; summer visitor to north-east. Europe **Population** 350,000 pairs.

Flight Reed looks hesitant, seldom travelling far. Showy white outer-tails the most obvious fieldmark. Can be mistaken for Lapland Bunting (right) in coastal fields in winter, but chunkier, skulking Lapland lacks obvious white in tail, has different voice and, when flushed, flies up strongly, often into distance.

◆ Breeds in reedy marshes, lakeshores and riverbanks, occasionally in drier habitats ◆ In winter, often forages in fields with other buntings and finches. Sometimes visits bird tables ◆ Hops quietly on ground or pops up on reed stem, spreading tail nervously ◆ Sings monotonous ditty, *zink-zink-zink tsirrr* (or variation) from top of reed, post or bushtop.

INDEX OF ENGLISH NAMES

Accentor, Alpine 206
   Hedge 206
Auk, Little 157
Avocet 95

Bee-eater 178
Bittern 16
   Little 17
Blackbird 217
Blackcap 235
Bluethroat 209
Brambling 277
Bullfinch 285
Bunting, Cirl 293
   Corn 289
   Lapland 290
   Little 295
   Ortolan 294
   Reed 296
   Rock 294
   Rustic 295
   Snow 291
Bustard, Great 92
   Little 92
Buzzard, Common 66
   Honey 56
   Rough-legged 67

Capercaillie 83
Chaffinch 276
Chiffchaff 240
Chough, Alpine 267
   Red-billed 267
Cisticola, Zitting 225
Crake, Baillon's 89
   Little 89
   Spotted 88
Crane, Common 23
Crossbill, Common 286
   Parrot 287
   Scottish 287
   Two-barred 287
Crow, Carrion 271
   Hooded 271
Coot 91
Cormorant 14
Corncrake 88
Cuckoo, Common 164

Great Spotted 163
Curlew 119
Dipper 205
Diver, Black-throated 2
   Great Northern 3
   Red-throated 1
   White-billed 3
Dotterel 99
Dove, Collared 158
   Rock 160
   Stock 161
   Turtle 159
Duck, Ferruginous 42
   Long-tailed 48
   Mandarin 55
   Ruddy 55
   Tufted 44
Dunlin 109
Dunnock 206

Eagle, Booted 69
   Bonelli's 69
   Golden 58
   Lesser Spotted 68
   Short-toed 59
   Spotted 68
   White-tailed 58
Egret, Cattle 18
   Great White 19
   Little 19
Eider, Common 46
   King 47
   Steller's 47

Falcon, Red-footed 71
Fieldfare 218
Finch, Citril 278
Firecrest 244
Flamingo, Greater 23
Flycatcher, Collared 246
   Pied 247
   Red-breasted 246
   Spotted 245
Fulmar 9

Gadwall 36
Gannet 13
Garganey 39

Godwit, Bar-tailed 117
   Black-tailed 116
Goldcrest 244
Goldeneye 49
Goldfinch 281
Goosander 53
Goose, Bar-headed 30
   Barnacle 31
   Bean 26
   Brent 32
   Egyptian 33
   Canada 30
   Greylag 29
   Lesser White-fronted 28
   Pink-footed 27
   Snow 31
   White-fronted 28
Goshawk 64
Grebe, Black-necked 7
   Great Crested 4
   Little 8
   Red-necked 5
   Slavonian 6
Greenfinch 280
Greenshank 122
Grosbeak, Pine 288
Grouse, Black 82
   Hazel 77
   Willow/Red 80
Guillemot 154
   Black 156
   Brünnich's 155
Gull, Audouin's 144
   Black-headed 137
   Common 135
   Glaucous 143
   Great Black-backed 138
   Herring 140
   Iceland 142
   Lesser Black-backed 139
   Little 133
   Mediterranean 136
   Ring-billed 134
   Sabine's 134
   Slender-billed 144
   Yellow-legged 141
Gyrfalcon 74

Harrier, Hen 62
   Marsh 61
   Montagu's 63
Hawfinch 275
Heron, Grey 20
   Night 17
   Purple 21
   Squacco 18
Hobby 73
Hoopoe 179

Jackdaw 268
Jay, Eurasian 264
   Siberian 266

Kestrel, Common 70
   Lesser 71
Kingfisher 177
Kite, Black 57
   Red 57
Kittiwake 132
Knot 103

Lammergeier 59
Lapwing 102
Lark, Calandra 188
   Crested 189
   Shore 187
   Short-toed 188
   Thekla 189
Linnet 284

Magpie 265
Mallard 37
Martin, Crag 193
   House 195
   Sand 192
Merganser, Red-breasted 52
Merlin 72
Moorhen 90

Nightingale, Common 208
   Thrush 208
Nightjar 176
Nutcracker 266
Nuthatch 256

Oriole, Golden 259
Osprey 76
Ouzel , Ring 216
Owl, Barn 165

Owl (cont.)
   Eagle 166
   Great Grey 171
   Hawk 167
   Little 169
   Long-eared 172
   Pygmy 168
   Scops 168
   Short-eared 173
   Snowy 166
   Tawny 170
   Tengmalm's 167
   Ural 171
Oystercatcher 94
Parakeet, Rose-ringed 179
Partridge, Grey 79
   Red-legged 78
   Rock 77
Peregrine 75
Petrel, Leach's 12
   Storm 12
Phalarope, Grey 127
   Red-necked 126
Pheasant, Common 84
   Golden 85
   Lady Amherst's 85
Pintail 40
Pipit, Meadow 197
   Red-throated 198
   Richard's 200
   Rock 199
   Tawny 200
   Tree 196
   Water 198
Plover, Golden 100
   Grey 101
   Kentish 98
   Little Ringed 96
   Ringed 97
Pochard, Common 43
   Red-crested 42
Pratincole, Collared 94
Ptarmigan 81
Puffin 157

Quail, Common 86

Rail, Water 87
Razorbill 155
Raven 269
Redpoll 283

Redshank, Common 121
   Spotted 120
Redstart, Black 210
   Common 211
Redwing 219
Robin 207
Roller 178
Rook 270,
Rosefinch, Common 288
Ruff 112

Saker 74
Sanderling 104
Sandgrouse, Pin-tailed 163
Sandpiper, Broad-billed 105
   Common 123
   Curlew 108
   Green 124
   Pectoral 105
   Purple 110
   Wood 125
Scaup 45
Scoter, Common 50
   Surf 51
   Velvet 51
Serin 278
Shag 15
Shearwater, Cory's 10
   Great 10
   Manx 11
   Mediterranean 11
   Sooty 10
Shelduck, Common 34
   Ruddy 33
Shoveler 41
Shrike, Great Grey 260
   Lesser Grey 261
   Red-backed 262
   Southern Grey 260
   Woodchat 261
Siskin 279
Skua, Arctic 129
   Great 131
   Long-tailed 130
   Pomarine 128
Skylark 191
Smew 54
Snipe, Common 115
   Great 114
   Jack 114

Snowfinch 274
Sparrow, House 272
  Tree 273
  Rock 274
Sparrowhawk 65
Spoonbill 21
Starling, Common 263
  Spotless 263
Stilt, Black-winged 95
Stint, Little 106
  Temminck's 107
Stonechat 213
Stone-curlew 93
Stork, Black 22
  White 22
Swan, Bewick's 25
  Mute 24
  Whooper 25
Swallow, Barn 194
  Red-rumped 193
Swift, Alpine 175
  Common 174
  Pallid 175

Teal, Common 38
Tern, Arctic 147
  Black 152
  Caspian 145
  Common 146
  Gull-billed 151
  Little 149
  Roseate 148
  Sandwich 150
  Whiskered 151
  White-winged Black 153
Thrush, Blue Rock 222
  Mistle 221
  Rock 222
  Song 220
Tit, Bearded 248
  Blue 254
  Coal 253
  Crested 252
  Great 255
  Long-tailed 249
  Marsh 250
  Penduline 258
  Siberian 251
  Willow 251
Treecreeper, Common 257
  Short-toed 257

Turnstone 111
Twite 282

Vulture, Egyptian 60
  Griffon 60

Wagtail, Grey 203
  Pied 201
  Yellow 202
Wallcreeper 258
Warbler, Aquatic 228
  Barred 234
  Blyth's Reed 231
  Bonelli's 242
  Cetti's 223
  Dartford 238
  Fan-tailed 225
  Garden 234
  Grasshopper 226
  Great Reed 231
  Greenish 242
  Icterine 224
  Marsh 230
  Melodious 224
  Moustached 228
  Orphean 233
  Pallas's 243
  Reed 230
  River 225
  Sardinian 233
  Savi's 227
  Sedge 229
  Spectacled 232
  Subalpine 232
  Yellow-browed 243
  Willow 241
  Wood 239
Waxwing 204
Wheatear, Black-eared 215
  Northern 214
Whimbrel 118
Whinchat 212
Whitethroat, Common 237
  Lesser 236
Wigeon 35
Woodcock 113
Woodlark 190
Woodpecker, Black 182
  Great Spotted 184
  Green 183
  Grey-headed 182

Woodpecker (cont.)
  Lesser Spotted 181
  Middle Spotted 185
  Syrian 185
  Three-toed 186
  White-backed 186
Woodpigeon 162
Wren 207
Wryneck 180

Yellowhammer 292

CODE OF CONDUCT

Today's birdwatchers are a powerful force for nature conservation. The number of those interested in birds rises continually, and it is vital that birdwatchers take seriously their responsibilty to avoid any harm to birds.

Birdwatchers must present a responsible image to non-birdwatchers who may be affected by birding activities and particularly those on whose sympathy and support the future of birds may rest.

The following points should always be borne in mind:

The welfare of the birds must come first.

Habitats must be protected.

Keep disturbance to birds and their habitat to a minimum.

When you find a rare bird, think carefully about whom you should tell.

Do not harass rare migrants.

Abide by the bird protection laws at all times

Respect the rights of landowners.

Respect the rights of other people in the countryside.

Make your records available to the local bird recorder.

Behave abroad as you would when birdwatching at home.